Cambridge Studies in French

THE KNOWLEDGE OF IGNORANCE

Cambridge Studies in French

General editor: MALCOLM BOWIE

THE KNOWLEDGE
OF IGNORANCE

FROM GENESIS TO JULES VERNE

ANDREW MARTIN

Fellow of King's College
Cambridge

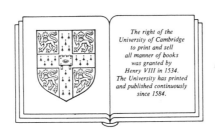

CAMBRIDGE UNIVERSITY PRESS

CAMBRIDGE

LONDON   NEW YORK   NEW ROCHELLE

MELBOURNE   SYDNEY

Published by the Press Syndicate of the University of Cambridge
The Pitt Building, Trumpington Street, Cambridge CB2 1RP
32 East 57th Street, New York, NY 10022, USA
10 Stamford Road, Oakleigh, Melbourne 3166, Australia

First published 1985

Printed in Great Britain at the University Press, Cambridge

Library of Congress catalogue card number: 84–29235

British Library Cataloguing in Publication Data
Martin, Andrew
The knowledge of ignorance: from Genesis to
Jules Verne. — (Cambridge studies in French)
1. French literature — History and criticism
I. Title
840.9   PQ103

ISBN 0 521 26556 8

WD

CONTENTS

GENERAL EDITOR'S PREFACE

This series aims at providing a new forum for the discussion of major critical or scholarly topics within the field of French studies. It differs from most similar-seeming ventures in the degree of freedom which contributing authors are allowed and in the range of subjects covered. For the series is not concerned to promote any single area of academic specialisation or any single theoretical approach. Authors are invited to address themselves to *problems*, and to argue their solutions in whatever terms seem best able to produce an incisive and cogent account of the matter in hand. The search for such terms will sometimes involve the crossing of boundaries between familiar academic disciplines, or the calling of those boundaries into dispute. Most of the studies will be written especially for the series, although from time to time it will also provide new editions of outstanding works which were previously out of print, or originally published in languages other than English or French.

PREFACE

Ignorance is like sin: most people profess to be against it, but few abstain altogether. The heretical character of some of the writers I shall be writing about is such that they are not only not against it, but would like to so maximize ignorance as to reduce knowledge to zero. Others, taking orthodoxy to a heterodox extreme, would prefer to make knowledge so all-encompassing that there is no room left for ignorance. In the one case, nothing but ignorance is the ideal; in the other, nothing but knowledge. But these two seemingly antagonistic camps are bound by a secret alliance: they share an obscure faith that knowing nothing and knowing everything are in some way equivalent, and a common abhorrence of the composite or intermediate state (which characterizes discourse) in which knowledge and ignorance commingle.

The title of this book is not intended to be mysterious. It does, however, incorporate various strands. The 'knowledge of ignorance', at its simplest, offers knowledge, or information, about ignorance. Secondly, the phrase denotes the attainment of ignorance (thus 'knowing' it as one knows joy, pain, etc.). Thirdly, it alludes to the privileged species of wisdom held to derive from the enjoyment of ignorance. And fourthly, the title signifies the apprehension or recognition of ignorance. The title, then, is simply an abbreviation, a more economical way of saying: 'the acquaintance with, acquisition of, enlightenment out of, and acknowledgement of, ignorance'. Ellipsis is, I think, a lesser evil than long-windedness.

The subtitle is similarly a slimmer version of a more obese ancestor. It originally boasted a triumvirate of abstract nouns, 'science, nescience, and omniscience', since omitted to avoid advertising the incredible. The existing subtitle, 'From Genesis to Jules Verne', might still seem like mere bravado. But it is at least more accurate (and briefer) than an earlier avatar – 'in some French Writers of the Eighteenth and Nineteenth Centuries' – and rather less fraudulent

vii

than one alternative suggested by my publishers – 'in French Literature'. The following text delivers, in fact, precisely what it promises, neither more nor less: it begins at the beginning of the Bible, goes on until it reaches Jules Verne, and then stops. But anyone expecting a comprehensive survey of the entire literary history spanning these extremes will be disappointed (although I trust that those who relinquish that expectation and read on will not be).

All books that claim to proceed 'from' something 'to' something else inevitably leave a lot out. The itinerary of this book differs only in degree by leaving in so little. The ordering of material obeys a narrative logic which is, moreover, less that of a history than of a work of science fiction: there are time-warps and hyperspatial jumps, as well as numerous black holes. Thus even what is left in is often left out of context.

This policy is not wholly accidental. Context is always a con-text: that is, a text that pretends to be something other than it is. To 'con' is to know (cognate with 'ken') but also to deceive, and may have some affinity with the French verb *cogner*. The contextualist purports to provide a foundation or origin to the text, a historical and intellectual prop for an interpretation. But contextualism conveniently forgets that the secondary or sub-texts it calls upon for endorsement are themselves in need of interpretation and thus engage the interpreter in an indeterminate interplay between texts. The con-text, converting circumstantial evidence into a canon, seeks to replace the circulation of sense by mere circularity, a tautological equation of texts, a hall of mirrors in which an interpretation encounters only reflections of its own argument. And since it makes a proper understanding dependent on acquaintance with the sub-texts invoked or the erudite commentary invoking them, the text in turn becomes fully accessible only to a closed circle of savants, initiates schooled in the incantations of the con-text.

While this esoteric knowledge is only a sophisticated mode of ignorance, it may be possible that ignorance, collapsing the putative foundation of the con-text, constitutes a kind of knowledge, a way out of the hall of mirrors, or at least a change of mirrors. Erudition, however wide, when tied to the con-text, is always too narrow. I will not therefore object too strongly if it is said of *The Knowledge of Ignorance* that there is more of ignorance than of knowledge in it. In an earlier incarnation, this text masqueraded as a scholarly dissertation; it now stands revealed as the mere book it always secretly was.

Nabokov wrote of Sebastian Knight that his prose was like his thought, which consisted of 'a dazzling succession of gaps'.[1] If the flattering epithet is set aside, the same might be said of this book, perhaps of any book, and certainly of this preface, which has indicated what is *not* in the text and sketched out a rationale of exclusion but has omitted to specify what *is* in it (an omission partially rectified by a rationale of inclusion in the introductory chapter). There is an aesthetics of omission; but one reason, perhaps the main reason, for the gaps in this book can be located in the gaps in the knowledge of its author. I am currently trying to fill in a few of these gaps and, as Verne said of his plan to describe the universe, this shouldn't take more than a century or so. Meanwhile, the gaps in the book will have to stay in.

Montesquieu said: 'il ne faut pas toujours tellement épuiser un sujet, qu'on ne laisse rien à faire au lecteur'.[2] This book, which follows that sound advice, can be read as the textual equivalent of a picture made up mainly of empty space populated by a few stray dots which need to be connected up before any intelligible form, or forms, can appear: I leave it to the reader to connect up the dots.

ACKNOWLEDGEMENTS

I am indebted to all those who have assisted in the genesis and evolution of this book: in roughly chronological order, to John Cruickshank, who opened; to David Kelley, who took over; to Christopher Prendergast, who encouraged; to Robert Bolgar and Terence Cave, who read and rectified; and to Malcolm Bowie, who advised and revised. The sections on Genesis and Jules Verne in particular have benefited from the generous erudition of, respectively, Melvyn Ramsden and William Butcher. I am especially grateful to King's College, Cambridge, for providing provocative interrogators and interlocutors, and for awarding me the Fellowship that made possible the final conversion from dissertation to book. My greatest debt of thanks is owed to Heather, who nursed the infant text, enthusing, musing, typing, editing, without ever losing faith, hope, or charity.

Earlier versions of the present sections on Genesis, and nutrition and cognition in Jules Verne, first appeared in *Philosophy and Literature* (Spring 1981) and *French Studies* (January 1983). The chapter on Verne also contains fragments of an article published in *Modern Language Review* (January 1982). I am grateful to the editors and publishers of these journals for permission to re-use this material (and for using it themselves in the first place).

Finally, I wish to thank all those, unnamed here, who have variously contributed, over the ages, to my knowledge of ignorance.

1

BEGINNING

'Begin at the beginning,' the King said gravely
(Lewis Carroll, *Alice's Adventures in Wonderland*)

To begin at the beginning is a desideratum difficult to obtain. In order to be able to begin at the beginning, it is necessary that there be a beginning to begin at, an *archē*, a state anterior to any process, a noun impervious to the verb: an intransitive beginning that precedes the transitive act of beginning.

The nostalgic recollection of an absolute origin has been endlessly and variously reiterated. The Old Testament records a divine Creation impaired only by human recreation. Plato postulates a paradise of intelligible ideas which the soul forgets in favour of acquaintance with sensible objects on its descent into the body. Rousseau alludes to an already long tradition (prolonged by Lévi-Strauss) of an uncorrupted state of nature prefacing the corruption of society.[1]

These disparate discourses, theological, philosophical, and anthropological, all share an archaeological configuration. Each articulates a linear sequence in which the prior is assigned priority. Each distinguishes between two beginnings, the one a degree zero of being exempt from becoming, the other the inauguration of a history characterized by the specification of a pre-history.[2] The text is retrospective, looking back to a time or space unoccupied by the text itself, a pre-text, which it is the function of the text to recall. Thus the archaeological text incorporates a teleology whose *telos* marks a recuperation of the *archē*: reunion, recollection, restoration: a reintegration of the future with the past, from which the present is alienated.

But the text itself marks an intermediate age between a temporarily lost plenitude and the moment of its reappropriation: it becomes identified with the displacement from an origin that it relates: the transition from virtue to sin, *epistēmē* to *doxa*, nature to

1

society, logos to discourse, speech to writing: it connotes a fall, a transgression, a loss. Thus while the beginning justifies the end, supplying a source of authority and a foundation to belief, morality, and epistemology, the text which invokes its name seems to render its restoration unrealizable. In consequence, the archaeological text generates an ambivalence towards writing, which it needs in order to articulate a desire, but needs to transcend in order to achieve consummation; its recurrent motif is frustration.

The beginning is therefore wanted but wanting, necessary but unobtainable. As Milton's Adam (who suffers from post-natal amnesia) observes:

> For man to tell how human life began
> Is hard: for who himself beginning knew?[3]

This difficulty is not, however, peculiar to man alone, but also seems to afflict his Creator. Genesis relates a beginning which has been identified as *the* beginning. The King James Bible begins:

In the beginning, God created the heaven and the earth.

But the New English Bible replaces this relatively simple, complete, declarative sentence with a more complex statement transferring the main verb from God to the earth by converting the act of creation into a dependent clause:

In the beginning of creation, when God made heaven and earth, the earth was without form and void, with darkness over the face of the waters.

The Anchor Bible (translated by E. A. Speiser) restores the main verb to God, but only by postponing its introduction until the third verse:

When God set about to create heaven and earth – the earth being then a formless waste, with darkness over the seas and only an awesome wind sweeping over the water – God said, 'Let there be light'.

These alternative translations derive from or exploit the grammatical ambiguity of the opening word of the Hebrew text, *bereshit* (corresponding to the phrase 'In the beginning' in the King James version). Hebrew lacks (or has lost) a genitive case or preposition; in order to indicate a possessive relationship between two consecutive words, it places the first in the 'construct' state, which may sometimes not be conspicuously different from its absolute state. *Reshit* has been read both as an absolute ('beginning') and as a construct ('beginning of'), since it remains identical in both forms.

Rashi, the eleventh-century Rabbinic commentator, reads it as the latter, making *bereshit* a property of the act of creating rather than of the moment in time at which it occurs: thus he rewrites the opening verse as: 'At the beginning of the Creation of heaven and earth', deferring the main clause (like Speiser) until the third verse.[4] According to Rashi, verse 2 implies that the waters were created before heaven and earth, so that verse 1 cannot relate a primordial generative act. Thus if verses 1–2 or 1–3 are taken as the syntactical unit, the beginning of Creation does not coincide with an origin: God does not begin at the beginning. Yahweh would then resemble other Mesopotamian demiurges who only impose order on a primeval chaos.[5] Borges cites the beginning of a Talmudic anthology which seems to confirm this interpretation: ' "It was only the first night, but a number of centuries had already preceded it".'[6]

Rashi has, however, been vigorously repudiated by Hirsch, who rewrites Genesis as follows: 'In the very beginning, God created . . .'. The advantage of Rashi's interpretation from a theological point of view, is that it does not ascribe the chaos depicted in verse 2 to the work of God. But this is outweighed, according to Hirsch, by its more serious disadvantages: the construct reading is

not only a metaphysical lie which has robbed the theories of mankind as to the origin of the world of truth i.e. of agreement with actuality, but is the much farther-reaching pernicious denial of all freedom of will in God and Man, which undermines all morality. If the material was there, was given to the world-former, He could only make the best possible out of that material but not the absolute best world. All physical and moral evil would then be in the imperfection of the material.[7]

God (as Nietzsche argues) appears to be determined by grammar: only if his action enjoys the status of an independent sentence, and is therefore originative, is he unlimited; if, on the other hand, creation is a dependent clause, then God too is subordinate to necessity. Only if *bereshit* is an absolute does God possess absolute dominion, whereas if it is a construct, then the created world in turn is only a construction upon a pre-existent base. The addition of a genitive to genesis restricts the divine autonomy proposed as a model to human morality: if God is not completely free, then neither is man. Nor, because the universe is not fully congruent with the designs of a Creator, can it correspond entirely with the creations or constructions of his creature. This reading of Genesis, says Hirsch, is not only false, it seems to make fallacy inevitable by

3

depriving human discourse, like the divine logos, of all 'agreement with actuality'. An origin is thus the indispensable ground of truth, the guarantor of verifiability.

However, even if read as an absolute, *bereshit* can only be translated as 'in *a* beginning'; 'in *the* beginning' would require *bareshit*, containing the condensed definite article.[8] The construct version, on the other hand, never takes the article, and can therefore be read as 'in the beginning of'. The choice is between indefiniteness and subordination. And in either case, the singularity of *reshit* is in doubt: God is an originator, a beginner, but not the only one; the divine origin is thus neither original nor unique. In the *Metaphysics*, Aristotle objects to the proliferation of origins. *Archē* signifies not only beginning, source, first cause, 'the first thing from which something either exists or comes into being or becomes known',[9] but also a principle of authority: sovereignty, rule, ruler. Too many *archai* imply bad government: thus Aristotle quotes Homer's *Iliad* in support of the view that 'the rule of many is not good; let one be the ruler'.[10]

In sum then, a non-archaeological genesis entails a degeneration into evil, falsehood, polytheism, pluralism, in a word, anarchy. As if in compensation, however, Genesis offers a firm distinction between a necessary, definite, unique human origin and an indefinite, contingent beginning. The Edenic pre-text prohibits the Tree of Knowledge; the Fall consists in eating of the forbidden fruit. Platonic theory also insists on a dichotomy between knowledge and ignorance but inverts their order of priority: the pre-natal Greek originally possesses knowledge of the *eidē* and only subsequently acquires ignorance on acquaintance with the world. Thus the two founding archaeologies of Western culture appear to present diametrically opposite images of human originality: in the one man knows nothing, in the other he knows everything.

But the archaeological text typically describes a circle in which beginning and end, genesis and apocalypse, nescience and omniscience are indistinguishably joined. Adam is bereft of the knowledge of good and evil, but until its acquisition there is no good or evil to be known. Thus although he knows nothing, there is nothing that he does not know (hence he is the intimate of God and able to name all creatures by their proper names). What cuts post-lapsarian man off from knowledge of his pre-lapsarian state is that he has knowledge. In order to know the unknown origin of unknowing he would have to transcend knowledge. But knowledge can only be brought to an end when it is completed, when there is nothing left to be known. Thus while primitive nescience shares the wholeness of omniscience, the attainment of omniscience coincides with the condition of nescience by achieving the restoration of an original intimacy with the universe. Similarly, according to Plato, only by relinquishing our (imperfect) knowledge of the world can (perfect) knowledge be recovered. Both Biblical and Socratic ignorance are species of wisdom. In short, to know nothing and to know everything appear as the two sides of a single page: one side is blank, empty, a *tabula rasa*; on the other is inscribed the thesaurus, the entire treasury of knowledge, the book of nature: the end of epistemology is conterminous with its beginning.

Baudelaire observes that 'tout poète lyrique . . . opère fatalement un retour vers l'Eden perdu'.[11] This is variously true of all the writers examined in this study. But their 'anepistemological' texts, postulating two symmetrical perfections, preceding or succeeding epistemology, alternate between or combine the nostalgic recollection of a pre-textual past in which writing has not yet begun and nothing is known, and the prophecy of a post-textual future in which writing is at an end and nothing is unknown.[12]

The second chapter of this study, ranging through a broad spectrum of exemplary works, traces a circular progression: beginning with the proposition that omniscience requires nescience, it ends with its converse, that nescience implies omniscience. The first three chapters of the Book of Genesis (a text to which all the other texts relate or allude) suggest that primal ignorance is the condition of virtue and beatitude, while knowledge, originating in the Fall, and the scripture that is its embodiment, are inherently sinful and tragic. The contradictory imperatives of Yahweh's epistemological prohibition and the serpent's advocacy of divine knowledge recur in the paradoxical *coincidentia oppositorum* of science and nescience, in which Greek and Judeo-Christian traditions intersect, and which was disseminated by Renaissance theologians and humanists (notably Nicholas of Cusa and Erasmus). The Renaissance couples the reverential reconstruction of an archive, the putative repository of wisdom, with an antipathy to books, alternately privileging Antiquity over the Middle Ages and the Golden Age over Antiquity.[13] Rousseau, a man of letters dedicated to the abolition of letters, represents at once a culmination and a condemnation of post-Renaissance culture: his dual utopias of nature and society replace communication by communion and invoke unknowing as the model of absolute knowledge.

The Bible, the Renaissance, and Rousseau embody temporal

hierarchies whose common function is to ascribe priority to one period over another (pre-lapsarian over post-lapsarian, *antiqua* over *moderna*, *sauvage* over *civil*). Chapter 3, devoted to thematically unified works of a restricted period, examines a spatial hierarchy. The primitive state postulated by Rousseau is located abroad in the decadent Orient, less a place than a *topos*, the *locus classicus* of ignorance. Hugo's *Les Orientales* articulates both the dominion of an enlightened, Platonic West over a benighted, Plutonic East, and the ascendancy of the self-apotheosizing poet over the universe. Napoleon's *mission civilisatrice* asserts the duty of French culture to educate and its right to annihilate the uncultured non-French, but postpones the Europeanization of the Arabs in favour of the Orientalization of the French. Napoleonic equivocation registers the central ambiguity of Orientalist discourse which, while it sanctions imperialism by the affirmation of epistemic supremacy, nevertheless displays an affection for, or affinity with, the intellectual degeneration it professes to abhor. Chateaubriand finds himself condemned (in the course of his *Itinéraire*) to either redundancy or repetition by Orientalism's exhaustive descriptions of the Orient. His frustrated craving for the renunciation of the thesaurus, a negation which would permit the affirmation of originality, is reflected in his celebration of the textual vacancy associated with the desert's negative landscape.

The central obsessions and images of anepistemological writing diverge in nineteenth-century French writing; but they appear to converge in the compendious fiction of Jules Verne. Chapter 4 therefore offers a close reading of his encyclopedic *Voyages extraordinaires* which, extending the temporal and spatial itineraries traced in earlier chapters to encircle the history and geography of the planet and the cosmos, incorporate a bibliography of contemporary literature, an index to the aspirations and anxieties of the age. Verne's scientific romances are less futuristic fantasies than nostalgic permutations of inherited categories and contraptions. Even Captain Nemo's submarine, the *Nautilus*, deviates from its historical model only by being spacious enough to accommodate a library and a museum alleged to assemble all the texts and objects generated by literature and science, art and nature. Thus the vessel is at once ark and archive. The vast Vernian *œuvre* is constructed on the model of the *Nautilus*: its transcendental ambition is to evoke the totality of things by articulating the totality of words available for their designation. The *Voyages*, anticipating the closure of the circle of knowledge, the attainment of omniscience, aim to supplant mimesis by mathesis, deploying science to abolish fiction. But the Vernian savant is always threatened, in the course of his journeys of intellectual discovery, by the catastrophic reduction of science to nescience. Finally, the fragmentation of scientific discourse suggests that knowledge and ignorance, science and literature, epistemophilia and anepistemophilia, are not mutually exclusive but inseparable. Accordingly, the final chapter goes on to consider why the end is as difficult to achieve as the beginning.

In each chapter, then, the anepistemological text repeats its attempt to articulate the hyperbolic desiderata of nescience and omniscience which belong outside the intermediate space of discourse. Writing cannot of course achieve the negation it affirms, cannot get outside itself, thus reconstituting a pre-scriptural origin or a post-scriptural conclusion. But, more damagingly, these ideal states are subtly corrupted and contaminated by being imported inside discourse. Each text sketches out a chiasmus[14] where the reversible polarities of knowledge and ignorance intersect, interlock, or interweave, incessantly displacing and replacing one another. Thus the text cannot attain a synthesis because it cannot even sustain an antithesis.

The same deficiency inevitably affects the following text. This study does not claim to do what it claims others fail to do. What it ought to be is a definition of the two distinct and incompatible concepts of knowledge and ignorance; what it is, is rather a demonstration of the difficulty of such a definition. The intentions and frustrations that characterize the anepistemological text apply equally to this book, which therefore does not so much say what its subject is, as show it.

The diverse texts considered herein share with the distant coordinates of a graph constructed from limited data the susceptibility to inclusion in alternative patterns spanning the conspicuous gaps between them. Conversely, it should be possible to introduce additional texts to support the structure of the argument. But in order to consider all the relevant texts it would be necessary to consider all texts because all are relevant. In order to complete this essay it would be necessary to complete the archive, to bring writing to an end, to close the hermeneutic circle which is the counterpart of the epistemological circle plotted by the texts under consideration.

In place of a synthesis, the tripartite central section, proceeding from an anthology through a corpus to an *œuvre*, affords three complementary and converging approaches to a pervasive intellectual mythology. The successive sections of the text correspond less to the consecutive moments of an evolution than to the interlocking concepts of a continuum of thought or writing: beginning and end, genesis and renascence, East and West, progress and decadence, science and literature. The methodology is strictly *bricolage*.[15] Thus although the text is not straight literary criticism, intellectual history, or philosophical treatise, it is not entirely *not* any of these either.

This study remains necessarily reductive: just as this text cannot exhaust all texts, neither does it pretend to exhaust any of the individual texts it alludes to. As Borges has observed: 'Literature is not exhaustible for the sufficient and simple reason that no single book is.'[16] The reverse, of course, is also true. The condition of incompleteness is not a problem to be resolved by either a longer or shorter inventory of items. Thus what follows (perhaps best categorized as a 'discourse') constitutes neither an extensive overview of the field nor an intensive *explication de texte*, but only (like the texts it examines) an intermediate text lodged between those two impossible ideals of completeness.

If the text can never constitute an origin, it seems inevitable not only that the ambition of hermeneutic archaeology, the excavation of an original meaning, should be ultimately unrealizable, but also that the present text should be far from original. Said's *Beginnings: Intention and Method* already deals amply with the phenomenon of beginnings; Kermode's *The Sense of an Ending* examines the varieties of ends; and perhaps no country between these limits remains wholly undiscovered. Situated at the intersection of countless other works which precede and exceed it, this study cannot but combine the preoccupations, techniques, and vocabulary of recent writers (its debt to Derrida and, to a lesser extent, Barthes, Foucault, Jakobson, Serres, will be evident) with other, more traditional, exegetical motifs. But the concept of 'influence' seems almost as mystical as that of 'originality', an astrological counterpart to archaeology. No prior critical text can have the last word any more than it can have the first: its judgement cannot be assimilated or reproduced undeviatingly. Thus just as the present study cannot transcend its predecessors, neither can it repeat them without qualification or question; it can be neither original with respect to the past, nor identical; it can escape neither dependence nor difference.

This opening chapter, an introduction to the text, a prolegomenon preceding a discourse, but preceded by a preface (itself, as Derrida observes, only nominally an 'hors livre'),[17] prefigures the intermediate status of the texts to be interpreted. 'The beginning', a place to begin at, is always a convenient fiction: it presents a past, a source, a point zero, pre-dating the beginning of a text which has already begun: it is inside a text which it only pretends to be outside. Thus it cannot provide a pretext, a justification, or an authority for what follows. The illusion of an origin prior to a beginning has already been exposed by Proust:

[mon soupçon] c'était que (alors que chaque jour je me considérais comme sur le seuil de ma vie encore intacte et qui ne débuterait que le lendemain matin) mon existence était déjà commencée, bien plus, que ce qui en allait suivre ne serait pas très différent de ce qui avait précédé.[18]

Just as there is no clear demarcation between youth and adulthood so there is none between pre-text and text in a novel which constitutes the book it professes to preface. There is no innocence, no privileged moment anterior and exterior to the text.

This text does not therefore begin at the beginning: it begins only when everything is already begun (but not yet ended): it begins (but also ends) where Dante began: 'nel mezzo del cammin'.

2

NESCIENCE AND OMNISCIENCE

Strange to know nothing
(Philip Larkin, 'Ignorance', *The Whitsun Weddings*)

2.1 Genesis

Theologically, epistemology stands condemned as irredeemably sinful because, psychologically, indistinguishable from vanity. What philosophy lacks, in theological terms, is humility, or, philosophically speaking, a systematic anepistemology: a theory of ignorance. Nor is it a simple matter to rectify this deficiency.

Scholarly indifference (springing from an enduring Platonic disposition to confuse knowledge with virtue) would suffice to render us more ignorant of the nature than of the condition of ignorance. But the ignorance of ignorance is also the consequence of an inexorable logic: on the one hand, the truly ignorant are inevitably ignorant of their own ignorance and so unable to give expression to their vacant state of mind; while, on the other, those articulate enough to propound a theory of ignorance, because they are also knowledgeable, are obliged to resort to their imaginations for their facts.

Yet further hazards impede the knowledge of ignorance: Pascal conceded that 'je puis bien concevoir un homme sans mains, pieds, tête . . . Mais je ne puis concevoir l'homme sans pensée'.[1] Analogously, it is possible that the absolute negation of knowledge, a *tabula rasa* of cognition, a degree zero of the intellect, is simply inconceivable. And it is certain that the first-person profession of ignorance (whether or not Socratically coupled with wisdom) is self-contradictory, since the acknowledgement, 'I am ignorant', implies my possession of at least one item of knowledge. Second-hand acquaintance with ignorance appears unobtainable; first-hand cognizance, untenable. In short, nothing is quite so unknowable as knowledge, unless it be the entire absence of knowledge.

The elements of one exemplary episode in the history of anepistemologies, linking the limits of knowledge and ignorance, may nevertheless be assembled by reference to the opening chapters of the Book of Genesis.

Here is one view of the Old Testament: it is a book of wisdom, written by wise men for wise readers, or to make the ignorant wise. Here is another: it is a sinful book, written and read by sinners.

If we take Yahweh[2] at his word, then the disconcerting truth is that both of these views are correct, and that the sages and sinners are one and the same. The equation of wisdom and evil is liable to seem suspiciously like a paradox. Of course, we know that the mere accumulation of knowledge and the susceptibility to sin are not mutually exclusive. We know that a sage can be a sinner; conversely, we know that the ignoramus does not of necessity covet his neighbour's wife. Nonetheless, if we do not, in the manner of Plato, consider knowledge synonymous with the Good, we do treat it, with quasi-Platonic reverence, as a sound or indispensable basis of moral conduct. Thus wisdom, *sophia*, relates the custody of knowledge to the exercise of an ethically discriminating conscience. Ignorance, it follows, is a condition which favours, if it does not entail, immoral conduct; it may be construed as *prima facie* evidence of undesirable propensities. The ignoramus, we may suspect, is a sinner at heart. Such are the prejudices of epistemic man.

It is therefore apt to seem mysterious, even inexplicable, that God should address to Adam the following injunction:

Of every tree in the garden thou mayest freely eat: But of the tree of the knowledge of good and evil, thou shalt not eat of it: for in the day that thou eatest thereof thou shalt surely die. (Genesis 2:16–17)[3]

Gerhard von Rad has written that 'to seek a purpose in the divine prohibition . . . is in our opinion not permissible; the question cannot be discussed'.[4] This *nolle prosequi* seems to be intended in two senses. First, von Rad believes that the issue cannot be resolved, can scarcely be raised, owing to a lack of pertinent evidence; second, he implies that even if the matter could, *per impossibile*, be rendered intelligible, it would be impious, even blasphemous, to do so. That human ignorance should form an integral part of the divine scheme of things seems, indeed, incomprehensible; however, unless some sense can be made of the affair, the deity's command is bound to appear not so much mysterious as merely arbitrary and capricious. Thus reticence on this point may in practice prove more

conducive to impiety than a frank attempt to solve the puzzle of
Yahweh's strict prohibition against the acquisition of knowledge.

The accretive genesis of the Book of Genesis, less swift and
coherent than the process depicted therein, compacting chronologically and ideologically remote strata of belief, and registering the
shifting stresses of alternative hermeneutical traditions, renders the
text notoriously susceptible to divergent interpretations. My own,
therefore, expresses not a necessary truth but only a possible one.[5]

The first three chapters of Genesis comprise two quite distinct
narrative cycles circumscribing contrary processes. These
sequences are not, however, alternative, but cohesive, separately
incomplete accounts of the business of creation. In the first,
Yahweh creates order out of chaos; in the second, man creates
chaos out of order, installs entropy in the cosmos. In the course of
this latter period, he also acquires the capacity to appreciate and
ultimately narrate the former. The punishment man's trespass
incurs turns out to be a fate worse than the capital sentence anticipated by God: not mere exile, but expulsion from Paradise combined with the compulsion to remember and remind others outside
what it was like inside. Man is tormented, like Dante's Francesca,
by memory: 'ricordarsi del tempo felice / nella miseria'[6] is his lot.
The recollection of happiness is the ground of our unhappiness;
what makes suffering finally intolerable is our accursed ability to
imagine things otherwise.

It remains obscurely scandalous that original sin should be
identified with the inclination to acquire knowledge. It is the inclination to avoid seriously entertaining this proposition that has led
many commentators to interpret man's misbehaviour as consisting
either in the quest for carnal knowledge or in the indiscriminate
transgression of a divine prohibition.[7] But the content of that prohibition is at least as important as its formal enunciation, and the
knowledge it seeks to outlaw irreducible to a matter of sex.

The opening chapters depict nescience as the *sine qua non* of
man's short-lived beatitude. Chapter 2 demonstrates ignorance to
be the object of Yahweh's approval; Chapter 3 is a lament for the
loss as much of ignorance as of divine favour. Virtue and ignorance
appear inseparable. This is a unique aspect of the Genesis account
of primeval history, startling in its seeming modesty when set
against other mythical texts describing creation. Ezekiel 28:12–19,
which contains an allusion to an alternative tradition, portrays man
as endowed with god-like wisdom, and banished from Eden for

12

numerous but unspecified iniquities.[8] In Genesis, on the other hand, it is ignorance that is god-given; man is created without innate ideas.

Before tasting the bitter fruit of the Tree of Knowledge, Adam (logic insists) is ignorant: he enjoys a state of primordial nescience. The narrative account of Eden reflects the difficulty of giving any positive content to this concept. The Yahwist, who is held responsible for most of this section of Genesis, appears remarkably reticent in comparison with exponents of rival myths steeped in fantastic local colour. Paradise remains scarcely characterized; nor is there any attempt to depict the psychological or moral condition of its occupants, except by implication. The only direct statement describing Adam and Eve's state of mind concludes with a negative: 'they . . . were not ashamed' (2:25). They are presented, in brief, as the negation of what they will be in the post-lapsarian stage. Their experience of life in Eden must be inferred from their experience outside.

Auerbach has argued that this rigorous suppression of detail is endemic to the Old Testament. Discussing the story of Abraham, he comments that 'everything remains unexpressed'.[9] However, although the Yahwist's discreet, parsimonious style is general, the minimal representation of psychic reality in Eden presents an extreme instance, a limiting case of narrative ellipsis, absolute zero on a scale of revelation. This lack of disclosure in Chapters 2 and 3 concerning God's favoured species corresponds to the account in Chapter 1 of the cosmos over which they are given dominion. The opening verses of Genesis are held by some to depict a process of *creatio ex nihilo*, by others to represent the ordering of the orderless raw material of the *tohu-wabohu* (without form and void); but, in either case, nothing is said of the featureless void that might be presumed to precede matter. Genesis abhors a vacuum. Yahweh must logically precede the universe of which he is Creator, but the narrative portrayal of the deity only proceeds when he is already engaged in creative activity. We are not informed how Yahweh spends the time, if there is any, prior to the first day of creation. God and nothingness appear incompatible. Similarly, Adam and ignorance (the internal, mental counterpart to the physical, external void), although logically coherent, are resistant to description. Just as Yahweh is describable only when the construction of his flawless idyll has begun, so the account of mankind only properly begins when Adam and Eve have set about its destruction. Chapter 2 is a parenthesis in the career of man in which God remains in complete control; Chapter 3 relates the forfeiture both of man's ignorance and God's domination. What remains is an exposition of the consequences of knowledge and freedom.

God and man, Adam and Eve, heaven and earth, nescience and omniscience: their one common denominator is that they are all couples: pairs of nouns. Many exegeses have artfully demonstrated the mystical relevance to the schema of creation outlined in Genesis 1 of the symbolically charged numbers 3 and 7: words, entities, events are ceaselessly affiliated to numerical permutations of these integers. But it could equally be shown, with less exercise of ingenuity, that the number 2, generating binary structures, dichotomies and couplings, is also fundamental to the Biblical universe.[10]

The process of creation is itself divisible into two distinct primary operations, each of which divides in turn into a pair of parallel secondary operations. The primary operations are, first, generative, and, second, transformational; combined they constitute the grammar of creation. The generative component consists of two recurrent procedures: immediate creation and mediate commandment. The former, with the verb *bara* (to create), implies the intimate involvement of Yahweh, and is reserved for such privileged entities as man and sea-monsters, or exceptionally spectacular gestures; Cassuto says that the use of *bara* stresses the 'wonder' of something.[11] The latter, a divine fiat soliciting the subjunctive ('Let there be') and the verb *asah* (to make), applies to inanimate things or lesser beings, such as cattle and 'every creeping thing that creepeth upon the earth' (1:26), which must be presumed relatively unwonderful.

Many of the entities thus generated are liable to undergo a further operation: transformation. Again, this phase of creation is reducible to twin procedures: division and combination. Without the transformational sequence creation would be incomplete or disordered.[12] Division (or, more specifically, bisection or bifurcation) and combination are the signs of creative economy: further, distinctive things and creatures are derived from existing *données*, instead of being summoned into existence by an additional act of creation: singulars can be made to yield plurals by division, or combined to produce another individual unit of the cosmos. Moreover, transformation is crucial to the intelligibility of the universe: a mere profusion of endlessly variegated, heterogeneous, unique and self-contained entities is thereby hooked into an orderly network of affinities, kinships, resemblances which fix the various elements of existence into a family relationship with each other (pointing to the singular progenitor of the vast plurality that is Creation).[13] Generative operations alone could only fill the *tohu* and *bohu* with further chaos; transformations, at the same time as they add to its diversity, substitute orderly genetic patterns for the sheer variety of the universe.

The repeated conjunction 'and'[14] suggests a succession of equal sequential actions constituting an arithmetical progression; it corresponds to the acts of immediate and mediate creation which are simply cumulative in effect, governing an operation of addition, and producing a prodigal but unstructured universe of disparate things. In contrast, the operation of division introduces an order of geometrical progression; generates manifold interconnections between the constituent parts of the total assemblage; multiplies distinctions and conjunctions, contrasts and continuities. Thus whereas the generative process is purely quantitative, the process of transformation is essentially qualitative.

But the created world, like the process of creation, remains dualistic in form. Systematically, thesis confronts antithesis: light is divided from darkness, day from night, heaven from earth, and the waters from the dry land. On a broader scale, the six active days of creation are divisible into two sequences of three days, balanced like the opposite sides of a mathematical equation, the first given over to the inanimate structuring of the universe, the other to the creation of its mobile or animate occupants. Man is conceived in Chapter 1 as the climax of creation, the culmination and completion of a series, the last word in perfection, virtually a twin of the Creator. Thus are God and man paired by the ubiquitous binary code. Chapter 2, in amplifying this account, concentrating on man alone after the broad perspective of Chapter 1 has sweepingly defined his place in the universe, shows man, uniquely, to be the issue of the second transformational procedure, combination. Man is not connected with other creatures or things by a relationship of opposition or identity; he is the lonely product of a synthesis. The tripartite structure of 2:7 ('And the Lord God formed man of the dust of the ground, and breathed into his nostrils the breath of life; and man became a living soul') dramatizes the combinative transformation which stands in contrast to the preceding phenomena of creation and division. In consequence, Adam internalizes external divisions: he embodies an elemental conflict.

The synthesis binds the incurably mundane to the absolutely sublime. The elements of earth and air can be combined, but they are not thereby deprived of their essentially contrary natures. Man is a meeting point, a space wherein two distinct orders of existence intersect and overlap;[15] he represents a blurring of identities, a kink in the smooth fabric of the universe, lacking the sharp definition of other items on the inventory of Creation. Categorially speaking, man is created impure.

Man's innate internal divisions are externalized by the Tree of Knowledge, whose position in the exact centre of the Garden corresponds to its crucial role in the drama of the Fall. Cassuto has demonstrated that the phrase 'the knowledge of good and evil' does not denote some abstract faculty of moral discrimination but rather a broad spectrum of action and experience. 'Good and evil' is in fact a nominal pairing (analogous in structure and import to 'heaven and earth') that accommodates everything that can be known.[16] And the manner of knowing is no less unrestrictive than the scope of the knowable. The verb *yada* (like the Greek *gignōskō*) is used of all kinds of knowing, including carnal knowledge; it makes no distinction between the intellectual and the sensual: thus we find 'Adam knew Eve' (4:1) as well as 'God doth know' (3:5). Genesis appears to incorporate an early instance of that *philosophie alimentaire* denounced by Sartre, according to which (according to Sartre), 'connaître c'est manger'.[17] But cognition is allied not only to nutrition but to coition. In the Hebrew tradition, knowledge is not located in some ideal, suprasensory world populated by philosophical souls but is, on the contrary, rooted in sensuous reality. Truth is not obtained via cerebral intimation or recollection: it is the fruit of a raw encounter with experience. Accordingly, the wisdom-fruit elicits an interest closer to lust than to either curiosity or appetite; and its consumption, the first joint activity of the couple, is the overture to a sexual union.[18]

Disappointingly, the forbidden fruit turns out to yield a poor epistemic harvest: not the omniscience promised by the serpent, but only the condition of consciousness in which knowledge is obtainable: it provides a means of access, heralds a departure rather than an arrival.[19] The discovery of nakedness that follows the assimilation of the fruit is a sign of transition, at once a symbol and a consequence of the humans' novel status: the couple have become self-conscious, objectified for each other, seeing themselves as they would be seen by others. Their gesture of concealment and evasion shows them behaving as they will behave in the public world beyond the Garden; they are already outsiders. Thus eviction from Eden is an objective confirmation of the externalization of self.

Another aspect of the phrase 'good and evil' is that, although grammatically it identifies the object of knowledge – what knowledge is actually 'of' – the connotative radiance of these substantives also qualifies the character of knowledge itself. Knowledge is morally ambiguous: it must be sacred since it is a property of the deity himself ('Behold, the man is become as one of us, to know good and evil' (3:22)); and yet, since Yahweh places it under an inflexible prohibition, its acquisition must be profane.

The prohibition against eating the fruit of the Tree of Knowledge poses an intolerable dilemma for the humans in Paradise and precipitates a rift in the overlapping elements of their being. Man is created a very close likeness of God; the Hebrew words *demut* (likeness) and *zelem* (image), cognate with verbs meaning to cut out or cut off, suggest an exact copy, a duplicate, a chip off an old block. Thus man, by virtue of his essence, inclines towards the nature of God, which includes omniscience. But he is created ignorant, and commanded to remain in this blissful state of intellectual and sensual vacancy. Clearly there is a conflict here between the propensity for, and the proscription of, cognition. It is the narrative function of the serpent – which constitutes a proleptic interpolation of post-lapsarian, epistemic man, an insertion of the corrupted future into the uncorrupted past, man as he is, tempting man as he was, to become as he will be: in short, an effect precipitating its cause – to shift conflict to crisis, and crisis to revolt. But the drama of temptation is almost redundant; the serpent, an allegorical intellectual, does no more than articulate the logic already implicit in Creation. God intended to mirror himself in man; but he neglected to endow his creature with knowledge equivalent to his own; man's disobedience consists in the god-like attempt to perfect God's imperfect art, to rectify an error or oversight of his Creator.

The analysis of the structure of Creation has indicated the binary rationale governing Yahweh's creation of man – the imperative that also issues in the creation of woman to partner Adam, an analogue of man. In the universe of Genesis, any singular entity, even the Creator, is constrained, in order to actualize its potential being, to seek a complementary being, a mate, a helpmeet, an *ezer kenegdo* (2:18), whose dual destiny, as commentators have shown, is to complete only by circumscribing its partner, to stand at once alongside and opposite, to act as both ally and antagonist.[20] The duty of the *ezer kenegdo*, in short, is not just to be half a couple but to be, in itself, double. The universal rage for coupling is one consequence of the transformational law of complementarity that generates the dualistic structure of Biblical reality. The law is of sufficient importance to merit the insertion of a didactic footnote into the main body of the text so as to make its interpretation quite unequivocal: Genesis 2:24, in an eerie, anarratorial voice which, like the serpent, belongs to the future,[21] states that the union of man and woman takes precedence over filial ties, that the couple enjoys preeminence.[22]

Jung's essay, 'Answer to Job', notes the internal application of this law to Yahweh by recalling the medieval view that God is a totality who, because he contains all possibilities, also contains all their opposites. Thus, if he is eternal and just, so he is simultaneously temporal and unjust, and so on. His nature, mathematically described, is akin to that of a parallelogram, consisting of equal and opposite forces.

One particular aspect of Yahweh's behaviour that Jung draws attention to is this: that although omniscient, he frequently acts as if, in Jung's phrase, he did not 'consult his omniscience';[23] he acts, apparently, as though he were ignorant of what he knows. Thus, for example, he can forbid Adam and Eve to eat of the fruit of the Tree of Knowledge and seem surprised when they nevertheless do so. While in principle having foreknowledge of their disobedience, his 'knowledge of good and evil' is restricted in practice to the one-sided opinion: 'behold, it was very good'. Or again, he may ask questions ('Where art thou?') to which he ought already, in principle, to know the answers. This apparent ignorance is super-inscribed upon God's activities in the world, eclipsing or casting a shadow over his actual omniscience. While man aspires to be God, God seems to play at being man. Thus, theologically, God knows the effects of his intervention in history; but, legally and aesthetically, must not be seen to know them, since such knowledge would make him guilty of complicity in the crimes of man, and, in addition, disrupt narrative sequentiality. Psychologically, he is split: in Jung's terms, conscious in one part of his psyche of what he is obliged to censor and suppress in another, he relegates knowledge to the unconscious, modulating his eternal omniscience by occasional nescience. Structurally, the narrative imitates Yahweh, in that it pretends to be temporarily ignorant of what it knows; conversely,

Yahweh imitates the narrative, by declining, by and large, to reveal the future.[24]

Yahweh, as he cannot help knowing, but refrains from disclosing to himself, is trapped by an unyielding logic. God must solve the problem (all the more problematic for gods) of how to acquire ignorance, for omniscience requires that he should know everything without exception, ignorance included. Jung's definition of God's pleromatic identity, which confers upon him the possession of antithetical qualities, and the universal algebra of complementarity entail the same consequence: that nescience is a supplement destined to complete knowledge: its *ezer kenegdo*.

There are two traditional answers to the question: Why does God outlaw the fruit of the Tree of Knowledge? The first is egotism. This is the serpent's answer: Yahweh is a god jealous of his divine pre-rogatives; he wishes to perpetuate his monopoly of omniscience and immortality. The second answer is altruism. Yahweh is a beneficent God, exhibiting kindly, paternal concern for his children. He knows that the acquisition of knowledge, the experience of the world beyond Eden, will bring them nothing but sorrow and seeks, out of goodness alone, to preserve their condition of blissful ignorance. His fears are borne out in the event, and Adam and Eve pay the price. Their expulsion from Eden is not the work of a vindictive god but the symbolic working-out of the suffering that goes with knowledge.

The considerations outlined in the preceding pages suggest an alternative answer. Yahweh's prohibition of knowledge arises from the deity's need and desire to realize the logical possibility, the logical necessity, of ignorance. Man is a device for discovering and experiencing the condition of ignorance. Omniscience is intoler-able; but nescience is not immediately accessible to God. Adam and Eve function as intermediaries who permit such access: they offer a vicarious respite from the burden of excessive knowledge. Unfortu-nately, they are too much like their Creator to endure indefinitely the primitive condition of ignorance; inevitably, they become con-sumers of the knowledge that Yahweh, through them, seeks to transcend.

It has been observed that God is not all-powerful because he can-not build a wall he cannot jump: God can do anything except fail; nor, it might be added, is he all-knowing because he cannot know ignorance: he can know everything except nothing. Man serves God as a means of circumventing these apparent limits to his limitless totality. Man builds unjumpable walls enclosing unknowable gardens on behalf of his omniscient and omnipotent Creator. This is his embarrassing *raison d'être*: to be ignorant and to fail.

But more than this, God's doomed experiment with human nescience, precisely because it was condemned to fail from the start – as God could not help but know – enables God himself to achieve failure. Man and woman, irrevocably flawed creations, are a visible refutation of all hypothetical circumscriptions of his infinite possibilities – which must include fallibility.

The insufficiently dialectical Jung observes that neither the Fall nor 'the Cain–Abel intermezzo' can be 'listed [among] the Creation's shining successes'.[25] But it follows, if the above argument is correct, that God's failure paradoxically constitutes a kind of success, *sub specie aeternitatis*, from the divine point of view, because it permits God to successfully fail. And it is doubly successful, because our failure, the Fall, obliges him, in the joyful act of creating a knowledge-seeking entity to whom he understandably, but unobeyably, forbids knowledge, to enact the ignorance of his own inevitable mistake.

Man is not only a model but also the means of ignorance: he is that creature of whose actions it is possible not to have foreknowledge. Omniscience, to attain completion, must embrace nescience, thereby condemning itself to incompleteness. God, a two-fold being like man, a *deus duplex*, although (as *Elohim*) capable of knowing all things, good and evil, nevertheless denies himself (as Yahweh) that epistemic absolute in order to know ignorance:[26] Yahweh, paradoxically, is therefore (in principle) an omniscient being who does not (in practice) know everything.[27]

Of course God's ignorance is never complete but only partial. But it seems that Adam, conversely, fails to conform to the model of absolute nescience. Rashi glosses 4:1 ('And Adam knew Eve his wife') as follows: 'And the man knew already before the events related above took place – before he sinned and was driven out of the Garden of Eden.'[28] The (Hebrew) perfect tense here, following a series of imperfects (coupled by 'and') acquires a pluperfect sense: the action it describes has already taken place previous to the event preceding. Knowledge (here, specifically carnal, and therefore general) is thereby reversed into the indefinite past. Hence Abraham ibn Ezra's remark that 'man did indeed possess great knowledge without eating of this tree'.[29] The account of creation in Chapter 1 omits the Eden interlude altogether, thus temporally and epistemologically overlapping Chapters 2 and 3 (hence, in 1:29,

God invites or commands man to eat from 'every tree, in the which is the fruit of a tree yielding seed' – the prohibition has already lapsed). But it does not then (as the 'Documentary Hypothesis' implied) constitute an unassimilated contradiction, but only a qualification: pure ignorance, the period of residence in Eden, belongs to a purely fictional moment, without duration: everything, and thus knowledge of everything, is already begun from the very beginning. Chapter 1 shows that Chapter 3 (eating of the fruit) is pluperfect with respect to Chapter 2 (abstinence): the Fall itself is post-lapsarian.

The serpent's prediction (3:4) and Yahweh's acknowledgement (3:22) of man's equality with God in the knowledge of good and evil recognize that they are both of epistemologically intermediate status: lodged between zero and infinity, their knowledge is incomplete. Thus ignorance stands to knowledge, as Adam stands to God and Eve to Adam, as its *ezer kenegdo*: at once adjacent and opposite, it extends only by restricting the scope of its counterpart: it anticipates and perpetually postpones the prospect of plenitude.

If knowledge is the root of sin, and perfect ignorance (which is certainly irrecoverable, perhaps imaginary) the prerequisite of virtue, it would seem to follow that the Old Testament itself, in so far as it pretends to be a repository of knowledge, is tainted. The Biblical text is one of the effects of the primeval tragedy that Genesis recounts, and represents an attempt to understand, to expiate, and redeem the fault that was its cause; but it is self-defeating, because in knowledgeably narrating, it only re-enacts the sin it is its hopeless ambition to annul.

The Old Testament is an intermediary plying between God and man, or between men, the rationale of whose mission springs from the cessation of unmediated communion. The Bible is a go-between charged with the task of procuring a rapprochement between former partners, but whose very articulation confirms a separation. More generally, the text is, at best, second-best: the consequence of a divorce, it embodies a sense of isolation and abandonment. Literature, in other words, owes its existence to the Fall, which is a falling-away (from perfection) but also a falling-out. Thus it only makes sense to speak of writing in the aftermath of original sin.

The pastoral, a literary invention, is characteristically antipathetic to literature. Paradise is pastoral, that is, it contains trees and animals, even humans (in minimal numbers), but no books. Adam can neither read nor write. But he, like his maker, has no need of literacy, since Yahweh sends him no written messages, hands him no scroll of parchment from a mountain-top (the implicit topology of Eden consists of a horizontal plane: nothing is hidden). The rapport enjoyed by this harmonious couple (later, trio) is (temporarily) flawless.

Scripture becomes possible at the same time that it becomes necessary, when this rapport has irreparably broken down. Holy scripture is an incessant reminder of our alienation from God, and an expression of nostalgia for the primordial condition of impeccable harmony between God and man. The Old Testament is thus both a confession of sin and a prayer for deliverance. It is a tragic text because the desire it embodies, for redemption and reunion, is doomed to frustration. Communion with God, the intimacy Adam enjoyed with Yahweh, presupposes the absence of books. Thus the book, though it proposes to heal the rift between the divine and the human, can only succeed in preserving or augmenting the distance between them. Ethically, all writing implies failure because it perpetuates the condition of sinfulness. In the beginning was the (spoken) Word ('Let there be light' precedes light);[30] but the scriptural formulation of that verbal origin signals the irrevocable transition (the decline) from the divinely-inspired, textless logos of Eden to the post-Edenic, secular textuality that afflicts mankind. The Oral Torah is the Law of God, but the Written Torah is the work of man (Moses): at once sacred and profane, it makes the logos decipherable, accessible to exegesis and hermeneutics, and therefore mysterious.

The nostalgic dream of an irrecoverable condition of nescience, alluded to in Genesis, recurs sporadically throughout the Old Testament. It is given its most plaintive expression in Ecclesiastes, whose pages echo with a despairing, alternately elegiac and cynical advocacy of ignorance, and reflect a profound disaffection for the sphere of socially sanctified education. Hence the melancholy lament that ends the first chapter: 'For in much wisdom is much grief; and he that increaseth knowledge increaseth sorrow' (1:18), and the quiescent self-negation of the conclusion (to which a later, less subversive peroration, commanding obedience to God's commandments, has been added): 'Of making many books there is no end; and much study is a weariness of the flesh' (12:12). The condition of reader is scarcely less suspect than the profession of scribe.

The worldly, literate wisdom of *hokhmah* (connoting coercive force, restraint) – repudiated by Ecclesiastes – is enshrined in the sentential, juridical strictures of Proverbs on the indispensability of epistemic maturity. The oppressive purpose of Wisdom Literature is to reconcile collective allegiance to a temporal community with the essentially individual and potentially anarchic belief in an eternal God; to suture Judaic social law with a spiritual creed by socializing and transcribing faith; to funnel divine authority into the rod of a secular ruler, supported by scribes, and thus render the true believer as subservient to his hieratic and political superiors as he is to God. (The Ecclesiastical advocacy of nescience is therefore worse than heretical: it is seditious, because it threatens to unravel the disparate threads of society, to unstitch the seam of morality, thus rescinding the jurisdiction over the believer of sage or priest.) But the authoritarian gesture of an epistemocratic *gendarmerie* contradicts the epistemic prohibition of Genesis. Thus there would seem to be a discrepancy between the rules of the Father and the city fathers, the divine commandments of the King of Heaven, and the civil ordinances of the kings of Israel: the interminable interpretation of the Word of God runs counter to the putative finality of the logos. This difficulty is recognized by Agur, who states: 'Every word of God is pure . . . Add thou not unto his words, lest he reprove thee, and thou be found a liar' (Proverbs 30:5–6). Agur, of course, then proceeds to add further words.

The New Testament, dramatically conceived, is the enactment of the conflict between the sacred and its licensed interpreters and intermediaries, precipitated by the entrance of an outsider proclaiming a means of direct access to God that circumvents constitutional channels. Scribes (along with Pharisees and tax-collectors) are seen as the *bêtes noires* of the faithful. The Pauline interpretation of events is encapsulated in the anepistemological inversion of *sophia*: 'If any man among you seemeth to be wise in this world, let him become a fool, that he may be wise' (1 Corinthians 3:18). Since knowledge precludes belief, the confirmation of faith implies the displacement of knowledge by ignorance. Genesis shows that omniscience inexorably entails nescience; conversely, the New Testament suggests that ignorance is a prerequisite of mystical revelation, of an insight into an eternal, divine truth inaccessible to quotidian cognition.

The exclusion of scripture from the scriptural paradise of Eden, and the explicit formulation of a critique of books in the Book of Ecclesiastes point to the post-Edenic significance of nescience. Relative or transitive ignorance is simply the ratio between known and unknown, the difference between what we think we know and what we think we ought to know; it is anticipatory, normative.

Absolute or intransitive ignorance – in a word, nescience – is, in contrast, a nostalgic, atavistic condition, as desirable (like omniscience) as it is unattainable; it may be provisionally defined as the state of being unacquainted with a cultural archive (the textual embodiment of knowledge, the sum of the *déjà-écrit*, what Russell calls 'knowledge by description').[31]

2.2 Renaissance

The Pentateuch distinguishes between a pre-lapsarian state, in which man enjoys intimate verbal communication with God, and a post-lapsarian state, characterized by writing, in which God has become elusive. Thus the Bible incorporates a scriptural abhorrence of scripture: it is a text calling, in one of its dissonant voices, for the annihilation of texts. A corresponding strategy occurs in Plato, who contrasts a prior (pre-natal) condition of unmediated knowledge of the Good, which may be recollected by means of the dialectic, with our existence in the sensible world, in which the truth is forgotten, an oblivion reinforced by writing, which is orphaned from its dialectical father.[32] The poet is a charlatan or magician who only appears all-knowing (*passophos*) because of our inability to distinguish between knowledge (*epistēmē*) and ignorance (*anepistēmosunē*): mimesis only multiplies the distance dividing the objects of experience, already copies, from their archetypal forms, the *eidē*.[33]

This antithetical structure of possession and loss, knowing and unknowing, presence and absence (of the Father), recurs persistently in the Renaissance, where it is translated into a history of culture, according to which, however, writing is the repository of all knowledge, not of *doxosophia* but of *sophia* itself. For the Bible and Plato, ignorance results from the fall into scripture and rhetoric; for the Renaissance, it is the consequence of a falling-away from true *eloquentia*, which may be reversed by the restoration of a lost archive.

The Renaissance seems to enact, even as it recalls, the Platonic theory of anamnesis: its privileged status depends on recollecting a temporarily forgotten thesaurus of ideas, identical with truth. Renaissance writing claims to recycle knowledge ignored by recent centuries (the *moderna*), a period which it therefore consigns to the perfect, completed past, even as it restores a pluperfect period (the *antiqua*) to the present. The Middle Age is denounced as a temporal interlude, an anachronistic supplement to Antiquity which has only to be transcended to renew the continuity of culture.

The medieval self-image, however, denied forgetfulness, discontinuity with the past: the pre-Renaissance was already a prolongation and a refinement of classical Rome, a *translatio studii*.[34] The project variously defined and undertaken by medieval writers was the rational reconciliation of authoritative texts. The ideal text (exemplified by the *summa*) would assimilate philosophy to theology, Aristotle (minus the *Poetics*) to Christianity, reason to revelation, and thereby generate a scripture commensurate with the universe, as irrefutable and definitive as Scripture, a symbol at once of supreme knowledge and salvation. The aim of the *summa* was to put an end to discord, to leave no room for disagreement. Thus scholastic theology, while dedicated to the Book, the Word, was intolerant of books and words, whose insidious plurality threatened to disrupt a unified system of belief in a singular God. Knowledge (the gift of God, not the acquisition of man) was already complete from the beginning: it required only contemplation, conservation, and dissemination.

Dante bridges the French scholasticism of the thirteenth century and the Italian humanism of the fourteenth. While Thomism (like Plato's Republic) exiled pagan poets for lying about the gods,[35] the *Commedia* reaccommodates them, but allocates them to the Limbo of the First Circle, while even the relatively mobile Virgil is not allowed to ascend to Paradise. The poem ('lo sacrato poema' (*Paradiso*, XXIII, 62)) is redeemed only by its submission to the task of supporting and revealing a strictly hierarchical Christian cosmos. Thus Virgil is conceived as the encyclopedic sum of human knowledge, bestriding arts and sciences, the 'savio gentil che tutto seppe' (*Inferno*, VII, 3); conversely, the cosmos constitutes a single encyclopedic volume, binding together innumerable scattered quires ('Legato con amore in un volume / ciò per l'universo si squaderna' (*Paradiso*, XXXIII, 86–7)).

The fourteenth-century Renaissance perpetuates Dante's view of the revelatory status of poetry:[36] it criticizes but perpetuates the thirteenth-century project by designating an alternative textual corpus as the treasury of wisdom.[37] The Parisian scholastics of the dark ages (that threaten to encroach on the present) appear as barbarians, their *ratio* only a species of blindness or ignorance, while the *oratio* of the (Italian) ancients affords the plenitude of true knowledge.[38] The Renaissance transcends the dichotomy of philosophy and rhetoric by redrawing the circle of learning, the *encyclios paideia*[39] drawn by the *summae*, so as to leave outside that which had originally left outside what was now inside. Just as Thomism sought to privilege discourse by excluding poetry, so the Italian poets in turn seek privileged status by excluding (the language if not the tenets of) Thomism. While the Middle Ages opposed Christian to un-Christian literature, the Renaissance draws a line between civilized and barbarian writers. But in each case, the Other is denounced for his ignorance by a discourse asserting a monopoly of wisdom and truth. Thus a three-fold periodization of time supports a two-fold division of discourse.[40] But if the Renaissance is a partial continuation of the Middle Ages it disdains, then its critique of scholasticism may in turn recur as self-criticism.

The reappropriation of knowledge claimed by the Renaissance is secondary to its claim to restore the past to presence. But a sense of the absence of the past infiltrates and contaminates the characteristic mode of self-identification of the Renaissance, the act of identification with Antiquity.[41] And the recognition of a dense zone of differences, a negation accompanying the affirmation, depriving the Renaissance of a textual proximity which would be its justification, coincides with the withdrawal of wisdom beyond the classical into a pre-textual age.

What distinguished the Renaissance was, by medieval standards, its lack of discrimination. Medieval Christianity was not inexorably hostile to all pre-Christian literature: certain pagan texts, compatible with dogma, could be salvaged, purified, and systematically Christianized.[42] The Renaissance humanists, on the other hand, departed from the principle of ideological selectivity: what was good was not so much what was virtuous but what was eloquent or merely ancient: ethical gave way to aesthetic or temporal criteria of judgement.[43]

The aesthetic principle of *copia*, a theory formulated and practised by Erasmus,[44] was central to Renaissance writing: it proposed the systematic assimilation and exploitation of the thesaurus of archival material that was the legacy of Antiquity. The writer would bring into play its vocabulary, grammar, and images in reworking the consecrated *topoi*. The sudden expansion of the archive had confronted the writer (the principal requirement of whose craft was that he should first be reader) with an embarrassment of riches; it was the function of the cornucopian text to incorporate, and thus exert control over, a multiplicity of alternative voices. But the sheer proliferation and diversity of available texts degraded the ideal of a comprehensive intellectual synthesis to a merely eclectic juxta-position of unreconciled manners and ideas. Moreover, the dis-integration of the collectively constructed but unified philosophical encyclopedia of the Middle Ages[45] was attended by a re-evaluation not just of particular textual authorities, but of the sacred authority of the text, now corrupted by *contaminatio*.

Ian McFarlane states that 'one of the battle-cries of the Neo-Latins and the Pléiade is directed against *le monstre ignorance*'.[46] Ignorance is a relic of the preceding dark ages destined to be banished by the more distant but also more brilliant illumination of the classical age. But the Renaissance does not present a unanimous encomium of knowledge.[47] Anepistemological writing, the learned defence of the monster ignorance, the bookish contempt for books, is a microcosm of the Renaissance universe, encapsulating its ambiguous allegiances. It exemplifies the tension between a prodigal archive and the renunciation of archival dogma, the fric-tion between scholastic form and humanistic content; and it com-bines an apparent negation with the evocation of a synthesis, the negation of a negation.

According to Aristotle, the desire to know is natural and praise-worthy; according to the Old Testament, curiosity led to man's dis-grace. Plato designates knowledge as the precondition of virtue; vice is the product of a lack of understanding about one's true interest.[48] Thus the Good is synonymous with absolute knowledge, while ignorance is the source of all evil. Genesis, on the other hand, suggests that ignorance is not merely conducive, but also essential to virtue. While the Greek tradition argues that it is enough to be wise in order to be good, the Bible asserts that it is enough to be good in order to be wise.[49] Morality is identified, in one case, with knowl-edge, in the other, with ignorance. It is a commonplace of the Renaissance, whose characteristic project it is to assimilate all previous statements, to reconcile these antithetical propositions by syllogistically reducing them to the paradoxical equation of knowl-edge and ignorance, science and nescience.[50]

Montaigne's *Essais* are, in one aspect, a late, concentrated embodiment of this ambivalent synthesis. The *Apologie de Raimond Sebond* is not just a simple critique of *le savoir* (*des autres*) combined with a celebration of *ignorance*, relying on canonical techniques of quotation, allusion, and paraphrase to support an argument attacking reliance on a canon: it argues that ignorance is in fact a superior mode of knowledge. Conversely, the acquisition of knowledge represents an increment in ignorance. In Scève's account of Eden, the inhabitants are thoroughly uninformed:

> Ensemble s'entr'aymant ignorans ne savoyent
> Par qui, à qui, pourquoy, et comment ils vivoyent.

Yet retrospectively, from the perspective of their subsequent intellectual development, they appear to have been comprehensively *au courant*:

> Ensemble dechassés du plaisant Paradis
> Dans lequel innocens divinement jadis
> Toute chose ils avoyent et nommee et connue,
> Ores toute incertaine en leur memoire nue.[51]

As they have put on clothes, so they have stripped their memory naked: they have forgotten all they ever knew, which is everything. Again, as in Genesis, the pluperfect is invoked: knowledge always precedes whatever time and tense the couple is currently in; as in Plato, knowledge can only be reminisced about. The Tree of Knowledge might more accurately have been named the Tree of Ignorance.

Gargantua's Letter to Pantagruel has often been invoked as an idealized statement of the most encyclopedic ambitions of Renaissance humanism.[52] But Rabelais's hyperbolic programme of studies nevertheless appears to strike at least one conspicuously discordant note. Gargantua enjoins his son to strive to achieve perfect knowledge: 'Et quant à la congnoissance des faictz de nature, je veulx que . . . rien ne te soit incongneu.' But he sums up his pedagogical advice by ambiguously concluding: 'Somme, que je voys un abysme de science.'[53] The phrase, *abysme de science*, denotes, now proverbially, a maximization of knowledge, and can be equated with the more common *puits de science*. Thus the optimistic father looks forward to the sinking of a well of science by his son, destined to irrigate and eradicate ignorance. But the etymology of *abysme*, deriving from the Greek *abussos*, bottomless, and its manifold negative senses of emptiness and perdition attach connotations of vacuity and even sinfulness to the term. Thus science may not be a well that one draws from so much as a pit that one is drawn into. In any case, if science is an abyss, without a *bussos*, baseless as well as bottomless, then it can never be filled, and cannot realize the plenitude of knowledge to which Gargantua vainly aspires[54] (a point he implicitly acknowledges when he proceeds to urge his son to desert his studies in favour of martial arts). But the phrase also hints at a further option: the *abysme de science* may constitute neither a well nor a pit but simply a void, an evacuation of science, a complete negation of knowledge which, like the Edenic nescience alluded to in the opening paragraph of the letter, may yet allow the unknower to accomplish the stated aim of omniscience.

The consequences of this *coincidentia oppositorum*, the attempt to reconcile the contradictory imperatives of Yahweh and the serpent, can be traced in numerous works located at the intersection of Greek and Christian traditions; two of the most influential are Nicholas of Cusa's *Of Learned Ignorance* and the *Praise of Folly* of Erasmus.

Medieval theology (and theology in general) oscillates between two distinct strategies. One, characteristic of the scholastic approach, generates a style of systematic theology, appealing ultimately for its validity to the criteria of philosophical legitimacy. It invokes a schema whose purpose is to reconcile metaphysics and reason, to base statements of an ontological order on the foundations of logic. *God*, a noun to which predicates can be attached similar in structure if not in substance to those attached to the noun *man*, say, or p or q, is installed at the head of a universal hierarchy of rational relations. The intention of this ordered exposition of absolute truth is to render intelligible to man the (only apparently) mysterious ways of God.

The other, more mystical strategy (which might be variously traced in the *theologia negativa* of Pseudo-Dionysius, Eckhart, *The Cloud of Unknowing*, and San Juan de la Cruz) emulates the first only in asserting, no less confidently, the existence of God. But it declines to translate the divinity into the anthropocentric symbols and concepts of language. To seek to systematize the deity is considered not only absurd but reductive, and in the last analysis, blasphemous. God is inaccessible, because infinitely superior, to our secular apparatus of thought (which is not the measure of all things); reunion with God will therefore exact a renunciation of intellect.

Nicholas of Cusa enjoys the singular distinction of contriving to embrace both these antagonistic tendencies simultaneously. In *Of Learned Ignorance* he assumes unconditionally the existence of God; pronounces him inexplicable, beyond the comprehension of man; whereupon he proceeds to outline an explanation of the deity for which he invites or demands our comprehension. Nicholas furnishes a complete deductive exposition of the relationship to the universe of a God who is admitted to be resistant to analysis by the tools of logical argument. He systematically refutes systems.[55]

Nicholas condenses his view of the divinity in a sentence that appears to exhaust all possible alternatives of opinion: 'the absolute maximum', he says, 'is beyond our comprehension yet intelligible, able to be named whilst remaining ineffable (*incomprehensibiliter intelligibile pariter et innominabiliter nominabile*)' (I, v, p. 14 (Heron translation); p. 11 (Leipzig edition)). This sentence registers the rivalry in the text between the Aristotelian logic which is the basis of discourse and the quasi-mathematical logic which seeks to displace it. In *Of Learned Ignorance* the rhetorical option of paradox, one of the devices of *elocutio*, is elevated to the plane of *dispositio*; thus a stylistic mannerism is converted into a structural strategy, the rationale of a method which Nicholas justifies as follows: 'in theology we must, as far as possible, forestall contradictories by previously uniting them in a simple concept' (I, xix, p. 43; p. 38). Thus the text aspires to the condition of God, whose nature it is to reconcile and transcend opposites.

One category in Barthes's three-fold typology of discourse, the *enthymématique*,[56] is particularly applicable to Nicholas: the enthymeme, in the sense of a licentious syllogism whose component premises are individually unreliable yet whose exemplary conjunction remains *ergo*,[57] seems to provide the pattern for his propositions. Moreover, the tripartite construction of the book reflects the quasi-syllogistic configuration of the textual dialectic. The symmetrical, orderly, triangular argumentation invokes the indubitable precision of mathematics, the structural elegance of geometry. At the level of *dispositio*, therefore, Nicholas's rhetoric rests its authority on its intellectual scruples, its conformity to classical models. Geometry, discourse, and the Trinity coincide.

The conspicuous formalism of the text, its mimesis of, and allusion to, mathematical patterns (which Nicholas holds, together with music, to underpin the construction of the universe and to reiterate the divine), respond to the desire for tautological certitude in theological matters. However, the text appears to enact the frustration of that desire. The flagrant improprieties of *elocutio* (multiplying paradox, oxymoron, *non sequitur*, and compounding the sin of self-contradiction by the disruptive conjunction of the finite and the infinite) run counter to the ponderous decorum of *dispositio*. At one level of ordering, Nicholas's discourse obeys the protocol of logical contiguity; at another, it violates or overleaps the decencies of persuasive disquisition. The friction between contrary manners is duplicated in the frequent ironic coupling of obstinately opaque statements and reflexive comments affirming their self-evidential transparence – phrases of the type 'It is clear that p', where p is any manifestly unclear proposition. The discontinuity between directions and indirections, as between a pseudo-logical superstructure and a sub-logical infrastructure, reproduces the frustration inherent in the negations of anepistemological theology.[58]

The mind, argues Nicholas, automatically aspires to truth. All empirical inquiry is comparative, approximate, conjectural: we climb towards the unknown or the uncertain on the steps of the (relatively) known and certain. But the ascent, proposed by philosophers, to the summit of knowledge, to ontological and theological truth, is condemned to failure. When we seek to know God or essences (the 'quiddity' of things) we are like owls trying to look at the sun, because there is no ladder of approximations and comparisons connecting the finite world (an aggregate, afflicted by plurality), which we know more or less, to the infinite world (a comprehensive unity), which we cannot know. Thus Nicholas restores transcendence to the transcendent. Truth is a circle[59] with which the intellect, merely a polygon of an unlimited number of sides, will never be perfectly congruent; its smooth circumference is resistant to the angular predications of discursive reason.

Our inquiry into the infinite will not, however, be entirely futile if it at least serves to acquaint us with our ignorance. In this way we acquire the condition that Nicholas calls *docta ignorantia*. But this is not to be confused with agnosticism. Nicholas never puts in doubt the existence of the deity; he refutes only the vain intellectual supposition that we can have any first-hand, intimate knowledge of God. Thus we *know that* God exists, but we cannot *know* God (in the sense of *connaître* as distinct from *savoir*): the mind always finally collides with the *murus paradisi* encircling the infinite. Moreover, Nicholas rests the logic of belief on precisely this unknowability: the implicit statement underlying his faith is *credo quia nescio*: knowledge (of God) and faith are mutually exclusive, theology and epistemology diverge.

For Nicholas, there are no Platonic forms to satisfy the intellect's insatiable desire for an eternal object of knowledge. Nicholas retains Plato's opposition between the sensible and the suprasensible, but deprives the latter of the qualification of intelligibility. Cassirer stresses that he thereby rehabilitates the quest for empirical knowledge of the world.[60] But all secular knowledge, according to Nicholas, whether 'sensual' or 'intellectual', synthetic or analytic, is not merely imperfect, unsatisfactory, but tainted: branded with the stamp of Adam. The price we pay for our epistemic impurity is to be cut off from knowledge of God, the supreme universal; ignorance therefore can only bring us closer to an apprehension of the deity. Thus Nicholas enumerates the contents of the senses, reason, and imagination, and asserts: 'we are compelled to eject (*evomere*) all that' (I, x, p. 22; p. 20). Correspondingly, in *De visione dei*, he argues that 'it behoveth then the intellect to become ignorant and to abide in darkness if it would fain see Thee'.[61] Knowing nothing and knowing everything are equivalent since, if truth is a circle, then the beginning of knowledge, original ignorance, coincides with its end, the epistemic minimum with the maximum.[62]

The *intellectus*, then, can attain infinity only providing the discursive *ratio* is in abeyance. This is one sense of *docta ignorantia*: theologically knowledgeable ignorance. But that conceptual possibility is itself placed in abeyance by the alternative sense of the phrase: ignorant knowledge. Our knowledge of the *maximum contractum* is ignorance of the *maximum absolutum*, but it is knowledge nonetheless.[63] Nicholas's negative theology is deprived of consummation by his positive epistemology: knowledge is inadequate, but also inescapable. As Koyré comments, 'la Docte ignorance est docte beaucoup plus qu'elle n'est ignorance'.[64] Thus the knowledge of ignorance prohibits, equally, pure ignorance and complete knowledge: the mind is permanently suspended between knowing nothing and knowing everything. The Incarnation is the ground of Nicholas's residual optimism; Christ represents a synthesis of the contingent and the absolute, the conjunction of the *maximum absolutum* and the *maximum contractum*: material proof that the rift between the knowable and the unknowable, between ignorance and knowledge, can be reversed. Thus the true renascence, a second genesis, must await the second coming: 'He in his great love will not abandon us; and when his glory shall appear will eternally satisfy us' (II, xiii, p. 122; p. 114). Revelation is always in the future tense.

Walter Kaiser has argued that in Erasmus's *Praise of Folly* 'for the first time, the implications of an ironic and paradoxical dramatization of Nicholas of Cusa's *docta ignorantia* were fully realized'.[65] 'No-one today', presumes L. F. Dean, 'would make Martin van Dorp's mistake of taking literally the ironical statements of the *Praise of Folly*.'[66] Both agree that Erasmus is ironic. But irony is easy, it is trivial, it is inevitable: all language, with its incessant displacements of sense, is naturally ironic. What is difficult, so difficult as to be virtually impossible, is to be sincere, to be un-ironic.[67] Erasmus speaks with the unreliable voice (the compendious voices) of Folly; but there is no writer that does not adopt a persona (the 'I' is always another), none that does not (like Whitman) contain multitudes. The effect of the *Praise of Folly* is to blur the boundaries between seriousness and joking: it is a serious joke. Thus the problem of exegesis is not solved by a premature recourse to inversions of its surface message or by splitting the text into arbitrarily defined zones of plenitude and vacuity: either strategy involves a process of gratuitous addition or punitive subtraction. Erasmus, in his prefatory letter, speaks not of a mock encomium (a defensive afterthought) but simply of an encomium. The work thus invites a naive, literal, Dorpian interpretation.[68]

The preface imparts the information that the encomium was composed 'recently, when I was returning to England from Italy (*ex Italia in Angliam*)' (Miller's translation, p. 1; Miller's edition, p. 67).[69] The two countries concerned are mentioned again in the subsequent text under the heading of *philautia*, the self-love of nations. The English, Folly observes, 'lay claim above all to good looks, music, and fine food'. The Italians, on the other hand, 'lay claim to literature and eloquence (*bonas literas et eloquentiam*) and on one point they all preen themselves most complacently: that, of all mortals, they alone are not barbarians (*barbari*)' (p. 69; p. 126). Thus *Anglia* and *Italia* are not the merely accidental designations of physical locations: they denote the opposite poles of a cultural geography. The distance between them is not just spatial but intellectual, ethical, aesthetic. While England gives priority to the gratification of the senses, feeding eye and ear as well as stomach, Italy represents itself as the lonely custodian of high art.

Erasmus can thus be seen as having travelled south in search of Mediterranean enlightenment and returning to darker Nordic shores laden with the fruits of the Renaissance. This interpretation is indicated by the comment that the *Praise of Folly* offered itself as a way 'to avoid wasting the whole time that I had to ride on horseback in *crude* and illiterate talk ('αμούσοις *et illiteratis fabulis*)' (p. 1; p. 67): any Museless (*amousos*) – uninspired or inartistic – discourse would be all the more unendurable after the *bonae literae* and *eloquentia* of Italy. At the same time, the genesis of the text coincides with the traveller's return to the uneducated state from which he set out; thus the preface is written 'from the country' (p. 5; p. 70), indicating the more pastoral England. From one perspective, Erasmus is (in the terms he offers) bringing wisdom back to folly; from another, he is giving up wisdom to go back to folly. Such are the alternative itineraries traced by the *Praise of Folly* itself. The journey across Europe appears, then, as more than an irrelevant autobiographical detail (a rare occurrence in the self-effacing Erasmus): it can be read not just as the immediate context of the text but as its intellectual schema.

The broadly tripartite structure of the *Praise of Folly*, noted by numerous commentators, corresponds to the stages of the journey. The first section constitutes and examines a point of departure: it presents a timeless Arcadia of happy morons, in which even the Greek gods (according to the paradigm of national characteristics) seem English. The middle section, beginning with the shift in attention from self-evident fools to 'those who have the appearance of wisdom (*sapientiae speciem*)' (p. 78; p. 138) and ending with the recognition that the encomium has temporarily turned into satire (p. 115; p. 176), is markedly censorious. The presence of princes, prelates, and popes suggests Rome. But the most numerous representatives of folly in this more urban, more urbane environment are the men of words, grammarians, rhetoricians, lawyers, poets, philosophers, theologians, on whom the State and the Church are to some extent dependent. The last part signals a return passage to the anti-intellectual emphasis of the first, but repeats earlier elements in a new key, shifting from carnal hedonism to mystical ecstasy. The text thus relates both spatial and temporal transitions: in Erasmus's version of history, a spiritual renascence occurs at the end of the Renaissance, while the Renaissance itself is relocated squarely in the midst of the middle period.

Nicholas remarks that movement can only be understood by reference to the immobile. The first and last phases in the evolution of folly, evoking respectively a beginning and an end, a birth and a rebirth, serve as fixed points, termini, along the textual journey. Erasmus again follows Nicholas in coupling antithetical concepts in a single term: the extremes of earthiness and otherworldliness are celebrated as twin aspects of folly. Both are linked by the proposition that the *idiota*, the unlettered layman, is (as he is for Nicholas and the New Testament) closer to God than the scholar, the fool more enlightened than the 'foolosopher' (*morosophos*) (p. 13; p. 74).[70] But the effect of paradox, the equation of opposite kinds of fool, as of ignorance and knowledge, depends on maintaining the antithetical character of the two terms involved. Thus the incarnations of folly are assigned parallel but mutually exclusive conditions.

The psychological youth of innocent, pleasure-seeking fools is associated with the historical primogeniture of the Golden Age.

Erasmus's account opposes instinct to education, nature to nurture: 'the simple people of the golden age, who were not armed with any formal learning, lived their lives completely under the guidance of natural impulses (*solo naturae ductu instinctique*)' (p. 51; p. 110). This passage stresses the exclusiveness of man's primordial constitution: people are *simplex* because they live under the sole command (*ductus*) and instigation (*instinctus*) of nature. Language is similarly unmixed: pure communication, it is exempt from the compound conditions of grammar, dialectic, rhetoric: 'What need was there for grammar when everyone spoke the same language, and when speech served no other purpose than to let one person understand another? (*ut alius alium intelligeret*)' (p. 51; p. 110). The singularity and uniformity of language correspond to an absence of differences between language users. Erasmus seems to suggest that disagreement only arises as a result of imperfect communication. The divisive 'learned disciplines' can only appear 'when the purity of the golden age (*aetatis aureae puritate*)' (p. 51; p. 110) has declined. As in Genesis, the rise in intellect coincides with a fall from integrity: discordant discourse originates in a certain impurity, a lack of complete rigour of definition: adult mankind is essentially adulterated. The other fools of the opening section are variously reminiscences of the Golden Age: also 'follow[ing] Nature as their only guide (*solamque naturam ducem sequi*)' (p. 52; p. 112), they too are *veridici*, truth-speakers (p. 55; p. 114).[71]

At the opposite end of the spectrum of fools are the Christian adepts who can transcend the physical world, absorbing the body into the spirit, and the spirit into the divine mind. Although devoted to the sacred in place of the secular, they are nevertheless prescribed the example of the English fools of the first section: 'stupid creatures lacking all intelligence, leading their lives according to the dictates of nature (*soloque naturae ductu*)' (p. 130; p. 186). Their ultimate object and model is, however, God: 'the pious strive with all their hearts to reach God himself, who is purest and simplest of all (*rerum omnium simplicissimum*)' (p. 134; p. 190). Just as the natural fools were nothing but nature, so the pious fools are nothing but piety, and while the former are seamlessly integrated with the created world, the latter relinquish it but regain access to the Creator.

These twin species of folly, the one dedicated to the earth, the other to heaven, are wholly opposite and therefore analogous. Each is integral, complete, self-sufficient: the fools exemplifying each genre are nothing but themselves, admitting no admixture of other-

ness. In the terms of the journey recounted, they constitute an
origin and a destination, stable and immutable loci on the map of
moria. But while the primitive and Pauline fools occupy points of
rest in the text, Folly's most characteristic feature is her mobility.
Her avowedly reflexive declamation specifies a succession of displacements. Folly is repeatedly described as a traveller. Thus she
asks: 'But why have I embarked (*ingredior*) on this sea of superstitions?' (p. 66; p. 126). The tropes that serve as Folly's vehicles not
only denote movement but typically connote speed: 'Even though I
am in a hurry (*propero*), I can hardly pass over (*praetercurrere*) in
silence' (p. 67; p. 126). Both verbs attribute a certain dash or haste
to their subject. This is appropriate to the course of her talk, which
moves in the metaphoric leaps and bounds of associations and
antinomies. Thus Folly is constantly seeking to move beyond any
particular fool: she observes that 'there is no bound or limit (*modus
neque finis*) to my praises' (p. 117; p. 178). And she concludes by
drawing attention once again to her tendency to transgress boundaries: 'I have long since forgotten myself and "have gone beyond the
pale".' The Lister commentary glosses the Greek phrase (here
translated by the phrase in double quotes), *huper ta eskammena
pēdō*, as follows: 'Id est, ultra limites salio' (p. 118; p. 194). The verb
in both cases is more energetic than the English allows: Folly
actively leaps over categorial restrictions.

In short, whereas the two principal kinds of folly that Folly holds
up for inspection and admiration are defined by their singularity,
exclusiveness, fixity, their intolerance of alternative modes of
being, Folly in person is notable for her multiplicity, inclusiveness,
mobility, permissiveness. Eschewing definition, Folly acts out her
character (a recurrent trope invokes a theatre or stage: all people
are actors). And the character she displays is alien to both the rustic
and religious states of folly to which she merely alludes. Thus the
Praise of Folly embodies a sharp contradiction between fools and
Folly, message and medium, saying and showing.

Folly often remarks that all men are fools; yet, as described here,
man in general is less like a fool than like Folly: 'man alone trie[s] to
go beyond (*egredi*) the bounds of his lot (*sortis suae limites*)' (p. 53;
p. 112). In her evocation of the Golden Age, Folly argues that
nature 'is completely adequate in every way (*nulla sui parte manca
est*), unless perhaps someone wants to leap over (*transilire*) the
bounds of human destiny (*mortalis sortis pomeria*)' (p. 52; p. 112).
But man, like Folly, is a bounder, a transgressor: complex and
therefore inadequate, unequal to himself, unable to attain the

simplex fullness of the primordial or transcendental fool. Like Folly, man appears permanently en route between the ideal, immobile locations permitting perfect communication among men or communion with God. He is thus implicated in the imperfect intercourse of the intermediate state depicted in the central section of the text where, instead of apparent folly issuing in wisdom, apparent wisdom issues in folly. Every man is a Renaissance man, because we are all *logodaedali* (p. 51; p. 110), sophists rather than *sophi* (p. 10; p. 72). In the last analysis, even Englishmen turn out to be Italians.

Folly suggests that *oratio* is the 'truest mirror of the mind (*minime mendax animi speculum*)' (p. 13; p. 74). Her own speech amply reproduces the shiftiness of the mind (*animus*); but it also registers the hesitations of the soul (*anima*). In superimposing the Platonic duality of body and soul onto the tripartite Pauline division of flesh, soul, and spirit, Erasmus discovers a remainder, a factor in one equation left unaccommodated by the other: in Erasmian writing the soul (*anima*) is typically dislocated, free-floating, condemned to *disponibilité*: an indeterminate shifter.[72] In a scriptural exegesis Erasmus notes that:

Paul divides the soul (*animam*) of man into three parts: into the flesh, which inclines to earthly things; the spirit, which strives towards heavenly things; and the soul (*animam*) in the middle which is turned now one way now the other.[73]

The description of the soul spinning incessantly from flesh to spirit and back again describes precisely the oscillating commitments of Folly.

Of Learned Ignorance enumerates three kinds of being: solar beings, 'bright and enlightened intellectual denizens', who, akin to angels, stand next to God; terrestrial beings, 'more gross and material'; and finally, lunar beings, who are conjectured to be 'betwixt and between' (*lunares in medio fluctuantes*) and, moreover, *lunatici* (III, xii, p. 116; p. 108). Again, Folly (recalling Ecclesiasticus) observes that while 'a fool changes like the moon (*stultus mutatur ut luna*), a wise man is immutable like the sun (*sapiens permanet ut sol*)' (p. 120; p. 180). The equivocal Erasmian soul, which is the man who is divided as well as one of his divisions, and is embodied and enacted by Folly, who is all men, is a Selenite, a Lunarian, a lunatic, intermediate between heaven and earth. Inconsistency is its fate. Such, too, is the condition of the Erasmian text, which is, as Chaloner observed, 'between game and ernest'.[74]

The *Praise of Folly* is the cornucopian text par excellence: accretive, loosely structured, digressive, vacillating, spanning the themes of sexual orgasm and divine beatitude, and the tonalities of eulogy and satire, it values inclusiveness above coherence, the abundance of doctrine above doctrinal consistency. Although more overtly humanistic in temper than the scholastically inspired *Of Learned Ignorance* and formally opposed to the austere geometrical rigidity of Nicholas, it shares with the earlier text a recalcitrant indeterminacy.[75] Dramatizing a pronounced mobility of meaning, it also proposes two stations, havens of security exempt from the perils of discourse. On the one hand, it recalls a pre-intellectual, pre-textual, pre-lapsarian age, devoid of differentiation, and looks forward to the rapturous ascent of the blessed spirit, freed from the *corpus* (both flesh and writing), to a textless logos. On the other, it places humanity in a state of perpetual displacement. Thus the invocation of ignorance joins the anticipation of wisdom in the double negation of the condition of ambiguity and prevarication of which Folly, embodiment of the soul, and the text are the persistent affirmation.

Of Learned Ignorance exhibits a parallel between a *nolle prosequi* issued against discursive inquiry into the divinity, and the hermeneutic impasse threatened by the text. Nicholas urges us to practise daily mortification if we are to crush the subversive desires of the flesh (*carnalia desideria*), the concupiscible power (*concupiscibilis potentia*) (III, vi, p. 145; p. 136). But the equally unruly intellect, which may otherwise allow itself to be deflected from its aim of reunion with God, must also be shriven of its epistemic desires (*intellectualia desideria*) (letter to Cardinal Julian, p. 174; p. 164). *Scientia* is deceptive, ultimately unsatisfying, a whore (*scortum*): 'there can be no marriage with a fickle woman, only with eternal wisdom (*aeternam sapientiam*)'.[76] The labyrinthine text that is *Of Learned Ignorance* is the instrument devised by Nicholas for inflicting a mortification and purification of the mind, quelling its epistemophile impulses: it solicits a *sacrificium intellectus*.

In *De visione dei*, Nicholas plays on the etymology of the word 'discourse' by comparing it to a dog running hither and thither (*discurrit*), seeking its master.[77] The restless, mobile condition of both *Praise of Folly* and *Of Learned Ignorance* would justify the same analogy: in both, writing is a running dog, a rover. Erasmus composes while 'riding on horseback' (p. 1; p. 67); Nicholas receives inspiration aboard a boat ('returning by sea from Greece' as Erasmus returned from Italy) (letter, p. 173; p. 163); God, on the other hand, the unmoved mover, 'is grasped only when movement ceases' (III, xi, p. 161; p. 152). For both Nicholas and Erasmus, God the Father is the personification of the Word, the authority, the *terminus ad quem* beyond contradiction whose presence would render writing redundant. Thus the text itself, shifty, godless, and contradictory, is bereft of authority.[78]

The Renaissance texts considered above present certain common themes and strategies that can of course be discerned in other, intellectually very distant traditions. Mahayana Buddhism, for example, distinguishes between relative and absolute modes of consciousness. To the former corresponds *maya*, the intelligible but illusory world populated by conventional forms (*rupa*) and designated by *nama*, the abstract names and classifications of descriptive discourse. To the latter corresponds *tathata* (literally, 'suchness', close in sense to *eccéité*), the world apprehended as pure being, synonymous with *sunyata*, the void, to the extent that it is evacuated of the mental discriminations which, allied to verbal representations, we mistake for truths. This distinction is the basis for the meaning of the condition, advocated by Zen, of *wu-hsin* (no-mind).[79] If *hsin* is contaminated by the delusions of *maya*, then it is not enough to negate the objects of consciousness: *hsin* itself must be transcended or transformed. Coinciding with the attainment of *wu-hsin* is *satori*, the ultimate objective and justification of Zen: the condition of 'enlightenment' (which displaces *maya* by *tathata*).

Were the strictures of Zen to be consistently observed, no Zen literature would be written, or, if written, could survive. And indeed, the ritualistic burning of books is an event frequently recorded in the annals of Zen. Its logophobia, more comprehensive in its disdain for language than Platonic logocentrism (which favoured dialectic) is invoked in the couplet:

> He who knows does not speak,
> He who speaks does not know.[80]

This utterance, declaring knowledge to be incompatible with its verbal transmission, appears to invalidate or prohibit all possible discourse (including itself). Rigorously implemented, the doctrine entails a rigid adhesion to monastic silence; thus it inhibits its own propagation. To Zen, all didacticism is anathema. It nevertheless accommodates a system of verbal instruction, based on the *koan* (literally, 'public document'). The *koan* seeks to negotiate a compromise between saying something and nothing. Assuming various truncated forms (the anecdote, the dialogue, the question), it invariably poses a problem or pseudo-problem, deprived by contra-diction or *non sequitur* of any possible solution, but which the aspir-ing novice is nevertheless called upon to solve. The violation of logical discourse is a device designed to shortcircuit the faculty of reason, and thus foster the condition of *wu-hsin* which is the necess-ary antecedent to *satori*.

The *koan* is also distinguished (like the *haiku*) by its brevity (thereby remaining close to silence). *Of Learned Ignorance* and the *Praise of Folly* can be conceived as extended *koans*, whose scepti-cism about language (exiled from wisdom) is, however, attended by irrepressible logophilia. Both impose restrictions or prohibitions on discourse which they cannot themselves obey; both resort to circu-lar, paradoxical and indeterminate modes of discourse, which, like the *koan*, are (in Suzuki's phrase) 'great baffler[s] to reasoning'.[81] Neither is merely a book about ignorance; their achievement is to elicit from the reader an acknowledgement of the condition of enlightened ignorance to which they allude.

But this enlightenment is only partial, for the texts demonstrate the folly of language without acceding to wisdom, admit the (incom-plete) ignorance of knowledge while deferring the (complete) knowledge of ignorance: they postpone alike *wu-hsin* and *satori*. But just as the renunciation of the text is the condition of either the eroticism of the body or the ecstasy of the spirit, so the renunciation by the text of its twin Biblical and encyclopedic ideals of revelation and completion prolongs the intermediate *jouissance* of *maya*.[82]

By reinstalling rhetoric and grammar in the midst of logic, the Renaissance infects philosophy with the instability of literature. The reconstruction of an archive thus involves an act of deconstruc-tion. The new beginning, illuminated by Antiquity, which would also be an ending, closing a cultural circuit with the past, recedes into the future, restoring the present to darkness. The *sapientia* which would justify the Renaissance is exiled from *bonae literae* and *scientia* and projected backwards or forwards in time. Instead of the past being made present, presence is made future. Both Nicholas and Erasmus set their texts in motion between a beginning and an end, the earth and the sun, a minimum and a maximum; they are denied the repose of the interlocking extremes of the closed circle of knowledge which cannot be added to, and the absolute zero which cannot be subtracted from.

Thus the Renaissance seeks to reject but seems to rejoin the *Medium Aevum*, the middle age of Dante, 'nel mezzo del cammin'. Clearly, the Renaissance could not coincide exactly with the classical age; more obscurely, it could not coincide with itself. The Renaissance, in short, is always pre-renaissance.

Erasmus posits England and Italy as limits on the scale of intellectual evolution; his text, however, is composed in neither country, but rather en route between them: presumably in France. France represents a median point on the cultural map, mid-way between North and South, with Paris, the symbol and fortress of medieval philosophy, at its centre. Thus it is to French writing that we might reasonably look for a prolongation of the dilemma of mediation.

Genesis and the Renaissance articulate two perfections, two ideal, fictional moments, denoting respectively an original *vacuum* and a final *plenum*, the one without duration, already past even as it occurs, the other always not yet. The writing of Rousseau reinvokes these polarities and seems alternately to construct and deconstruct a bridge between them.[83]

Rousseau's immediate literary environment, in his own estimation, is bounded and overlooked by the Renaissance. The French Enlightenment, argues Jean-Jacques, is not distinct from the Renaissance, but only its almost redundant résumé: eighteenth-century France is a pleonasm of the *quattrocento*. In Rousseau's imagery, the Renaissance is the dawn of the day of which contemporary France is the evening. His intention is to announce the closure of an age, the end of the Renaissance day. But the metaphor of renewal is itself derived from the Renaissance. Rousseau advertises himself as the first truly post-Renaissance writer, but re-enacts the quintessential configuration of the Renaissance itself.

His writing redefines and expands the Renaissance concept of *docta ignorantia*; but its critique of a corrupt, book-oriented post-Renaissance culture acquires an intensely personal, private intonation: an onto-theological argument undergoes an egocentric introversion. Nicholas and Erasmus, their identities obscured by multiple citation or impersonal formalism, conform with their mystical, almost ineffable doctrines by encouraging mystification; Rousseau, in contrast, committed to expressing his individuality, insistent on the indissolubility of his life and his writing, experiences incomprehension as an attack on his integrity, and also as nemesis. Thus he specifically rejects the rhetoric of paradox and irony.

But his destiny is to be torn between vocation and conviction: he proposes to afford perfect understanding via language that language is an instrument of imperfect understanding. The Buddhist doctrine opposing speech to knowledge is echoed in Rousseau's belief that 'généralement, les gens qui savent peu parlent beaucoup et les gens qui savent beaucoup parlent peu' (*Œuvres complètes*, IV, p. 666). But Rousseau would abhor a *koan*, on grounds of both unintelligibility and excessive brevity. Like Papageno (in *The Magic Flute*), although remorsefully conscious that silence is stipulated as the unique testimony to wisdom, he is unable to stay silent for long. His mission of self-affirmation compels him to perpetuate the cardinal sin (according to his own standards) of literary discourse. An exile haunted by inexorcizable guilt, Rousseau thus seems to relive rather than merely relate the drama of the Fall.[84]

2.3 Rousseau

Borges omitted Rousseau from his list of Kafka's precursors. Jean-Jacques can nevertheless be claimed as an ancestor of Joseph K. Rousseau's unremitting sense of persecution prefigures the first sentence of *The Trial*: he, too, suspects that 'someone must have been telling lies (*verleumdet*) about him'. He is perpetually on trial (so it seems to him), unjustly arraigned for unspecified crimes.[85] Rousseau's consciousness of a malevolent universal Other converts all friends into enemies only pretending to be friends. Thus he prefers frank declarations of hostility to equivocal silence, explicit accusations to hypocritical professions of good will. He seems to encourage and even gloomily enjoy the injuries inflicted by others since they consolingly confirm his low opinion of the world.

Rousseau needs others to confirm his high opinion of himself, to reflect in their gaze his hidden being, and therefore demands to be judged; but, exposed to the public eye, he is invariably misjudged. Rousseau's first line of defence against his massed accusers is verbal self-exculpation. But he lacks the (contemptible) fluency required for self-advertisement, the ability to market the commodity of character at its proper value. Thus words also betray him: they fail to testify to his essential innocence, projecting only defective, deflated images of his true self. Confronted by misunderstanding and misinterpretation, the front line of vocal self-defence already in ruins, Rousseau turns to writing as a refuge against attack. The pen is mightier than the tongue; thus Rousseau claims that, although an ineffective conversationalist, 'je ferais une fort jolie conversation par la poste' (I, p. 113). Writing is conceived as a means of retreating from society while remaining the object of public attention: a way, in short, of being simultaneously absent and present. Rousseau is a self-avowed *Robinsoniste*: his insular ideal is a desert island devoid of other inhabitants. His privileged places of residence (notably, L'Ile de Saint-Pierre) are those that come closest to realizing this ideal; yet he is incapable of cutting all ties with ill-intentioned humanity: his texts are like so many messages sent back to the shores of society.

The project explicitly espoused by Rousseau's writings is self-vindication: the rectification of erroneous opinions concerning their author.[86] But the vocation turns out to be as insecure and precarious as was the writer's physical presence in society. Rousseau is acutely conscious of the risks attendant upon taking up the pen. All moral criticism of his person is redundant or malicious. But this is no less true of literary criticism. Attempting to forestall the one, Rousseau invites the other. All writing allows or demands a response, an interpretation, a judgement. Thus the text is not unassailable, not self-evident or self-sufficient, but just as vulnerable to attack as its author. The reader is always a latent misreader, critic, enemy; his weapons are misattribution, distortion and misinterpretation. Just as Rousseau actively solicits the judgement he fears from his fellow citizens, so, as a writer, he both requires and resents readers, who must bear witness to his self-portrait, but who, by reason of incompetence or malevolence, threaten to misunderstand.

At the end of the *Confessions*, Rousseau proclaims that whoever, in spite of having read his autobiography, 'pourra me croire un malhonnête homme est lui-même un homme à étouffer' (I, p. 656). The objective of his writing is precisely to stifle such hostile voices, to put an end to false rumour. The writer seeks to disarm his critics by anticipating all possible criticism. Rousseau admits that everything he writes refers ultimately to himself; and, he might have added, to itself. His writing is not only autobiographical but auto-exegetical, systematically reflexive.

The model for this technique is Saint-Preux, the prolific correspondent of *La Nouvelle Héloïse*. In the exclamatory letter (II, pp. 146–7) written while awaiting the arrival of his mistress in her 'cabinet' and impatiently speculating about an imminent night of bliss, he subjects everything to instantaneously composed commentary: not merely the prospective lover's 'transports' or (more improbably) the appearance of Julie, but the process of commentary itself: 'Quel bonheur d'avoir trouvé de l'encre et du papier!' Like the underwear Saint-Preux fondles, the ink and paper serve as a fetish, a substitute for the absent beloved; but they continue to displace her even when she is present. While Julie walks in, the writer obsessively continues his letter, so preoccupied by the act of recording his emotions as to be almost indifferent to their object. Thus the drama of intense (because anticipated) experience is rivalled and overshadowed by the drama of writing: the text becomes the subject of the text.[87]

In Rousseau, proliferating self-analyses are coupled to analyses of those analyses; introspective statements generate a series of further statements, each amplifying, revising, or reviewing its predecessors. Thus *La Nouvelle Héloïse* closes, as though reluctantly, by opening out into a copious preface.[88] The author apologizes for the paradox of placing a preface at the end of a book, but explains that the commentary on the text had become so prolonged as to risk incurring the displeasure of the impatient reader if placed at the beginning. Thus an exposition of the novel gives rise to an exposition of the exposition. The Rousseau text is typically enclosed, as if for additional defence, in an envelope of prefaces and postfaces.[89]

Just as each sentence in some way qualifies another, so each essay or letter is a more extended qualification of a previous work. Every text constitutes a post-scriptum. Thus does Rousseau's *œuvre* feed upon itself. Writing becomes a compulsion, a mechanism inducing the writer to write further in order to add retrospective support to a prior text. He will write to explain what he has written. The fear of misinterpretation is thus an instrument of scriptural proliferation, of *copia*. When, in defence of his epistolary hero's prolixity, Rousseau states that the passionate writer 'n'a jamais achevé de dire; comme une source vive qui coule sans cesse et ne s'épuise jamais' (II, p. 15), he is also speaking (as ever) of himself. He finds it difficult or impossible to finish a text because the more he says the more there is to be said. Any conclusion is only a temporary point of repose not a definitive terminus. At the end of the fourth of the *Lettres écrites de la montagne*, Rousseau promises to confine himself to just one more, terminal letter; the sixth begins apologetically: 'Encore une lettre, Monsieur, et vous êtes délivré de moi'; the seventh, eighth and ninth omit all mention of the promise of brevity. Again, the inconclusive conclusion to the *Confessions* looks forward to their continuation: 'On verra dans ma troisiéme partie si jamais j'ai la force de l'écrire' (I, p. 656). Predictably, Rousseau has anticipated the observation of his dilatoriness: 'Je suis en racontant mes voyages comme j'étois en les faisant; je ne saurois arriver' (I, p. 172).

However much he interprets himself, the writer cannot exhaust the susceptibility to further, divergent interpretations of his text.

Rousseau's reading of himself, like his writing, cannot be conclusive: it is still liable to be ignored or refuted. The succession of mutually supporting texts remains therefore unsupported. Moreover, Rousseau's defensive strategy appears ultimately self-defeating: the very multiplicity of self-descriptions, begotten by the desire to prohibit or postpone description by others, demands the interpretative intervention of the reader in order to be reconstituted as the portrait of a singular individual.[90]

Writing was advertised as a means of reappropriating an identity of which Rousseau had been divested by others; once again, however, he faces the prospect of dispossession. As a citizen he was subject to slander; now, as a writer, he is still more subject to libel. Thus Rousseau's relationship with the reader recapitulates and seals his relationship with society.

Unable to count on the literary intelligence or rectitude of his audience, Rousseau points the reader towards an intangible entity (*essence*, *cœur*, or *âme*), a transcendent self beyond the text. He asks finally to be judged neither on what he says or writes (nor on what he does), but on what he is. Precisely because he begins by abhorring the defective moral judgement of his fellows, he is obliged in the end to submit to that judgement from his readers, whom he alternately flatters ('lecteur sensé' (I, p. 561)) and despises ('lecteurs vulgaires' (IV, p. 323)). Rousseau seeks to encircle his texts in a ring of anticipatory reviews, but finds himself trapped instead in the social circuit of inexorable and uncertain *opinion*.

The law of reflexivity requires that Rousseau should convert the source of his scriptural anxiety into a subject of his writing. Thus the texts, whose initial function is to criticize scurrilous attacks upon their author's integrity, also incorporate a critique of textuality. Rousseau's work invokes two contexts in which the sins of society and of writing may be redeemed, in which the text can be closed, and identity sealed off from attack: nostalgically, a pre-intellectual, pre-social world bereft of the knowledge of good and evil; prophetically, a de-socialized society, rendering writing and criticism redundant: a pre-textual past and a post-textual future. The first presupposes a state of perfect ignorance, the second a state of perfect knowledge. Rousseau consistently equates these two perfections, a primitive anepistemology and a transcendent epistemology. Starobinski (following Engels) infers that the structure of Rousseau's thought is essentially dialectical, that the resolution of a state of conflict both within the self and society is predicated on an assumed synthesis (of nature and culture, knowledge and ignorance). But Rousseau's solutions usually turn out to be as problematic as the problems they offer to solve.

The indictment of man and all his works consistently gives way to panegyric: a contemptuous sociology, the dissection of a dystopia, is counterpointed by exalted histories and prophecies, the celebration of utopias. But the evocation of ideals is invariably accompanied by a sustained critique of idealism, the construction of fantasies (of Genesis and Renaissance) by their systematic deconstruction.[91]

According to Starobinski's reading, the *Discours sur l'origine de l'inégalité* 'recompose une Genèse philosophique où ne manquent ni le jardin d'Eden, ni la faute, ni la confusion des langues'.[92] The essay (a 'version laïcisée, "démythifiée" de l'histoire des origines') only repeats Scripture by translating it into a more anthropological language. But according to Rousseau, the primordial state sketched in Genesis does not coincide with the *état de nature*; although temporally antecedent, it is intellectually more advanced. Rousseau remarks that 'il est évident, par la lecture des Livres Sacrés, que le premier Homme ayant reçu immediatement de Dieu des lumieres et des Preceptes, n'étoit point lui-même dans cet état [de nature]' (III, p. 132). In his view, Adam is already endowed (or over-endowed) with knowledge even before the encounter with the serpent: hence his capacity for conversing with God and for naming animals. Genesis, then, presents only an incomplete evacuation of *eloquentia* and *scientia*.

But this is equally true of those expositions explicitly concerned with the state of nature. Previous writers on the subject 'parloient de l'Homme Sauvage et ils peignoient l'homme Civil' (III, p. 132). Rousseau does not, however, attempt to rectify this error, and thereby describe a conceptually consistent primitive state which would be the true antithesis of civilization. Rather, he shows why such an intention is doomed to failure; his brief, ambiguous descriptions are a mosaic of quotation and allusion exposing the illusions of prior genetic theories. Notoriously, Rousseau begins by renouncing reality ('Commençons donc par écarter tous les faits' (III, p. 132)) and declaring the imaginary character of his account. But the evocation of a state of nature is not simply a fiction or hypothesis, but rather the demonstration of an impossibility; thus the *Discours sur l'origine de l'inégalité* functions as a *reductio ad absurdum* of the notion of origins.[93]

Characteristically, the vertiginous series of prolegomena ('dédicace', 'préface', 'avertissement' and introduction preceding the 'Première Partie') that preface and delay the *Discours* ambivalently assert both the wisdom and the folly of the textual enterprise. A clear exposition of the state of nature is necessary in order to clear away the 'monceaux de Sable mouvant' surrounding the 'Edifice' of 'établissemens humains' and reveal 'la base inébranlable sur laquelle il est élevé' (III, p. 127). But this requirement is unsatisfiable: 'c'est en un sens à force d'étudier l'homme que nous nous sommes mis hors d'état de le connoître' (III, p. 123): the more we know, the less we can know about the *état primitif*, which is defined by the absence of knowledge. Thus the project the text assigns itself appears at once indispensable and unrealizable. Rousseau states that he does not flatter himself that he has seen what is 'si difficile à voir . . . J'ai hazardé quelques conjectures, moins dans l'espoir de resoudre la question que dans l'intention de l'éclaircir et de la reduire à son véritable état' (III, p. 123). The *Discours*, then, is less about the state of nature than about the problem of defining such a state ('qui n'existe plus, qui n'a peut-être point existé, qui probablement n'existera jamais' (III, p. 123)).

A well-known passage in the *Contrat social* (Geneva manuscript) asserts that:

la paix et l'innocence nous ont échappé pour jamais avant que nous en eussions gouté les délices; insensible aux stupides hommes des prémiers tems, échappée aux hommes éclairés des tems postérieurs, l'heureuse vie de l'âge d'or fut toujours un état étranger à la race humaine, ou pour l'avoir méconnu quand elle en pouvoit joüir, ou pour l'avoir perdu quand elle auroit pu le connoitre. (III, p. 283)

The ignorant would always be too ignorant and the knowledgeable too knowledgeable to attain the knowledge of ignorance; the ignoramus has only to attain the knowledge of ignorance (thereby becoming knowledgeable) in order to forfeit it forever. Here, there is no middle way running between ignorance and knowledge. But in the *Discours*, ignorance and knowledge are themselves conjured away: there is nothing but a middle way. The idea of nescience is declared not just unknowable but inconceivable, a concept without a content, while omniscience is prohibited by the prohibition of mere knowledge. I cannot know that I know nothing, so much is clear; the *Discours* adds to this commonplace the more opaque double assertion that I cannot know nothing, nor can I know anything. The text, by taking a fiction seriously, enacts the theory of language and society it articulates.

In Starobinski's reading of the *Discours*, the *sauvage* is seamlessly integrated with nature: nothing separates a psychology and an
ecology; fallen man, *l'homme civil*, on the other hand, is alienated
from nature. But precisely this dichotomy is put in question by
Rousseau. Derrida and de Man have shown how the constants of
pity and liberty already place the savage in a state of transgression
with respect to nature. More generally, Rousseau shows that if we
postulate a savage who is the complete negation of civilized man
then there is no way of closing the gap between them, bridging
nothing and something, 'pures sensations' and 'simples connaissances' (III, p. 144). Rousseau's technique in the *Discours* is to
accept the hypothesis of a degree zero of society, thought, and
language, then elaborate its consequences, which turn out to be
incompatible with the development of society, thought, or
language. The text constructs a series of binary models setting up a
diametrical opposition between nature and culture, ignorance and
knowledge, silence and discourse and ascribing logical and
chronological priority to the first of each couple, only to reveal them
as self-destructive.

This technique is first applied to technology. If we suppose the
savage to be utterly non-instrumental in his relations with his
environment, a passive receiver rather than a doer, it would be
necessary also to suppose that 'les instrumens du Labourage fussent
tombés du Ciel entre les mains des Sauvages' who would have to be
instructed in their uses, in 'toutes choses . . . par les Dieux, faute de
concevoir comment ils les auroient apprises d'eux-mêmes' (III, p.
145). But even then, without the institution of property, the savage
would revert to pure savagery: 'En un mot, comment cette situation
pourra-t-elle porter les hommes à cultiver la Terre, tant qu'elle ne
sera point partagée entre eux, c'est à dire, tant que l'état de Nature
ne sera point anéanti?' (III, p. 145). The *Discours* consistently
repeats this gesture of *anéantissement*: the narration of a temporal
transcendence entails a logical negation.

This structure of argument clarifies the sense of the much disputed section on language. As in the case of liberty, perfectibility,
and instrumentalism, Rousseau demonstrates that in order for there
to be language, language should always already have been.
Between silence and language would stretch a 'tems infini': either
non-discursiveness and discourse are separated by eternity, or man
has always been discursive; thus pre-discursive man is inconceivable. Rousseau supposes 'cette première difficulté vaincue', crossing 'l'espace immense qui dut se trouver entre le pur état de Nature

et le besoin des Langues' in order to reveal a further difficulty: 'si les Hommes ont eu besoin de la parole pour apprendre à penser, ils ont eu bien plus besoin encore de savoir penser pour trouver l'art de la parole' (III, p. 147). Starobinski comments that Rousseau formulates this difficulty 'pour indiquer un nouvel "espace immense" intervenant entre le "besoin des langues" et les langues instituées' (III, p. 1324). But the consistent pattern of argument implies rather that either this space is uncrossable (the 'franchissons l'espace immense', like the 'supposons cette difficulté vaincue', contains a *per impossibile*), or there is no space.

Again, the text espouses an idea it condemns as untenable, that of an invention of language *ex nihilo*. The 'premier langage', the 'cri de la Nature', proves not to be 'd'un grand usage dans le cours ordinaire de la vie' (III, p. 148); therefore, it must be replaced by conventional signs. But this assumption leads to a further infinite regression: any convention governing meaning would require a prior convention in order to be understood: thus 'la parole paroît avoir été fort nécessaire, pour établir l'usage de la parole' (III, pp. 148–9). The next section, concerning the problem of naming, similarly cannot be taken at face value; rather, it appears as a satirical parody of a nominalist theory, a caricature of an argument.

As before, Rousseau asserts a temporal and logical distinction which collapses under the weight of its own contradictions. Literal denomination, the Adamic attribution of 'noms particuliers' to individual things ('Si un Chêne s'appelloit *A*, un autre Chêne s'appelloit *B*' – the intrinsic improbability is heightened by the foregrounded selection of overtly philosophical rhetoric), is held to precede conceptualization, the assimilation of particulars to *idées générales* (which, as de Man observes, involves a metaphorical operation, substituting one term for another).[94] But Rousseau is quick to point out 'l'embarras de toute cette Nomenclature': the transition from proper nouns to generic terms would require 'des observations et des définitions, c'est à dire, de l'Histoire Naturelle et de la Métaphysique, beaucoup plus que les hommes de ce tems-là n'en pouvoient avoir' (III, p. 149). Rousseau mockingly describes 'les premiers Inventeurs . . . nos nouveaux Grammairiens' going about generalizing their exclusively particular language 'par des moyens que je ne conçois pas'. The inventors, having first noticed nothing but differences ('ils avoient d'abord trop multiplié les noms des individus faute de connoître les genres et les espéces'), then proceed to ignore them entirely ('ils firent ensuite trop peu d'espéces et de genres, faute d'avoir considéré les Etres par toutes leurs diffé-

49

rences' (III, p. 150). In brief, the entire schema distinguishing names and classifications, the literal and the metaphorical, dissolves into absurdity. Referentiality merges with conceptualization, while differences and resemblances blur into a generalized process of comparison.

The section on language concludes with an appeal to the reader to consider problems which the writer considers insoluble:

> Quant à moi, effrayé des difficultés qui se multiplient, et convaincu de l'impossibilité presque démontrée que les Langues ayent pûnaître, et s'établir par des moyens purement humains, je laisse à qui voudra l'entreprendre la discussion de ce difficile Problême, lequel a été le plus nécessaire, de la Société déjà liée, à l'institution des Langues, ou des Langues déjà inventées, à l'établissement de la Société. (III, p. 151)

This passage sums up the preceding section and supplies the link to the account of society. Each of the antitheses opposing *l'homme naturel* to instruments, ideas, language has been successively stretched apart and shown to spring back to form a continuous band; the same compression affects the relation of society and language, which in order to exist must be telescoped together into interdependence.

Thus, on the one hand, *l'homme sauvage* is not the opposite of *l'homme civil* but his mirror-image, already involved from the start in communication and community.[95] And on the other, the destiny of society described in the Second Part of the *Discours* coincides with the linguistic model described in the First Part. The systematization of differences and resemblances, inherent in the structure of language, inevitably extends to human relationships; such is the process constitutive of inequality and its attendant vices. Perfectibility and liberty, imperfectibility and inequality are all enfolded in the patterns of language and unfolded in the history that it is the function of the Second Part of the *Discours* to relate. But as in the first, the consecutive structure of the narrative is less the translation of the successive stages of an evolution than the unravelling of a network of necessities and possibilities structured by discourse, and simultaneously present at every moment. The *Discours* presents a diachronic transcription of a synchronic state of affairs.[96]

Thus the structure of the text is not linear but circular. Having recounted and contested the notion of a pre-textual man enjoying privileged and immediate access to nature, Rousseau considers the complementary notion of a natural post-textual discourse claiming proprietorial rights over truth: 'C'est ici le dernier terme de l'inégalité, et le point extrême qui ferme le Cercle et touche au point d'où nous sommes partis: C'est ici que tous les particuliers redeviennent égaux parce qu'ils ne sont rien' (III, p. 191). Rousseau's excavation of the foundation of the *droit naturel* has exposed only the 'sable mouvant' of discourse; deprived of any transcendental authority, right may nevertheless be enforced with might by 'le Despotisme': 'sitôt qu'il parle, il n'y a ni probité ni devoir à consulter, et la plus aveugle obéissance est la seule vertu qui reste aux Esclaves'. The naturalization of the textual 'Loi' can only be achieved by superimposing coercion on an illusion. Thus the original 'Etat de Nature' of the savage and the conclusive 'nouvel Etat de Nature' imposed by political terror are fictions included within the operation of a discourse which precludes the legitimation of any *ordre naturel*.[97]

The *Discours*, parodic, satirical, critical, exposes the imperfections implicit in the concept of the two perfections of nescience and omniscience, zero and absolute knowledge. Rousseau's archaeology eliminates the *archē* in which ignorance entails the knowledge of nature, while his teleology discredits the *telos* in which the savant recovers that primal proximity. Language is not a function of man, which he can transcend as he preceded it; rather man is a function of language, himself an *idée générale* as inseparable from discourse as he is unreconcilable with nature. While man is stripped of the credentials of primitive integration, language is deprived of any grounding in pure referentiality. All language incorporates *idées générales*; but these *idées* themselves originate in language: 'il faut donc parler pour avoir des idées générales' (III, p. 150). Thus language not only transcends the world of things, incorporating a metaphysics, but constitutes a metalanguage, founded on the shifting sands of its own terms. The Fall related by Starobinski is absent from the *Discours*; as in Genesis, original man is already fallen, equipped with *lumières* as with language; but here all discourse, not just Scripture, denotes a divorce.[98]

Again like Genesis, Rousseau's texts obsessively issue an epistemological prohibition. In Rousseau's writing, knowledge, because it relies on the complicity of language, shares with the arts and sciences the status of a mode of mediation testifying to a state of alienation (of which the faculty of judgement afflicting the persecuted individual or misinterpreted writer is the further effect and symbol). Empirical statements are imperfect because innumerable:[99] they may express truths (verified by reference to other statements), but never the truth, which although infinite is (like the other nouns Rousseau champions: *vertu*, *liberté*, *justice*) singular. Books blind us to the book of the world. Knowledge, affiliated to *opinion*, the current cultural *doxa*, is therefore, in a sense, already anepistemic. The anepistemological gesture, the flight from the text towards a pre-textual origin or a post-textual conclusion, an *anéantissement* or a totalization of knowledge, seeks to satisfy the desire for anepistemological reappropriation of plenitude only imaginable within, but excluded by, the text.

Rousseau's *œuvre*, throughout its various preoccupations with politics, religion, and education, persistently reiterates the configuration of the *Discours*, in which the mediate, intermediate condition of knowledge is condemned by the standards of nescience and omniscience, each intertwined with nature, and condemned in turn, by the condition of knowledge, to unattainability.

Rousseau's histories, prophecies, and proposals invariably envisage a modification of society. *Emile* seeks to recreate the state of nature by expelling society from the consciousness of an evolving individual, whose reclusive existence is deliberately modelled on Robinson Crusoe. The child is proposed as the living equivalent of the *sauvage*. '*Infans*' (IV, p. 299), notes Rousseau, denotes the absence of speech (Derrida restates this conception thus: 'L'enfance . . . c'est le non-rapport au signe').[100] The procedures specified by the theory of *éducation négative* – the prohibition of books, the cultivation of sensual experience – are designed to preserve a prior isolation from language and reinforce immediate proximity to the world, unmediated by received knowledge. But ignorance, if it must be learned, has already been forgotten; it becomes unattainable (like *wu-hsin*) from the moment it is necessary to strive to attain it because the attempt (whose origin is mental) to purify the mind is itself impure. The child is transformed at last into an image of his governor, equipped with rational disdain for the opinion of mankind, but, equally, nostalgically attached to, and therefore utterly separate from, his infantile ignorance (which he aims to recapture vicariously, evanescently, like God, through producing children).

Only if time could be terminated, and if the governor and, by extension, all humanity, came to resemble the hypothetical Emile (rather than the reverse), might the transformation be averted. These precisely, are the premises of Rousseau's arguments for social reform, which imply the closure of history and the resolution of society into an individual, a collective citizen. According to Cassirer, the second *Discours* concedes the possibility of a synthesis between the virtues of pre-social man and the advantages of civilization; the *Contrat social*, its logical extension, then seeks to reconcile nature and culture by constructing a society devoid of the flaws inherent in society and permitting the individual the full development of his intellectual and moral powers without incurring the vices of intellect: Rousseau looks forward, in this interpretation, to a revival of a (fictional) golden age.

The *Contrat social* provides for the prolific satisfaction of an urge for intimacy by housing innumerable souls in a single body: the body politic. Rousseau's characteristic resolution of the choice between solidarity and solitude is to conceive an extreme form of solidarity which would also be equivalent to solitude, a society which would be identical to an individual, a community whose heterogeneous members would merge to form a transcendent, corporate unity. But the *Contrat* juxtaposes without combining two analytical modes, the one ahistorical and metaphysical, the other historical and empirical; as in the *Discours*, purely theoretical solutions vanish at the level of political practice. The alienation of man from nature in the *Discours* and the sign from the object in the *Essai* reappears, in the *Contrat*, in the disjunction between the ideal and the real. The *volonté générale* is (like nature) only capable of representation and therefore doomed to misrepresentation. Plurality and fragmentation, which are inevitable,[101] condemn the body politic to renewed exile from self-evident truth, from the proximity to nature which is the prerogative of social singularity. Thus the voice of the general will is infallible but eternally mute.

Salvation, the reversal of the Fall, the redemption of self and society, predicated on the reinstitution of our putative pre-intellectual intimacy with the world and with others, is, if not feasible, at least imaginable. So it is logical that Rousseau's discourse should issue in an explicitly fictional text, that his cultivation of letters, and the genre of the letter, should culminate in an epistolary novel. *La Nouvelle Héloïse* variously projects the vocation of intimacy and solidarity along the axis of a sequestered community of *belles âmes*, a microcosm of the unrealizable integrated society.

The text represents a sustained if oblique elaboration of the themes of knowledge and ignorance. All Rousseau's writing plays upon the interdependence of coition and cognition: Saint-Preux's initial career as Julie's unofficial 'maître d'études' signals his dual epistemic and erotic status in a text which, like Genesis, posits an equivalence between the knowledge of good and evil and carnal knowledge, between verbal and sexual intercourse. Thus *La Nouvelle Héloïse* operates as a sexual parable of the dilemma of epistemic man. The anepistemological ideal examined in Rousseau's writing, of attaining the state of knowing without the impediment of knowledge, of being simultaneously ignorant and knowledgeable, is mirrored in Julie's exactly analogous fantasy of loving without ever having loved, of possessing without being possessed, of being an amorous virgin. She strives to obey the imperative enunciated in *Emile*: 'jouis à la fois de l'amour et de l'innocence' (IV, p. 782). Her double negation of philosophy and passion is allied to an emotional affirmation of the feasibility of a complete spiritual communion exempt from physical intimacy. She confines eroticism to the epistolary intercourse of correspondents.

The structure of reconciliation recurs in Julie's ambition to overcome all internal and external antagonisms. Clarens, the paternal household where she endeavours (vainly) to unite in hierarchical harmony an aggregate of disparate individuals, resembles the precivilized state from which all differences are absent. Julie's régime of self-suppression extends to the management of both the estate and the house. The secluded garden that she names 'Elysée' proclaims the conjunction of nature and culture in its variety of domesticated wildness and cultivated naturalness. The problem which the principles of domestic economy (strict segregation of the sexes, constant surveillance, isolation from the outer world) claim to solve – the counterpart to controlling the landscape – is how to stop the servants running wild. While the invisible hand of the gardener guards against the appearance of enforced symmetry and sinuously disguises overt linearity, the comparable art of the benevolently despotic master (or mistress) is to 'cacher' the 'gêne' of the domestics 'sous le voile du plaisir ou de l'intérêt' (II, p. 453).

The human landscape of Clarens foregrounds an illusion of asexual stasis against an horizon of strict emotional discipline. Julie's submission to paternal authority is less the sign of an incestuous attachment (as Tanner argues in *Adultery in the Novel*) than a willed prolongation into adulthood of the sexual neuterdom and indifference that Rousseau associates with childhood. Julie's dilemma is that her philosophy of disincarnate union, innocent love, is constantly refuted by the history of a liaison (with Saint-Preux) that she would like to forget (and wishes to perpetuate). Like *l'homme civil* laying claim to the naturalness of his discourse, she represents a post-lapsarian being clinging to the illusion of pre-lapsarian innocence. Thus she conceives her marriage as a renascence, the recovery of a lost innocence.

Starobinski asserts that 'le roman nous offre le spectacle d'une dialectique qui aboutit à une synthèse'.[102] But in fact the text only traces the ramifications of a would-be but truncated dialectic finally deprived of synthesis. Saint-Preux stresses the presence of an insoluble contradiction: 'Tu as voulu concilier la tendresse filiale avec l'indomptable amour; en te livrant à la fois à tous tes penchants, tu les confonds au lieu de les accorder, et deviens coupable à force de vertu' (II, p. 336). The split between *la volonté* and *le cœur* renders Julie guilty, in her own eyes, of the double sin of lust and hypocrisy. Her death, a *mort heureuse*, apparently self-willed (the boating accident is less a cause than a pretext), represents a deliverance from eternal vigilance over her libido and the agony of self-contradiction. Death, moreover, holds out the prospect that, disencumbered of the opaque flesh, the transparent soul will at last accede to that absolute proximity to the beloved for which the letter is an imperfect substitute. Dead, the lover will at least no longer have to write. Julie, like *l'homme sauvage*, attains in life only a fiction of innocence, a pseudo-ignorance: the letter holds her attached to that which she condemns.

Repeatedly, the Rousseauiste text begins by prescribing and ends by proscribing (or, more ironically, first proscribes then prescribes) the impeccable, asexual, apolitical, atextual ignorance that is conterminous with absolute knowledge, an *archē* that is also a *telos*: in the terms of the *Contrat*, a total alienation of knowledge that would be identical with a total restitution. And it is precisely because it is unattainable that it is also irresistible. If reality is always imperfect, then perfection is necessarily unreal; as Julie writes: 'il n'y a rien de beau que ce qui n'est pas' (II, p.693). Ignorance is implicated in an indissoluble and reciprocal liaison with the experience of love. In the *Confessions*, love appears as an illusion sustained by an imagination dependent on the absence of the loved one. Carnal knowledge, possession, the satisfaction of desire, spells the death of desire. It is the function of ignorance (or innocence) to promote the operation of the imagination and hence the desirability of the beloved. Conversely, ignorance, if it is to be desirable, must remain unknown. Julie's theory that 'on jouït moins de ce qu'on obtient que de ce qu'on espere' (II, p. 693) implies, consolingly, that to wish for ignorance is perhaps preferable to the fulfilment of that wish since it enables the aspirant to savour at least the lack of that condition of which, being ignorant, he would, inexorably, be unaware.

According to Rousseau, to have knowledge of something is to duplicate in the cognitive mode the act of appropriation signified by 'Ceci est à moi' in which the proprietor–the knower–remains quite distinct from his property – the known. To attain absolute knowledge, the verb *avoir*, mediated by the disjunctive genitive, must be replaced by *être*: it is not enough merely to *have* knowledge of something, one must *be* that which is known. Thus self-knowledge provides the paradigm for knowledge of the world. But the nature of the self falls under the same interdict as Nature, with similarly disruptive epistemological consequences.

In the *Confessions*, Rousseau confesses that 'il y a des lacunes et des vides que je ne peux remplir qu'à l'aide de recits' (I, p. 130). The self is incomplete, and can only be completed by way of an encounter with discourse; but discourse is not capable of completion either. The integrated, singular self is a destination located at the far end of an interminable journey through writing. Autobiography could only be conclusive if it were possible to 'tout dire', to exhaust the number of possible statements about a personality: 'Je n'ai qu'une chose à craindre dans cette entreprise; ce n'est pas de trop dire ou de dire des mensonges; mais c'est de ne pas tout dire, et de taire des vérités' (I, p. 175). The autobiographer's prolixity is therefore attended by frustration, but also by guilt. The possibility of self-affirmation is seen to depend on a lack of self-definition, of a *nom propre*. While all statements about the self are grounded in rhetoric, the self is only a structure of deceits, and the claim to innocence only another rhetorical gesture. Thus the *Confessions* relate the adventures of a guilty conscience in search of crimes sufficient to justify its expression.

It is the function of the autobiography to generate the false opinions it proposes to refute. The self is constituted by the same fate that afflicts the other transcendent unities immortalized in Rousseau, Nature and the *volonté générale*, condemning itself, in the same movement in which it condemns other entities, to disintegration: like the 'corps politique', '[il] commence à mourir dès sa naissance et porte en lui-même les causes de sa déstruction' (II, p. 424).

Thus in the *Dialogues*, Rousseau resigns himself to perpetual misunderstanding and misrepresentation, relying for rehabilitation on an unreliable posterity or the final judgement of the 'arbitre suprême' (I, p. 989). Rousseau's scriptural consciousness seems to lodge within itself an archetypal and irrevocably hostile reader. The writer is also his own most severe critic: 'Jean-Jacques et celui qui le croit malhonnête', as Foucault observes, 'sont noués dans une même étreinte mortelle.'[103] Fearful of equivocal silence but incapable of self-vindication, Rousseau is driven to impersonate his accusers, 'cumulant contre moi toutes les charges imaginables' (I, p. 663). Rousseau himself is responsible for telling lies about Jean-Jacques.

Rousseau's anepistemological discourse permeates the oratory of the Revolution it predicts. But the Revolution also implements the programme of non-discursive action advocated but left unspecified by the first *Discours*. Hence the consequence noted by Thibaudet, namely that 'la proclamation de la République française coïncide en effet avec l'abolition de la République des lettres'.[104] The Romantic rejection of the Enlightenment (for which everything is knowable, and what is unknowable does not exist) is performed in Revolutionary annihilation. The abrogation of the rights of literature was not accidental; the attack on conventional discourse was a necessary concomitant of a rational campaign of subversion. *La Nouvelle Héloïse* indicates that the social hierarchy is buttressed by the tyranny of language encapsulated in the arbitrary power conferred by titles. Saint-Preux, a *quidam*, is doomed to impotence and poverty and itineracy by his lack of a noble name (a deficiency dramatized in the text by the postponement of his identification). Name and rank were the symbols not just of aristocratic privilege but of a comprehensive control over the consecrated forms of language. Literature, written by, for, or under the protection of, the nobility, represented a narrow-based monopoly vulnerable to expropriation. Similarly, written legislation objectified the inequality it codified and sought to perpetuate.

Rousseau invokes money as a recurrent metaphorical vehicle for language: words are the inflated but intrinsically worthless currency of social transaction, displacing and devaluing their referents. The yield on an investment in language, the accumulation of socially sanctified knowledge, was bound to reinforce the disparity of classes by the creation of a dominant intellectual elite. Knowledge (tied to the conjugation of the verb *avoir*) was a species of property inimical to equality.

Accordingly, the Revolution tended to be inimical to knowledge;

its anti-intellectual purpose was to actualize, historically, the myth of an original society, democratic by virtue of universal ignorance. The reply to Lavoisier's request (recounted by Carlyle) for a stay of execution on the grounds that a vital experiment remained unfinished – 'la République n'a pas besoin de savants' – may be apocryphal but it would have been perfectly consistent with Revolutionary ideology.[105] The severance from an intellectual past was symbolically accomplished by the guillotine, a more drastic accomplice of Ockham's razor, dispensing with redundant entities: a quintessentially Cartesian blade, definitively dividing body and mind.

But the Revolution could only postpone not renounce its epistemic inheritance. The installation of a repermutated social hierarchy was accompanied by a reaffirmation of intellectual inegalitarianism. Thus the Revolution also retraced Rousseau's circular transit from savage to civil society. It was no longer knowledge but ignorance which was condemned to abolition. But the persistence of ignorance offers to knowledge an indispensable confirmation of its continued superiority. And if it was virtually expunged from France, the vestiges of nescience, the outcome of regression postulated but declared impossible by Rousseau, might nevertheless be located abroad, in a remote elsewhere; more specifically, in the decadent Orient: the esteemed cradle of civilization, birthplace of the arts and sciences (and origin of the Renaissance), now demoted by the Occidental Romantic imagination to the last outpost of ignorance.

Rousseau acclaimed Socrates' profession of ignorance. But the 'I' and ignorance are forever irreconcilable, since the claim 'I know that I do not know' is self-refuting. Thus the self-avowed ignoramus is always insincere. Ignorance is partly an effect of grammar: incompatible with the first-person pronoun, it is almost inseparable from the third-person plural: I am not ignorant (neither, of course, are *you*); but *they* are. Such is the premise of nineteenth-century Orientalism.

The Renaissance typically defined its superiority in opposition to an inferior intermediate period, lodged anachronistically between the wisdom of the past and its reincarnation in the present. Orientalism reiterates the cultural nationalism of Petrarch while permutating his terms. The France that was for the humanist a nation of (scholastic) barbarians supplants Italy as the custodian of culture, while barbarianism is exiled eastwards. The epistemological dichotomy of knowledge and ignorance is transposed from a temporal into a spatial dimension, the dualism implicit in the periodization of history rearticulated in a repartition of geography.

Proceeding from the premise that knowledge is possession, Orientalism translates the proposition of epistemic supremacy into an enterprise of global appropriation. Both verbally and militarily, 'France laboured to promulgate the forms which correspond to her national mind as universally binding.'[106] The elimination of difference, and the eradication of ignorance, would be achieved by duplicating the (textual) exhaustiveness of the *Encyclopédie* and the (spiritual) expansiveness of the Rousseauiste ego in the (imperial) acquisition and domination of space.

The earlier sections on Genesis and the Renaissance illustrated some of the hazards impeding the renunciation of intermediacy and incompleteness in favour of the conditions of an original nescience, exemplified by a *tabula rasa*, or a conclusive omniscience, embodied in a permanent thesaurus: the binary (but equivalent) alternatives of a zero that cannot be subtracted from and a unity that cannot be added to. Rousseau offered a confirmation of that analysis. This study will proceed in accordance with Rousseau's method: the first part having dismissed an antithetical model of knowledge and ignorance as a fiction, the next part will consider the practical ramifications of that illusory theory.

3

THE OCCIDENTAL ORIENT

Enough of science and of art
(Wordsworth, 'The Tables Turned')

3.1 Heliotropes

Nicholas of Cusa observed that the centre of the universe always appears to coincide with the position of any observer.[1] Thus from a terrestrial point of view, the sun is merely a satellite of the earth. This state of affairs was noted in passing by Nietzsche who, contrasting our simple concepts of Being with our complex experience of Becoming, remarks that 'the situation is the same as with the motions of the sun: in that case error has our eyes, in the present case our language as its perpetual advocate'.[2] But it is clear that language is also the stout defender of a reassuring solar mythology: our retarded rhetoric has still not caught up with the Copernican revolution; it remains obstinately Ptolemaic. The metaphor that depicts an animated, personified sun rising and retiring in accordance with the rhythms of humanity domesticates and perpetuates a geocentric delusion.

The word 'Orient' derives from the Latin *oriens*, signifying 'sunrise' or 'rising sun', and hence, by association, the East; (conversely, *occidens*, issuing in 'Occident', signifies sunset or the West). On exclusively etymological grounds, therefore, it is possible to state that the Orient does not exist; more generally, it can be shown that the Orient, in the elastic cultural and geographical senses we attach to the term, is an invention, a palpable figment of a Europocentric imagination.[3]

The language we commonly employ to refer to the sun incorporates an obsolete cosmology; scarcely less archaic and inexact are our terms for describing the planet Earth. We typically speak of it as though it had not three dimensions but two, as though it were not an imperfectly spherical globe with a couple of depressions at opposite

60

ends, but a flat, rectangular plane. Terrestrial consciousness is inscribed with a bipartite symmetrical atlas centred on Europe. The lines of longitude measured east and west of an imaginary straight line, the Prime Meridian, passing through Greenwich and the poles, are more than mere navigational conveniences: they are the geographic delineation of a global prejudice. Just as the illusion of the sun's motion has been rendered canonical by linguistic habit, so the Orient has been converted by the chance ascendancy of Occidental cartography into an ontological absolute.

In the light of the inescapable association of the Orient with the rising sun, it is bound to seem improbable that, in the preface to his early sequence of poems, *Les Orientales*, Hugo should recall that the inspiration for the subject of the Orient came upon him 'd'une façon assez ridicule, l'été passé, en allant voir coucher le soleil' (*Œuvres poétiques*, I, p. 578). Hugo appears to posit a causal connection between a percept and a concept: on the one hand, the sight (the illusion) of the sun setting on the horizon, and, on the other, the idea of the Orient.

Hugo's predilection for the crepuscular is legendary. Musset writes that Mardoche

> se couchait, précisément à l'heure
> Où (quand par le brouillard la chatte rôde et pleure)
> Monsieur Hugo va voir coucher Phoebus le blond.[4]

Mme Hugo's biographical remarks[5] tend to confirm the poet's own declarations (in *Feuilles d'automne* and elsewhere) that the setting sun functions as Hugo's muse, engendering a mood receptive to any poetic subject. But the phrase 'd'une façon assez ridicule' indicates Hugo's awareness of the apparent contradiction in the juxtaposition of a dying sun and the portion of the planet whose defining attribute is to be the birthplace of the sun. Barrère argues that the preface is therefore not to be read *à la lettre*: 'Tout d'abord, c'est et ce veut être un défi au bon sens: l'espace, il l'a dit, appartient au poète qui peut rêver de l'orient à Paris; mais aussi bien du soleil, sans le voir.'[6] But the 'Prélude' to the *Chants du crépuscule* suggests that this *prima facie* incongruity conceals a sense of aesthetic appositeness, a correspondence between perception and intuition:

> L'Orient! L'Orient! qu'y voyez-vous poètes?
> C'est peut-être le soir qu'on prend pour une aurore.
>
> (I, p. 831)

The Orient, in Hugo's imagination, is paradoxically the land of the

61

setting sun, of twilight, more in harmony with the night than the day. This perspective originates in the mental dominion of a metaphorical *soleil* over the empirical sun.

It would be superfluous to rehearse all the figurative formations in which the words 'sun' or 'soleil' have appeared.[7] It will suffice here to recall that the most pervasive solar metaphor, or heliotrope, is that due to Plato, who identifies the sun as the son and semblance of the Form of the Good, which is the supreme cause and object of all knowledge.[8] Typically, the sun has been coupled with all the intellectual and spiritual faculties denoted by the word *esprit*. For the Renaissance, the sun was indistinguishable from the circle, the figure of the encyclopedia, signifying 'toute entière perfection qui gist en la vraye cognoissance des bonnes Lettres et Sciences'.[9] Such is the *soleil*, for instance, whence emanate the *lumières* held (notably by eighteenth-century French writers) to characterize eighteenth-century France. Derrida, linking it with the *nom propre*, designates the sun as 'le père de toutes les figures. Tout tourne autour de lui, tout se tourne vers lui.'[10]

While the literal sun may appear to rise in the Orient, *Les Orientales* suggests that it is this figurative, Platonic sun that Hugo imagines to have set there: culturally, intellectually, spiritually, politically, the sunlit yet benighted Orient has sunk into a condition of darkness, of *ténèbres*. In Plato's terms, it is located in the cave of ignorance. The West, in contrast, has internalized the sun.[11]

Butor, among others, has noticed that 'à la fin du XVIIIe siècle, la métaphore du jour et de la nuit était fort répandue: au point de vue religieux, le jour du christianisme s'opposait à la nuit du paganisme, au point de vue esthétique, l'âge d'or de l'"antique" à la "nuit" du Moyen-Age'.[12] Perhaps both the senses of *nuit* specified by Butor, each connoting a certain lack of enlightenment,[13] are conflated in the letter sent by Fénélon to Bossuet: 'Je vois déjà le schisme qui tombe, l'Orient et l'Occident qui se réunissent, et l'Asie qui voit renaître le jour après une si longue nuit.'[14] Nicholas of Cusa discovers in the Saracens the epitome of debauchery and sin, the *concupiscibilis potentia* which is the distinguishing feature of those terrestrials most remote from the solar beings who are closest to God: they are doomed to be tormented by fire. Similarly, Dante condemns all infidels to Hell. Because God is represented (like Plato's Good, in solar terms) as the ground of truth, faith is equated with knowledge, and the absence of faith with ignorance. It is this unacquaintance with divine truth for which the heathen, even the virtuous ones, are necessarily punished.[15]

The title of one chapter in Volney's seminal *Voyage en Egypte et en Syrie* echoes Nicholas and Dante and states the unifying principle of future studies: 'Des arts, des sciences [negligible thereabouts] et de l'ignorance [superabundant]'. Mahomet is pictured as the archetypal Oriental:

Il faut le dire: de tous les hommes qui ont osé donner les lois aux peuples, nul n'a été plus ignorant que Mahomet; de toutes les compositions absurdes de l'esprit humain, nulle n'est plus misérable que son livre.[16]

The function of Volney's book is to render more analytical, official and canonical the demarcation already explicit in St Paul's classification of Greek and Barbarian (assessed by virtue of their knowledge or ignorance of Greek) as, respectively, *sophos* and *anoetos* (Romans, 1:14; the Vulgate gives *sapiens* and *insipiens*, the King James 'wise' and 'unwise'):

Il suffit d'observer que cette ignorance répandue sur toutes les classes, étend ses effets sur tous les genres de connaissances morales et physiques, sur les sciences, sur les beaux-arts, même sur les arts mécaniques. Le plus simples y sont encore dans une sorte d'enfance.[17]

Thus the Orient is close to the state of nature: 'tout enfin retrace la simplicité des premiers temps'.[18] Volney institutionalizes the Orientalist tone of condescension and outlines a rudimentary blueprint of the invasion for which his work is an ample apologia. Napoleon's attempted annexation of Egypt and Syria at the end of the eighteenth century, although a military failure, made the Orient seem more intimately available to French culture.

Orientalist discourse, existing in a kind of symbiotic relationship with colonialist ideology, and attaining its most expansive articulation in the nineteenth century, has elaborated a set of congenial and intertextual theories about the Orient – traversing scholarly, political, philosophical, economic, literary and historical writing – which tolerate, encourage, or justify an active policy of foreign domination. The Orient is consistently represented as drastically inferior to the West, displaying the barbarism that it is the moral duty of civilization to eradicate and replace by a society modelled on itself. The ignorance predicated of the Orient is subsumed in this overall project of constructing a basis for French (or British) hegemony. The East is intellectually (and morally and spiritually) incompetent, backward; it is decadent; this condition solicits the intervention of French knowledge and know-how, whose mission it is (variously conceived in pedagogical, cultural, medical, religious terms) to educate, regenerate, enlighten, cure, redeem (Volney's verb is *naturaliser*, synonymous with *franciser*). France is destined to assimilate the Orient while eliminating the Oriental, to Europeanize the Arabs, to turn night into day.

Schwab writes that 'L'Orient est l'Autrui de l'Occident.'[19] And like the Sartrian *autrui*, its repression permits the expression of the repressing consciousness. The French shaping of the Orient, by instituting or consolidating an antithesis between an Us and a Them, a *là-bas* and an *ici*, an *étranger* and a *patrie*, is instrumental in the dramatization and imposition of a fixed and favourable identity assumed by France.[20] According to the mythology of mainstream Orientalism, the Orient, the incarnation of nescience, is deemed to await instruction by France, the exponent of omniscience. France is an ideal, a norm, a *plenum* to which the Orient stands as a *vacuum*: but it needs to demonstrate its epistemic plenitude by geographical expansion, realigning its frontiers to coincide with the universal horizons of its knowledge.[21] France already dominates the world, it is simply a question of translating that theoretical pre-eminence into practice. France (it is asserted) is already culturally complete, but (it is admitted) might be more complete still. Thus on the one hand, the Orient seems to invite transformation; on the other, it offers the opportunity of a transformation to the transformer. Both terms of the equation are therefore unstable.

Under the aspect of colonialism, the country to be colonized has to be endured rather than enjoyed until it has undergone conversion and basks in the full *rayonnement* of the *soleil* of French *civilisation*. But in an epistemological terms, the Orient may be seen not as a temporary hell but already a potential paradise: precisely that primitivism which the colonial ideology claims to subject to a civilizing metamorphosis is the principal attraction. The Orient, then, presents the double image of decadence and desirability; it encompasses both primordial civilization and rampant barbarism, both wisdom and ignorance; it is the object both of a *topophilie* and a *topophobie*.[22] Moreover, the shifting evaluations of the East imply a re-evaluation of the West. The West, in describing the East, is always ultimately referring to itself, constructing an image which it alternately refutes and reflects.

Historically, the ascendancy of Orientalism and the rise of Romanticism coincide; thematically, they are interdependent.[23] Lamartine speaks for a generation when he affirms that the Orient is 'la patrie de mon imagination'.[24] Thus the history of French adventurism in the East is simultaneously a chapter of literary history tracing the adventures of the novelistic and poetic imagination. Imperialism and writing, the note-taking *voyageur* and the armed *conquérant*, all figure as accomplices in a single enterprise of description and domination: as Martel observes of Napoleon, 'la plume et l'épée vont de pair'.[25] But Orientalism is premised on the transcendent value of the cultural archive, a classical conviction questioned in Romantic writing.[26] These divergent assessments of the French *soleil* are illuminated against the darkness of the Oriental *nuit*.

3.2 Hugo

'J'irai là-bas', wrote Baudelaire (in 'La Chevelure'). *Aller*, in this context, is not a verb of motion: it denotes a purely intellectual or imaginative displacement. The future tense (one of many in the poem) looks forward to a destination which has not yet been attained. The 'chevelure' of the poet's mistress is a mnemonic mechanism whose function it is, in part, to recall or call up a lost paradise. But Baudelaire's idyll is less a place than a prospect, an approach, a passage, a continuing experience that has not yet reached a conclusion, not even, perhaps, a beginning (the poem opens with a present participle ('moutonnant'), moves through the imperative and the subjunctive, and closes on an interrogative ('n'es-tu pas . . . ?')). His poetry values arrivals and departures less than the anticipation or discovery engendered by the condition of being in transit. The ideal Baudelairean journey would be one in which disembarkation (with its inevitable disappointment) was indefinitely deferred, and the imagination, unrestricted by the perceptible presence of *l'étranger*, savoured the dislocation of permanent travel.

In the same way that the evanescent spectacles evoked by the mistress's hair seem ultimately to count for less than the more durable possibility of their evocation, the abstract, content-less process whose end-product they are, so the image of the Orient is less powerful, less radiant than the paraphernalia of transportation. While 'La langoureuse Asie et la brûlante Afrique' connote an indifferent voluptuousness, a vague, generalized, indolent gratification of the senses, by contrast, thrust, energy, vitality are assigned to a cluster of 'rameurs', 'voiles', 'mâts', to the 'houle' and the 'roulis' (and, correspondingly, the 'chevelure' or 'parfum'), the compliant slaves or vehicles of the passive *voyageur*, which comprise the *primum mobile* of the Baudelairean universe. The chief attraction of the Orient is its distance, or, in the parallel terms of the sexual analogy that links the exotic with the erotic, the opportunity it provides of a prolonged postponement. The Orient offers an approximation to the unrealizable ambition of the interminable journey or perpetually unconsummated (and therefore undiminished) desire. Hence the opposition between a tangible, present, carnal *ici* that, like satisfaction, spells the death of desire, and a remote *là-bas*, 'Tout un monde lointain, absent, presque défunt'. Typically, an immediately accessible metropolis or prostitute, decaying or corrupted, is the occasion for revulsion or ennui while an invisible, inaccessible, and therefore desirable Orient is (like Baudelaire's 'Passante') apprehended as the location of a nostalgic or oneiric ideal.

In the nineteenth century, the *paradis artificiel* of the Orient was a publicly available opiate, the destination of a trip that could be undertaken in domestic comfort. Hugo, like Rousseau, like Baudelaire's *voyageur*, preferred not to arrive; unlike them, he preferred, in addition, never to depart. His poem 'A un voyageur', which pretends to welcome back a returning traveller (but with conspicuous mockery), relates how the poet

> moins heureux et moins sage
> Attendait des saisons l'uniforme passage
> Dans le même horizon,
> Et comme l'arbre vert qui de loin le dessine,
> A sa porte effeuillant ses jours, prenait racine
> Au seuil de sa maison! (I, p. 729)

Yet for Hugo too, temporarily rooted to his doorstep though he may have been, the Orient was a seductive locale, 'l'oasis où je rêve' of 'La Chevelure', a site destined to minister to his insatiable thirst for a mythology.

Rousseau feared that maps, globes, atlases would usurp the sovereignty of place. The Orient constitutes an exemplary case of textual displacement: composed of myth and reportage, it had acquired the canonical status of a pure signifier, the knowledge of whose signified was a hindrance to its description, as irrelevant as an actual triangle to a proof of the Pythagoras theorem. As Baudelaire recognized, to arrive *là-bas*, to discover the identity of, or possess the elusive woman, was the formula of disenchantment. Orientalism furnished Hugo with that tautological knowledge of the Orient which was compatible with perfect ignorance of Oriental reality.

Thus it was not necessary to visit the Orient in order to write authoritatively about it; more strictly, it was necessary not to visit it. The ahistorical, ageographical, fabulous essence of the Orient on which Hugo's poetry is predicated carries the implication that it is indispensable for the writer to stay at home, lounging on his doorstep, if his ideal, epical archetypes of valour and villainy are to remain uninflected, uncorrupted by empirical existence. (Conversely, it follows that the essential Orient cannot exist without the creative reconstruction effected by the poetic imagination.) Rousseau extolled (but denied) presence; Hugo prizes absence.

The preface to *Les Orientales* testifies to what Schwab, following Edgar Quinet, calls 'la Renaissance orientale': the virtual obsession with Orientalia common to scholarship and society by the turn of the nineteenth century: 'Au siècle de Louis XIV on était hélléniste, maintenant on est orientaliste' (I, p. 580).[27] The major polemical burden of the preface is a critique of the decorum criticism: that there are proper and improper subjects for poetry. Hugo asserts the freedom of art to engage *any* subject (and thus *even* the Orient). He condemns the imposition of 'limites de l'art' (I, p. 578), but implicitly acknowledges their existence by placing the Orient outside those limits, in transgression of aesthetic laws. Thus he seeks to incorporate the non-aesthetic within art, to import the outside inside. 'A quoi rime l'Orient?' he asks, parodying the sceptical critic, but he implies that the very lack of a rhyme or reason ('il n'en sait rien'), and thus its deviation from classical rules, is what makes the *topos* irresistible for him.

For almost the entire duration of one very protracted sentence, Hugo appears to discard the Orient in favour of Spain: 'pourquoi n'en serait-il pas d'une littérature dans son ensemble, et en particulier de l'œuvre d'un poëte, comme de ces belles vieilles villes de l'Espagne, par exemple, où vous trouvez tout'. The 'tout' is then broken down into its component parts: promenades beneath orange trees along river banks, festive squares, tortuous streets, labyrinths of buildings, noisy markets, cemeteries, tinselled theatres, a scaffold (from which still dangles a skeleton 'qui craque au vent'), and, in the centre, dominating the town and visible for miles around, a great gothic cathedral. The enumerative syntax, indefinitely extendible, is finally interrupted by a dash, which splits off from the rest of the sentence at the same time as it introduces 'la mosquée orientale', situated 'à l'autre bout de la ville' (a location mirrored by its position in the sentence) and 'cachée dans les sycomores et les palmiers' (I, p. 579). Spain, then, turns out to be subsumed in the

Oriental (the East begins south of the Pyrenees; thus part of the Orient lies to the west of France); but its visibly Oriental aspect is concealed, discreetly hidden away at the far end of town behind a mass of trees.

Hugo modestly concedes that he cannot hope to duplicate the diversity of the Spanish town: 'si on lui demandait ce qu'il a voulu faire ici, il dirait que c'est la mosquée'. *Les Orientales* thus presents itself as Hugo's attempt to 'faire la mosquée'. Hugo, that is, will emulate the mosque: his work will be to the classical aesthetic what the mosque is to the rest of town. To do the mosque is also to visit it, and thereby make central what has hitherto been marginal. But doing the mosque involves, perhaps principally, constructing or reconstructing the original edifice, keeping it firmly in place at the opposite end of Western culture, out of sight. The stated programme therefore accommodates disparate projects, entailing both display and concealment, a disposition alternately of remoteness from and proximity to the Orient.

Hugo professes a 'vive sympathie de poète . . . pour le monde oriental' (I, p. 580) (although his attitude towards the Orient in his later works oscillates between the extremes of fanatical partisanship and indifference, exaltation and the derision of exaltation). One reason for the lure of the East for Hugo is suggested by the dialectical interplay, in the last paragraph of the preface, between Orient and Occident. Jean-Pierre Richard, in a short essay concerned chiefly with Hugo's prose, reiterates the view that 'dans l'arsenal des figures hugoliennes, il en est une cependant qui domine, en quantité comme en valeur, toutes les autres: c'est, on le sait, l'antithèse'.[28] In Hugo (as in Nicholas of Cusa), antithesis is less a simple rhetorical device than a ubiquitous structural principle. Its ambiguous dualism operates equally in the manicheistic tendency of his later verse and in the tenets of his political ideology.[29] But it is similarly implicit in the fundamental premise of Orientalist wisdom, the cultural, geographical, literary, philosophical demarcation between East and West. The conduciveness of the Orient to the prodigal play of antithesis makes it a naturally sympathetic locale for the proliferation of Hugolian polarities.[30]

Les Orientales rests on a scaffolding of structural oppositions which supports both the unity of individual poems and their overall effect of homogeneity. Many of the poems depict a literal conflict that is the external counterpart to an inner, psychological antagonism: a state of war in which Greek is set against Turk, and, more generally, European against Oriental. The determinant of discord is discovered in the intrinsically bellicose character of the Oriental, whose bloodthirsty, lustful, rapacious figure stalks through the poems. The will to power, it appears, is a racial trait of the composite Oriental man just as servility and susceptibility to Western charm are the immutable distinguishing features of Oriental woman (evidenced in 'Adieu de l'hôtesse arabe'). Both these propensities are dramatized against the backcloth of the encounter of Christian, civilized Europe with the barbaric, heathen East, which it is destined to conquer or convert.

The preface, on a scholarly note, declares that 'Jamais tant d'intelligences n'ont fouillé à la fois ce grand abîme de l'Asie. Nous avons aujourd'hui un savant cantonné dans chacun des idiomes de l'Orient, depuis la Chine jusqu'à l'Egypte' (I, p. 580). Asia is conceived of as an inexhaustible archaeological trench, a site to be excavated by imported European spades. But the pursuit of academic knowledge is metaphorically tied to military support; the Orient is also an encampment, a front, an intricate network of far-flung outposts in which each indigenous language must be subjugated by militant scholars, annexed in the name of an epistemic empire guarded by an intellectual army billeted abroad.

Intercontinental strife, which is the staple source of narrative drama (battles and duels, pursuits and escapes, triumphs and defeats, winners and losers etc.), is installed within a grid of moral, optical, geographical, climatic, theological, and epistemological polarities (at articulating which, the alexandrine, with its twin hemistiches set apart by an audible and visible caesura between them, is virtuosically adept): day/night,[31] *lumière/ombre*, sin/virtue, sea/land, desert/oasis, hot/cold, wet/dry, divine/human, knowledge/ignorance. These headings obscure the passage of metaphorical traffic via the multiple junctions and interchanges between neighbouring couples. Thus, for example, the essentially optical opposition of light(ness) and dark(ness) occurs in contexts as diverse as the intellectual (enlightenment contrasts with benightedness), the moral (the powers of good and evil), the existential ('la nuit du trépas'; 'ténèbres' rhyming with 'funèbres'), and the racial.[32]

The endless interplay of bilateral images promotes the production of striking effects: the opposites that clash in antithesis may reunite in paradox or oxymoron – the poetic equivalent of Hugo's tragi-comic theatre – blending the sublime and the grotesque. But these provisional, almost accidental syntheses (such as occur in Spanish towns) scarcely blur the sharply defined frontiers along which Hugo's epic antagonists are aligned (hence Hugo's abomination of 'accouplements hideux' ('Le Feu du ciel', I, p. 590). At the level of argument, the preponderance of the either/or structure issues in the drama of the choice:

> Choisis enfin, avant que ton Dieu ne se lève,
> De Jésus et d'Omar, de la croix et du glaive,
> De l'auréole et du turban.

('Les Têtes du sérail', I, p. 604)

But the decision rarely involves a dilemma (unless you are like Sultan Achmet, and your Spanish concubine demands conversion in exchange for her favours ('Sultan Achmet', I, pp. 656–7)).[33]

At the level of style, contemporary critics were quick to criticize the allegedly *pittoresque* character of the poems. Hugo was censured for offering nothing more edifying than a 'poésie pour les yeux', for adopting a 'matérialisme poétique' devoid of intellectual content.[34] Throughout the poems, it is true, Hugo displays a painterly preoccupation with the subtleties of shade and colour, contour and perspective. The opening poem, 'Le Feu du ciel', invokes the episode in Genesis of the destruction of Sodom and Gomorrah as a pretext permitting the inconspicuous, virtually invisible narrator to adopt a bird's-eye view (or, more strictly speaking, the point of view of a cloud), and conduct an elevated ordnance survey of the Oriental landscape. With remarkable indirectness, as if the destination and ostensible purpose of the divinely-directed cloud (namely, to incinerate the sinful cities) were irrelevant, the cloud travels, by a roundabout *route touristique*, from West to East (running parallel to the Danube, '[qui] coule / De l'occident à l'orient' ('Le Danube en colère', I, p. 678)), duplicating the passage of the poetic imagination, over sea, desert, Egypt, corn, naked ebony virgins. Thus are some of the main landmarks on the subsequent itinerary introduced.

The narrator's meagre, physical presence is concentrated in the repeated references to his organ of vision: the ubiquitous *œil* is the unsung hero of the poem. What the narrative relates, essentially, is the adventures of an eye. Persistently, the roving, Cyclopean, all-seeing eye is drawn to anatomical and architectural detail. Hugo proposes a poetry of surfaces; but the verbal geometry which is its consequence exalts the *rond* over the straight line and the angle ('le romantisme, c'est . . . le plein et le rond').[35] If the Orient is apprehended as a décor or façade to be measured and recorded with technical proficiency, Hugo's draughtsmanlike precision nonetheless does not exclude an overt predilection for the voluptuous, feminine contours of domes, spheres, aqueducts and spirals, counterpointed by the more masculine linear geometry of pyramids, spires and pillars. Not that the vagrant eye wholly approves of them: 'Ces ponts, ces aqueducs, ces arcs, ces rondes tours, / Effrayaient l'œil perdu dans leurs profonds détours' ('Le Feu du ciel', I, p. 590). Hugo is consistently attracted by what he nevertheless claims to find repellent, as if the Orient were some kind of self-imposed endurance test. *Les Orientales* flatters (or appals) the senses with a profusion of sights and sounds (the quality of which it often strains to reproduce in the lay-out and phonology of the verse) and, to a lesser extent, of tastes and smells (which can only be referred to). In sum, the Orient is presented as an intelligible hierarchy of sensorial (architectural, pictorial, olfactory) data.

The Oriental, the inhabitant of the Orient, is similarly perceived as a constellation of surfaces and angles (and odours); the stone of the buildings, the canvas of the tents, and the sunburnt skin of the natives are all inspected by the indiscriminate, ubiquitous eye (and nose). Thus the poems embody a physiognomy of the Oriental, who is defined by his texture, colour or design: his visible aspect. The Arab, like his architecture, is all surface. One recurring word points up this conspicuous superficiality of identity: *le front*: the character of the individual is imprinted perceptibly, as though branded, on his forehead. The Oriental is flatly two-dimensional; in geometrical terms, he is the mere sum of his coordinates.

But if the Oriental is superficial, he is not abstract or lightweight; on the contrary, he is dense, grossly substantial, massive, made of too too solid (and sullied) flesh. In the confrontation of European and Oriental, the conflicting elements engaged (Bachelard would say) are those of earth and air. The European is all lightness and spirit: he is aerial, mercurial, almost gaseous. In 'Adieux de l'hôtesse arabe', the 'voyageur blanc', this 'bel oiseau passager', is not just inaccessible, restlessly mobile, as his Arab hostess complains, but actually invisible, a nebulous absence, the distant, intangible object of desire (I, pp. 647–8).

'Lazzara' (I, pp. 642–5) is a tale of a Turk's lust for a white girl, probably Greek, who is young, tall, svelte, vivacious, and, above all, fleet-footed. The poem repeats the refrain, 'Comme elle court!', and elaborates the point: 'Elle va, court, s'arrête, et vole.' She appears more bird-like than the birds, who would give up their wings for her feet. She is, inevitably, like the European male, desirable: 'Certes, le vieux Omer, pacha de Négrepont, / Pour elle eût tout donné.' The disdain in this line is audible: 'le vieux Omer', poor old impotent Omer, still chasing girls at his age, or, rather, not so much chasing – he could never keep up with her – but just wishing he could. 'Certes', to be sure! how could he not covet and wish to bag this white bird? 'Négrepont' hints overtly at his racial remoteness from the European, and a darker colour than the alabaster of the girl. A long and detailed list of the things he would give up to obtain the girl (including ships, horses, pistols, tiger skin, concubines, Albanians, French, Jews (and their rabbi), even his Spanish woman – too dark-skinned) asserts the priority of desire over materialism, but nevertheless contrives to stress the pasha's sheer materiality. Thus his clothes are 'tout ruisselant de pierreries': he is so loaded with stones he can hardly move; 'ruisselant' therefore strikes an ironic note. But the pasha is a heavyweight even without clothes: the silver butts of his 'lourds pistolets' have been worn down by his 'main rude'. This may explain why the girl is running so hard: to get away from the pasha's abrasive hand. The concluding stanza is pitiless with the Turk: the girl is abducted by a passing 'klephte', a Greek or Albanian brigand unweighted by belongings (other than air, water, gun, and liberty): giving nothing in exchange, he merely runs off with her (an act impossible for the ponderous pasha).

The poet asks himself, 'Que suis-je?', and answers his own question: 'Esprit qu'un souffle enlève' ('Enthousiasme', I, p. 606). He is volatile, a leaf carried on the breeze. The European (and especially the poet) is closer to heaven than to earth. While the lumbering, earth-bound Oriental is all exteriority, pure mass, the incorporeal, vaporous European is all interiority and insubstantiality; the one is Plutonic, the other Platonic. Curiously, therefore, it is rather the European who is inscrutable, mysterious, profound; the Arab is unfathomable because he is not even shallow.

Descriptive oppositions lend symbolic support to the account of the respective capacities of French and Oriental cultures and their representative citizens. There is no description that is not also normative, the vehicle of a tacit judgement, no colour or combination of colours that is not simultaneously a fragment of a coherent metaphysic. Thus style is subordinated to the demands of the cultural antithesis that is the central premise of the poetry.

The imagery of *Les Orientales* has attracted the criticism that it is, too often, gratuitous, excessive, the uncontrolled overflow of a reservoir of figuration. The Hugolian object or action, it is true, is rarely unescorted by simile, with the effect that a poem (such as 'Mazeppa', with its swift succession of 'comme's) will frequently consist of a dual series of separately identifiable and virtually autonomous strings of tenors and vehicles. The inflated image, overshadowing the object which is its foundation and insufficient justification, appears to float loose from its mooring in a literal ground, in the company of an accumulating consortium of other such dislocated images. Simile and metaphor, thus invested with considerable logical independence, exceed and dominate their tenors, cutting perpendicularly across the plane of dramatic narrative.

The equivalent importance accorded to literal and figurative universes initiates a state of rivalry between them in which the former may be the loser. Thus the malefic tropical sun which poses a threat to the Icarus-like European in 'Adieux de l'hôtesse arabe' ('Garde-toi du soleil / Qui dore nos fronts bruns, mais brûle un teint vermeil' (I, p. 648)) takes second place in the collection to the beneficent tropological sun which is successively Napoleon, Muse, poetry and civilization. The interplay of these dual suns is anticipated in the opening poem, where, before the contemplative eye,

> L'astre-roi se couchait. Calme, à l'abri du vent,
> La mer réfléchissait ce globe d'or vivant,
>   Ce monde, âme et flambeau du nôtre;
> Et dans le ciel rougeâtre et dans les flots vermeils,
> Comme deux rois amis, on voyait deux soleils
>   Venir au-devant l'un de l'autre. (I, p. 588)

In the remainder of the collection the two 'rois' are less 'amis' than adversaries seeking to usurp one another. Barrère considers that 'tout le recueil est un hymne au soleil';[36] but precisely the singular status of the sun is in doubt. In *Les Orientales*, at least two suns, the cosmological object and its reflection in a 'mer de poésie' (I, p. 580), compete for pre-eminence. If, as Riffaterre argues (*contra* Barrère),[37] the Orient characteristically appears in a nocturnal mode, this is because the local sun has been eclipsed by its superior Western counterpart.

According to two poems, 'Novembre' and 'Rêverie', the process of inspiration depends on the successful outcome of a struggle for primacy in the poet's mind between a view of Paris (cold, wet, gloomy) and a vision of the shimmering Orient. Both poems link the Orient with sunlight and warmth: 'Novembre' asserts that the extinction of light in autumn, when days are shortened and fog and smoke fill the sky, prohibits further *Orientales*: when the sun disappears, so too does the Orient. In 'Rêverie' on the other hand, faced with similar seasonal and climatic conditions, the poet strives (subjunctively) to summon up the contrasting image of a 'ville mauresque'. But the apparent drift of these poems is deflected in the course of the argument. In 'Novembre' the fading of light is the occasion not only for the poem as a whole, thus making the loss of inspiration the subject of composition, but for a prolonged and detailed recapitulation of Oriental archetypes; and the recollections Hugo evokes in place of the Orient to satisfy his frustrated muse (a typically Hugolian inversion: the poet inspires the muse) include a memory of Spain – in Hugo's reckoning, a part of the Orient. The Moorish town of 'Rêverie', initially described in the second stanza as 'éclatante', a radiant construction which 'déchire ce brouillard avec ses flèches d'or', appears itself, by the end of the third stanza, 'brumeuse', like the 'ciel d'automne', like Paris (I, p. 679). These poems reveal a predilection for darkness and a secret affinity between obscurity and the East which is sustained less secretly elsewhere in the collection.

The inflammable cloud of 'Le Feu du ciel' is pre-eminent among the special effects of *Les Orientales*. It does not blot out the sun, since it accomplishes its mission by night, but rather turns out to constitute a rival star by virtue of its destructive fire. Elements of this scenario, an Oriental locale by night, suddenly illuminated, as if by flares, for the purpose of retribution, recur in various combinations throughout the poems. Darkness pervades *Les Orientales*: *les orientales* are seductively dark-skinned, 'Belles comme les beaux soirs' ('Le Feu du ciel', I, p. 587); Istanbul, like Sodom and Gomorrah, incestuous sisters 'dormant dans la brume des nuits' (I, p. 590), is steeped in nocturnal 'ombre' (I, p. 598); the common epithet attached to cloud, fingers, Babel, trees, lace, and chaos in 'Le Feu du ciel', namely, 'noir', is also attracted to (for example) eyes ('Lazzara', I, p. 644), blood ('Marche turque', I, pp. 631–3 and *passim*), and two rocks ('Nourmahal-la-Rousse', I, p. 651). Natural sunlight in the Orient is almost always obscured, shaded, dimmed, outshone by alternative sources of radiance (fire, but also blades or blood), or supplanted by purely conceptual suns.

The point has often been made that Hugo sometimes takes the part of the Orientals, speaking with their voice, as if this were proof of innocence and a guarantee of fair play. But Hugo's alternative personae nevertheless generate a highly unified set of themes and images. The celebration of Napoleon in 'Lui' is balanced by 'Le Poète au calife'; both invoke the trope of the 'astre impérial' in describing their respective emperors. But in Napoleon's case, his imperial star 'se lève à l'orient' so that 'l'Egypte resplendit des feux de son aurore' (I, p. 684), while in the case of the caliph, the last stanza introduces the disruptive motif of a 'triste pensée' which cools the 'radieux Noureddin':

> Telle en plein jour parfois, sous un soleil de feu,
> La lune, astre des morts, blanche au fond d'un ciel bleu,
> Montre à demi son front nocturne.   (I, p. 681)

While Bonaparte rises with the dawn, inaugurating a fresh beginning, the sultan, even in the midst of day, is already preparing for night (and perhaps death). Hugo effects a reversal of the etymological and geographical properties of Orient and Occident: the Western sun is always rising in the East whereas the Eastern sun is always, if risen, on the brink of setting.

The persistent sunsets of *Les Orientales* appear, moreover, like the arrival of the incendiary cloud, to prefigure blood-letting. In 'Le Voile' (I, pp. 623–5), the slaughter of a girl by her four brothers for lifting her veil in the presence of a stranger is preceded by the ominous statement: 'Le soleil était rouge à son coucher ce soir.' The distinctive colour of the East, set against shades of black, is the red of the declining or dying sun and of blood: thus 'l'Europe se tournait vers le rouge Orient' ('Navarin', I, p. 607). Europe seems like a further incarnation of the cloud and the four brothers; so too does Hugo.

'Le Voile' embodies the fantasy central to Hugo's text: a veiled, dark, sensual, Oriental, feminine form is tantalizingly unveiled, then definitively reveiled.[38] This event is not simply recalled in the course of the dialogue between the girl and her brothers, cited as evidence for the charge of impropriety and grounds for punishment, but, in addition, acted out, in duplicate. According to the defendant, she was 'Cachée aux regards téméraires / Des giaours et des albanais', and, although her 'voile un instant s'est ouvert', the mysterious man in the green caftan (alluded to by her brothers) 'n'a point vu mes traits dévoilés'. The brothers never bother to question this stout denial; rather, as if frustrated by the lack of evidence or a confession, they proceed to enact the crime. The merely verbal interrogation of their sister is supplemented by more physical probing. Their flashing eyes, 'comme des lampes funéraires', are reflected in their gleaming blades: 'Déjà trois fois, hors de l'étui . . . / Les lames des poignards ont lui.' The girl is first undressed by their gaze, rendered 'faible et nue en [leur] pouvoir', before being run through, as if lasered, by their knives. Having received 'quatre poignards dans [son] flanc', she apostrophizes, regretfully, her 'voile blanc', as if it had been lost as a result of her wounds. Finally, another veil is unfurled, condemning her to irrevocable darkness: 'sur mes regards qui s'éteignent / S'étend un voile de trépas'.

'La Bataille perdue' (I, pp. 633–6) combines a number of recurrent themes. Rodrigo, the hero of the *romance* on which the poem is modelled, has become Reschid, another pasha (the Spaniard becomes, or already was at heart, a Turk), who bewails the loss of troops and possessions after military defeat. The possessive pronoun is again conspicuously frequent: the tragic manner is undone by the mocking attention to Moslem materialism. The poem offers an evident contrast between the quick and the dead, but although the pasha is still alive, it is as though he has suffered a fate worse than death: being stripped of all his worldly goods. Yesterday, Reschid mourns, I had castles, I had beautiful cities, thousands of Greeks to sell to servile Jews; I had great harems and arsenals. Today I have nothing: 'Allah! je n'ai plus même une tour à créneaux!' A sad fate, Hugo asks us to reflect, to be left without even a crenellated tower to one's name (a crenellated tower – obviously much prized among Turks – is one of the things old Omer offers to give up for Lazzara).

Reschid is forced to flee 'Comme un voleur qui fuit troublé dans les ténèbres': reduced to a furtive cat-burglar, he can only operate at night (the pasha, probably overweight, clearly objects to the necessity for urgent motion at any time). But the whole poem repeats or anticipates this translation to the nocturnal mode. Stanza 7 begins: 'Quoi! c'était une armée, et ce n'est plus qu'une ombre!' The army has become a shade: its shadiness is presented in contrast to its previous brilliance: the camp was 'éblouissant à voir'. But the pasha is reminded, seeing the fallen stretched out by their horses, of similar previous scenes when they 'dormaient à leur ombre aux haltes de midi!' The past seems to have been a rehearsal for the present: the soldiers taking their siestas in the shade of their horses were only practising for the big sleep (just desserts, perhaps, for failing to find shade for their beasts). The information conveyed in the first stanza, that at night there would be so many fires lit in the camp that it seemed the sky had rained down stars on the sombre hill, suggests that the Orientals were vainly struggling, with their artificial lights, to postpone the inexorable descent of darkness. Now 'Les noirs linceuls des nuits sur l'horizon se posent': the aged metaphor of night falling like a shroud is rejuvenated by reference to the death of Reschid's battalions who have sunk with the sun. Their rigorous exclusion from light is definitively sealed by their enclosure in a black box: vultures swoop down, 'passant leur bec entre leurs plumes noires', before tucking in to supper.

These two poems, 'Le Voile' and 'La Bataille perdue', encapsulate the events described in the opening and closing poems of *Les Orientales*. In 'Le Feu du ciel', the 'immense entassement de ténèbres voilé' (I, p. 591) of Sodom and Gomorrah is brilliantly lit up by the 'lueur sanglante' of the cloud ('chaque colonne / Brûle et tourbillonne / Comme un grand flambeau' while the tiara of the priest 'Prend feu comme un phare' (I, pp. 593–4)); but the veil is finally brought down once more: 'Ainsi tout disparut sous le noir tourbillon' (I, p. 595). The first stanzas of the last poem, 'Novembre' (I, pp. 686–8), systematically echo the last stanzas of the first: in Sodom and Gomorrah, 'Sur leurs débris éteints s'étend un lac glacé' (the alliterative conjunction of 'éteint' and 'étend' recurs in the closing lines of 'Le Voile') while in Paris, Autumn shortens the days, 'Eteint leurs soirs de flamme et glace leur aurore'. Expiring light and expanding ice: such are the distinguishing features of the world according to Hugo. The same vocabulary is applied to both the fall of the sinful cities of the plain and Fall in Paris: 'feu', 'tourbillonne', 'inonde', 'Flots', 'fumée', 'noirci'. The fourth stanza of 'Novembre' recalls the Biblical episode again: 'plus d'ardente Gomorrhe / Qui jette un reflet rouge au front noir de Babel': again a cloud obliterates the Orient. But not all light is quite snuffed out: in the final stanza, Hugo defines 'quinze ans' as 'l'âge où l'œil s'allume et brille'. Thus at the end of *Les Orientales*, as darkness closes in all over the world, only one solitary thing remains alight, penetrating the gloom like a beacon: the laser-like eye of the poet. Glaring down over the Orient, in place of the truant sun, is Hugo's all-pervasive, Occidental eye.

The high status granted to metaphoricity has a two-fold effect: both to suggest the objectivity of the figure and to stress the figurativeness of the object. Bachelard's concept of the image as any significant product of the verbal imagination, irrespective of its rhetorical function as tenor or vehicle, is eminently applicable to Hugo. The implication, that perception and intuition, truth and invention are indistinguishable, corresponds to Hugo's assessment of his own method.

As Richard remarks, there is, in Hugo, a 'paysage de la rhétorique' corresponding to a 'rhétorique du paysage'.[39] This rhetorical landscape,[40] and especially its plethora of metaphor, emphasizes the sheer textuality of *Les Orientales* and, indeed, of the

Orient itself. A long tradition of literary and historical interest (culminating in Volney, Byron, Chateaubriand and the translations of Edgar Fouinet) has made available, or inevitable, a vast and consecrated compendium of narratives, characters, and motifs, heterogeneously transcending national and geographical boundaries. And Hugo's allusive text, teeming with references to the Orientalist canon, points to its own intertextuality.[41] The voluptuous metaphor functions as the visible sign of the poet's self-conscious imagination at work on his inherited material, the outward manifestation of what Hugo consistently refers to as his *rêve* or *rêverie*. Whenever the persona of the poet is explicitly introduced in any poem, it is precisely this capacity for dream that is highlighted. The poet is a spontaneous, irrepressible dreamer ('Tout me fait songer' ('Enthousiasme'), 'je rêve dans l'ombre' ('Fantômes'), 'je rêve à la fenêtre' ('Rêverie') (I, pp. 606, 667, 679)). It is his prodigal unconscious, the unfathomable psyche that is the fount of creativity, in a word, Hugo's *âme*, which distinguishes the poet from his subject.

The Orient is the stuff that dreams are made of; but, according to the dreams, it is a materialist universe par excellence. Thus the Oriental inhabitant, typically the Arab or the Turk, is defined in terms of a lack; what he lacks is an unconscious or a soul, of which he has been relieved by poetic amputation: he lacks what Hugo characterizes elsewhere as a *vide*, the *abîme* that is the site of reverie. He is not advanced or bright enough even to be the victim of *maya*. The Oriental is, or ought to be, illiterate, still at the oral phase: 'Adieux' notes that Arabs 'sans en faire, écoutent les récits' (I, p. 647), but the 'Marche turque' condemns the man who 'sait lire' as a coward (I, p. 633). The coarse, gross, sensible reality of the Oriental is necessarily transmitted via the metamorphic vision of the poet, who is the appointed ambassador of oneiric truths that would, without him, remain unspoken because undreamed by a soulless, inarticulate Orient. The Orient does not dream, it is dreamed. Hugo conceives his task in terms of a mission, a duty, divinely ordained, whose accomplishment depends on the poet being a free-floating spirit, a cloud, a citizen of the dream world.

Jakobson writes that 'l'œuvre poétique doit en réalité se définir comme un message verbal dans lequel la fonction poétique est dominante';[42] Richard affirms that 'écrire, d'abord, pour [Hugo] c'est faire être le chaos . . . Mais c'est aussi le dominer scripturalement, le contrôler par l'acte de nomination même . . . Le langage s'offre . . . comme le chaos . . . mais l'espace aussi où l'homme se rend maître, ou du moins signifiant de son chaos.'[43] Together, these

two statements specify a relation of domination between the signifier and its signified, and between the poet and his signs. This
arrangement reproduces the primacy assumed by *Les Orientales* of
the white, ethereal European (exemplified by the poet) over the
'noir chaos' ('Le Feu du ciel', I, p. 588) of sand and sultans, of
the spiritual, dreaming West over the dreamless, carnal Orient. But
the two hierarchies intersect in the metaphor: the metaphor is the
sign not only of poetic distinction, of genius (as Aristotle maintained),[44] but of aesthetic, epistemic, and cultural domination.

The material, visual, sensual world, veiled in darkness and populated by veiled, dark-skinned houris, which represents for Hugo at
once a seductive temptation to the libido and a threat to the soul, to
be briefly unveiled only before being wiped out by redemptive fire,
is held to be inferior, by the poetic ego, to the potential of the
unconscious for originating dream, fantasy, mythology, vision.
Thus the antithesis of West and East, the demarcation between 'les
deux moitiés du monde' (which Bounaberdi's 'regard', like Hugo's,
'Embrasse d'un coup d'œil' ('Buonaberdi', I, p. 682)), is portrayed
as an immutable opposition between the metaphysical and the
physical, articulate wisdom and dumb ignorance, metaphor and the
metaphorized. The Orient is at once intellectually negligible, in
need of re-education, and the occasion for literary exaltation.

'Il aime le soleil', says Hugo of himself in the preface to *Les
Rayons et les ombres* (I, p. 1021). Hugo's beloved sun is (*inter alia*)
the Platonic origin of his 'beau rêve d'Asie' ('Novembre', I, p. 686),
the source of intellectual illumination that oversees its transition to
language, and the eye of the sky, the externalized image of the
poet's panoptic organ, the model of 'le grand œil fixe ouvert sur le
grand tout'.[45] The immediate, sensible world, to whose confines the
Oriental is restricted, is an illusion or a distraction; dream is the way
to discovery, the means of access to unseen truths, the condition in
which the dreamer's 'yeux plongeaient plus loin que le monde réel'
('Extase', I, p. 680): the vision of God occurs at night, when the sun
is displaced by the solar eye of the poet. By extension, poetry, the
purest expression of the soul and the public record of the private
dream, is not only visionary, mystical, eternal,[46] veridical, but the
textual embodiment of privileged knowledge, a reflection of divine
omniscience.[47] And metaphor is the hallmark of the poet's self-
apotheosis, the elevation of the dreamer to the status of seer.
Savoir, penser, rêver: these verbs are so many synonyms for the
experience of ontological revelation which is vouchsafed to the
poet; of them, Hugo can therefore declare: 'tout est là' (I, p. 1022).

Thus Hugo's text asserts the epistemic domination of the enlightened West over the benighted East and locates that superiority in the text. But the heliotrope, the axis of poetry, rises only after sunset, at night, in the absence of *hēlios*, and is therefore attracted to the congenial environment of the Oriental eclipse, which tolerates or encourages dream. As in Nicholas, it behoveth the intellect to abide in darkness. Thus *Les Orientales*, in joining Hugo to the Oriental, the heliophile to the heliophobe, dramatizes a miscegenation, an 'accouplement hideux'. The poet expresses a preference for the moon over the sun, and then continues:

> J'aime ces chariots lourds et noirs, qui la nuit,
> Passant devant le seuil des fermes avec bruit,
> Font aboyer les chiens dans l'ombre.
> ('Enthousiasme', I, p. 606)

Poetry is akin to the barking of shade-enshrouded dogs (again, as in Nicholas, dogs are discursive), called forth by the passing of heavy, dark, noisy, nocturnal vehicles (a description which suggests they may be transporting fleeing pashas).

'Là, en effet, tout est grand, riche, fécond, comme dans le moyen-âge, cette autre mer de poésie' (I, p. 580): the Orient, then, according to the preface, is comparable to the Dark Ages; but it is also of greater antiquity than Antiquity, and is therefore given chronological priority over Greece and Rome: the West is perceived ultimately as a derivative of the East. According to this archaeological structure of filiation, the atextual Orient, the prolongation of a pre-literate beginning, is the 'source' at which the poet may slake his thirst: at once an origin and the spring which finally empties into the sea of poetry. The Orient, in short, by virtue of its baseness, supplies a ground to metaphor, a foundation to literature. The oneiric *abîme* whence the text emerges discovers its image in the 'grand abîme' of the East.[48] On the one hand, the aesthetic is indistinguishable from the epistemic; on the other, unknowing becomes not only the immoral subject of poetry but also its indispensable first condition.

According to Hugo, Napoleon, like Hugo, is a dreamer: 'Bounaberdi' pictures him looking down on the world from a great height – the exalted position of the poet, the eye, the sun – and dreaming of invisible armies. For Napoleon, as for Hugo, the Orient procures a state of impersonal nostalgia in which a constellation of literary and historical memories drawn from a purely textual universe is recollected. He informs Mme de Rémusat that 'en Egypte . . . je rêvais toutes les choses'; to this essentially Hugolian perspective, he adds that 'je voyais les moyens d'exécuter tout ce que j'avais rêvé'.[49] Napoleon's Oriental project seeks to coerce a literary metaphor into history.

3.3 Napoleon

Truth, according to Nietzsche, is an illusion about which one has forgotten that it is an illusion; language consists not in observational statements but rather in 'a mobile army of metaphors'.[50] Napoleon's Oriental expedition sought to demonstrate the truth of an illusion by equipping a metaphorical army with cannon and powder and an armada to ship it *là-bas*.

The essential premise of Napoleonic imperialism was the comprehensive superiority of France over a decadent, enfeebled Orient. The destiny of cultural (philosophical, moral, physical, political, economic, gastronomic, literary, scientific) primacy, invoked as the rationale of foreign intervention, required for its fulfilment that this theoretical pre-eminence be translated in practice into a military victory on the field of battle. But if this was a necessary condition of establishing for all time the validity of a conventional wisdom, it was ultimately insufficient. The definitive and sufficient proof of intellectual hegemony (without which, it was held, a merely military domination was both valueless and impossible) lay in the reciprocal process of translating an empirical reality back into a textual empire, perpetuating and petrifying an otherwise transitory state of affairs in durable language.

Thus the subjugation of a country was to be supplemented by scriptural fortification, the healing 'congelation and coagulation of an original mass of similes and percepts' that Nietzsche perceived to be the requisite of man's 'repose, safety and consequence'.[51] Hence the double character of Napoleon's Egyptian adventure, his conduct of a war on two fronts, military and intellectual.[52] A martial campaign was designed to project the outward veracity of a textual assertion; at the same time, the fragile political manifestation of imperial philosophy would be buttressed by a scholarly regime.

Nietzsche maintains that the relation between subject and object is 'aesthetic'; that is, that an understanding by the one of the other calls for the operation of 'an intermediate force, freely composing and freely inventing'.[53] Napoleon similarly conceived his role as an intermediate, creative, shaping force in the encounter between

81

West and East, subject and object. He pronounced himself a creator, a supreme practitioner of the art of war, an inventor of history. But he was also a historian, a copious writer and rewriter of histories. Napoleon was at once warrior and scholar, a man of war and letters, both the author and the hero of his texts. Thiers declares that 'Napoléon est le plus grand homme de son siècle, on en convient, mais il est aussi le plus grand écrivain'.[54] Napoleon was certainly the greatest writer of his period in terms of sheer quantity: his complete works (combining the standard edition of the *Correspondance*, plus supplements, with the numerous subsequent collections of *inédits*) run to around fifty volumes. As Tomiche comments, 'peu d'hommes ont autant écrit'.[55] Even fewer, perhaps, have produced such a diverse *œuvre*, comprising not just histories, letters, memoirs, articles, proclamations, orders, bulletins, and assorted notes, but short stories, a novel (unfinished), Socratic dialogues, and Rousseauiste *discours*. Strictly speaking, however, he was less a writer than a dictator, in the verbal sense of the word: he usually had secretaries attend to the task of recording (or rectifying) his words for posterity.

The singularity of the man, the conviction that he was a *phénomène* rather than a mere epiphenomenon, was integral to the Romantic reading of his personality. But, at least in the context of his Oriental programme, Tolstoy was probably right to argue that if Napoleon had never existed he would have had to be invented. If the occasion of the Egyptian expedition was the conjunction of one man's monumental ambitions and the Directory's determination to frustrate them,[56] it was inevitable (as further French adventures in Africa and the East, of which the Egyptian excursion was the forerunner, suggest) that Orientalist theory, once formulated, should be tested in imperialist practice. Napoleon can be seen less as the author of a historical scenario than as a star performer, at liberty to make adjustments to a script. He is an improvisor on a standard theme: the champion of, but also the detached commentator on, an established discourse.

The chief protagonist of Napoleon's Oriental histories is invariably himself. The narrator characteristically refers to himself as agent in the third person: Bonaparte (as the name suggests) is a good part to play, a distinct personality with which Napoleon only happens to coincide. In designating himself author of the future he derives his authority from authors of the past, reinterpreted to justify the present. He was not only a prolific writer but a prodigious reader: everywhere Napoleon went, a *bibliothèque portative*, in addition to artillery, was sure to go.[57] And his writing (considered both thematically and stylistically) is fed by the recollections of his disparate reading. In connection with Egypt the name of Alexander figures prominently among the most recurrent historical allusions. Thus General Bonaparte announces to his army shortly before disembarkation that 'la première ville que nous allons rencontrer a été bâtie par Alexandre. Nous trouverons à chaque pas des souvenirs dignes d'exciter l'émulation des Français' (*Correspondance*, IV, p. 198). It is true that the capture of Alexandria is militarily expedient; but, equally, it is a factor in Napoleon's equation of himself with Alexander. The identification with historical personages becomes an obsessive gesture: Napoleon is also the reincarnation of, variously, Caesar, Charlemagne, Frederick the Great, Joan of Arc, and Jesus Christ. He is not a nostalgic in search of times past; rather, he seeks to collapse the past, anachronistically, into the present. In Napoleon's telescopic approach, history appears indistinguishable from autobiography. His task in Egypt is not just to annex space but to recover lost time, to reappropriate and invest in his own person the forty centuries which, so he reminds his troops before going into battle, gaze down upon them from the heights of the pyramids (IV, p. 240).

If Napoleon invokes Alexander as his model or rival it is because his classical predecessor is an exponent both of martial expertise and the philosophy of the *mission civilisatrice* which is the altruistic alibi of imperialism. According to Napoleon, Alexander did not belong to that category of uncivilized invaders who would generally restrict the scope of their activities in foreign lands to looting, rape, and murder: his victories were attended by the benefits for the host country of an encounter with a superior culture. The Orient, it follows, would accrue similar advantages from the advent of France.

The theory of the civilizing mission is set out in the 'Prospectus' to *La Décade égyptienne*:

Nous ne vivons plus dans ces temps où les conquérants ne savaient que détruire là où ils portaient leurs armes: la soif de l'or dirigeait toutes leurs actions; la dévastation, les persécutions, l'intolérance les accompagnaient partout. Aujourd'hui au contraire, le Français respecte non seulement les lois, les usages, les habitudes, mais même les préjugés des peuples dont il occupe le territoire. Il laisse au temps, à la raison, à l'instruction, à opérer les changements que la philosophie, les lumières des siècles ont préparés, et dont l'application devient chaque jour plus prochaine.[58]

The Frenchman, more an anthropologist than a soldier, will (unlike his less scientific precursors) respect the integrity of local culture (even if this is grounded on mere superstition and error); time and reason, however, will not be so respectful. Coercion is redundant, because conversion is inevitable, the irresistible effect of the propagation of *lumières*. The proclaimed objective of civilizing the uncivilized, an epistemic teleology predicated on the unassailable intellectual authority of an enlightened France over a barbaric Orient, is the rationale that underwrites the long-term expansion of the French Empire.[59] The transmission of culture is destined to consolidate a prior military advantage, to reinforce the submission of the native population by securing their willing acquiescence to fate. The subject race will be expected to recognize the necessity of the French archive to their *amélioration, prospérité, bonheur*, and even *salut*. Thus printing-presses were indispensable weapons in the struggle for control over the Orient.

Just as historical figures appear as anticipations of Bonaparte, so too Napoleon's fictional characters offer mirror-images of his character and career. In 'Le Masque prophète', an early short story based on an episode in Marigny's *Histoire des Arabes*, he delivers a brief eulogy on the noble Prince Mahadi, who reigned in Baghdad in the year 160 of the Hegira:

ce prince, grand, généreux, éclairé, magnanime, voyait prospérer l'empire arabe dans le sein de la paix. Craint et respecté de ses voisins, il s'occupait à faire fleurir les sciences et en accélérait les progrès, lorsque la tranquillité fut troublé par Hakem, qui, du fond du Korassan, commençait à se faire des sectateurs dans toutes les parties de l'empire.[60]

In the Egyptian variant of this story, Napoleon assigns the part of Hakem, the insurrectionist who threatens the growth of knowledge, to the evil Turkish beys who provide the immediate pretext for French intervention. Napoleon, on the other hand, is a would-be Mahadi: a benevolent, pacific, patriarchal ruler, concerned principally with promoting research and education, and only moved to violence by unruly troublemakers. In Egypt, he adopts the name by which he is popularly known: Sultan El-Kebir, The Great Sultan (XXIX, p. 540), and glories in the title of 'le Père du feu' (XXIX, p. 532). The image encodes the double character of the Napoleonic expedition: fire is, from one point of view (the Egyptian), what comes out of the barrels of muskets and cannon; from another (the French), it offers illumination, warmth. Thus Sultan El-Kebir, Father (or source) of Fire, is both sun and gun, both educator and corrector. His status as 'Membre de l'Institut', following his more conventional designation 'Bonaparte', is frequently given precedence over his rank of 'Général en chef'.[61] Napoleon commonly represents himself as the ambassador of the exact sciences: not just a warrior but a 'guerrier civilisateur', wielding not just a sword but 'une épée lumineuse'.[62] The true general is also, of necessity, a scientist, attuned to the laws of the universe to which those of history conform; he is a mathematician, skilled in computing his chances.

A scientific intonation and terminology emerge consistently from Napoleon's letters and campaign notes of the period (even the early *Discours sur le bonheur* deploys such recondite vocabulary as 'ichtyophage' and 'rhizophage').[63] His self-consciously erudite 'descriptions' display their credentials in a fondness for diagrammatic geometrical comparisons (which invoke, *contra* Hugo, the straight line and the right angle) accompanied by arithmetical computation. But this detached, measured statement of empirical data is syncopated by hyperbole, self-hypertrophy, and gross generalization (the world, they, we, are thus or thus). Thus the Napoleonic text mingles the abstemiously realistic and the intemperately metaphysical, reflecting the 'mélange' discerned in the author by Mme de Rémusat, of 'habitudes géométriques' and 'rêverie', the analytic and the *romanesque*.[64] Stylistically, Napoleon's Oriental writings can be considered to represent his mature middle period, falling between the early excesses and the strict austerity of the later works.[65]

Napoleon's thought and action favour the symbolic. Thus the armada that crossed the Mediterranean (led by his flagship, which anticipated its destination by its name, *L'Orient*) was only in part a means to an end; it was also an evocation of that end. It was at once a fighting machine, an instrument of coercion and transportation, and the prefiguration of an ideal, a microcosm as well as the harbinger of the society it proclaimed as model. Its most significant nonmilitary contingent was the *Commission scientifique et artistique* consisting of 167 eminent or at least distinguished savants (the most eminent having generally declined the honour of escorting Napoleon's army) drawn from every sphere.[66] Their presence was justifiable on pragmatic, technical grounds: their assembled knowledge and skills would assist in the execution of a military campaign; and poets would immortalize Bonaparte's exploits in verse. But the savants served above all as figureheads, intellectual status symbols:

they were luminaries in the firmament of French culture; they were the icons of a secular faith in the *pouvoir* of *savoir*; they were extensions and reflections of their erudite *chef*.[67]

In his first proclamation[68] to the people of Alexandria (2 July 1798), Napoleon (blending judicious piety, scrupulous reasoning, and unsubstantiated assertion) expounds the case for the installation of a government of the most knowledgeable, a Platonic republic, an epistemocracy whose guardians will be chosen according to the disinterested criterion of intelligence:

tous les hommes sont égaux devant Dieu; la sagesse, les talents, et les vertus mettent seuls de la différence entre eux. Or quelle sagesse, quels talents, quelles vertus distinguent les Mamelukes, pour qu'ils aient exclusivement tout ce qui rend la vie aimable et douce?

This state of affairs is worse than a crime, it is a mistake. The French are the means by which a just and rational rectification of past errors will be achieved:

Tous les Egyptiens seront appelés à gérer toutes les places: les plus sages, les plus instruits, les plus vertueux gouverneront, et le peuple sera heureux.

(IV, p. 191)

Here a critique of the past and a long-term prediction of the future serve as a covert *plaidoyer* for a short-term colonial government of the present peopled by the superlatively knowledgeable French. The syntactical proximity of *sagesse* and *vertu* reflecting their semantic affinity implies that they are Platonically inseparable.

Napoleon's initial proclamation notified the Alexandrians that his troops were the involuntary tools of divine retribution, visited upon the wicked beys, who had insulted the French and tyrannized the Egyptians. A later proclamation to the inhabitants of Cairo further inflates these claims. Here Bonaparte has been promoted from the rank of heaven's scourge to God's chief minister. Simultaneously appealing and threatening, Napoleon declares that he has been given his orders by God and that 'le destin dirige mes opérations'. The text culminates in the assertion that:

Je pourrais demander compte à chacun de vous des sentiments les plus secrets du cœur, car je sais tout, même ce que vous n'avez dit à personne; mais un jour viendra où tout le monde verra avec évidence que je suis conduit par des ordres supérieurs et que les efforts humains ne peuvent rien contre moi.

(V, p. 221)

Like the Hugolian *œil* (and like the disincarnate soul according to Rousseau's Julie), the Napoleonic *je* enjoys immediate knowledge of the deepest recesses of other minds. It is a commonplace of Orientalism that the West knows more about the East than the East knows about itself; and it is received wisdom that French *clarté* and *lumières* execute a divine imperative that makes their adoption by the Egyptians a condition of salvation. Thus Napoleon's statement that he shares with God his prerogative of absolute knowledge can be seen as a histrionic extension of a prior *donnée*.

'Je veux tout savoir' is a characteristic phrase in the *Correspondance*, and the confident assertion, 'Je sais tout', is not restricted to exclusively Oriental occasions.[69] In Egypt, more specifically, Napoleon's pseudo-omniscience is a facet of the role he assumes as chief representative of the *Commission* and the *Institut*, which in turn represent the entire span of the French intellectual arc, an animate *Encyclopédie*; thus Napoleon is perceived, within the symbolic envelope of his singular personality, to contain the epistemic plenitude of an impersonal cultural universe. It is this principle of comprehensiveness that informs the monumental, encyclopedic study which was the collective enterprise of the *Institut*, *La Description de l'Egypte*.[70] And it recurs in Hugo's vision (which coincides exactly with the ambition of its subject) of a Napoleon fusing the Christian West with the Islamic East, bestriding both halves of the world.[71] Hence also the frequency in Napoleon's vocabulary of the word *univers*. The word and the project of acquiring universal power or knowledge consort with a sympathetic stylistic mannerism: the fondness for universal propositions, superlatives, absolutes, generalizations.[72]

The profession of first-person (singular or plural) omniscience is invariably complemented by the ascription of third-person nescience; in a universe of omniscient beings, omniscience would be unknowable for want of contrast, and therefore impossible. Although fleeting allusions to Oriental ignorance[73] are scattered throughout his work, it is only in the *Œuvres de Saint-Hélène* that Napoleon delivers a full-scale exposition of the underlying theory. With a characteristic synthesis of pedantry and aphoristic *non sequiturs*, Napoleon enumerates the differences between the French and the Arabs, conveniently located in their contrasting religions, which become symbolic of civilization and barbarism. On the one hand,

la religion chrétienne est celle d'un peuple très civilisé. Elle élève l'homme; elle proclame la supériorité de l'esprit sur la matière, de l'âme sur le corps.

The Christian exaltation of the philosophic soul and its recommended mortification of the flesh anticipate an afterworld wherein 'jouissance' is 'toute spirituelle'. Mahomet, on the other hand, reintroduces a version of Christianity to the East whence it originated, but promises a paradise of milk, shade, and 'divines houris' in compensation for a harsh existence: a sensual variety of afterworld modified to meet the peculiar demands of his market:

Il s'adressait à des peuples sauvages, pauvres, manquant de tout, fort ignorants; s'il eût parlé à leur esprit, il n'eût pas été entendu.

(XXIX, pp. 475–7)

Intellectual contemplation of the impalpable is all very well for the Greek (and, by derivation, the Frenchman); but it would be wasted on the Arab. This theory removes the contending parties in the Platonic antithesis[74] of an intellectual, cognitive soul and a concupiscent body from the sphere of the individual and redistributes them, respectively, to the western and eastern hemispheres of the globe, inhabited by congenitally antithetical beings. The Frenchman is (in principle) all disinterested ascetic *esprit*; the Arab, all lustful carnality. According to Napoleon, there is, *pace* Rousseau, no innocence in ignorance;[75] rather, it is the soulful, highbrow European who is already prematurely disincarnate.

Although Napoleon has established that it would be futile (as it was for Mahomet) to address the mind of Moslems, it is nevertheless assumed to follow from this assumed cultural disparity that the more primitive population would be the beneficiary of the *trésors*, the intellectual thesaurus, possessed by the more sophisticated culture (while the latter would partake of the *trésors*, of a more material kind, of its hosts). Economically expressed, the philosophy of the Egyptian expedition rests on a law of supply and demand – the French boast an abundance of a commodity that the Orient lacks, namely, civilization – and, inescapably, on a law of exchange. Thus the enterprise of colonialism would be mutually beneficial; fortuitously, self-interest and altruism coincide.

Intellectually, the relation between the professorial French and the unlearned Arabs replicates that between the Rousseauiste *gouverneur* and his *élève* while reversing the priority of nature over culture. Napoleon readily resorts to the metaphor of 'teaching x a lesson', where x is anyone who has incurred his displeasure or posed an obstacle to the French advance. But the same trope might equally describe the purpose of the entire campaign, which is represented as educative (although education presupposes discipline), a conquest over ignorance.[76] Napoleon adopts the character he assumes in 'Le Souper de Beaucaire', a Socratic dialogue in which 'Le Militaire' dialectically defeats all-comers at dinner only to have an interlocuter return to the fray at breakfast: '[il] avait bien des doutes à proposer, et moi bien des vérités intéressantes à lui apprendre'.[77] His subordinates share this vocation to teach: a brief, poignant, and incredible elegy on Cafferelli recalls that 'il périt glorieusement au siège de Saint-Jean d'Acre, en prononçant, à son lit de mort, un très-éloquent discours sur l'instruction publique' (XXIX, p. 365).[78]

The main institutional agency of the educational enterprise was *L'Institut de l'Egypte*, a local, colonial manifestation of the metropolitan archetype, of which Napoleon appoints himself vice-president. The 'arrêté portant création de l'Institut' outlines its primary objective as 'le progrès et la propagation des lumières en Egypte' (IV, p. 383). Its other functions will include conducting research (on the environment, industry and history of Egypt) and giving expert technical advice to the government (on such problems as baking bread, making beer, producing gunpowder, purifying the Nile). But there is to be a two-way traffic, conducted both ways by France: on the one hand, enlightenment will be spread abroad; on the other, in exchange, Egypt will be subjected to scholarly appropriation. Under the auspices of the *Commission*, and on the pretext of a general acquisition of information, the savants are entitled to remove any objects of artistic or scientific interest: antiquities, artefacts, obelisks, sarcophagi, mummies, parts of pyramids.[79] But if the *Institut* is an instrument of expropriation, it is also an exhibition, a showcase, a living museum of, and monument to, French culture and intellect.

The theory of cultural transmission, which is more of the nature of a physical law than a blueprint for its operation, presumes that an invisible cultural gravity is at work. The recipient nation is an empty vessel into which, via the medium of imperialism, so much cultural liquor will flow from the donor nation, the reservoir of knowledge.[80] But if the transmission of culture is inevitable, it seems also interminable: if the cultural liquor pours forth, then the cultural level of the two vessels, dispenser and receiver, should eventually even out; but then, since the putative demand would have been satisfied, the logic and the morality of the initial intervention, which supposes a disparity in levels, disappears. That such an eventuality is either not envisaged or indefinitely postponed[81] suggests that some imperfection in the system will prevent its adequate operation: it seems as if the receptacle is not just empty but cracked: it has a hole draining away French fluid, implying the need for constant replenishing. The instillation of culture is self-perpetuating.

Napoleonic imperialism rests on two propositions. The first, projecting relative (Arab) beliefs onto the axis of (French) knowledge, pronounces the Egyptian ignorant; the second supposes that he will be sufficiently impressed or seduced by the exhibition of French reason to succumb voluntarily to French rule. The first implies an absence or poverty of judgement, a state of uneducatability; the second requires the discrimination necessary to recognize, and the wisdom to submit to, a higher intellect, a disposition to be educated. Thus the civilizing mission can only be accomplished if it does not need to be; but if it needs to be then it cannot be accomplished because Arab ignorance is bottomless. As Rousseau makes clear, the gap between nescience and knowledge is unbridgeable.

The concept of decadence is proposed as the bridge between the twin predications of the Arab: that he is devoid of, and impatient for, learning. Napoleon maintains, in his assessment of his Egyptian achievements, that 'il avait reporté les sciences et les arts à leur berceau' (V, p. 97). Egyptian society has become barbaric because as the arts and sciences grew older they abandoned their native land and travelled west.[82] The task of France would be to return these errant children, now having attained adulthood and French citizenship, to their original home. Although historically the Egyptian has declined from an erstwhile position of cultural eminence, he retains some innate, hereditary afterglow of his ancestors' former glory and, hence, a mute, as yet unfulfilled desire for intellectual attainment; it remains only for the French to reactivate this dormant aspiration, and to (inadequately) satisfy the renewed thirst for erudition, if they wish to obtain respectful, grateful subservience. Like Socrates' slave-boy (in the *Meno*), the Arab ignoramus would not need to be taught anew, but simply reminded of what he has forgotten; the spectacle of French *savoir* and *savoir-faire*, like a reflection of himself in an earlier incarnation, would ignite the recollection of a dim memory.

It is true, however, that the reluctant or disobedient Oriental might stand in need of additional reminders. Sir Walter Scott comments cynically that 'Buonaparte did not trust to the superiority of science to ensure the conquest of Egypt. He was fully provided with more effectual means.'[83] Judged on his actions, it appears that Napoleon took the view that although the pen is mightier than the sword, cannon and musket are even mightier. Power is certainly the bottom line in this editorial observation by the *Courier de l'Egypte* on a plan requiring all Egyptians to wear a rosette in French colours:

Le succès obtenu dans cette affaire par Bonaparte prouve que tous les hommes, même les moins instruits, et par conséquent les plus accessibles aux préjugés et aux préventions, ne sont jamais insensibles au langage de la raison et de la douceur, surtout lorsqu'il se trouve dans la bouche de celui qui a entre les mains la force et le pouvoir.[84]

French soldiers were not all sweetness and light, but the advertised image of a civilized and civilizing army, consisting mainly of intellectuals, required that force should not only be exerted, but should not always be seen to be exerted.

The *mission civilisatrice* proposed, at its crudest, the Francification of Egypt: 'l'Egypte pouvait devenir en peu de temps non seulement une colonie, mais en quelque sorte une province français, et offrir à ses nouveaux habitants l'image de leur propre patrie'.[85] Just as Alexander and the Romans had been recommended to the French for emulation, so now France (itself a copy) was envisaged as the pattern on which the rejuvenated Egyptian society would be modelled: Egypt would become a mirror reflecting the image of France. Discretion, however, required that the project of transformation be initiated by a denial that any transformation was intended. The French military would not, beyond redressing grievances and enhancing prosperity and well-being, interfere with the quotidian life of the inhabitants. A veteran of the Egyptian campaign, in Balzac's *Curé de campagne*, recalls this philosophy in the speech he attributes to his General:

Mes enfants, les pays que vous allez conquérir tiennent à un tas de dieux que vous allez respecter parce que le Français doit être l'ami de tout le monde, et battre les gens sans les vexer. Mettez-vous dans la coloquinte de ne rien toucher d'abord; parce que vous aurez tout après! Et marchez![86]

The theory of beating people without vexing them came up against a powerful obstacle in practice: that the mere sight of a heathen was often enough to vex the faithful of Islam. In order to achieve their ends the French would need to be more than merely friendly and diplomatic: they would need to disappear.

But such a manifest presence, however self-effacing, could attain imperceptibility (like omniscience among gods) only when Egyptians, involuntary hosts, resembled their French guests. And such a metamorphosis, even if it were attainable, was not instantly available. Some measure of rapprochement was nonetheless indispensable if the 'barbarians' were not to denounce them as barbarians. Therefore, reasoned Napoleon, if they cannot become like us, we shall become like them. Thus was born the paradoxical instrument of the Europeanization of the Arabs: the Orientaliz-ation of the French. The French would be converted to Islam; Bonaparte, Sultan El-Kebir, Hugo's 'Mahomet d'Occident', espouses the Koran, and Menou becomes a Moslem, while special dispensation is arranged to reconcile uncircumcised, wine-imbibing, former infidels with the faith. Napoleon supports his claim to superior knowledge by identifying himself not as the rep-resentative of the West but rather as the disciple of the Prophet, or the minister of Allah:

depuis que le monde est monde, it était écrit qu'après avoir détruit les ennemis de l'Islamisme, fait abattre les croix, je viendrais du fond de l'Occident remplir la tâche qui m'a été imposée . . . dans le saint livre du Koran, dans plus de vingt passages, ce qui arrive a été prévu, et ce qui arrivera est également expliqué.   (V, p. 221)

Bonaparte is the champion of Islam not of Christianity, the apostle of the Koran not the Bible. Thus he informs the Pasha of Aleppo that 'nous ne sommes plus de ces infidèles des temps barbares qui venaient combattre votre foi; nous la reconnaissons sublime, nous y adhérons, et l'instant est arrivé où tous les Français régénérés deviendront aussi vrais croyants' (IV, p. 489).[87] The projected con-version of the Orient is supplanted by the conversion of the Occi-dent. According to Napoleon, it is not the East after all, but the West which requires regeneration. In his writing the sense of the verb *changer* oscillates between the transitive and the reflexive: in order to convert, the would-be converters must first themselves be converted.

Hakem, the anti-hero of 'Le Masque prophète', stricken with facial disfigurement and blindness, takes to sporting (for cosmetic purposes) a silver mask, which he claims is designed to 'empêcher les hommes d'être éblouis par la lumière qui sortait de sa figure'.[88] When his besieged and hopelessly outnumbered forces face imminent defeat he informs his troops of a nocturnal conversation with God (whose 'Envoyé' he purports to be) in which he receives divine advice to dig wide trenches around their encampment as a means of trapping the enemy. But the trenches are destined not for the opposition but for his own side: rather than endure capture and humiliation, Hakem poisons his remaining troops en masse, hauls them into the lime-filled graves they have unwittingly dug for themselves, puts a match to a tub of vitriol, and finally plunges into the flames.

Although Napoleon assigns himself the victorious role of Mahadi, the wise and pedagogically-oriented calif, there are still closer parallels with Hakem. Bonaparte, Member of the *Institut* as well as Commander-in-chief, like Hakem, wears a mask or many masks: although partially blinded (by the 'fluide magique [qui] nous cache les choses qu'il nous importe le plus de connaître'),[89] Napoleon claims to emit or transmit light ('J'étais le soleil'),[90] to enable others to see the light; like Hakem, he is an emissary of God, possessed of privileged or prophetic information, on a mission to restore and purify the (French or Islamic) empire; and he admits to at least intending to poison some of his own (plague-stricken) troops (at Jaffa). In what looks like a reminiscence of 'La Masque prophète', Napoleon reports (in a letter to the Directory) that he has quelled a rebellion in Syria led by a man calling himself 'l'ange El-Mahdy' (V, p. 462). Finally, in the manner of Hakem, facing ultimate defeat, or at best stasis following reverses in Syria, he ditches his army. He does not, however, commit suicide.

Napoleon declares the Arabs 'soumis' (XXX, p. 84), and the French conquest of Egypt irreversible, before returning to France: 'Sa personne était désormais aussi inutile en Orient qu'elle était nécessaire en Occident: tout lui annonçait que le moment désigné par le destin était arrivé' (XXX, p. 81). What announced this moment, more specifically, were the newspapers, mischievously supplied by Sir Sidney Smith, recording details of French defeats in Italy. Although omniscient with respect to the Orient, Napoleon lacked information about events in Europe; thus, '[il] passa la nuit dans sa tente à dévorer ces papiers, et résolut à l'instant même de passer en Europe, pour remédier, s'il en était temps, aux maux de la patrie et la sauver'.[91] Doctor Bonaparte is called away by an emergency: he must administer to the urgent needs of his patient, the sick-man of Europe. Having saved the East, he must return to save the West. Just as he was guided on his foreign travels, and perhaps persuaded to depart, by his reading about the Orient, so, similarly, he is prompted to return by his reading about the Occident. Napoleon, alternately Mahadi and Hakem, General Bonaparte and Sultan El-Kebir, Messiah and Mahomet, shifts incessantly between rival archives. Thus the voyage home, back across the Mediterranean, finds him in the tranquil company of his *bibliothèque portative*, 'renfermé la plus grande partie du jour dans

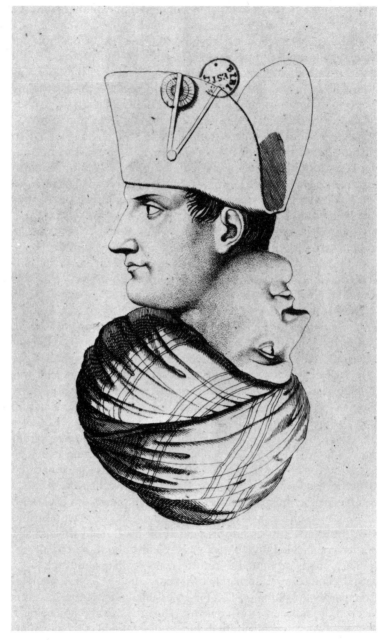

Napoleon wearing two hats
de Vinck, Cabinet des Estampes, Bibliothèque Nationale, Paris

94

sa chambre, où il lisait, dit Genteaume, tantôt la Bible, tantôt l'Alcoran'.[92]

But no rapprochement is achieved between the rival cultures. Kléber, who is obliged to stay on and take his leader's place, discovers, contrary to Napoleon's sanguine view of matters, 'une population très ennemie, soupirant après le moment d'égorger tous les Français' (XXX, p. 102). He has the meagre consolation, as he suffers the fate he foresaw for Frenchmen, of being proved right. The knife that splits Kléber's back seems to mark the failure of the programme of fusion between East and West.[93]

In the correspondence, the memoirs, and the strategies of Napoleon, as in the poems of Hugo, the Oriental psyche is negatively reconstructed, pictured in terms of a deficiency. This lack is represented as the *sine qua non* of French interest and intervention; thus Fourier argues that 'l'Egypte n'est pas seulement utile par ce qu'elle possède, elle l'est encore par ce qui lui manque'.[94] Hugo deprived the Arab of an unconscious, or a European and specifically poetic soul, that would provide access to eternal truths; according to Napoleonic doctrine, what Arabs most conspicuously lack is a *cogito*. They cannot think because they are not French. Thinking is a peculiarly French prerogative. The nationalistic, xenophobic species of Cartesianism inherent in French colonial ideology, *je pense donc je suis Français*, entails, inversely, that if I do not think, not only am I not French, but also, strictly, *je ne suis pas*. Imperialism contains a selective solipsism. At best, the existence of an Arab is a superfluity, almost an aberration; to erase it is equivalent to rectifying an omission of nature. A putative ignorance is the justification for genocide. The Egyptian adventure therefore combines education with annihilation.

But the cultural and epistemic status of Napoleon himself is in doubt. Napoleon's Egyptian transformation from European to Oriental parallels his transition from Corsican to Frenchman. In his first writings, the young Bonaparte vigorously asserts his Corsican identity and condemns the French in Corsica as alien invaders; later, as he rises through the ranks, however, he relinquishes his ancestry in favour of French citizenship. Thus while in 'Sur la Corse' he recapitulates the ways in which *we* (Corsicans) have been repressed by *you* (French), in 'Position politique et militaire du département de Corse au 1er juin 1793' he recommends ways in which *they* (Corsicans) can be more efficiently repressed by *us* (French).[95] Napoleon, like his pronouns, is a shifter: he is not only socially but culturally mobile, his nationality as changeable and ambiguous as his allegiances. He embodies the attitude he ascribes to Corsicans: 'Il faut être d'un parti: autant de celui qui triomphe, de celui qui dévaste, pille, brûle; dans l'alternative, il vaut mieux être mangeur que mangé.'[96]

Rejected as a pseudo-Oriental by the Orientals, Napoleon nevertheless does not seem unequivocally French to the French: Sainte-Beuve notes that Napoleon '[est] sorti d'une île à demi sauvage'.[97] Mme de Rémusat based her contention that 'au fond, il [Napoléon] est ignorant' on his lack of 'manières': 'Il ne sait ni entrer ni sortir d'une chambre; il ignore comment on salue, comment on se lève ou s'asseoit.'[98] Napoleon found confirmation for his inherited conviction that the Arabs were ignorant in the observation that 'ils ne connaissent même pas une paire de ciseaux . . . Ils ne connaissent point l'usage des moulins' (IV, p. 252). In one case, an absence of etiquette, in the other, of technology, furnish circumstantial evidence for the identical charge. In both cases, the presumption of ignorance (which aspires to the condition of an absolute) is founded upon the perception of a relative difference, the accused's failure to belong to a specified cultural order, permeated by an orthodoxy of rules and regulations, social or scientific, on his nonconformity to an established paradigm; in a word, his ignorance (like knowledge, culturally specific) is reducible to abnormality.

L'autre, especially that most alien manifestation of otherness the French call *l'étranger*, is deemed to be ignorant until proven otherwise. Thus the unmannerly Corsican general appears to the quintessentially metropolitan Mme de Rémusat just as much an exotic and untamed savage as the Oriental appears to Napoleon. But the same normative, third-person law applies equally against the French: Napoleon realizes that they risk appearing, according to an Arab code, no less *barbares*, *infidèles*, even *ignorants*, for all their balloons and electricity and printing-presses.

There are only two alternatives: 'il fallait se rembarquer ou se concilier les idées religieuses, se soustraire aux anathèmes de l'islamisme' (XXIX, p. 479). The expedition can only be saved if the French subordinate their cultural traditions to those of Islam. But if they do, then there is no longer any justification for the French presence. Unless the claims of the French to be true believers, not infidels, are believed, the civilizing mission must fail; but if they are, then it must be futile. Napoleon admits to Las Cases that had his policy been successful serious consequences would have followed:

'Je prenais l'Europe à revers, la vieille civilisation européenne demeurait cernée, et qui eût songé alors à inquiéter le cours des destinées de notre France, ni celui de la régénération du siècle!'[99] It is Europe, after all, which has degenerated, and stands in need of regeneration: the East, it appears, serves as a metaphor, an *image* of the Western *patrie*. To conquer Egypt would be to 'prendre l'Europe à revers': the Orient, then, is not distinct from Europe but rather a part of its anatomy: the back side, its concealed, rather embarrassing verso. Thus the civilizing mission finally exchanges the missionary approach to the East for an advance on the rear of Europe. The West is already Orientalized: the explicit substitution of the practice of Orientalization for the principle of Europeanization blows away the tissue of epistemological legitimacy enveloping the Orientalist exercise.

Napoleon informs Las Cases that his Egyptian proclamation constituted 'du charlatanisme', adding, 'mais du plus haut'.[100] But the perpetual succession of *mensonges* and masks displayed in the *Correspondance* seems to make sincerity, or the reconstruction of Napoleon's beliefs, impossible.[101] His vaulting ambition has the virtue of remaining ideologically pure, irreducible to any of the philosophies under whose colours it temporarily parades. His attitude towards history is strictly utilitarian: 'J'étudiai moins l'histoire que je n'en fis la conquête; c'est-à-dire que je n'en voulus et que je n'en retins que ce qui pourrait me donner une idée de plus, dédaignant l'inutile, ne m'emparant que de certains résultats qui me plaisaient.'[102] Napoleonic history is not the teleological absolute of Orientalism: the future is infinitely malleable, while the past likewise complies with the imperatives of the present.

Léon Bloy's view that 'l'Histoire est comme un immense Texte'[103] reiterates Napoleon's. Conversely, every text is a history and, accordingly, for Napoleon, not inviolable, but always liable to reinterpretation: 'il fallait convaincre, gagner les muftis, les ulémas, les chérifs, les imâms, pour qu'ils interprétassent le Coran en faveur de l'armée' (XXIX, p. 479). If Napoleon subscribes to the authority of a text it is not in virtue of any Hugolian conviction of its transcendent truth but because he is pragmatically aware that its power consists precisely in its susceptibility to conscription in disparate causes.[104] The conception of discourse championed by Napoleon is militaristic: language comprises an army of metaphors capable of mobilizing to coerce reality into order, but fundamentally treacherous, disloyal, equally capable of being turned against their user. Napoleon is conscious of the power of words: 'Vous savez combien les mots font aux soldats', he writes to a subordinate (VI, p. 178); but also of their unreliability: 'La langue française n'est pas une langue faite', he observes, and adds, regretfully: 'J'aurais bien dû la fixer.'[105] The general can be out-generalled by language. In particular, the vocabulary of a cultural hierarchy proves to be a double-edged weapon.

Just as Nicholas shows that centrality is an illusion determined by the observer's position in the universe, so the strategies of Napoleon suggest that the classifications of knowledge and ignorance, civilization and barbarism, do not designate fixed bodies but are relative to a system of discourse. Throughout Bonaparte/Sultan El-Kebir's oscillating commitments to Alexander and Mahomet,[106] the Bible and the Koran, the polar opposites of *civilisé* and *barbare* are constants, but the respective nouns to which these epithets are attached are variables. The West, from being educator, governor, guru to the East, becomes its pupil, its servant, its disciple.

But this reversal of roles only dramatizes the ambiguity already inherent in the imperialist concept of the reciprocal process of exchange: France, the embodiment of Europe, which is the embodiment of the world, is projected as the *telos* of civilization; at the same time, it originates in the Orient and is returning to its sources, equipped with an army of savants, to seek regeneration. On the one hand, the aim of French expansionism is to universalize French culture; on the other, that culture is itself borrowed, degenerate, susceptible to transformation.

Napoleon's achievement in Egypt is to have inflated and exploded the systematic dualism of Orientalist rhetoric. The propagation of culture envisaged by Condorcet is postponed in favour of the renunciation of culture proposed by Rousseau. As the flow of cultural liquor is reversed, so too history and language appear equally reversible. In approaching Europe from the rear Napoleon inverts the symbolic value of the continent: Europe does not dominate the world, rather it needs dominating. If the figure of Bonaparte recurs so obsessively in the Romantic imagination it is, in part, because he seems to condone the rewriting of the cultural archive. This is a task which Napoleon personally undertakes: dissatisfied with what he perceives as overwriting among the works in his *bibliothèque portative*, he sets about rectifying and reducing the canon: thus, in his copy of *La Nouvelle Héloïse*, words, sentences, whole paragraphs are boldly crossed out, and abbreviated, rephrased, or simply omitted, while one line elicits in the margin the damning comment: 'phrase fausse'.[107]

But like Rousseau, Napoleon relapses into the figures he condemns. He imagines, or pretends to imagine (in his writing the distinction is negligible), that the French colonization of Egypt heralds a new dawn on the dark continent (Egypt is perceived as part both of the Orient and Africa). *La Décade égyptienne* publishes a poem, purportedly translated from an Arab source, supporting this view: 'Enfin nous voyons luire sur nous l'aurore du bonheur: les temps fixés par Dieu sont arrivés; une atmosphère de félicité nous environne; l'astre brillante de la victoire qui dirige les guerriers français a répandu sur nous son éclatante lumière.' These 'quelques étincelles', remarks the translator, suggest that the Arab muse might be 'digne' of a 'petite place' in the 'empire littéraire' of the European muses.[108] But if the putative cultural illumination is inhibited by a rival sun, 'le soleil brûlant du tropique' (XXIX, p. 451), it is certainly obscured by the inescapable 'nuées d'arabes' (IV, p. 252), who are so benighted that, seeing the sun of enlightenment, they see and do not perceive: they are too ignorant to know what is good for them.

Egypt, Napoleon admits in his memoirs, appears to have survived unassisted by the French; but what prosperity might it not have enjoyed if only it had been 'assez heureuse pour jouir, pendant dix ans de paix, des bienfaits de l'administration française!' (XXIX, p. 428). The same applies, *a fortiori*, to an Egypt blessed with fifty years of French domination:

la civilisation se serait répandue dans l'intérieur de l'Afrique par le Sennaar, l'Abyssinie, le Dârfour, le Fezzân; plusieurs grandes nations seraient appelées à jouir des bienfaits des arts, des sciences, de la religion du vrai Dieu, car c'est par l'Egypte que les peuples du centre de l'Afrique doivent recevoir la lumière et le bonheur. (XXIX, p. 430)

There was a time when the sun never set on the French empire; but in Egypt at least the brief star of Occidental light and happiness quickly expired.[109] Although Hugo continues to maintain that Napoleon's imperial star is rising in the east,[110] Napoleon III sees in his illustrious predecessor's memoirs not a dawn but a sunset: 'Tels les derniers rayons du soleil couchant derrière l'immensité de l'océan éclairent le ciel, telle la pensée de Napoléon Ier éclaire l'avenir' (I, p. v). It is a fitting and almost inevitable conclusion to the career of Napoleon that his death, according to Las Cases, should coincide with the dying of the sun: 'C'est le 5 mai, vers six heures du soir, à l'instant même où le coup de canon annonçait le coucher du soleil, quand sa grande âme a quitté la terre.'[111]

The moribund imaginary suns of Hugo and Napoleon continue, fitfully, to irradiate the avowedly nocturnal writing of Chateaubriand, in his account of the Orient. The imperialist's case, invariably dignified by a solar mythology, is vitiated by the improbability of a dialectic that pretends to reconcile a claim to invisible spiritual authority over the carnal foreigner with a visible imperative of material exploitation. The Romantic imperialist embodies an intensified form of this dilemma since his attraction to the East is partly occasioned by his private disillusionment with those Western values to which he publicly subscribes in his capacity as ambassador. Such is the position, in particular, of Chateaubriand (who at once deplores and succumbs to the Napoleonic dalliance with Orientalization).

3.4 Chateaubriand

Napoleon Bonaparte is one of a trio of legendary figures who populate the most reverential and the most censorious pages of Chateaubriand's *œuvre*; the other two are God and Chateaubriand. His detailed study of the Emperor in the *Mémoires d'outre-tombe*, although less hostile than *De Buonaparté et des Bourbons*,[112] still distances its author from its subject by the accumulation of adverse judgements. But Chateaubriand is an inveterate contriver of rapprochements. And, like Hugo (like Lamartine, like Balzac), he cannot resist the temptation to detect frequent parallels and affinities between Napoleon's career and his own: Chateaubriand sees himself as the Napoleon of literature;[113] he sees Napoleon, in turn, as the Chateaubriand of politics.

Their *œuvres* display demonstrable similarities of language. Thematically considered, Chateaubriand's *Itinéraire de Paris à Jérusalem et de Jérusalem à Paris* often reads like a recapitulation of imperialist dogmas. Thus, for example, Chateaubriand's defence of the Crusades is reminiscent of Napoleon's comparison of the Christian and Islamic religions. Chateaubriand, rebutting the attitude of fashionable scepticism about Christian motives, affirms that:

Il s'agissait, non seulement de la délivrance de ce Tombeau sacré, mais encore de savoir qui devait l'emporter sur la terre, ou d'un culte ennemi de la civilisation, favorable par système à l'ignorance, au despotisme, à l'esclavage, ou d'un culte qui a fait revivre chez les modernes le génie de la docte antiquité, et aboli la servitude? . . . L'esprit du Mahometisme est la

persécution et la conquête; l'Evangile au contraire ne prêche que la tolér-
ance et la paix.   (*Œuvres romanesques et voyages*, II, pp. 1052–3)[114]

Again, East and West are divided along an artistic, moral, and intellectual frontier whose very existence requires that it be crossed
(from West to East) by an altruistic, Christian army charged with
rehabilitating and re-educating a race of malevolent heathens. Presumably this worthy objective was not wholly achieved since the
process must be repeated by Napoleon's army. Thus, while arguing
(in the chapter of the *Mémoires* devoted to the subject) that the
Egyptian expedition was a pointless sideshow, and admitting that its
main result was massacre, rape, pillage, Chateaubriand nevertheless maintains that the Orient must have benefited from the salutary
presence of the senior Western power. Echoing Napoleon (who is,
however, denounced as an insincere imperialist, bent on mere self-
glorification), he claims that the French sowed the germs of civilization, brightened the Islamic darkness with Christian light, and
breached the wall of Barbarism.[115]

The anxiety of the reader familiar with even a small number of
French texts of the period purporting to describe the East for the
edification of the West, is that the Orientalist seems doomed to
repeat a sequence of scarcely permutated *idées fixes* articulated by
a set of automatic metaphors. But in this case precisely the same
anxiety is shared by the writer. The dilemma for Chateaubriand is
that although (and because) the Orient is an irresistible topic, it has
already been exhaustively treated by those that have gone before
him. He suspects that there is nothing more to be said on the subject, nothing to be added to the mass of pre-existing material; or
that, if there is, he is not competent to say it. At the same time, one
of his most intransigent aesthetic imperatives concerns originality,
which alone can bear witness to the existence of an individual soul.
Aesthetic, linguistic originality, and temperamental, psychic individuality, are interdependent: individuality without originality is
doomed; originality without individuality is inconceivable. Thus
ego and text are mutually supportive (or destructive).

The *Itinéraire* is steeped (like all Chateaubriand's work) in an
enviable erudition. Chateaubriand, not without pride, reminds us
that he has had 'la patience de lire à peu près deux cents relations
modernes de la Terre Sainte, les compilations rabbiniques, et les
passages des anciens sur la Judée' (II, p. 981). He is fully equipped
with all the necessary information about the countries he visits
before he sets foot out of France.[116] Increasingly, he suspects that

his own trip is redundant. Wherever he travels, he cannot help stumbling across the literary or physical traces of his predecessors. Not only is he conscious of following in the footsteps of illustrious men; he is equally conscious of a predetermined discourse, an unavoidable library of encyclopedic descriptions, antiquated metaphors and motifs, scholarly analyses, travellers' stories, and more or less imaginative expositions all clustered round the subject of the Orient, and to whose definitive collective doctrine he is duly subservient. His route is bestrewn with his reading.

Moreau has argued that 'son imagination a besoin de se sentir soutenue par des anciens textes'.[117] Support for this view can be drawn from Chateaubriand's favourable evaluation of the same trait in other writers:

je vois que tous les poètes épiques ont été des hommes très instruits; surtout ils étaient nourris des ouvrages de ceux qui les avaient précédés dans la carrière de l'épopée: Virgile traduit Homère; le Tasse imite à chaque stance quelque passage d'Homère, de Virgile, de Lucain, de Stace; Milton prend partout, et joint à ses propres trésors les trésors de ses devanciers.

(II, p. 1111)

This sounds like an unequivocal advocacy of imitation, of the Renaissance principle of erudite poetry, of intertextuality: Chateaubriand appears content to subsume himself in a community of like-minded (and suitably elevated) authors. And, in practice, it is indeed from the established corpus of Oriental scholarship that he derives his authority; he invests his predecessors with such prestige that he holds the falsity of a statement to be less important than its conformity to a tradition: 'il me suffit d'être à l'abri sous leur autorité: je consens à avoir tort avec eux' (II, p. 708). In the last analysis, poetic, literary truth overrides scientific objectivity, good faith with the past outweighs fidelity to the present; thus contradiction is rejected, with contempt, as mere perversity: 'Que dirait-on d'un homme qui, parcourant la Grèce et l'Italie, ne s'occuperait qu'à contredire Homère et Virgile?' (II, p. 1031).

Books are Chateaubriand's most constant companions on his travels ('c'est en effet la Bible et l'Evangile à la main que l'on doit parcourir la Terre Sainte' (II, p. 1031)), and yet the sense of a tradition is far from being an undiluted source of comfort, security, and inspiration for this writer. A trivial but emblematic event reveals ambivalent feelings towards the literary canon. The better to savour his view of the (ruined) Temple, Chateaubriand produces a copy of *Athalie* from his pocket and proceeds to reread the text with special attention to the passages related to that same (still intact) edifice. The rapture afforded him by Racine gives way, in the present, to a paralysing revulsion from writing: 'La plume tombe des mains: on est honteux de barbouiller encore du papier après qu'un homme a écrit de pareils vers' (II, p. 1088). The paralysis is, of course, only temporary: Chateaubriand's nerveless fingers recover in time to record his inability to write: writer's block is good for a couple of lines. But the feeling of inferiority, uncharacteristic of Chateaubriand, will recur, for it is not simply the unsurpassable quality of some of his predecessors' writing that is the cause of his anxiety and problematic aesthetic: it is its sheer quantity. The weight of documentary matter wearies the writer overburdened with books, who carries not only the Bible in his hand but Racine in his pocket.

The genre of the travel book proposes the adequate translation of a perception into a description. The problem for the Oriental traveller is that any perception he may enjoy is certain to be preceded, and to that extent conditioned by, a superabundance of prior descriptions, which his own description is constrained to replicate, thereby producing that copy of a copy denounced by Plato as third-hand mimesis. Berkeley resolved the being of an object into its being perceived; the being of an Oriental object is resolvable into its being described, and, moreover, its being already described. Description is not the externalization of perception; rather, perception is the internalization of description: cognition consists in recognition. The major difficulty confronting the travel writer in the mysterious East is that it is no longer sufficiently mysterious. The trouble with the Orient, Chateaubriand realizes with apprehension, is that it is a cliché.

Thus he arrives in Egypt (or at the Egyptian stage of his exposition), fearful that he will be unable to write, or at least write much, because unable to write anything that has not already been written:

Que dirais-je de l'Egypte? Qui ne l'a point vue aujourd'hui? Le Voyage de M. de Volney en Egypte est un véritable chef-d'œuvre dans tout ce qui n'est pas érudition: l'érudition a été épuisée par Sicard, Norden, Pococke, Shaw, Niebhur et quelques autres . . . j'ai moi-même dit ailleurs tout ce que j'avais à dire sur l'Egypte. (II, p. 1136)

Chateaubriand's admiration for his predecessors (including himself) cannot conceal an admixture of exasperation, even of antipathy; he is dependent for his facts upon their judgements, but resents the condition of dependence. The writer's perception of his aesthetic predicament receives its clearest expression with regard to his visit to Jerusalem:

Ici j'éprouve un véritable embarras. Dois-je offrir la peinture exacte des Lieux Saints? Mais alors je ne puis que répéter ce que l'on a dit avant moi: jamais sujet ne fut peut-être moins connu des lecteurs modernes, et toutefois jamais sujet ne fut plus complètement épuisé. (II, pp. 1017–18)

The account that follows unavoidably comprises a mosaic of annotated extracts from prior accounts cemented by occasional observations from the author. Thus the *Itinéraire* is exegetical in construction.[118] The writer is condemned, it seems, either to reiterate or distort; but neither alternative is satisfactory since he cannot bring himself to forgo either the essential information given by previous writers or the freedom of the creative spirit that they threaten to take away in exchange. A prisoner of his precursors, Chateaubriand dreams of escape.

Thus there is a felt sense of relief, mingled with the opposite apprehension of error, occasioned by a relatively unstudied subject:

Si la multitude des récits fatigue l'écrivain qui veut parler aujourd'hui de l'Egypte et de la Judée, il éprouve, au sujet des antiquités de l'Afrique, un embarras tout contraire par la disette des documents. (II, p. 1165)

The 'disette' consists in there being, to Chateaubriand's knowledge, a mere thirty or so accounts of the area, which, however quantitatively abundant, fail (for once) to exhaust the matter of the 'antiquités'. Thus Chateaubriand can licitly, and proudly, declare his originality: 'On peut donc dire que le sujet que je vais traiter est neuf, j'ouvrirai la route: les habiles viendront après moi' (II, p. 1165). The author's task is to blaze a trail: he is an advance scout to be succeeded by a troop of scholars. For once, the tables are turned (a claim qualified in the third preface by his discovery of a document already covering the field).

The metaphor underlines an analogy (persistent in the work of Rousseau, another of Chateaubriand's precursors and idols) between the process of writing and the experience of travelling. Literal displacements reappear transposed into figurative vehicles of the author's progress; thus the *Itinéraire* presents a certain itinerary of composition. The frequent sliding from the past historic (of action) to the present (of contemplation) and back again, blurring the distinction between *now* and *then*, reflects and reinforces the interplay between the journey and its narration. All Chateaubriand's texts in which the writer is also the traveller present an ambiguous assessment of travel, which reflects the pervasive ambivalence towards the writing of his literate predecessors. In the preface to *Voyage en Amérique*, the author depicts travellers ancient and modern as the discoverers to whom we owe our knowledge of the world. They are creators, giving substance and shape to the unknown, clothing with reality the bones of our theoretical speculations:

Christophe Colomb dut éprouver quelque chose de ce sentiment que l'Ecriture donne au Créateur, quand, après avoir tiré la terre au néant, il vit que son ouvrage était bon: *vidit Deus quod esset bonum.* Colomb créait un monde. (I, p. 637)

But the golden age of discovery is past: nothing, fears Chateaubriand, remains to be discovered; our knowledge of the world is complete. Drake and the rest of his ilk 'ne laissent plus un écueil inconnu' (I, p. 643). Again, praise is charged with regret: the panegyric on past achievement is also a lament on the impossibility of present emulation:

Je viens me ranger dans la foule des voyageurs obscurs qui n'ont vu que ce que tout le monde a vu, qui n'ont fait faire aucun progrès aux sciences, qui n'ont rien ajouté au trésor des connaissances humaines. (I, p. 663)

Chateaubriand's evaluation of his own humble status on his journey West could equally apply to his journey East: the literary thesaurus is already complete and can no longer be added to, only subtracted from.

On the one hand, Chateaubriand is compulsively drawn to a kaleidoscopic variety of landscape.[119] On the other, his attitude is not devoid of hostility or scepticism towards travelling and travellers (common to Pascal, Hugo, and Lévi-Strauss). Reality rarely fails, in the end, to disappoint, while the Oriental traveller in particular must carry with him, like Aeneas setting out from Troy with a past generation on his back, the burden of antecedent accounts of the Orient. In these circumstances, the text is bound to become introverted.

In the *Itinéraire*, the journey is relatively painless, fraught only with the occasional party of marauding bandits or fleet of pirates or some crazed and avaricious Turk or Arab (all disdainfully outgeneralled by the seemingly invulnerable Frenchman). Travel becomes almost tediously effortless:[120] nothing is inaccessible (unless rendered so by the cunning manoeuvres of some devious native guide, who thereby incurs Chateaubriand's just wrath and indignation). All the traditional hazards, difficulties, and excitements of the journey are transferred to the act of recording the journey. And the element of risk involved elevates the writer in place of the traveller to the status of hero of the story.[121] Thus the *Itinéraire* effectively relates an arduous tour through a variety of exotic texts in which the heroic author encounters and recruits or conquers other writers. The last page, for example, recalls the persistent valour beyond the call of duty that has distinguished the writer's enterprise:

un grand nombre de feuilles de mes livres ont été tracées sous la tente, dans les déserts, au milieu des flots; j'ai souvent tenu la plume sans savoir comment je prolongerais de quelques instants mon existence.

(II, p. 1214)

The *Itinéraire*, then, is in part the self-congratulatory record of how it came to be written.

The reasons for Chateaubriand's itinerancy may be political, religious, or psychological;[122] his justifications are literary. A journey, in his view, is only ever as good as the narrative it gives rise to. Once overcome, the difficulties encountered by the writer en route – at once practical (how to write in a storm?) and theoretical (the proliferation and apparent sufficiency of prior narratives) – can only add to the (evanescent) satisfaction of arriving at a destination: the last page. Thus the reflexivity of the text contributes to the dramatization of the author.

The writer proclaims his subjectivity as the fundamental subject of all his writing: 'Je parle éternellement de moi' (II, p. 702).[123] And he recommends that the *Itinéraire* be considered more in the nature of an autobiography than a geographical or cultural dissertation (II, p. 859). He is not a travel writer but rather a travelling writer. Chateaubriand's textual egocentricity is epitomized by his habit of defining the meaning of a place for him in terms of his meaning for it, which issues in the curious stylistic mannerism of the description of a hitherto unvisited place or thing bent magnetically towards his previous absence from the place or thing described. Thus: 'Asie, partie du monde qui n'avait pas encore vu la trace de mes pas, hélas! ni ces chagrins que je partage avec tous les hommes' (II, p. 925). The interjection 'hélas' is so placed that Chateaubriand may be regretting his 'chagrins', the fact that he shares them with all men, or, more probably, that Asia has not yet had the opportunity to witness them.

The prominence of the Chateaubrianesque *moi* is conceived as a partial solution to the problem of the conflict between exhaustive antecedent scholarship and the unoriginal craving for originality. The genre of the *voyage* necessarily contains at least two constituents: *le voyageur* and *l'étranger*. In the case of the Orient, says Chateaubriand, the latter is already excessively annotated; therefore he undertakes to write about the former, namely, himself. The emphasis on the subject as subject-matter, the introversion of Chateaubriand's writing, is ostensibly vindicated by the suspicion that there is nothing else left to write about. If the individual is a unique being then it follows that any account of self, assuming it is adequate to its subject, must be original. But originality is the condition of adequacy.

It is by way of metaphor, suggests Chateaubriand, that originality might be attained. Thus Chateaubriand envisages himself as a crusading *chevalier errant* doing battle, on behalf of art, with the pre-existing 'army of metaphors, metonyms and anthropomorphisms' that already confronts him like an enemy. Of the purpose of his trip, Chateaubriand writes that 'j'allais chercher des images, voilà tout' (II, p. 701); and he records, with satisfaction, that he 'revient à ses foyers avec quelques images nouvelles dans la tête et quelques sentiments de plus dans le cœur' (II, p. 709n). 'Sentiments' succeed 'images': the novelty of the image seems to be less the means of expressing feelings than the prerequisite of their release. Thus the literary ambition of the *Itinéraire*, which translates into a pilgrimage the theory developed in *Génie du christianisme* of a literature renovated by belief (following the philosophical impieties of the eighteenth century), is implicated in a programme of emotional renewal.

The image of the *désert* which dominates Chateaubriand's conception of the Orient is an improbable candidate for the rank of *trouvaille*. Lévi-Strauss remarks that 'le survol de l'Arabie propose une série de variations sur un seul thème: le désert'.[124] And given its prominence even in those of Chateaubriand's works quite unconnected with the Orient, the *désert* scarcely constitutes an *image nouvelle*. Rather, it appears as the precondition of novelty, the ground of metaphorical originality.

Napoleon perceived an incongruity between the potential riches of the country of Egypt and the actual indigence, material and intellectual, of its inhabitants: while the land is 'belle', 'fertile', and so on, the people are 'laids', 'misérables', and so on. He posits an antithesis between an inanimate and almost immaculate milieu and its animate and defective tenants. The same structure of opposition recurs in Chateaubriand, who supplements Napoleon's observation by the addition of his own reaction: one of indignation (one of the most frequently performed in his repertoire of emotions), almost of outrage. The apparent discrepancy between Orient and Orientals dismays him, as though paradise had been invaded by alien beings (which according to Chateaubriand is precisely what has happened):

> quand on songe que ces campagnes n'ont été habitées autrefois que par des Grecs du Bas-Empire, et qu'elles sont occupées aujourd'hui par des Turcs, on est choqué du contraste entre les peuples et les lieux; il semble que des esclaves aussi vils et des tyrans aussi cruels n'auraient jamais dû déshonorer un séjour aussi magnifique. (II, p. 944)

Chateaubriand's abhorrence of what he perceives as an anomaly testifies to a theory of the environment: he requires that there exist a correspondence between place and populace, a visible congruity such that each would be an adequate expression of the other.[125]

The Nile episode gives expression both to Chateaubriand's patriotic nostalgia and the intimate liaison he postulates between landscape and society. Observing an orderly, symmetrically arranged grove of palm-trees, on the bank of the river, he reflects:

> Les palmiers paraissaient alignés sur la rive, comme ces avenues dont les châteaux de France sont décorés: la nature se plaît ainsi à rappeler les idées de la civilisation, dans le pays où cette civilisation prit naissance et où règnent aujourd'hui l'ignorance et la barbarie. (II, pp. 1134–5)

On the one hand, nature, imitating art, evokes a cultured society; the society, on the other, is entirely uncultivated. Thus a gap has opened up between the beauty of mother nature and the ugliness of human nature. But the palm-trees also indicate the solution to the problem they pose, by duplicating the French vocation of recalling civilization to its source.[126] Chateaubriand is a perfect embodiment of the French role: a mobile extension of the *château* (his name recalls an ancestor's home: (Baron) Brien's castle), a noble vehicle of its seigneurial values. His ideal space, his *locus amoenus*, would similarly eliminate any discrepancy between form and content.

The perceptible discontinuity of *milieu* and *peuple* in the Orient reflects the conflict which permeates the text between past and present. Chateaubriand's chronological schema admits three ages of man, to which the stages of a civilization correspond: *enfance/jeunesse*; *maturité*; and *décadence*. The Orient he perceives and reviles has attained a state of advanced senility, almost of moribundity: it prefigures its imminent condition of carrion by being fed upon by vulturine Turks. The Orient he imagines and admires has at least two things in common with France: that it is absent; and that (like himself) it is, or was, mature: that is, at the peak of its cultural productivity.[127] Both the present (but absent) France and the lost (but recoverable) Orient are the apotheoses of the values of civilization, while the present (insupportable) Orient vividly embodies a decline.

Thus while the classical Orient and modern France coincide, the modern Arab, by infringing the aesthetic law of Chateaubriand's environmental logic, appears preposterously out of place:

> Nous passâmes par le canal de Menouf, ce qui m'empêcha de voir le beau bois de palmiers qui se trouve sur la grande branche de l'ouest; mais les Arabes infestaient alors le bord occidental de cette branche qui touche au désert libyque. (II, p. 1141)

The intelligibility of the conjunction 'mais' depends on our understanding that the invisible palm-trees, potentially beautiful, even supposing they had not been blocked from view, would in any case be deprived of all beauty by the proximity of disharmonious Arabs. The verb *infester* denotes the illicit, provisional character of the Arab presence: they do not belong by right to the area which they choose to inhabit: they are mere interlopers, destined to be expelled just as the French are destined to return, trespassers on the banks of the Nile, who have wandered away from the territory allotted in accordance with their uncultivated nature, and designated in the closing phrase: the 'désert libyque'. An earlier passage (whose opening line places the East under Western surveillance) recalls that:

> j'avais sous les yeux les descendants de la race primitive des hommes, je les voyais avec les mêmes mœurs qu'ils ont conservées depuis les jours d'Agar et d'Ismaël; je les voyais dans le même désert qui leur fut assigné par Dieu en héritage . . . l'Arabe, pour ainsi dire jeté sur le grand chemin du monde, entre l'Afrique et l'Asie, erre dans les brillantes régions de l'aurore, sur un sol sans arbre et sans eau. (II, pp. 1013–14)

In this case, the rationale of secret harmonies is endorsed by divine fiat: the desert is the predestined habitat of the Arab, who is doomed to wander in search of trees and water (but is prohibited from ever legally attaining either).

The hierarchy of moral absolutes in which ethical and ethnic categories overlap, providing for the assured enunciation of *sententiae* about a collective soul or psychology (all Turks are corrupt, all Arabs stupid), interlocks with a relative aesthetic schema linking man's identity and destiny to his native surroundings. Man and his environment are bound by mutual sympathy: while the human subject is reducible to the sum of his ecological correlatives, geography is charged with moral and psychological connotations. It is enough to observe the landscape in which a people is set in order to acquire knowledge of its true character: the eminently fathomable inner nature, the collective essence of the Arab population, is visibly displayed in the outer nature to which Chateaubriand's God has eternally consigned it. The Arab is turned inside out, his mind externalized for inspection, projected outwards upon his environment. Intangible qualities of mind, emotion, morality, are no longer imagined to reside, inaccessibly, within the individual: they are publicly engraved upon a physical terrain: Chateaubriand's Arab shares with Hugo's the property of being all surface.

But the chief attribute of the Egyptian desert is its emptiness: it is the negative landscape par excellence: devoid of content, stripped bare, denuded. And the same is metaphorically true of the Arab: he is bereft (as the desert is of soil, vegetation, water) of rational thought, a moral code, political ideas of justice, liberty, democracy.[128] He professes 'une religion qui a brûlé la bibliothèque d'Alexandrie, qui se fait un mérite de mépriser souverainement les lettres et les arts' (II, p. 1053). Systematically philistine, the only book he has neglected to destroy is the Koran, perhaps because 'il n'y a dans le livre de Mahomet ni principe de civilisation, ni précepte qui puisse élever le caractère: ce livre ne prêche ni la haine de la tyrannie, ni l'amour de la liberté' (II, p. 908). Motivated only by animal self-interest, he presents, in short, a negative mental landscape that finds its exact equivalent in the form of the desert. What the Arab and the desert have most in common is vacancy: the Orient is characterized by a dual geographical and human barrenness; the Arab is an intellectual Sahara. The Arab's lack of culture is reflected in the uncultivated nature of the land he inhabits. Chateaubriand thus exploits an agricultural etymology to provide a visible counterpart of educational underdevelopment or decay, to encode ignorance. Hence the mission of the cultured and cultivating French: to scatter the good seed. The Oriental stands in need of fertilization.

In contrast to the Arab, Chateaubriand himself retains an

inexhaustible interiority which is the prerogative of the European. His identity is shaped by his childhood environment of Brittany, but he remains nonetheless a free agent, ecologically speaking, whose indeterminacy is mirrored in his endless travelling: he is never *chez lui* ('presque un étranger dans mon pays' (II, p. 770)), only a detached spectator in any territory. The Chateaubrianesque *je* is as limitless as the world. And while the hollow, superficial, infertile Arab mind is symmetrical with the desert, a flat, wide, empty plain, Chateaubrianesque immanence and profundity appear to find an objective correlative, a system of common denominators, in the *ruine*.

The vocabulary of ruins is extensive and ubiquitous in the *Itinéraire*: the travelling author is incessantly drawn to *débris*, *vestiges*, *remnants*, *décombres*, and more particularly to symbols of death, the *tombe*, *tombeau*, *cimetière*, or *sépulcre*. The crumbling edifice, the evocative remains of an ancient architecture, the grave: each allows for the expression of melancholy and the operation of the retrospective mode of thought and feeling to which the *Itinéraire* gives priority; and each offers an exact image of the pervasive mutability, the rise and fall of civilizations, which is a central theme of the book.[129] The writer's sense of personal affinity with ruins springs from the perception not only that both are presently endangered and ultimately doomed to disappear, but also that both are laden with culture and history: both, in short, are *plena*, distinguished by their labyrinthine complexity, their wealth of irrecoverable meaning, their indecipherability. The secrets of the self are buried deep within the individual: hence the frequency of the verb *ensevelir*: René 's'ensevelit' in the depths of a forest, his memories and emotions are 'ensevelis' within him (just as 'palais' are 'ensevelis' in 'poudre') (I, pp. 117, 122). Similarly, the meaning of the *grotte*, which is the privileged space of the ruin, is essentially subterranean and, chronologically, buried in the past, requiring excavation or evocation by the erudite observer.

Structurally, plenitude implies the contrast of vacancy. It is this juxtaposition of an inner cornucopia of feeling and an outer vacuity that inspires René's *ennui*: in *René*, a 'cœur plein' meets a 'monde vide' (I, p. 1). An analogous disposition of forces is evident in the *Itinéraire*: the inward, vertical, vertiginous fullness of the ruin is foregrounded against the outward, horizontal horizon of the desert. Likewise, the aristocratic French pilgrim stands out from the crowd of Oriental humanity. The time-spans of civilizations and citizens are condensed in an architectural image: the monument – temple, *château*, Chateaubriand – which becomes a ruin which is then engulfed in the desert.

Richard asserts that 'l'imagination de Chateaubriand se livre donc à une grande mise en scène de l'absence. Autour du moi elle étend un désert de négativité.'[130] The hero of the *Itinéraire*, unlike the Arab, is never the mere reflection of an environment. Chateaubriand's elaborate network of analogies entails a real or imagined rapprochement of the self and a shifting milieu. Hence the affinity of the author with ruins does not exclude a sense of sympathy with their setting. Thus he concludes his recapitulation (in the *Mémoires*) of his Oriental adventures with this coda: 'Je n'ai devant les yeux, des sites de la Syrie, de l'Egypte, et de la terre punique, que les endroits en rapport avec ma nature solitaire; ils me plaisent indépendamment de l'antiquité, de l'art et de l'histoire.' He identifies these timeless, artless places quite specifically: 'Les pyramides me frappaient moins par leur grandeur que par le désert contre lequel elles étaient appliquées.'[131] The *Itinéraire* depicts Chateaubriand as a Christ-like figure wandering in the wilderness. His contempt for the Arab conceals a clandestine envy which finds expression in his unconcealed admiration for the Frenchmen, the residue of Napoleon's expeditionary force, who have become Mamelukes (the guardians of the old regime they were supposed to depose) and have 'vécu longtemps dans le désert avec les Bédouins' (II, p. 1145).[132] The dual passion for the crumbling edifice and the immortal desert reflects an ambiguity of commitment.

In the *Itinéraire*, Chateaubriand parades his allegiance to the values of a *civilisation* which is conterminous with France; but he nevertheless senses and declares his kinship with an uncivilized past: hence his self-description: 'Moi, Barbare civilisé' (II, p. 833). Chateaubriand's consciousness of a hybrid self, a dual personality, issues in the image he reserves for himself of the 'androgyne bizarre'[133] and induces both Thibaudet and Butor to affirm that there are 'two Chateaubriands'.[134] His symmetrical journeys westwards and eastwards, tabulating the rise and fall, the birth and the decay of new and old cultures, enable him to find an outlet for the antinomial poles of his personality and give expression to the antagonistic values of civilization and barbarism whose respective emblems are plenitude and vacuity, erudition and ignorance.

Thus Chateaubriand's Oriental travels involve a process of exchange: like Napoleon, he is a European (but above all, a Frenchman, a patriot, championing France versus England and the rest of the world) exporting Western culture to the East; at the same time, he tries on the identities of the lands he visits, enacting the destinies of Egypt and Greece: 'peut-être le génie des nations s'épuise-t-il; et quand il a tout produit, tout parcouru, tout goûté, rassasié de ses propres chefs-d'œuvre, et incapable d'en produire de nouveaux, il s'abrutit, et retourne aux sensations purement physiques' (II, p. 887). The *Itinéraire* merges the fate of civilizations with the evolution of an individual: the growth to maturity, the full flowering of genius, inevitably entails exhaustion and decay; but decline, in turn, implies a cyclical return to an original state of pure sensation, the recovery of a lost childhood (thus Chateaubriand's progress through space coincides with his regress through time). In Chateaubriand's literary epistemology, books are conceived of as foods feeding the literate mind: the fertilizers of culture. But the *Itinéraire* shows that the author's surfeit of erudition can give rise to a state of congestion, of intellectual indigestion or creative constipation. Chateaubriand, cursed by excess, is too crammed with potential material to make any use of it. Trapped in the labyrinth of his own learning, he seeks to free himself of the accretions that surround and stifle the self: to eliminate overabundant knowledge.

The desert seems to represent precisely such a deliverance because its transcendent emptiness calls up, in accordance with Chateaubriand's eco-logic, its concomitant in the observer of an immanent evacuation. His fascination with the desert springs from an urge to relinquish the tradition of which he is ambassador, the ambition of inner, mental *déracinement* (an uprooting both of *racines* and Racine) corresponding to his physical exile. The desert purifies the world of its descriptions: it is the Orient minus Orientalism.[135] Thus the primal condition of nescience – the negation of a cultural archive, the incineration of libraries – censoriously ascribed to the Arab, also constitutes the secret consummation of Chateaubriand's aesthetic. His plenitude may be a satiety that causes the suspension of creativity; the desert, by voiding, regenerates the jaded spirit.

Chateaubriand has alleged the search for new Muses as one reason for his journey East; later he admits that 'naturellement un peu sauvage, ce n'était pas ce qu'on appelle la société que j'étais venu chercher en Orient: il me tardait de voir des chameaux et d'entendre le cri du cornac' (II, pp. 923–4). Both programmes are fulfilled in the contemplation of the desert: 'L'Egypte m'a paru le plus beau pays de la terre: j'aime jusqu'aux déserts qui la bordent, et qui ouvrent à l'imagination les champs de l'immensité' (II, p.

1148). The arid, empty sands are a fertile source of inspiration: the *désert*, aesthetically, is adjacent to the measureless *champs* of the literary imagination; both literally and analogically, it is the ground of the novel, the *nouveau*: the camel, the cornac, and the freshly-minted metaphor.

Thus the *désert* is not exclusive to the Orient: it appears rather as a universal constant in Chateaubriand's work, a permanent companion of the author, conjured up on all his travels. Visiting the mausoleums of the Pharaohs, Chateaubriand recalls the tombs of Ohio:

> je commençais alors le voyage, et maintenant je le finis. Le monde, à ces deux époques de ma vie, s'est présenté à moi précisément sous l'image des deux déserts où j'ai vu ces deux espèces de tombeaux: des solitudes riantes, des sables arides. (II, p. 1144)

Semantically, *désert* is not reducible to the geographical sense of a mere expanse of sand or rock; it is sometimes indistinguishable from Rousseau's primitive forest,[136] inhabited by *sauvages*. The *désert* of the New World, writes Butor, is 'l'équivalent de l'anglais *wilderness*. Il n'évoque nullement la stérilité, le Sahara; au contraire ce désert est caractérisé par la splendeur de sa flore. Il s'agit d'un lieu que la société humaine a laissé intact.'[137] Thus the remote phases of civilization, the nascent and the moribund, together and in parallel with the phases (recollected or projected) of Chateaubriand's childhood and senility, are united by the single ambiguous image of the *désert*.[138] The desert, then, marking the absence of culture and the pre-eminence of nature, is ubiquitous, at once empty and full, sterile and fertile: a cornucopian void.

Chateaubriand traces the ancestry of solitude and nescience to Biblical sources; he discerns their coincidence in the myth of the Garden of Eden to which allusions are scattered throughout his work. Chateaubriand's desert, which is also a garden, is, like Adam's pre-lapsarian paradise, blissfully purified of the nomenclatorial anxiety that is sinful, literate man's secular, sublunary malediction. Here the writer can finally achieve his ambition of absolute originality: only in the Edenesque *désert* is he able not only to 'voir à nu' (like the first Western travellers in the East) (I, p. 633), but also to summon 'la parole primitive que Dieu a donné à l'homme avec l'existence' (I, p. 786), the ideal language postulated and refuted by Rousseau, which closes the rift between sign and object.[139] Thus the new world of the imagination seeks an origin in the old.[140]

The *désert*, metonym of the Orient (with which it is contiguous), and metaphor of the Arab (to whom it corresponds), thus stands as the symbol of originality. 'Où y a-t-il du nouveau? Est-ce en Orient?' Chateaubriand asks, and answers by the imperative 'Marchons-y.' But there is nothing new under the sun: the sun (the West, civilization, the knowledge enshrined in discourse) is the symbol of the old: its canonical *lumières* threaten to deprive language of its access to novelty. Chateaubriand's literary pilgrimage therefore imposes further conditions: 'puisque nous cherchons de nouveaux soleils, je me précipiterai au-devant de leur splendeur et n'attendrai plus le lever naturel de l'aurore'.[141] Chateaubriand heads eastwards towards the benighted Orient to escape the rising of the sun; the desert can only achieve the complete negation of obsolete culture at night: Chateaubriand's ideal landscape would be sunless. Writing accordingly becomes a nocturnal enterprise: Chateaubriand describes himself as 'courant le jour et écrivant la nuit' (II, p. 1017). Symmetrically, in the American forest, with the rumble of Niagara echoing 'de désert en désert', he discovers inspiration at night: 'c'est dans ces nuits que m'apparut une muse inconnue' (I, p. 302). Chateaubriand's muse, like Hugo's, operates under cover of night.

Genette has noted that 'l'imagination poétique s'intéresse davantage à la nuit qu'au jour' and that the explicit preference for night over day constitutes 'un choix coupable, un parti pris de l'interdit, une transgression'.[142] In Chateaubriand, it represents an inversion of the Orientalist project, an attempt to infiltrate the East into the West: to incorporate the Oriental *nuit* into the Occidental *jour*. Genette has also noted that the antithesis of day and night is 'un paradigme défectif' since 'la relation entre jour et nuit n'est pas seulement d'opposition, donc d'exclusion réciproque mais aussi d'inclusion: en un de ses sens, le jour exclut la nuit, en l'autre, il la comprend'.[143] Semantically, at least, Chateaubriand's anti-Orientalist intention seems eminently capable of fulfilment, since day already incorporates night.

But, conversely, as Blanchot remarks, 'la nuit ne parle que du jour'.[144] If the day cannot exclude the night, neither can night exclude day, since it is a fraction of the diurnal cycle. Even when the sun is absent from Chateaubriand's desert, it is supplanted by the moon. The writer is nocturnal, and therefore (according to Nicholas's classifications) a lunatic, an owl who cannot tolerate the sun. The narrator of *Les Natchez* apostrophizes the moon, calling on it to 'découvrir à ta lumière les secrets ravissants de ces déserts'

(I, p. 167). But of course the moon does not emit light, it is only a pale reflector of the sun: its light is derivative. Thus the Chateaubrianesque desert, the scene of original writing, the primordial metaphor, cannot escape solar reflection.[145]

Language then, even as it appears in its raw, metaphorical, Oriental state, is already irradiated by the Occidental sun of culture. And the Oriental desert, the chief exemplar of the *désert*, in which all its senses overlap, itself reflects the destructive effects of the sun. The *désert* is not distinct from the *ruines* it accommodates but is itself a vast ecological ruin, the remnant of an indeterminate process of dissolution. The desert (of Greece as well as of Egypt) is not a pure negation, a primitive state of nature, but the residue of a fertile, civilized past. The desert is not just the location of tombs but the paradigm case of the *tombeau*.[146] Thus writing reverts from the ambition of originality to the recognition of mortality. The metaphor is a ruin of language, not a fresh construction but the destruction of inherited forms, a monument to the past, the wreck of an irrecoverable originality: the text, in turn, seems to Chateaubriand like a tomb, 'un temple de la mort'.[147] In the introduction to the *Mémoires* (whose full title suggests less an autobiography than a post-mortem), Chateaubriand declares that he always imagines himself, while writing, to be seated in his coffin. The writer (as Nietzsche said of himself) is born posthumously, deprived of a birth.

But the writer seems equally deprived of a definitive death. Just as Chateaubriand regrets the derivativeness of his own writing, so, symmetrically, he fears its duplication. He realizes (reflecting on the ruins of the Parthenon) that 'je passerai à mon tour: d'autres hommes aussi fugitifs que moi viendront faire les mêmes réflexions sur les mêmes ruines' (II, p. 876). He laments not so much the brevity of life as its prolongation in others: the prospect of individuality is debased by the eternal recurrence of the author's preoccupations and expressions. Chateaubriand cannot be a pioneer, the first to discover and describe the Orient; neither can he be the last, 'le dernier historien' (II, p. 1019) or 'le dernier Français' (II, p. 769) to make the pilgrimage to the Holy Land: hordes of literary tourists are already following in his tracks.[148]

The *Essai sur les révolutions* bemoans the severance from a past (because it severs authority). All Chateaubriand's writing confirms the condition of exile from a point of origin. However, in *Génie du christianisme*, Chateaubriand advances historical proofs upholding the validity of the Biblical account of Genesis, arguing that man and the world are relatively recent inventions, that the preponderance of ruins does not demonstrate the antiquity of civilization but only the speed at which it decays. In order to refute the paleontological objection involving the apparent age of the earth, he resorts to a theory of 'vieillesse originaire'.[149] If the Creation occurred recently but the earth is ancient, then 'Dieu a dû créer, et a sans doute créé le monde avec toutes les marques de vétusté et de complément que nous lui voyons.' The Creator creates a mature universe of ancient forests, ageing animals, a reef-filled ocean, and a man thirty years old, eliminating an 'insipide enfance' on apparently aesthetic grounds, since 'la nature, dans son innocence, eût été moins belle qu'elle ne l'est aujourd'hui dans sa corruption'. The primordial world is 'à la fois jeune et vieux'; the beginning incorporates an infinite past;[150] everything which is now has always been. Thus Chateaubriand preserves Genesis only at the cost of abolishing genesis,[151] condemning youth, innocence, novelty, in short, the negative moment of a pure origin, as artistically intolerable. The logos emerges *in medias res*; such is, *a fortiori*, the case of discourse, The writer, born amid the ruins of culture and language, is the image of the Creator because he only creates what is already old.

3.5 The Oriental Occident

In Orientalism, a relative, genitival ignorance, an ignorance *of* something, specifically, the French thesaurus, is converted, by the equation of a singular culture with the civilization and history of the world, into an absolute. Hugo, Napoleon, and Chateaubriand all retrace 'cette autobiographie gigantesque' analysed by Schwab, 'que l'Occident du XIXe siècle a commencé d'intituler "la civilis-ation"'.[152] While decadence defines the Orient, *civilisation* is equated with the rise of Western Europe, encapsulated in the French nation. In turn, the attraction for Romanticism of Oriental otherness resides in the opportunities it furnishes for self-dramatization. The Orient is a pretext for the differentiation of an identity: Hugo's dreamer and poet, Napoleon's omnipotent emperor and omniscient messiah, Chateaubriand's aggressive patriot. Above all, the Orient is the 'théâtre'[153] in which are played out characterizations of the Occidental archive.

Hugo's literary philosophy identifies poetry with the sun of supreme knowledge, whose ascent coincides with Western ascend-ancy over the East; Napoleon shifts from externalizing civilization to internalizing barbarianism; Chateaubriand makes the oscillation and interchange between East and West, night and day, the subject and symbol of his writing. Each of these writers espouses the programme of exporting the commodity of Western culture to the East, but each, in return, smuggles Eastern contraband into the West. Oriental nescience, in particular the renunciation of culture, stands out not just as a damning characteristic of an alien race, the rationale of an ideology and the dignification of an appetite for power and space, but also as the precondition of the enlightenment associated with artistic originality, the source of 'nouveaux soleils'.[154] Re-educating the East is a pretext for de-educating the West.

Thus the literary Occident both disdains and exalts the Orient, the site of desert, darkness, negation. But even the Orient, frustratingly, is never truly Oriental but already traversed by Occidental discourse: its desert remains populated by ruins, its darkness illuminated by reflected light, its negation incomplete. The journey to the Old World repeats the disappointment of the journey to the New, where Chateaubriand's dream of imitating the savage is frustrated by the lack of a suitable Rousseauiste model.[155] But if the Orient, the destination of a journey or pilgrimage, turns out on arrival to be already Occidental, the Occident from which the writer departs turns out on his return to be already Oriental.

The desire for regeneration in the East reflects a sense of the decadence of Western culture. Chateaubriand finally agrees with Hugo that it is superfluous to travel East in search of the uncivilized:

la civilisation actuelle décomposée ne passe pas par la Barbarie; elle se perd en elle-même; le vase qui la contient n'a pas versé la liqueur dans un autre vase; c'est le vase qui est brisé et la liqueur répandue.[156]

The Oriental receptacle seemed to have a hole in it preventing the complete transmission of cultural liquor; but the disintegrating Occidental dispenser is itself a leaky vessel from which nothing can be poured and which, equally, cannot be filled. The task of civilizing the East is unrealizable because the West has not yet finished the task of civilizing itself. Thus the Orient is not finally the Other for the West, but only its reverse side, its *alter ego*, its double.[157] The disorientation of the East is coupled with a reorientation of the West.[158] This is why Baudelaire and Hugo can speak of going *là-bas* without moving an inch: for France, the Orient begins at home.

French Romantic writing registers a pathology of the sun. Reflected and dissolved in Hugo's nocturnal 'mer de poésie', the harbinger of death and defeat for Napoleon, the *astre-roi* is usurped by the moon or, worse, multiplied in Chateaubriand's firmament. The sun is always metaphorical, cooled by a system of substitutions eclipsing and transforming its meaning.[159] The Orient, at once *la patrie du soleil* and *la patrie de l'imagination*, dramatizes the demise of the figurative sun of the West. The sun, invoked as the guarantor of knowledge, counterpart of the Good and origin of the Cartesian *lumière naturelle*, is always liable to disappear from view. But if we cannot observe the sun directly (as Plato warned and Napoleon discovered) without suffering the penalty of blindness or death, we can never entirely escape its lingering reflection. It is the characteristic affliction of writing always to anticipate or recall a sun which it can neither possess nor preclude: *occidens* and *oriens* mark its recurrent limits.

Nicholas of Cusa described discourse (just as Napoleon describes the Oriental savage)[160] as a dog; Hugo associates poetry (and the Orient) with the twilight of sunset: it is not a dog but *entre chien et loup*. Chateaubriand brings writing to an end at sunrise. The *Mémoires* trace the period between these two moments: although the preface promises an account of 'les rayons de mon soleil, depuis son aurore jusqu'à son couchant',[161] the text traverses not the interval from dawn till dusk but from dusk till dawn: Chateaubriand's birth is recorded as the 'pâle reflet . . . d'une immense lumière', and the writer lays down his pen and prepares for death with the moon still visible at six in the morning: 'Je vois les reflets d'une aurore dont je ne verrai pas se lever le soleil.'[162] The entire text, while very long, is only an anticipation: even by the end it has not properly begun. The span of the scriptural moment is recorded in Baudelaire's 'Hymne à la beauté': 'Tu contiens dans ton œil le couchant et l'aurore.'[163] For these writers, writing occurs only when the sun is no longer or not yet visible, although its rays are. Chateaubriand's metaphorical suns recur in his vision of the stars of the Milky Way ('un océan à vagues de soleils'): 'la distance de ces étoiles est si prodigieuse que leur éclat ne pourra parvenir à l'œil qui les regarde que quand ces étoiles seront éteintes, le foyer avant le rayon'.[164] But it seems that the rays of the *soleil* suffer the same fate as those of the 'soleils': to be cut off from their source, the reflections of an extinct star.[165]

This universal solar sickness entails a malady of writing. Orientalism is constitutionally equivocal: it traces the decay of a duality into an ambiguity. Chateaubriand's shuttling between *oriens* and *occidens*, both physical and textual, constitutes a circular journey in which, as for Hugo (in his *Post-scriptum*), 'il ne fait pas jour, le jour, et il ne fait pas nuit, la nuit'.[166] The day and night of West and East are never nothing but, unequivocally, day or night, since the sun controlling those metaphors is never either wholly present or absent. This uncertainty allows for the stable articulation of neither Hugolian antithesis nor synthesis; thus the ruling prepositional construction of Chateaubriand's work is neither *ou/ou*, nor *et/et*, but rather *entre*:[167] his writing traces a Rousseauiste *voyage* in which the writer is always in circulation between a point of departure and a destination, a commuter forever in transition.

Orientalism, as it adds to the Oriental minimum and subtracts from the Occidental maximum, disclosing the content of a void and the emptiness of a plenitude, seems to deprive knowledge of an origin and an end. Nevertheless, nescience and omniscience remain throughout the nineteenth century the rival patterns on which French writing is alternately modelled: it is the business of literature to fix the thesaurus for all time or to transcend it, either to say everything (Balzac) or nothing (Flaubert). The compendious fiction of Jules Verne, which extends the journey East to encircle the solar system, and spans the poles of science and literature, nescience and omniscience, seeks to encompass these alternative aesthetics: to say everything and nothing.[168]

The obsessive gesture of nineteenth-century writers in France consists in affiliating their fictions to the enterprise of science. Science enjoyed power, credence, prestige. Literature, in contrast, lacked the privileged epistemological status of science, and appeared to accomplish no visibly useful or (more importantly) profitable function. Science, accordingly, became the object of literary envy. So it was inevitable that certain novelists, in search of a justification of their art, should pose as quasi-scientific analysts of human relations or the soul. Their novels (resting on a fictitious inductive model of the scientific enterprise) would be sociological or psychological documents dictated by objective realities.

That science exercised a fascination and even a formal influence over the literature of the period, and operated as a major alibi for its practice, is a commonplace of literary history; more neglected is the fact that it also began to appear as a constitutive element of imaginative writing.[169] If, formally, the novel was to be the encyclopedia of existence, its panoramic vision informed by a set of scientific and fabulous theories about men and society, then, thematically, it would also include an inventory of the activities, the uses, and the products of science. Moreover, if the novel was to be the purveyor of truth, then science would stand as guarantor of its illusory verifiability, the valuta of fictional coinage.

In the *Voyages extraordinaires* of Jules Verne, science is assigned a triple role: the subject of imaginative extrapolations, it is also the underwriter of the plausibility of such imaginings and, ultimately, of the legitimacy of the text; and, finally, it serves to provide the linguistic raw material from which Verne constructs his literary technology.

Science and literature share at least one common denominator: their substantive resonance is, in part, a consequence of their insubstantial hollowness: each is devoid of a single identifiable referent; each, like a Platonic Idea, constitutes a conceptual archetype whose objective manifestations are inevitably pale shadows or defective copies of the real thing, which is unreal, and therefore, indestructible. While science and literature are invested with the permanence of impalpability, the book and the machine, on the other hand, are inherently impermanent, in a word, disposable: the one, eminently palpable, dependent for its transmission on the technology of the printed page, shares the pulpable destiny of paper; the other, likewise inscribed upon the material world, is equally vulnerable to the logic of mutability and decay.

It is the structurally identical drama of entropy, the ceaselessly increasing disorder of the empirical universe (or, in information theory, a measure of the uncertainty of a message), set against an ideal order of the intellect (wherein no message is uncertain), that is enacted in the scientific fictions of Jules Verne.

In the *Voyages*, while literature aspires to the condition of science, science aspires to the condition of omniscience. But an alimentary epistemology translates the distant prospect of omniscience into the more immediate practice of omnivoracity.

4

THE SCIENTIFIC FICTIONS OF JULES VERNE

Je hais les voyages et les voyageurs   (Lévi-Strauss, *Tristes tropiques*)

4.1 Nutrition and cognition

L'univers est égal à son vaste appétit   (Baudelaire, 'Le Voyage')

Il faut . . . manger trop   (Verne, *Les Enfants du capitaine Grant*)

In the *Voyages extraordinaires* of Jules Verne, only the ordinary remains extraordinary. The imaginary itineraries traced in these far-flung fictions have become too quotidian, too routine, insufficiently improbable to be fantastic; while those automotive marvels that are their indispensable accessories, now overtaken by the future they strove to anticipate, have ceased to be marvellous. But Verne's adventures in the banal continue to astonish. And his compendious novels contain nothing so commonplace, nor so singular, as their cult of nutrition.

Few writers have managed altogether to exclude eating from writing. Some have sought to make a virtue of necessity by converting the indifferent occasion of a meal into a textual device subservient to the articulation of plot, theme, or character.[1] Two nearly antithetical culinary aesthetics are exemplified in the fictions of Rabelais and Flaubert. The Rabelaisian *fête* or banquet, whose lavish congeries of food and drink solicit hyperbolic notations and protracted inventories, is a pretext for Epicurean and nominal prodigality. In contrast, the characteristic menu of Flaubert (more a *gourmet* than a *gourmand*) is at once more restricted in the range of individual dishes offered and less random in their arrangement, privileging grammatical symmetry over lexical abundance. The respective cuisines celebrated by these writers emphasize, gastronomically, the quantitative and the qualitative, rhetorically, the metaphoric and the metonymic: the standard regimen of the one is chaotic but cornucopian, of the other, conservative but orderly.[2]

Rabelais would envy and Flaubert disdain the extravagant heterogeneity, the exoticism, the sheer indiscriminateness of the infinitely various diets prescribed in the polyphagous novels of Jules Verne. It would be difficult to name any other writer whose textual menu extends not only to such delicacies as elephant's tongue (and feet), kangaroo's tail, and seaweed, but also to assorted organs and limbs subtracted from walrus, polar bear, and armadillo.

The *Voyages*, at once rigorously literal and densely symbolic, abound in microfigures, reflexive images duplicating in miniature the configuration of a text or texts, emblematic résumés of plot or theme. One such condensed *tableau*, unsavoury but also exemplary, occurs near the opening of *Les Enfants du capitaine Grant*, in an episode where a shark is ritually disembowelled; the unflinching narrator comments: 'il est d'usage à bord de tout navire de visiter soigneusement l'estomac du requin. Les matelots, connaissant sa voracité peu délicate, s'attendent à quelque surprise, et leur attente n'est pas toujours trompée.'[3] Analogously, the Vernian *œuvre*, afflicted with a narrative compulsion to reveal what is secret, to expose for inspection occulted caverns and compartments, is destined to tabulate the surprising dietary input of various human, but no less voracious, consumers. Verne, in all things almost pathologically exhaustive, addicted as much to enumeration and taxonomy as to food, obsessively catalogues and classifies the contents of those miscellaneous meals devoured by his itinerant heroes.

The series of novels comprising the *Voyages* involves their protagonists in interminable dislocation; for the duration of their adventures they are exiled, rocketed to the moon, spun around the globe, or driven to its extremities: compelled, in brief, to strive for the unattainable condition of ubiquity. And to their displacements correspond equivalent transformations of their daily régime. Thus the extent of what one critic has aptly designated the Vernian 'dépaysement culinaire'[4] is a reliable marker of their location and distance from home. Domesticity is gauged by reference to a norm of traditional home-cooking;[5] conversely the more bizarre the fare, the more remote the environment. In each case, the constituents of the meal reflect the nature of the milieu, absorb and exhibit an array of local colour.[6]

Thus the *Voyages* compose a gastronomic guide to the globe, an alimentary atlas. The eponymous island of *L'Ile mystérieuse*, a microcosm of an entire continent, or of the world, a utopian site accommodating representative specimens of a vast range of fauna and flora, provides a correspondingly lavish, international cuisine.

The islanders' table is itself a microcosm, amply confirming Brillat-Savarin's statement that 'un festin savamment ordonné est comme un abrégé du monde'.[7] The gradual colonization of the island is measurable by the progressive domestication of the meals, which, initially confined to the *lithodomes* that are the harvest of beach-combing, eventually expand to include bread, wine, and the post-prandial pipe.[8]

It is the peculiar property of Verne's exiles that, being torn from their beloved *patrie*, they are consequently denied the national or provincial diet that is their birthright; the origin of their keenest anguish (and pleasure) is that they are condemned to perpetually eat native, to sample the cooking of the lands their routes traverse. Brillat-Savarin remarks that whereas animals tend to adhere to an exclusive diet, eating either vegetables or flesh or grain, but not all of them together, 'l'homme, au contraire, est omnivore'.[9] But while resident natives are restricted to the products of a unique locale (and therefore characterized and conditioned by their diet),[10] the distinguishing feature of the Vernian traveller's *vaste appétit* (the verification of humanity's privileged rank in Brillat-Savarin's digestive cosmogony) is its absolute inclusiveness.

The *voyageur* is capable of eating virtually anything (one of the *Chancellor*'s raftees is reduced to chewing on fragments of leather); but his quintessential desire, the omnivore's dream, is no less than to eat everything, to leave nothing (even the inedible) untasted.[11] Vernian man aims to get the outside inside: to get outside the outside. Just as, geographically, there is no site, however inaccessible, that Verne's globe-trotters can bear to leave untrodden or unscrutinized, beyond the frontiers of scientific cartography, so there is no animal or vegetable (even minerals are not excluded *a priori*), however unsavoury, that is not, in principle, assimilable. The travellers' appetites are as universal as their itineraries; their stomachs are the most supple feature of their typically inelastic constitutions and characters.

The demand of the Vernian appetite for ubiquitous satisfaction seems not merely incidental to an itinerary, the condition of a journey; it tends to displace other, logically prior motivations of travel, to become not a means but an end. The *voyageur* does not eat in order to travel: he travels in order to eat.[12] The spacious geography across which the Vernian consumer is propelled houses multitudinous objects; the most searching question to which they can be subjected is this: *Ça se mange?*

In Verne's economy overproduction (of food) determines a market of overconsumers: supply generates demand. On the journey to the North Pole, Clawbonny observes that, 'dans les régions arctiques il faut manger beaucoup; c'est une des conditions non seulement de la force mais de l'existence'.[13] The roving protagonists, often reluctant to imitate native manners, subscribe enthusiastically to this dietary imperative. But the cold climate is scarcely more than a pretext for their systematic overindulgence. Abnormal eating is the traveller's norm, not a local, momentary aberration. 'En manger raisonnablement', says Paganel, referring to the profusion of edibles, 'ce serait de l'ingratitude envers la Providence, il faut en manger trop.'[14] Although rudimentary value judgements invariably attend the consumption of a meal (usually 'excellent' – the adverse, critical epithet is rare), it is plain that quality is subordinate, in the *Voyages*, to sheer quantity.

Gluttony, then, becomes a positive virtue. The operation of a moral law converts the business of eating from a pleasure or a necessity to a duty. Ethically, the institution of the *repas* denotes the fulfilment of an obligation; ritualistic and reverential in character, it permits both access to the bounty of a world charged with divinity and the experience of communion with one's fellow consumers. The Vernian mess has the quality of a mass.

Considered with respect to their structural position in the economy of the text, the meals distributed throughout the *Voyages* are remarkable for their regularity and frequency. Genette has observed that 'très schématiquement, on peut dire qu'un récit, quel qu'il soit, peut raconter une fois ce qui s'est passé une fois, *n* fois ce qui s'est passé *n* fois, *n* fois ce qui s'est passé une fois, et une fois ce qui s'est passé *n* fois'.[15] The second case, where an event occurring with a certain frequency is related with that same frequency (what Genette calls the *type anaphorique*), is characteristic of Vernian catering, where narrative *discours* and *histoire* are commensurate. A polar traveller points out that 'dans les récits des voyageurs arctiques, il [est] toujours question de repas'.[16] The arctic narrative is the model of the Vernian text. The function of the thrice-daily refreshments is to enable the fast-moving narrative to pause, expand, expound and digress, thus generating additional, secondary, tangential narratives in the shape of dinner-table anecdotes. Meals are stops ('halte[s] de réfection'),[17] incursions of immobility into the sphere of travel, stations along a route, regular punctuation marks in the narrative syntax. While their contents specify an exotic locale, their predictability and punctuality temper the unfamiliar with the flavour of the quotidian.

In summary, Verne's strict nutritional scheme demands of his heroes the unrealizable objective of eating everything, in impossible quantities, as often as possible.

Verne's global excursions resemble less a sightseeing tour or a scientific investigation than a prolonged hunting and fishing expedition through a seemingly inexhaustible game reserve. From an anthropocentric point of view, however, the beneficent ecology of the *Voyages* is not without hazard. Nature is a universal restaurant in which the interminable feasts are always *gratis* and *à la carte*. But the replete customers may be obliged to pay in kind: inveterate consumers, Verne's protagonists run the risk of being themselves consumed. The Vernian repast is reversible, susceptible to a reciprocal process of exchange. The denizens of the lavishly stocked larder of the world enjoy a dual status: edible providers of instant replenishment, they are also liable to dine off the would-be diner. The passenger has only to step outside the security of his vehicle to be assailed by tigers, bears, sharks, giant squids: an endless parade of man-eaters no less gluttonous than he.

This precarious state of affairs is the origin not only of recurrent fantasies and anxieties, but of a collective carnivorous destiny. There are no vegetarians in Verne, except involuntary ones; the *voyageur* shows a marked preference for fauna over flora. Verne subscribes to the doctrine, purveyed by Brillat-Savarin, that a regular intake of animal flesh is nutritionally indispensable to the wellbeing of one's own: he asserts 'la nécessité pour le carnivore de refaire sa chair et son sang par l'azote contenu dans les matières animales'.[18] But the traveller's appetite is predisposed, irrespective of the need to replenish his depleted reservoir of nitrogen, in favour of those animals that are also carnivorous, and more especially, anthropophagous, and which are consequently declared 'de bonne guerre'.[19] The whole of nature, *chez* Jules, is a conjugation of the verb to eat, in both the active and the passive moods. The cardinal rule governing the nutritious but predatory environment of Verne's reversible restaurant is: eat or be eaten.[20]

Hence the pervasive oral component in the *Voyages*, which display a consistent fascination with, and terror of, *la gueule*: mouths, jaws, mandibles, tongues, and, above all, teeth (thus sharks are a favourite object of contemplation): 'leurs lèvres s'avancent en pointe, leurs dents qui se découvrent, prêtes au rapt violent, déchireront comme des dents de carnassiers, avec la voracité brutale des bêtes'.[21] These ruthless incisors belong not to sharks but to starving sailors, about to tuck into a purely human (and still conscious) meal. The meal is in theory an occasion for the fortification of *camaraderie*, of solidarity; but the indiscriminate exigencies of appetite threaten to disrupt temporary harmonies by compelling the underfed to fall on and feast off each other.

Vernian man is not merely definable by what he eats; he is liable to become what he eats. Verne warns that if we eat nothing but vegetables, or even fish, then we are apt to become bloodless, brainless, inert. The converse metamorphosis implies that those who partake abundantly of animal flesh will have a corresponding potential for bestiality. Eschewing vegetarianism, they more readily resort to cannibalism. It is only the proliferation of alternatives and the exercise of restraint that prevents the practice of interconsumption, common among savage foreigners, from extending to civilized Europeans.[22] The most extreme case of this expedient is that of the would-be cannibal, who, bereft of candidates for the pot, is reduced (like Jynxtrop and Kazallon of the *Chancellor*) to feeding off his own famished flesh, drinking his own thinning blood. It is not merely the wish to avoid being eaten alive himself that inspires in Vernian man a horror of cannibalism. The devouring of one's neighbour and, *a fortiori*, of oneself, infringes the Vernian rule that proper nutrition shall be conditional on the variety of its constituents. The essential ingredient of the Vernian recipe is *la différence*. Thus the utopia of polyphagy is opposed by the dystopia of anthropophagy (or worse, autophagy), diversity by repetition.[23]

While humans are chiefly preoccupied with determining the relative edibility of their environment, they are at the same time uneasily aware that they are themselves eminently edible. It is for this reason that the Vernian *gourmet* has to eat on the run; he is an addict of fast-food: prolonged sloth, torpor, immobility, invite the attention of man-eaters; only by virtue of his greater mobility can he hope to escape the jaws of rival consumers. Fortunately, the largely carnivorous input of the human digestive system appears to comprise one hundred per cent protein, utterly unfreighted with roughage, a mass instantly and comprehensively converted into an output of pure energy. In the diurnal cycle of Verne's chaste, constant, economical world, there is no recycling, no waste, no discrepancy in the equation of comestibles and productivity: the subtraction of fuel from food leaves a zero remainder. Whether on (or under or over) land or sea, the *voyageur* remains indefinitely continent. Like his imaginary machines, Verne's digestions are absolutely and inexplicably efficient: they give rise neither to surplus-value nor pollution.[24]

But the priority of movement, involving the expenditure of energy, inevitably serves to reinforce the nutritive cycle. As Brillat-Savarin writes:

Le mouvement et la vie occasionnent dans le corps vivant une déperdition continuelle de substance; et le corps humain, cette machine si compliquée, serait bientôt hors de service, si la Providence n'y avait placé un ressort qui l'avertit du moment où ses forces ne sont plus en équilibre avec ses besoins. Ce moniteur est l'appétit.[25]

Vernian man must eat in order to avoid being eaten; but the energetic avoidance of being eaten requires him to eat still more. The monitor or spring of appetite is thus perpetually hyperactive, over-sprung: the *besoins* of the *voyageur* invariably exceed his *forces*: he is always hungry. The Vernian text is constructed on the same pattern: it is a *machine* afflicted with disequilibrium.

Jules Verne has himself figured as the protagonist of numerous biographical texts. And the character they depict bears many resemblances to the characters he invented; one common denominator is their immoderate addiction to food. *Jules Verne* by Jean Jules-Verne tells the tale of an undernourished literary apprentice in Paris, gorging himself at occasional feasts *chez les Dumas*, who succumbs to pathological gluttony as he attains success and financial security, and is confined for his sins, in a dyspeptic and diabetic old age, to a frugal diet.[26] The biographer also places the bulimia of his subject and his subject's subjects in an intimate relation of cause and effect. This supposition is less self-evident than the fact that both Verne and his characters face a simple and identical problem: how to pass the time between breakfast, lunch, and dinner. Verne's solution is to invent characters suffering from this problem; their solution is to translate their obsession with consumption into a vocation of intellectual assimilation. Thus a further common denominator of all Verne's heroes (which, again, they share with their creator) is the hunger (or thirst) for knowledge.

In an earlier chapter, I recalled Sartre's denunciation of the 'philosophie alimentaire', whose central premise, according to Sartre, is: 'connaître c'est manger'.[27] Verne is liable to attract Sartrian censure, since his writing proceeds demonstrably from the premise of a nutritive epistemology: consciousness is conceived on the model of the digestive system as an apparatus dedicated to the automatic internalization of external objects. Thus diet, no less than travel (the two are effectively inseparable), furnishes an organizing metaphor, in the *Voyages*, for the accumulation of knowledge. Nutrition and cognition, the two major activities on the Vernian *voyage*, are serviced by an identical vocabulary and coupled by a unitary philosophy.

This relation can be traced in Verne's archetypal fictive physique. An over-oxygenated, euphoric astronaut en route to the moon elicits the following statement: 'Tout en lui, estomac et cerveau, était surexcité au plus haut point.'[28] The nominal phrase in apposition implies what the *œuvre* as a whole continually reiterates: that the human anatomy, in the *Voyages*, incorporates only two internal (and no external) organs: the stomach and the brain. The innovatory Verne is the first among French novelists to excise the *cœur* quite so ruthlessly from the novel: all his heroes, not just his villains, are heartless. Or rather, the heart has not utterly disappeared, but has simply been displaced, occluded by other organic matter, as in the case of the *matelots*: 'il leur fallait une nourriture substantielle, car on peut dire qu'ils avaient le cœur au ventre'.[29] There is a view which maintains that Verne's fiction was new simply because it was the old with a lot left out. But this redistribution of physiological priorities suggests that distinctively different orders of interest and attention are inaugurated by the *Voyages*. Verne's writing champions a hierarchy of values distinct from the Romantic anthropocentric tradition; emblematically, it suppresses romance.[30]

If sailors appear to have hearts in their bellies, anthropophagous Maoris, in contrast, have brains (not their own) in theirs, for eating the intellectual organ of one's vanquished enemy is a privileged ritual among the New Zealanders: 'On hérite ainsi de son âme, de sa force, de sa valeur, qui sont particulièrement renfermées dans la cervelle.'[31] The brain, like the stomach, is a container, accommodating the soul, etc., which are chemical substances, not nebulous, extra-material entities. And the desirable, savoury contents of the brain can be absorbed by the process of digestion. But they are also initially acquired by an analogous process of cerebral nutrition.

The transaction between eating and apprehending is witnessed in the recurrent character of the savant (such as Clawbonny and Paganel) who is also, and no less brilliant, a cook: a processor of food and information: a *chef*. Metaphorically, it is usually the more intellectual that is envisaged in terms of the more carnal phenomenon. Thus Axel: 'J'avouerai que je mordis avec appétit aux sciences géologiques; j'avais du sang de minéralogiste dans les veines.'[32] The image is cannibalistic: it seems that Axel's enthusiasm for rocks stems from eating a mineralogist. A similar procedure results in the identification of algebraists as 'mangeurs d'x'.[33] More generally, scenes are portrayed as banquets, *fêtes des yeux*, wherein the verb *dévorer* is synonymous with *regarder*. Books, conceived of as vehicles of information, are, of course, conventionally predicated with the attributes of meals.[34] The substitution of *manger* for *lire* will occur obsessively in Verne's *œuvre*. But, through the operation of a characteristic manoeuvre, Verne converts a metaphorical vehicle into a literal tenor. In *L'Ile à hélice*, he imagines a type of disreputable newspaper destined to 'distraire un instant, en s'adressant à l'esprit . . . et même à l'estomac', and fulfilling this double function by way of being printed on an edible paste in chocolate-flavoured ink.[35]

For Verne, the progress of science, like the maintenance of corporeal health, is dependent on the multiplication of its inputs, or, more exactly, on their interminable addition. Knowledge, in this light, appears as essentially cumulative, a stockpile or summation, the end-product of a process of epistemological accretions, a corpus fed on the eminently assimilable data of the physical universe. This perspective suggests an explanation for Verne's mania for extensive lists, congeries of esoteric nouns: the Vernian inventory is the menu offered by the restaurant of nature for the sustenance of science.

Verne's *romans scientifiques* are suffused with a mythological and religious imagination. Scripture is regularly called into play, explicitly and implicitly, as a reservoir of archetypes, moral aphorisms, and narrative *exempla*. The book of Genesis in particular is a frequent source of quotation and allusion. So the figures of Adam and Eve recur as points of reference, as symbols, as metaphors, in comic and serious moods. Their ubiquity in the *Voyages* parallels that of Verne's savants, who undergo a recognizably Edenic encounter with experience: indifferent to, or disdainful of, prohibitions and limitations, urged on by the serpent of appetite, they regale themselves with the fruit plucked from every tree in the garden, especially *l'arbre de la science* (and not declining, in addition, beasts of the earth, fowl of the air, and even, occasionally, creeping things). The compulsion, perhaps pathological, to eat everything, corresponds to the admirable, but perhaps sinful ambition to know everything. Polyphagy and polymathy, bulimia and epistemophilia, obey a single corporate impulse.

Verne translates into fiction Yahweh's statement that 'the man is become as one of us' (Genesis 3:22): the Vernian savant gravitates irresistibly towards the condition of omniscience and the status of deity. The Vernian hero is a Job who does battle with his tormentors; to those divine questions intended to belittle puny humans – 'Hast thou entered into the springs of the sea? or hast thou walked in the search of the depth?' and 'Hast thou perceived the breadth of the earth? declare if thou knowest it all'[36] – he replies confidently in the affirmative. Hence the assertion that closes *Vingt mille lieues sous les mers* (apparently transposing Job to Ecclesiastes): 'Aussi, à cette demande posée, il y a six mille ans, par l'Ecclésiaste: "Qui a jamais pu sonder les profondeurs de l'abîme?" deux hommes entre tous les hommes ont le droit de répondre maintenant. Le capitaine Nemo et moi.' Verne's scientists thus carry out the programme set out by Flaubert's 'Science': 'Je veux savoir tout, je veux entrer jusqu'au noyau du globe [*Voyage au centre de la terre*], je veux marcher dans le lit de l'Océan [*Vingt mille lieues sous les mers*], je veux courir à travers le ciel, accroché à la queue des comètes [*Hector Servadac*]. Oh! je voudrais aller dans la lune pour entendre sous mes pieds craquer la neige argentée de ses rivages et pour descendre dans ses crevasses souterraines [*De la terre à la lune*; *Autour de la lune*].'[37]

In the *Voyages*, the higher the protagonist ascends the variously projected tree of knowledge (or, conversely, reflected on the retina of Verne's convex imagination, the lower he descends its inverted image: the abyss), the more aerial (or more subterranean) its fruit, the closer he approximates, perhaps blasphemously or parodically, to God. This strategy and philosophy are given axiomatic expression in the early short story on the Faustian model, *Maître Zacharius*, by the slogans magically appearing across a clockface: 'Il faut manger les fruits de l'arbre de la science' and 'L'homme peut devenir l'égal de Dieu.'[38] But no less than the youthful, fugitive Jules, hunted by a wrathful father (after stowing away aboard an ocean-bound schooner),[39] the overweening *voyageur* courts the attentions of nemesis. The final maxim flashed up on Zacharius's clock announces: 'Qui tentera de se faire l'égal de Dieu sera *damné* pour l'éternité.'[40]

The quest for knowledge entails the destiny of exile from the enclosure of the garden.[41] Pursuing his claim to divinity, the truth-seeker must relinquish his claim to security and stability; his possession of knowledge, like the satisfaction of Vernian voracity, is strictly provisional, precarious, jeopardized by conflict with physical limitations and barriers, and contradictory ethical regulations, by the prospect of a catastrophic fall from grace, by famine, and, ultimately, by the restoration of a condition of ignorance. Intellectual *besoins* typically exceed the *forces* available to satisfy them. The desire for plenitude (physical repletion and epistemic completion) may be frustrated by *inanition*, an inner void. Knowledge, even as it expands to consume the universe, is being gnawed away from within. Thus cognition, by the same token as its twin, nutrition, is subject to the sway of reversibility.

The dream of omniscience coupled to the practice of omnivoracity; and, reflected in the mirror of negation, involuntary abstinence haunted by the nightmare of nescience: such are the main coordinates of Jules Verne's oneiric and chiastic career.

4.2 The omniscient author

The works of numerous nineteenth-century French writers profess an ambition to exhaust all the possible predicates of any one or more of a cluster of nouns: history, Paris, women, the future. Such transcendent intellectual programmes are, however, easily transcended by Verne's monumental project: to exhaust all possible nouns.

Just as Marx would expound the economically-framed laws of dialectical history, so Comte, for whom sociology was indistinguishable from the sum of everything human, embraced (he thought) the history of thought, deciphered its evolutionary laws, and was thus in a position to predict its future, which happened to be identical with his personal intellectual present. Dumas, imagining a hero doomed to immortality, conceived the (inevitably unfinished) *Isaac Laquedem*, in which the procession of humanity through time would be attended by an eternal spectator.[42] Balzac's *Comédie humaine* proposed the detailed elucidation of an entire society during a crucial phase of its history, which (it was held) would also constitute a timeless metaphor of mankind. No matter how extensive their range, or how comprehensive their vision, what all these writers share in common, in the last analysis, is that each is reductivist and essentialist. They could not afford to be otherwise; for their projects to stand a chance of completion, the innumerable phenomena of existence needed to be portrayed as the enumerable incarnations of a few archetypes. The more ambitious Verne, disdaining all diminution and exclusion, renounces the profile of localized pseudo-totalities, mere monads, in favour of the undiminished, inclusive description of the physical universe.

The nineteenth century marks the conjunction of expansive conceptual designs with the formal spaciousness of the novel. The

Voyages, a fictional sequence more euphoric and hyperbolic than Balzac's and Zola's, which seems to travesty by espousing their implicit aesthetic, aims imperiously at stretching the novel to accommodate nothing less than everything. What others had accomplished partially, Verne would complete.

The immoderate nature of that aesthetic programme has been famously evoked by Hetzel in his 'Avertissement', where he baldly proclaims that the purpose of Verne's *œuvre* is to execute a singular plan, namely, to

résumer toutes les connaissances *géographiques*, *géologiques*, *physiques*, *astronomiques*, amassées par la science moderne, et de refaire, sous la forme attrayante et pittoresque qui lui est propre, l'histoire de l'univers.[43]

Verne's own accounts of his immodest proposal are no less uncompromising. His task, he writes, in the brief 'Souvenirs d'enfance et de jeunesse', is to 'peindre la terre entière, le monde entier, sous la forme du roman'. Verne opines that such a task is not impossible; a century or so might suffice to accomplish it. His stark conclusion is this: 'C'est bien difficile.'[44]

Verne seeks to realize Laplace's ideal of collecting all the data in the universe (thereby acquiring knowledge of the past and the future as well as of the present). To encompass the totality of things, he proposes to articulate the totality of words available for their designation. Thus he belongs to that class of writers for whom in order to say anything it is necessary to say everything. *Tout dire*, Rousseau's autobiographical ideal, stands as the ruling imperative of the *Voyages*. But Verne reiterates the scientific apprehension of language rendered equivocal by usage. He is particularly apprehensive regarding metaphor; hence Paganel's warning to a youth (criticizing Chateaubriand's comparison of *flamant* and *flèche*): 'Ah, Robert, la comparaison, vois-tu bien, est la plus dangereuse figure de rhétorique que je connaisse. Défie-t'en toute la vie; et ne l'emploie qu'à la dernière extrémité.'[45] Mere linguistic constructions must be supported by the unshakeable foundations of mathematics. Thus in Verne's fiction, mimesis is supplemented or supplanted by mathesis, whose task it is to accommodate the plurality of the world within a unitary discourse. The principal figures of the *Voyages* are not the tropes of rhetoric but the integers of arithmetic and the model structures of geometry. Science seeks to emulate mathematics; literature shares the origins of dream: Verne, assimilating literature to science, offers a mathematical dream or an oneiric mathematics.

Leibniz invokes man as his model of God. The distinction between man and God is relative, not absolute, and corresponds to the distinction between truths of reason and truths of experience, respectively exemplified by mathematics and history. Whereas we, largely ignorant, have perfect cognizance of only a part of reality, God, intellectually unlimited, apprehends the whole: for the divine mind, the miscellaneous physical facts of time and space are as self-evident as the laws of geometry are for us.[46] Thus the epistemological attainments of man and God differ only in degree not in kind, in quantity rather than quality. Verne inverts the equation and eliminates the difference: following Genesis, he invokes God as his model of man, and expands the intensive knowledge of mathematics to incorporate the extensive world. The basic cognitive manoeuvre of his novels consists in situating the contingent data of the empirical sphere under the tautological umbrella of mathematics, projecting the light of *a priori* certitude into the shadows of the *a posteriori*, displacing the qualitative by the quantitative.

Verne is a modern Pythagoras, the disciple of mathematical mysticism. For Pythagoras, all things were numbers. Similarly, for Verne, numbers are not merely the yardstick of truth, they are the ultimate reality, more immutable and eternal than the heavenly bodies. Numbers are the key to understanding the universe because the key to understanding is measurement; they open a channel of communication between human intelligence and things. Arithmetic is thus fundamental to both physics and aesthetics, to beauty and truth, since it offers at once an ideal of precision and intelligibility, and a practical tool for grasping reality. Verne (the Buddhist might say) is in the thrall of *maya*.

Vernian man, as Foucault has observed, is a *homo calculator*:[47] he subordinates the task of description to the technique of computation. Thus there is a whole chapter in *Vingt mille lieues sous les mers*, modestly entitled 'Quelques chiffres', devoted exclusively to the narrator's analytical formulation of the construction, dimensions, and technical capabilities of the *Nautilus*. Throughout their many volumes, the *Voyages* display a fascination with sheer quantity, with enormous, almost inconceivable numbers. Thus a Vernian narrator refers admiringly to the 'méduses microscopiques observées par Scoresby dans les mers de Groënland, et dont ce navigateur évalue le nombre à vingt-trois trilliards huit cent quatre-vingt-huit billiards de milliards dans un espace de deux milles carrés'.[48] Such extreme precision verges on incomprehensibility, so Verne obligingly elucidates in a footnote: 'Ce nombre échappant à toute appréciation de l'esprit, le baleinier anglais, afin de le rendre plus compréhensible, disait qu'à le compter, quatre-vingt mille individus auraient été occupés jour et nuit depuis la création du monde.' Verne seems to retrospectively elide all trace of innumerate innocence: Adam and Eve would have been better off computing. All Verne's characters are afflicted, to a greater or lesser degree, with this numerical intoxication; but it is perceived as a virtue not a vice. Human distinctiveness and dignity are derived, in the Vernian universe, precisely from the ability to quantify time and space. The heroes of *L'Ile mystérieuse*, whose first task is to measure the meridian and plot their position, know that Ayrton, the other castaway they eventually rescue, has been reduced to a state of animal savagery because he no longer knows what year it is. The visible signs of this obsession are omnipresent: watches, clocks, barometers, speedometers, altimeters, etc. Asked how much he had written, Verne is reputed to have replied: 'At least three yards.'[49]

But Verne is finally dissatisfied with the simple arithmetical quantification of randomly distributed, multifarious objects. He seeks to limit his seemingly limitless subject by containing infinity within the conjugation of a finite number of fixed patterns. Thus intolerance of unassimilable contingency is allied to the cultivation of a geometrical rhetoric and a reverence for machine-tooled objects. T. E. Hulme has lucidly characterized this attitude, which he associates with the expression of religious values:

The disgust with the trivial and the accidental characteristics of living shapes, the searching after an austerity, a monumental stability and permanence, a perfection and rigidity, which vital things can never have, leads to the use of forms which can almost be called *geometrical*.[50]

In order to make this analysis consistent with Verne's *œuvre*, it would only be necessary to omit the timid adverb 'almost'.

Pierre Macherey has called the *Voyages* 'les aventures de la ligne droite'.[51] Michel Serres, on the contrary, has discerned therein only successive variations on the theme of the circle ('Il n'y a pas une ligne droite chez Verne, pas une seule').[52] But the mission of Verne's composite traveller is less exclusive than either view suggests: to discover and retrace the infinite line postulated by Nicholas of Cusa which would be simultaneously a straight line, a triangle, a circle, and a sphere (and therefore equivalent to the *maximum absolutum* and the *maximum contractum*);[53] he dreams of being, like the God of Nicholas's mathematical theology, simultaneously at the centre and at the circumference of the all-embracing sphere that is the universe.

Two novels revolve around agents whose dual and complementary ambitions, to descend to the centre of the earth and to circuit the circumference of that imperfect spheroid, comprise a comprehensive impersonation of the deity of Nicholas; they are *Voyage au centre de la terre* and *Le Tour du monde en quatre-vingts jours*.

4.3 Planet Earth

Although Vernian man, physiologically speaking, is heartless (and bereft of a Vernian woman to make good this deficiency by her cardiac abundance), *le cœur* is not wholly absent from the *Voyages*: it resides in the sphere of the non-human, transferred to the possession of things, located at their cold and invisible centre. Thus the novelistic tradition of the sentimental romance of *les âmes* (temporarily lodged in *les corps*) is supplanted by the scientific romance of *les choses*.

While the phenomena of nature, in Balzac, are assimilated to the phenomena of human society, pressed into service in a battery of reflexive, analogical accessories, they are relieved, by the Vernian transformation of figurative vehicles into literal tenors, of their burden of metaphoric anthropocentrism. While men are often reduced to the status of things – all exteriority – things are vitalized, become more complex, unpredictable: they constitute part of the personnel, the true *dramatis personae* of Verne's fiction.[54] Balzac concentrates on unravelling the labyrinthine intricacies of the *pour-soi*; Verne's proclaimed mission is to dramatize *l'être-là* of the *en-soi*, the autonomous being and presence of the alien world. The latter's *Voyages extraordinaires* constitute a quasi-scientific rival to the former's quasi-mystical *œuvre*, a sort of *Comédie inhumaine*. They elaborate a system in which man, implicitly, is no more than a single element (or combination of elements) among others, just as in cosmology the world is just another planet: Verne is to Balzac what Copernicus is to Ptolemy. Whereas Balzac's fully adjectivized decor is notoriously permeated with the qualities of the humanity whose backcloth it is, men and things in Verne (despite the mediation of number) are alienated from each other by the absence of common epithets. Vernian objects are never mere psychological or sociological hieroglyphs, ultimately displaced by their Rosetta stone of connotation, but intractable unknowns, requiring inspection and analysis.

The subtitle given to the *Voyages extraordinaires* is 'Voyages dans les mondes connus et inconnus'. *L'inconnu* represents the area in which Verne's imaginary landscapes and inventions are inscribed; but, curiously, his fiction dramatizes the urge to reduce and eliminate that abhorrent, uninspected space, to do away with the very possibility of fiction. The persistent ideal foregrounded in Verne's novels anticipates the enclosure and annexation of the unknown by the familiar and expanding boundaries of the known. For the Vernian savant, the unmapped, the uncodified portions of reality pose an intolerable and provocative threat to his authority (founded on cartography and codification). So long as there remain undiscovered countries, unexplored regions of the earth, so long as unseen objects and creatures persist unnamed, resisting colonization by the empire of science (in whose domain knowledge is synonymous with possession), the dominion of epistemic man is unstable, susceptible to usurpation.

In the *Voyages*, the unknown, and its human correlative, ignorance, are figures in the negative landscape of the partial void. For Sartre, the *pour-soi* of consciousness, loaded with its anguished freight of self-conscious *néant*, is mocked by the massive solidity of the *en-soi*, things whose outside and inside are identical and continuous.[55] For the non-anthropocentric Verne, the reverse is true: while the conscious observer is reassuringly wholesome and selfconsistent, untroubled by self-doubt,[56] unconscious matter is alarmingly vacuous. For both, the stone is a recurrent point of reference: the Sartrian text depicts it as unified, authentic, soulless; the Vernian, on the other hand, discovers an absent centre beneath a deceptive surface which, weakened by internal vacancy, is liable to cave in or burst open. The Vernian *pierre* is brother to the truant Sartrian Pierre.[57]

While humanity is almost exclusively superficial, unambiguous, decipherable, the non-human, in contrast, is pervaded by the mystery of hollowness. Axel, apprentice savant and youthful companion to Professor Lidenbrock in *Voyage au centre de la terre*, is initially, prophetically, engaged in labelling and arranging in their display cases 'toutes ces pierres creuses au-dedans desquelles s'agitaient de petits cristaux'.[58] Later, situated in a subterranean cavern glitteringly illuminated by his party's lamps, he imagines himself to be travelling through 'un diamant creux'.[59] *Le creux* seems to exercise a magnetic attraction over Verne's metallic *voyageurs*: it is at once alarming and irresistible.

The world itself constitutes a paradigm case of hollowness. Discontinuous, porous, perforated, its surface is ruptured by innumerable orifices – volcanic craters, chasms, abysses, gulfs – indicating the covert presence of an enticing *profondeur*, and pointing down into *grottes*, caverns, intraplanetary spaces mirroring the void of interplanetary space.[60] Our honeycomb globe presents the dangerous and voluptuous feature of multiple orality: its crust is envisaged as a series of mouths, *bouches* or *gueules*. A frugal diet can change 'l'estomac en un gouffre profond';[61] the Vernian law of reciprocity requires that the 'gouffre', conversely, should be an 'estomac'. Like the voracious, anthropophagous beasts that populate the *Voyages*, the telluric *entrailles* (ravaged by intestinal seismic disturbances) threaten to swallow up (*avaler*, *engouffrer*, *engloutir*) innocent bystanders. But Verne's travellers are not even innocent; they tend to suffer from the complex of Empedocles: accomplices of their consumers, they plainly wish to be swallowed up. Thus the fanatical Captain Hatteras has to be forcibly restrained from launching himself into the crater which turns out to occupy the North Pole.

Physical and intellectual vacancies are intimately related: the abstract enterprise of filling in the gaps and interstices of knowledge is translated into the mission of tabulating or vanquishing the plethora of orifices that inhabit nature. The libidinous occupation of the *voyageur* consists in occupying any available apertures. As in Genesis, the acquisition of knowledge is inseparable from carnal discovery. Thus the volcano is, among other things, the gateway to the sphere of Eros.[62]

Almost invariably, the novels of the *Voyages* state a problem, in Verne's own term, an *énigme*, often posed by the discovery of a more or less mysterious text, whose sense or solution has to be tested or attained by means of a journey. In *Voyage au centre de la terre* the intellectual dilemma of a runic cryptogram to be decoded (inviting the decoders to repeat the encoder's Orphic descent), spatially transposed, assumes the form of a labyrinth to be explored.[63] The stages of the journey, its directions and indirections, the entanglements in, and eventual re-emergence from the labyrinth, correspond to the successive phases of the formulation, the mystification, and final elucidation of the enigma. In the terms proposed by Barthes in *S/Z*, the 'hermeneutic' and 'proaïretic' codes intermesh. In other words, the characteristic narrative structure of the *Voyages* effects a synthesis of the detective novel (a genre whose elaboration in the stories of Poe, Verne admired) and the adventure story, a composite form whose distinctive feature is the interdependence of discovery and displacement.

The scientific puzzle that Professor Lidenbrock proposes to resolve by his speleological journey is whether or not the earth is hollow. While most geologists, it is admitted, favour the view that the core of the earth is molten, and therefore inhospitable to visitors, Lidenbrock postulates a thermal frontier beyond which the subterranean explorer can disport himself at ease. But although the narrative repeatedly anticipates an answer, the question is never satisfactorily resolved. Lidenbrock and Axel (in common with the majority of *voyageurs*) fail to reach their appointed destination, and the concluding statement by the narrator (Axel) manages to be firmly inconclusive, while supporting received scientific opinions: 'je crois et je croirai toujours à la chaleur centrale; mais j'avoue que certaines circonstances mal définies peuvent modifier cette loi sous l'action de phénomènes naturels'.[64] The Lidenbrockian hypothesis is clearly a necessary premise or pretext for the fabulation of the story, but it also registers the recurrent suspicion, amounting to an obsession, shared by so many of Verne's emissaries, that all objects conceal a vacuity at their centre.

The journey records a double excursion, at once spatial and temporal, down into the earth and backwards in time. Darkness, a sign of the tyranny of the unknown, is as intolerable to the Vernian explorer as an unplumbed depth. Thus the technological ingenuity of the savants is dedicated to maintaining and expanding a central point of light (like an island) in the midst of a measureless circle of night. The subterranean *voyageurs*, like the electrically-powered beam of Captain Nemo's submarine, the *Nautilus*, banish obscurity by constantly extending the area of illumination, pushing in front of them a pool of transparency that renders their environment not only visible but eminently decipherable.

The lightless underground world acquires through the intervention of men the luminous intelligibility of a pellucid manuscript or book. Repeatedly, the constituents of the earth are enumerated in a scriptural or textual metaphor: 'Toute l'histoire de la période houillère était écrite sur ces sombres parois, et un géologue en pouvait suivre facilement les phases diverses.'[65] The contents of the huge but determinate book of nature are readable and, hence, nameable: 'Je mettais sans hésiter un nom à ces os gigantesques.'[66] Paleontology, in short, is conceived in paleographical terms, as a fossilized orthography readily disclosing its secrets to the hermeneutic eye of the reader.

Thus the savant's craving for information is temporarily assuaged. And while the contents of the earth are consumed by the visitors from the surface, it cannot consume or contain them. Humans prove to be unfit for telluric consumption: avidly swallowed up, they give rise to intestinal disturbance, a digestive upset, and are consequently regurgitated: 'repoussés, expulsés, rejetés, vomis, expectorés dans les airs'.[67] Descent into the interior via the crater of the extinct Sneffels is mirrored by reascent to the exterior via the chimney of an erupting Stromboli (aboard the remarkably durable remains of a wooden boat).

The volcano participates doubly in Verne's binary topology of prominences and cavities: it is a hollow pyramid connecting the heavens with the underground inferno; and it is a two-way sliproad onto the dual carriageway of human traffic leading into and out of the earth's core. Like the ocean depths, the contents of the volcano are accessible, either through descent into the interior or as a result of eruption evacuating the earth of its mysterious, desirable, but also potentially lethal insides. The Vernian law of reciprocity requires that not only should man urgently plumb the depths of the planet, but that the earth's core should equally strain to escape from secrecy, burst through its fragile skin and so stand revealed in the sight of men. Science and nature, here at least, by reason of their opposite inclinations, harmonize. Finally, the volcano is the entrance to an inverted universe; and it preserves an imprint of that inversion, comprising a portion of the subterranean world violently everted and solidified, the abyss turned inside out by an explosion. Conversely, the outer world appears to have slipped inwards, and been turned upside down: like a mirror-image of the volcano, a portion of the external surface occurs internally in the shape of a gigantic cavern, equipped with its own Mediterranean and pseudo-firmament.

Paradoxically, the more deeply the *voyageurs* descend into the earth, the further they advance (not retreat) in its history; while the shallowest levels of the crust display evidence of the most remote periods, man, earth's most recent creation, is discovered at the lowest point visited. Descending, the text implies, is synonymous with (re)ascending 'l'échelle de la vie animale'.[68] The baffled Axel (it is the duty of at least one member of any expedition to be perpetually baffled or ignorant in order that he, and his *alter ego*, the reader, should be educated) inquires how it is that animal life belonging to the 'périodes secondaires' can be located *beneath* the incandescent rock formations of the 'époque primitive'? Lidenbrock replies:

A une certaine époque, la terre n'était formée que d'une écorce élastique, soumise à des alternatifs de haut et de bas, en vertu des lois de l'attraction.

Il est probable que des affaissements du sol se sont produits, et qu'une partie des terrains sédimentaires a été entraînée au fond des gouffres subitement ouverts.[69]

The professor subsequently refines his theory by surmising that the progressive cooling of the globe produced 'des cassures, des fentes, des failles, où dévalait vraisemblablement une partie du terrain supérieur'.[70] The alternating motions of ascent and descent are thus linked by a systematic rhythm of undulation whose kinetic force is derived from the physical instabilities and discontinuities of the planet.

The moral that what goes up must come down governs the balloon journey and the climbing expedition, while its converse rules the subterranean explorations and the itinerary of the *Nautilus*. It is a characteristic curiosity of the *Voyage au centre de la terre* that Axel's 'leçons d'abîmes' in preparation for his descent into the earth consist in the repeated ascent of a clock-tower.[71] But it is the lunar journey, above all, that confirms the apparent equality of contrary directions: *monter* (from the earth) and *tomber* (towards the moon) are encompassed by a single trajectory. The two events are not alternatives but twins, the simultaneous components of an indivisible coupling. Opposite motions are not merely mutual reflections, causally connected or temporally contiguous: it seems, in Verne's paradoxical cosmogony, as if they are equivalent, identical, rigorously interchangeable phenomena. Like acceleration and gravity in Einstein's system, ascent and descent, in Verne's, can be difficult or impossible to distinguish. All motion is relative: cosmologically speaking, there are no ups and downs, only motion through de-referentialized space.

The elasticity of movement in the *Voyages* has inspired the opinion that the central figure of Verne's *œuvre* is the sine-curve.[72] But the systole and diastole of ascent and descent should not be seen in isolation from the conjunction of other antithetical and complementary processes. Thus, in *L'Ile mystérieuse*, in the flight from a Confederate camp which leads, after the ascent by balloon, to a descent into isolation and imprisonment on a remote island, the theme of escape is mirrored by that of sequestration. Again, the notion of interiority, of enclosure, constantly precipitates that of transcendence, and vice-versa. In the *Voyages*, it is virtually impossible to get outside one thing without simultaneously getting inside something else: every exit entails an entrance. Thus the wave-like configuration of the sine-curve, like the Vernian journey, is subordinate to the more general law of reversibility (to whose operation the earlier account of nutrition has already testified). This law governs, moreover, the decoding of the cryptogram (itself a figure of the journey), which transposes vertically a horizontal arrangement of letters, subsequently retransposed into the horizontal plane, that must be read backwards from the bottom upwards, and from right to left. The circle, in which beginning and end are invisibly dissolved, affords a further amplification of the geometry of indefinite reversibility.

Circularity is programmed into the mobile hardware of *Le Tour du monde en quatre-vingts jours*. The circuit of the earth is the barely anthropomorphized translation into geographical vocabulary of a figural abstraction, an ideal of geometrical and mechanical perfection; the adverb elicited by the verb *voyager* is *mathématiquement*. Thus the circumnavigatory Phileas Fogg is perceived as an efficient machine: 'Il ne voyageait plus, il décrivait une circonférence. C'était un corps grave, parcourant une orbite du globe terrestre, suivant les lois de la mécanique rationnelle.'[73] The Vernian hero is recklessly confident of his geographical vocation: to demonstrate his insouciance, Fogg accepts and encourages potentially ruinous bets on his ability to put into practice his *prima facie* implausible theories. But Fogg's project proposes more than a simple maximization of global speed, as specified by the wager: it challenges the contingency of the material world, defies the arbitrary flux of *l'imprévu* – obstacles and interruptions, delays and disasters both mechanical and human in origin – that chance opposes to the sequential clarity and temporal rigour of *Bradshaw's Railway, Steam Transit, and General Guide*, the international timetable that is Fogg's preferred reading matter. The tour represents the successful application of a Euclidean discipline to matter, denotes the transportation of pure into applied mathematics. And the completion of the circuit in the period allotted, achieving the chronometric precision prescribed by a train schedule, flaunts a scientific triumph over the vagaries of time. Thus the journey effects a salutary purification, a sanitization of the empirical.

Fogg's itinerary, exhausting all available means of transport, binding the globe with a 'chaîne de communication',[74] seeks to encompass and interconnect discrete locations: distant continents, countries, cities, like the coordinates of a graph, are aligned by the draughtsmanlike inscription of a circle across their surface. But motion about the terrestrial sphere incorporates not only disconnected points but the perfect parallel lines of the American railways and the triangular Indian subcontinent.[75] Fogg can therefore be seen as the emissary of Nicholasian geometry, the assembler of a compendium of patterns that constitute, in sum, a description of the universe.

The aim of the *Encyclopédie* is to accomplish a geodesic journey around the sphere of knowledge: it is a textual circle, the archival embodiment of that figure's closed, corporate geometry. Encirclement, it follows, is the geographical, spatial homologue of encyclopedian exhaustiveness and epistemological enclosure. But, in the diverse forms of the grand (global) tour, it also underlies the teleology of the *Voyages*. Thus circumnavigation is the encyclopedic manoeuvre par excellence, and the diagrammatic incarnation of the Vernian quest for a totalization of knowledge. Truth for Verne, as for Nicholas, is a circle.

In both *Voyage au centre de la terre* and *Le Tour du monde en quatre-vingts jours*, narrative structure coincides with the relative mobility of the protagonists, their progression or delays, their directions and indirections. Verne's problem, perhaps the problem of any writer, is only partly how to complete the text, to say everything; it is also how not to complete it too soon, not to say everything at once. 'Raconter', remarks Serres, 'c'est éviter le court-circuit.'[76] Specifically, in the *Voyages*, Verne's task is to enhance the importance of destinations by postponing their attainment, and to interrupt and retard the journey sufficiently to allow or justify, en route, erudite excursions around the scientific archive. Thus the multiplication of impediments, obstacles, errors, red herrings, etc., obeys a didactic function. The devious narrative, begetter of frustrations, opposes a series of countervailing objects and situations to the purposiveness of the *voyageurs*.

In *Le Tour du Monde*, Phileas Fogg is relentlessly pursued around the globe by a detective, Fix, who (as his name suggests) plans to arrest our hero – on suspicion of theft – and supposes his journey to be a flight, motivated by the desire to elude justice. The intended arrest is, however, itself arrested, held in suspension by the delay or annulment of the requisite *mandat d'arrestation*, until Fogg returns to England, where Fix recovers jurisdiction. But prefigurations of the event are evenly distributed along the route, in the shape of human stratagems or mechanical failure. And the actual arrest, one of two deceptive, premature conclusions (the other is Fogg's seemingly overdue return to London, following his release from custody, his innocence of the charge established), prefigures the actual conclusion, when Fogg is successfully restored to the Reform Club, his point of departure, the circuit closed and the text terminated. Fogg and Fix, as the alliteration on their names implies, form a comic couple; literally inseparable ('On eût dit qu'un fil le [Fix] rattachait à cet homme [Fogg]'),[77] they are mutually indispensable in the economy of the narrative. Fix is a shadow, an *alter ego*, a mirror-image of the chief protagonist, characterized by the same abstract, impersonal persistence: against his quarry's will to motion, he opposes the will to immobilization. Like the procedures of ascent and descent, these twin characters embody equal and opposite forces locked in a ceaseless struggle for primacy.

In *Voyage au centre de la terre*, the fastest, most direct route to the appointed destination describes a perpendicular with respect to the surface; but this hypothetical ideal is rarely attained in practice, proving either untraceable or impracticable. Thus the increasingly impatient Lidenbrock is deflected from his projected path by circuitous detours, indirect or erroneous byways, and, most redundantly, by merely horizontal routes, involving the fatigue of displacement without the compensation of bringing the destination any nearer. Understandably, the professor 'pestait contre l'horizontalité, lui, "l'homme des verticales"'.[78] The antithetical planes of travel, alternately vertical and horizontal, correspond to the shifting phases, or gears, of narrative progression, of advancement towards, and postponement of, an anticipated ending.

These persistent narrative structures, which it is not difficult to discern elsewhere in the *Voyages*, with their binary contrasts between verticality and horizontality, and circulatory mobility and arrest, are not, however, arbitrary: they embody Verne's alternative models of human history.

4.4 Perpendicularity and circularity

Like all Verne's iterative images, his twin models of history are diagrammatic and geometrical. One, occupying the vertical plane, depicts man at a perpendicular angle to the rest of the world;[79] the other, occupying the horizontal, confines him within the circumference of circular time.

Verticality projects a theory of human evolution as continuous progress in the form of a gradual transition from the purely carnal to the purely cerebral, analogous to a rectilinear ascent from a flat surface. Man is pictured climbing upwards through time, swinging from rung to rung of a Jacobian ladder or ever higher on a scaffolding of his own invention. The central verb in this theory is *monter*, denoting an activity prominent in many of the *Voyages*: all the *voyageurs* are climbers by choice or necessity; with obsessional frequency, they undertake to scale mountains, volcanoes, walls, obstacles of all kinds. But only European man is situated squarely at the top of the evolutionary *échelle*: dark-skinned foreigners, together with intelligent orang-outangs, inhabit some obscure intermediary rung.

There is, in fact, considerable ambiguity concerning the position of man in relation to animal life. Being less preoccupied with ideological coherence than with intellectual comprehensiveness, Verne is free to make glancing references to rival theories of evolution. The *Voyages* play off against one another, rather than choose between or reconcile, at least two available accounts: the Darwinian, supporting the image of a single but complex ladder, or tree, with upper and lower rungs or branches occupied respectively by man and ape; and the Lamarckian, resting on a premise of separate development, and isolating man on an independent ladder of his own, quite divorced from other species. Darwinism represents a horizon of possibility and anxiety: while it is only hypothetical that man evolved out of lower animals, it is certain that he is capable of evolving into one; he has an inalterable potential for degenerating into bestiality. Thus, on the one hand, even the primitive Australian is free of an ignoble ancestry: 'Entre la brute et l'Australien existe l'infranchissable abîme qui sépare les genres';[80] but, on the other, shipwrecked sailors behave brutishly: 'C'est un instinct béstial qui nous entraîne et que nul ne peut réprimer. Il semble, en cet instant, que nous n'avons plus rien d'humain.'[81] There is no evidence sufficient to arbitrate between the alternative hypotheses; instead, it is the responsibility of man to prove himself, by his intellectual endeavours, uniquely human. The *voyageur*, consequently, is under an obligation to transcend Darwinism, and establish his Lamarckian credentials.

In Vernian evolution, not only is man a privileged species, but within that category certain classes, or races, are more privileged than others; and only outstanding members of those doubly favoured groups are capable of activating their full potential for development. The ladder is narrow and competition for the occupation of its highest rungs intense. The chief apprehension of the climbers concerns the danger of a sudden and involuntary descent, *la chute*. At or beyond the bottom of the ladder lie the measureless *gouffres* that threaten to swallow up the careless or reckless or unlucky climber.[82]

If Verne's reversible itineraries allow of one distinction between motion upwards and downwards, it is that while the latter is potentially interminable, condemning the victim to an infinite fall in bottomless space, the former appears to provide for a terminus. Verne's theory of progress postulates a finite ladder terminating in a platform or plateau: a lateral departure from the anguish of perpendicularity, a horizontal space supporting a condition of stasis free from the danger of falling that afflicts the vertical. Analogously, *manger* is succeeded by *dormir*, the post-prandial snooze, and epistemic consumption by the satisfaction of intellectual plenitude. Thus the Vernian climber and truth-seeker looks forward to the completion of his monumental task.[83]

The successful climber should, in principle, be rewarded by *repos*; at the end of his ascent he can relax. Hence the ideal state of satiation and inactivity devoutly wished for by the Zartog (Doctor) Sofr-Aï-Sr at the conclusion of *L'Eternel Adam*:

Mais le jour viendrait-il jamais où serait satisfait l'insatiable désir de l'homme? Le jour viendrait-il jamais où celui-ci, ayant achevé de gravir la pente, pourrait se reposer sur le sommet enfin conquis?[84]

But these questions are of course rhetorical: they predict a negative response: they look forward only to the endless repetition of an onerous task. In their sceptical or frankly pessimistic mood, the *Voyages* depict the climber not as a Hillary who, having conquered his Everest, is allowed to rest on his laurels, but as a Sisyphean toiler, condemned to repeat the periodic motions of ascent and descent. All motion in the vertical plane then comes to seem irrelevant or illusory. *L'Eternel Adam*[85] is effectively a negation of verticality, subordinating all evolutionary theories of progressive man to a horizontal model of history as a circle.

In this short story, the 195th anniversary of the empire of the Mahart-Item-Schu (over a virtually unrecognizable earth in a remote century of the future) is being celebrated by a gathering of intellectuals and scholars, 'une pléiade de savants', who proudly tot up 'le bilan du savoir humain'[86] (a characteristically nineteenth-century pastime), each specifying the triumphant attainments of his own speciality. Sofr-Aï-Sr, an exemplary member of the scientific community, ponders the mystery of man's evolution, and, despite conflicting archaeological evidence implying the prior existence of defunct civilizations, adumbrates a reassuring, optimistic schema of human progress in accordance with the vertical model: life (he asserts) débute par les formes les plus simples, et va toujours se compliquant pour aboutir finalement à l'homme, son expression dernière et la plus parfaite. L'homme, à peine apparu sur la terre, commence aussitôt et poursuit sans arrêt son ascension. D'une marche lente mais sûre, il s'achemine vers sa fin, qui est la connaissance parfaite et la domination absolue de l'univers.[87]

The very existence of man is itself an instance of evolution's inherent teleology, its capacity to achieve definitive perfection, and seems to herald a conclusion to man's striving, a *fin* denoting the accomplishment of a vocation. Man, the hopeful traveller, will arrive at his appointed destination; his journey is inevitable but not interminable; his knowledge of the universe moves inexorably towards completion.

But these reported opinions are inflected by narratorial interventions, dissenting footnotes interrupting and disrupting this self-congratulatory hymn to humanity. On the upper part of the page, we are informed that man is greater than the immense universe of which he is the predestined master; while lower down, that his contemporary representatives 'ignoraient encore le téléphone et la lumière électrique'[88] – in Verne's technological universe, a damning indictment. Moreover, although the Zartog yearns for intellectual plenitude, dreams of possessing 'la vérité intégrale', he is uneasily aware that his own knowledge is far from complete; in particular, he realizes that his theory of human development is still only a fragile hypothesis rather than an impregnable truth. And with the discovery of an ancient manuscript, Sofr's vertical model is shattered.

Skipping over the long years of deciphering, the narrative initiates an internal, secondary narrative, the translated text of the unearthed document. The text-within-the-text, in its opening section, displays an exact parallel with the opening of the outer text: it recounts (this time in the first person) the congregation (around a dinner table) of a number of men who complacently applaud the unsurpassed scientific achievements of mankind: 'On s'accorda sur ce point que l'humanité avait atteint un niveau intellectuel inconnu avant notre époque, et qui autorisait à croire à sa victoire définitive sur la nature.'[89] The sense of *déjà-lu* for the reader corresponds to the sense of *déjà-vu* for the primary narrative's protagonist, reader of the secondary narrative. The secondary narrator is the double of the Zartog: a prematurely assertive savant and advocate of evolutionary verticality. He, like Sofr, scoffs at the hypothesis of prior civilizations, and the apprehension that the present one might be utterly destroyed. The action of the inner narrative then over-

147

takes that of the outer; the next sentence reads: 'Ce fut à cet instant précis que survint le cataclysme.'

The double hubris of the dual protagonists suffers instant deflation; both sets of parallel histories and prophecies are simultaneously overthrown. A small group of survivors from the earlier, duplicate civilization is isolated on an island, where its members rapidly regress into animality, amnesia, and inarticulacy. The threat of famine is accompanied by total intellectual decadence.[90] In terms of Verne's fictive physiology, stomach and brain enjoy a state of harmonious equilibrium in the healthy body; the Platonic future predicted by the savant envisages the triumph of brain over stomach; but the pathological deterioration that may be mankind's alternative fate reverses the equation: 'notre vie cérébrale est abolie. Manger, manger, c'est notre but perpétuel, notre préoccupation exclusive.'[91] Man's epistemological appetite is rendered subservient to simple nutrition.

At the level of the primary narrative, the Zartog's optimism gives way to doubt, then to despair. Perceiving the analogy between his and his double's civilizations, he realizes that far from man necessarily ascending a ladder into a cornucopian future, he is trapped in a futile iterative loop, doomed to repeat the illusions and disillusionment of his predecessors. The resonant final sentence declares that '[il] acquérait, lentement, et douloureusement, l'intime conviction de l'éternel recommencement des choses'.[92] In the *Voyages* abstract ideas are invariably articulated in graphic forms; here, the vision of palingenesis (whose legendary correlative is Atlantis), supplanting the evolutionary concept of vertical, progressive history, is embodied both in the symmetrical structure of the double narrative and in the image of the island, like the secondary, inner narrative, enclosed within a circle: 'ce seul point solide du cercle immense décrit par l'horizon'.[93] The circumnavigational enclosure of the globe, a symbolic acting-out of the programme of intellectual completion, transposed from the spatial dimension into the temporal destiny of historical circularity, presupposes an ineluctable regression to intellectual zero: as in Nicholas, a maximum and a minimum coincide.

In *L'Etre et le néant*, Sartre asserts that the 'cercle . . . est la caractéristique de la situation en général';[94] his analysis is perfectly applicable to the experience of the Vernian traveller. In the Sartrean metaphysic, circularity, with its implication of purposeless, directionless dynamism, exhausting the desire for revolution in mere rotation about an axis, stands as a coefficient of absurdity; and it is the affliction visited upon the sinners of Dante's Hell (and repeated in Eliot's 'Wasteland': 'I see crowds of people walking around in a ring'). No less pervasive in the *Voyages*, the geometry of the circle, representing a check to the *voyageur*'s linear ambitions, traces the path of tragedy and futility. The deflection of the lunar capsule (in *Autour de la lune*) from its intended linear trajectory into an orbit around the moon confirms the tendency of verticality to decline into circularity.

Verne's novels hinge on a conflict between intention and achievement, or, diagrammatically, between the vertical and horizontal planes, between perpendicularity and circularity. The consequence of this interplay, in geometrical terms, is the helix or spiral. The descensional pull of gravity and the centrifugal force of revolution, frustrating Vernian man's evolutionary will to ascend, convert his ideal of vertical motion into the practice of spiralling upwards (or downwards): unable to climb directly up the sheer face of his chosen or appointed obstacle, he is obliged to ascend circuitously: he does not climb a ladder so much as describe a cone. The subterranean journey ('nous descendions une sorte de vis tournante')[95] is condensed in the single image of the *maelstrom* (the outcome of the tension between opposing tides and currents), which terminates (temporarily) the submarine voyage of the *Nautilus*: as the vessel is sucked down by the whirlpool, 'il décrivait une spirale dont le rayon diminuait de plus en plus'.[96]

Like Goethe's answer to Eckermann's remark that human thought and action seem to repeat themselves, going round in a circle: 'No, it is not a circle, it is a spiral',[97] Verne's upward spiral seems to offer an optimistic counterpoint to the pessimistic vision of pure circularity; the *voyageurs*, after their sojourn in a rotary hell, will be allowed to accompany Dante on his ascent towards paradise. But the rule of reversibility implies that the spiral can as easily lead downwards to perdition as upwards, like a Mountain of Purgatory, to salvation.

The Vernian savant meets with a dilemma: frustrated by the iterative loop of circular time, he strives in vain to attain the epistemic plateau of timeless, intellectual plenitude which, if he were to attain it, he would discover to be circular: an encyclopedic transcription of the circumference of knowledge. Thus encirclement appears as both an unattainable objective and an inescapable fate. The spiral affords no solution to this predicament, but rather reinforces it: like its material incarnations, the cyclone and the whirlpool, an object of terror, bereft of a terminus, it promises only the perpetuation of circularity.[98]

4.5 Ark

The observation Apollinaire is alleged to have made of Verne's writing: 'Quel style! Rien que des substantifs!'[99] scarcely exaggerates the facts. Grammar itself is subordinated to the demands of the noun, with the result that nominal enumeration (congeries, lists, inventories) becomes the privileged rhetorical mode. But the device of congeries, linear and cumulative, evinces a purely additive structure. Syntactically, the conjunction loosely binding objects together is *et*; mathematically, the sign of connection is '+'. Thus Verne's nominalist environment suffers from discontinuity, the same heterogeneity that is reproduced in the *voyageur*'s diet: things appear to be related only by their arbitrary proximity.

The words most commonly deployed (in genitival constructions) to characterize any association of objects are *amoncellement*, *entassement* and *agglomération*; they signify an aggregate, a random assortment of items, self-contained and independent, a community of neighbouring rather than related members, only provisionally held together by some tenuous unifying force: 'Les rochers cramponnés les uns aux autres ne se maintenaient que par un miracle d'équilibre. La montagne n'était, à vrai dire, qu'un amoncellement de pierres tombées de haut . . . Cette île . . . n'était due qu'à l'agrégation successive des déjections volcaniques.'[100] Matter itself, in Vernian physics, is friable, the texture of over-yeasted bread, liable to crumble. All objects and beings appear to consist of a temporary reunion of other autonomous objects and beings, apt to revert to the primeval chaos from which they sprang (for circular time implies that Genesis awaits us in the future).

The Vernian universe therefore resembles the Biblical Creation after the generative but before the transformational phase. Spontaneously, the world presents to the *voyageur* a structureless prodigality; it is the business of the savant to discern the structure of necessity concealed within its chance collocations, to reveal the secret affinities of things. Taxonomy serves as the means of ordering the proliferation of words and things generated by Verne's nominalist disposition. The world is organized syntagmatically, as a linear string of articles, enabling it to be read as a book; the purpose of classification is to reorganize things paradigmatically, to sort them out into sets. Thus Verne's most taxonomic statements can be said to represent eruptions of the vertical into the sphere of the horizontal. *Vingt mille lieues sous les mers* has been called an ichthyological novel; it is also, more particularly, a taxonomic text, in which a journey of circumnavigation is intersected by perpendicular inventories.

Of the trio of characters surrounding the central, enigmatic figure of Captain Nemo, Ned Land, master harpoonist, is the most consistently materialist, the most carnal, the hungriest. His professional status indicates (for Vernian man seamlessly unites being and doing: he is never alienated from his labour) that he is essentially concerned with the business of hunting and catching a commodity; but he is no less intent on consuming what he catches. He is the epitome of omnivoracity, of indiscriminate dietary habits; his stomach is the physical counterpart to those epistemic voids that Verne's more scientifically oriented agents are committed to filling in. While Ned's individual *telos* is reducible to the attempted satiation of an insatiable appetite, his two companions, Professor Aronnax and his domestic, Conseil, are assigned the task of taxonomic tabulation. But the processes involved, the demand for food and for information, are homologous; Ned's division of fish into two classes, the edible and the inedible,[101] is the equivalent, in a comic, sensual key, of scientific procedure.

A pause in the narrative formulation of the initial *énigme* posed in *Vingt mille lieues sous les mers* – what is the true nature of a putative marine monster? (which turns out to be not the gigantic whale postulated by Aronnax but the submarine *Nautilus*) – finds the narrator (Aronnax) poring over his 'chères et précieuses collections': 'Je m'occupais donc, en attendant, de classer mes richesses minéralogiques, botaniques et zoologiques, quand arriva l'incident du *Scotia*.'[102] The sentence is a distillation of the entire text; its syntactical priorities and the juxtaposition of imperfect and past historic tenses prefigure the subsequent pattern relating classification and plot: the business of taxonomic ordering, an activity spanning the whole voyage, is a continuous process interrupted by occasional events. The question of the relative priority of observation and action, placing in competition the ambition to taxonomically exhaust the contents of the ocean and the desire to escape imprisonment in a submarine, becomes itself an integral part of the intrigue. While Ned Land, bored by the monotonous diet of fish (*le régime ichtyaque*), craving meat and dry land and repose from the circulatory motion around the world, urges flight, Aronnax is reluctant to pass up the opportunity to explore the ocean at such close quarters, or leave the job of classification incomplete (*achever* is the most imperative verb in the vocabulary of the Vernian professorial elite).

Vingt mille lieues sous les mers is unique among the *Voyages* for incorporating character (a character, Nemo) into the hermeneutic code, which is otherwise reserved for abstract, scientific problems; Nemo is the sole psychological puzzle of the novels. More typically, character is reduced to the capacity to exercise a function (generally the installation in the realm of nature of the same rigidity that distinguishes humanity).[103] Exemplary, in this respect (as if to counterbalance the exceptional opacity of Nemo), is Conseil. His simple and exhaustive *raison d'être* is classification ('classer, c'était sa vie');[104] thus he sacrifices his identity to the requirements of his taxonomic vocation. In the heated debate between Ned Land and Aronnax, he self-effacingly abjures the right to vote: 'deux personnes seulement sont en présence', he declares; even the habituated Aronnax has never before seen him 'annihiler si complètement sa personnalité'.[105] Attacked by a shark, which would also like to annihilate his personality, he 'le rangeait, non sans raison, dans la classe des cartilagineux, ordre des chondroptérygiens à branchies fixes, famille des sélaciens, genre des squales'.[106] In the *Voyages*, the enterprise of taxonomy constitutes a kind of heroism.

It is one of the chief characteristics of the Vernian planet that its population of objects and beings is endlessly proliferating; like the single grain of wheat (in *L'Ile mystérieuse*) that grows to reproduce itself several million-fold, they are self-multiplying. Even the polar North displays a tropical profusion of creatures; Clawbonny looks into the sky and sees the following: 'Les oiseaux volaient en bandes innombrables, pareilles à des nuages épais et gros de tempêtes . . . tous les spécimens de la grande famille aquatique . . . avec des proportions gigantesques . . . ces monstres aériens'; he looks down into a diaphanous sea mirroring the heavens, and observes 'cet élément sillonné par toutes les espèces . . . les monstres marins'.[107] This cornucopian abundance is beneficent since it promises the eternal satisfaction of appetite. But nature is potentially hazardous, and the image of the storm cloud, together with the emphasis on the monstrousness of the innumerable beings, and (later) their ambiguous *puissance*, suggest a sinister, maleficent aspect.[108] The overflowing, immeasurable, dangerous world of monsters and sharks, if it is to be rendered anodyne and intelligible, fit for human consumption, must be contained.[109] Containment, or enclosure, is the objective and rationale of Verne's scientific taxonomy.

The *Nautilus* is both observatory and trawler, netting and hauling aboard the immense variety of sea-creatures visible through its inspection glass. Whether through visual or tactile contact, it falls to Conseil and Aronnax to sort them, to redistribute them to their correct compartments of existence. The act of classification is the instrument of multiple containment. The category is a verbal *filet*, while the paragraph, often composed of a single lengthy sentence, laden exclusively with categorical substantives, is the typological accomplice of the classificatory sequence: it too is a net, trapping a plethora of entities. Thus the narrative events of *Vingt mille lieues sous les mers* are interspersed with enumerations of species and recitations of the taxonomic identity of individual ichthyological specimens. Aronnax includes in his inventories three fundamental categories of fish: those he has seen, those he has only glimpsed, and, finally, 'ceux que la vitesse du *Nautilus* déroba à mes yeux'.[110] He is careful to allude not just to those the *Nautilus* has caught but also to those that, although absent, taxonomic exhaustiveness renders deserving of mention. Thus the parade of names, on their first appearance, is already ordered in accordance with a hierarchy of classificatory criteria: the *Nautilus* appears to traverse a non-ecological space in which the dispersed members of a species are magically reunited.[111] The voyage of twenty thousand leagues beneath the sea (contrary to popular misconception, the length of the journey, not its depth) expands and articulates Clawbonny's instant revelation of 'toutes les espèces'; the vertical, after all, can only be expressed horizontally.

The dominant preposition in *Vingt mille lieues sous les mers*, perhaps in all the *Voyages*, is *dans*. The taxonomic enclosures effected by classification represent, at most, only a species of the genus of containment. The action of the text is located in the struggle between rival containers. If the nets of the Nautilus contain the denizens of the sea, the all-containing sea in turn engulfs the submarine. The incarceration of the guest captives, as of the discreetly invisible crew, is a metaphor for the danger of containment affecting their container. The itinerary of the *Nautilus* encompasses the seven seas; but having briefly moored at the South Pole, the submarine is itself encompassed, immobilized, and imprisoned by ice. Aronnax hallucinates: 'Il me semblait que j'étais entre les formidables mâchoires d'un monstre qui se rapprochaient irrésistiblement.'[112] The vision of eating as an allegory of containment anticipates a literal event: the struggle with the ice is succeeded by combat with a giant squid[113] which first engulfs the submarine, then its passengers. The undersea voyage, no more than the overland trek, cannot annul that stark alternative – eat or be eaten! – that is the basis of Verne's nutritional philosophy. Aronnax's verdict on the 'cachalots' – 'Ils ne sont que bouche et dents'[114] – adequately describes the innumerable monsters that lurk in the path of the *voyageurs*.

The *Nautilus* is the instrument of their containment. Paradoxically, the spectators securely situated behind the observation window, gazing out on the depths, gain the impression that, far from their vehicle being at the mercy of the aquatic environment, it is they who are doing the containing, and the ocean is their containee: 'nous regardions comme si ce pur cristal eût été la vitre d'un immense aquarium'.[115] The submarine's capacity for containment is dual: both external and internal. Internally considered, it is at once prison and refuge; although potentially (and in the case of Nemo, actually) a tomb, it grants the shipwrecked mariners salvation from drowning. The inner world of the *Nautilus* is a model of security, offering protection from the dangers of the outer world (primitive humans as well as sharks). And like all Verne's vehicles, it affords comfortable, even luxurious accommodation. Pascal affirmed that all human misery stemmed from man's inability to stay at home, 'en repos, dans une chambre'.[116] In the *Voyages*, man's ceaseless urge for mobility results in exposure to misfortune, most notably, to being devoured. But Verne's solution to this problem is to devise a means of travel permitting the traveller to be simultaneously in motion and *en repos*. Thus the Vernian vehicle is, in essence, a mobile home outside of which the traveller, if he is wise, rarely ventures, or does so only at his peril.[117]

But the *Nautilus* is more than a hotel; it is referred to as 'une arche sainte',[118] a designation whose twin senses (like those of 'vessel') evoke the submarine's double status as both a vehicle of salvation and a receptacle of revered documents. The library aboard the craft is a microcosm of the nineteenth-century archive; its voluminous shelves contain 'tout ce que l'humanité a produit de plus beau dans l'histoire, la poésie, le roman et la science'.[119] No less ample, the 'salon' constitutes 'un musée dans lequel une main intelligente et prodigue avait réuni tous les trésors de la nature et de l'art'.[120] Thus the submarine is sufficiently capacious to accommodate all the texts and objects generated by literature, science, art, nature. Verne invents a ship the size of an island (see *L'Ile à hélice*); but the *Nautilus* is constructed on the dimensions of the world: it is the matrix of an ideal order, of the chaotic planet rationally rearranged, the *summum bonum* of the cult of classification.[121]

The *Nautilus*, the ark, the combined submarine museum and library, is a compressed replica of Napoleon's Egyptian fleet, a seaborne encyclopedia:[122] armed with electricity and torpedoes, it assembles a comprehensive repertoire of objects and artefacts. But the function of this vehicular archive is not merely to exhaust the cultural spectrum of past and present, or to transport it abroad, but also to eliminate the unpredictable horizon of the future; the definitive aim of its captain is to fix civilization inalterably in time: 'Je veux croire que l'Humanité n'a plus ni pensé ni écrit.'[123] Secure inside the *Nautilus*, Nemo's microculture is removed for all time from the realm of contingency and mutability. The chef of the *Nautilus* adopts the same strategy towards food as his captain towards the arts and sciences: 'Mon cuisinier est un habile préparateur, qui excelle à conserver ces produits variés de l'Océan . . . Voici une conserve d'holothuries.'[124] His art is essentially one of conservation, of rendering the changeable permanent.

It is possible that the future will tolerate further technological progress; but this is unlikely, since surely nothing, or next to nothing, remains to be invented: 'Nous sommes d'un temps où tout arrive – on a presque le droit de dire où tout est arrivé.'[125] The future is almost a thing of the past; but that 'presque' is a point of stress in the sentence, adverbially fracturing and corroding the verbal optimism: it does not exclude decay and degeneracy. Time is on the side of change. The dual role of the Vernian container is to enclose and compress nature and culture, and to exclude and suppress time:

Afin de leur assurer une éternelle durée, ces tableaux sont placés à l'intérieur de vitrines où le vide a été préalablement fait . . . Grâce à ce climat sans pluies ni brouillards, groupes, statues, bustes, peuvent impunément résister aux outrages du temps.[126]

The closed, confined, well-ordered space (of *vitrines*, submarines, classifications, *cerveaux*, orbits) assumes, in the *Voyages*, the status of a double symbol, at once temporal and aesthetic: it is the physical counterpart to the closure of history that is the prerequisite of epistemic totalization; and it is an image prefiguring the completion of Verne's fictional enterprise.

4.6 Archive

Verne's fiction is constructed on the model of the *Nautilus*: it is a library of quotations, allusions, references: a bibliography of nineteenth-century science. Verne's technical vocabulary, in turn, proposes a verbal equivalent to the transparent and commodious glass cases of the submarine museum. The unfolding of the hermeneutic and proaïretic codes (the alliance of problem-solving and travel) is underpinned, in the *Voyages*, by the conspicuous presence of a *code culturel*, in which the accredited *savoir* of experimental and inventive science has supplanted the collective legacy of *sagesse* as the adequate object of reverence and the ultimate guarantor of literary credibility.[127]

Verne, like Nemo, is a collector: he collects esotericisms. Allotte de la Fuÿe's biography pictures the youthful literary apprentice engaged in assembling the rudiments of a scientific terminology: 'Dans sa chambre du Boulevard Bonne Nouvelle, il est . . . en train de se substantifier.'[128] The reflexive verb indicates that the substantive has become part of the substance of the writer. The museum of the *Nautilus* furnishes a pretext for the performance of a learned vocabulary: the collection of things is a platform for exhibiting an onomasticon, a collection of names, whose unfamiliarity and, perhaps, incomprehensibility, reflect their exoticism. Thus the conchology section is a pretext for Verne's vast repertoire of recondite nomenclature:

enfin des littorines, des dauphinules, des turritelles, des janthines, des ovules, des volutes, des olives, des mitres, des casques, des pourpres, des buccins, des harpes, des rochers, des tritons, des cérites, des fuseaux, des strombes, des ptérocères, des patelles, des hyales, des cléodores, coquillages délicats et fragiles, que la science a baptisés de ses noms les plus charmants.[129]

This incantatory recitation is completed, and the almost liturgical reverence banished, by the arithmetical lament of the accountant: 'chiffrer la valeur de cette collection était, pour ainsi dire, impossible'. The insertion of the phrase 'pour ainsi dire' registers embarrassment that a 'chiffre' should not, on this occasion, be forthcoming. The noun stands as Verne's lexical integer.

It is tempting to dismiss (and edit out in abridged versions) the teeming jargon that punctuates, say, *Vingt mille lieues sous les mers*; but this strategy of exclusion would be inconsistent with the tenets of the *Magasin d'éducation et de récréation* (under whose innocent banner the *Voyages* first appeared), evoked in its motto: 'L'instruction qui amuse, l'amusement qui instruit.' It is an indication of the importance Verne himself attaches to the articulation of his pedantic terminology that he is prepared, temporarily, to suspend the amusement of the reader, to risk inflicting ennui. Verne anticipates and seeks to disarm the naive objection (whose essential truth, however, he does not deny) that certain long-winded passages are simply boring, and defends erudition, 'cette nomenclature un peu sèche, mais très exacte',[130] an arid vocabulary of the ocean, on the grounds of precision.

But although Verne's writing explicitly declares its exactitude, his novels not only fail to exclude vagueness: they resort to it regularly, almost systematically, as if the machinery of the Vernian imagination had to be frequently lubricated with euphemistic, elliptical or plain evasive generalities. The ambiguous conclusion to the *Voyage au centre de la terre* is symptomatic of a widespread antipathy towards clarity. A similar imprecision veils the working of Verne's innovatory vehicles. The actual ignorance of a pseudo-omniscient narrator is dissolved in the ripples of a pseudo-explanatory discourse. Question: how is it possible to enhance the relatively weak motive force of electricity sufficiently to power the *Nautilus*? Answer: a cunning system of levers. Likewise, insoluble problems (in the terms in which they are posed) concerning the trip to the moon are overcome by unspecified technical ingenuity. Thus Vernian containers are also arcana; obscurity is the *sine qua non* of their power to enchant.

A characteristic note of anxiety is sounded whenever there arises an apparent antagonism between codified knowledge or consecrated theory and the expansiveness of a fictive imagination, whenever dream overruns the frontiers of mathematics. Butor's assessment of science fiction registers the dual nature of the *Voyages*: 'C'est un fantastique encadré dans un réalisme.'[131] It is precisely in those disputed border areas where the frame appears no longer able to contain invention that Verne is most reticent.[132] Verne permits himself only the most modest extrapolations and anticipations. Thus he criticizes Poe for transgressing physical laws, and objects that H. G. Wells resorts to the transparently fantastic device of anti-gravity metal to get his space-travellers to the moon, whereas he, Verne, constructs a giant cannon, loads it with a hollow cannon-ball, loads that with passengers, and points the whole lot at the moon before touching it off: 'I make use of physics', he concludes, 'He invents.'[133] Unfettered invention seems to Verne to be a form of mendacity.

On the other hand, Verne flaunts a self-confident contempt for the restrictions of verisimilitude. He explicitly discards *la vrai-semblance* in favour of *le vrai*: he claims he is concerned not with the appearance of truth (a hypocritical second-best) but with truth itself. He assigns to the future the responsibility for conferring retrospective plausibility on the seeming fictions of the present: 'Si notre récit n'est pas vraisemblable aujourd'hui, il peut l'être demain grâce aux ressources scientifiques de l'avenir.'[134] But nothing in the *Voyages* is quite so implausible as their profession of implausibility. Despite the advertised renunciation of *vraisemblance*, the improb-able is scrupulously eschewed: the unknown turns out, on inspec-tion, to resemble the known; the future is a mere extension or repro-duction of the present world. The diminution and eventual exclusion of *l'inconnu* to which the Vernian savant looks forward is thus fictionally anticipated. *L'invraisemblable* in the *Voyages* denotes a deviation from purely literary conventions defining the appropriate subject matter of literature, and the espousal of scien-tific criteria of inclusion.

In the course of his Herculean labours of description, the Vernian narrator issues frequent admissions of inadequacy. Rare is the chapter without at least one instance of good-humoured renunciation of the descriptive mission, of declarations that the pen (like the paintbrush) is incapable of conveying fully an experience or a truth. The Vernian world appears to be partially afflicted with *l'indescriptible*. It is evident, however, that, even in the loquacious, almost euphoric assertion of indescribability, Verne suffers no anxiety on this account. The resilience of narratorial descriptive confidence depends on a distinction between what does and what does not need to be reliably described and the coincidence of descriptive capacity with the former.

Vingt mille lieues sous les mers contains a brief item of literary criticism. After the chapter relating the encounter with the giant squid, and culminating in the devouring of the unfortunate sub-mariner. Aronnax discloses a certain apprehension regarding his authorial adequacy: 'J'en ai revu le récit. Je l'ai lu à Conseil et au Canadien. Ils l'ont trouvé exact comme fait, mais insuffisant comme effet. Pour peindre de pareils tableaux, il faudrait la plume des plus illustres de nos poètes.'[135] This passage sets up a double distinction between 'fait' and 'effet', and poetry and prose. Prose is declared the province of the 'fait', poetry (and painting), that of the 'effet'.

Facts are what constitute the composite world minus its human inmates; effects derive from the conjunction of man and thing; facts are no less than everything that is the case; effects are transient human noumena, phenomenological aberrations, epiphenomena contaminated by rampant subjectivity.

Verne therefore feels at liberty to invent the activities of his fictional characters, to elaborate fantastic plots, since humanity and illusion are, in any case, inseparable; but he is constrained to describe with all possible fidelity the decor his personnel explore. He is free, for example, to imagine a journey to the moon, but is not permitted to give a fuller account of the moon's surface than has already been ratified by scientific inquiry. The lunar projectile fails to land, and passes over the 'dark side' of the moon when it is, in any case, dark, unillumined by the sun, and therefore invisible to the frustrated astronauts. An exploding asteroid briefly turns night into day, permitting a glimpse of the hitherto unseen lunar landscape, which appears to include seas and forests and to be equipped with atmosphere. But the vision is no sooner enunciated than retracted, condemned as 'une illusion, une erreur des yeux, une tromperie de l'optique', or, at best, 'une observation superficiellement obtenue' to which the observer cannot reasonably 'donner une affirmation scientifique'.[136] Similarly, in *Voyage au centre de la terre*, the apparent sighting of a man beneath the earth's surface is qualified, withdrawn, and denounced as unscientific. The model for these adventures is Phileas Fogg: the travellers travel but rarely see anything. For Verne, the *descriptible* is bounded by what has already been described; the *scriptible* is identical with the *déjà-écrit*. Thus Verne's fiction seems less anticipatory than nostalgic. Even the future world of *L'Eternel Adam* is technologically prior to the late nineteenth century.[137]

Structurally, the Vernian text is analogous to the filing system in which Verne stored his voluminous scientific material: it is haunted by the phantoms of barely assimilated data cards, crammed with lateral digressions where disparate facts are expounded with impartial didacticism, and punctuated by footnotes of tangential pedantry. The Vernian *récit* is, in essence, a recitation, an immense index of recorded information, a thesaurus of recondite nomenclature. The odysseys of the *voyageurs* read like a series of expeditions, at different angles, through a consecrated scientific archive.[138]

The undulating landscape of Verne's inhuman comedy is comparable to that in Dante's *Comedy*; and the definitive and exhaustive vision of the universe sought by Verne is not dissimilar in outline from that mystical insight vouchsafed the purified Dante at the close of *Paradiso*. But Verne's ambition to bind the universe together in a volume is mediated, not, as in the case of the disembodied Dante, by direct access to the divine, but by a comprehensive reading of scientific texts. Thus his fiction recalls that intention, alluded to, derided, and periodically espoused by the stories of Borges, 'to construct an absolute book, a book of books that includes all the others like a Platonic archetype, an object whose virtue is not lessened by the years',[139] 'un libro total',[140] a compendious text that, like the Library of Babel, would be indistinguishable from the universe. Verne is a bibliophile (whose recurring fantasy is the resurrection of the incinerated Alexandrian library), a lexicographer, a collector of words and phrases and theories; in Serres's term, he is a *doxographe*.

Science, in Verne's view, holds out the prospect of realizing the ideal implicit in the linear theory of history, and in Nemo's library and museum: that nothing more should be thought or written. The *Voyages* are bound to express a pervasive yearning that time should have a stop, since the mere passage of time suffices to condemn the pretended totalization of available knowledge, which is the putative justification of the fictional sequence, to be perpetually out of date. The function of science is to abolish the unpredictability of the future. At the culmination of a finite process of replacing and refining erroneous or inadequate hypotheses, the savant stands to attain a fixed plateau of certitude enabling him to enunciate definitive, irrefutable statements about the world. Scientific discourse would then be an impregnable fortress, eternally secure against the tyranny of time: 'Assez. Quand la science a prononcé, il n'y a plus qu'à se taire.'[141] Thus the writer too, who is symbiotically attached to, or identical with, the savant, would be enabled to complete his colossal and otherwise interminable task of exhaustive description, and to lapse at last into consummate silence. Science promises to release the anguished writer, afflicted with a sense of infinite possibilities, from the burden of imagination, and to accord him a final tranquillity. But the *Voyages* are pervaded by the disappointment of expectations; they enact the tragedy of unkept promises.

4.7 Remainders

The main constituents of Verne's fictional *maya*, the instruments devised to attain the twin objectives of mimesis and mathesis (the naming and numbering of the elements that compose the universe), have now been enumerated. It only remains to observe that these means and their appointed ends are incommensurable.

Vernian science entails an heroic but doomed enterprise to encompass experience by intelligence. Phileas Fogg, for example, although he wins his wager by circling the globe within the period allotted, fails to assimilate time to chronicity: his preconceived 'programme', determined by reference to a railway timetable, is too inflexible – like the watch he keeps regulated according to the Greenwich Meridian – to take account of the day gained travelling eastwards. All his careful calculations still leave a remainder. Scientific discourse is revealed to suffer from the same rigidity as Fogg.

The creations of God differ irremediably from the inventions of man by virtue of their geometrical imperfections; the universe may be the work of a prolific artist; it is not the work of a geometer. While machines, buildings, even men (who appear self-constructed), manufactured according to draughtsman-like blueprints, are eminently describable, the unreconstructed material world frustrates accurate delineation to the degree that it deviates from our abstract, analytical models.[142] Thus the earth is not a sphere but only a spheroid;[143] things only resemble, in an approximate way, the imaginary constructs of circles, triangles, spheres.

Arithmetic, similarly, is found to be wanting. In *De la terre à la lune*, the narrator concludes an elaborate calculation by asking: 'Qu'ajouter à ces nombres si éloquents par eux-mêmes?', to which he answers: 'Rien!'[144] Figures promise to do away with the necessity of words; it should be possible to reduce the world to an equation. But the obsession with numbers characterizing many of the *voyageurs* receives a definitively ironical critique in the figure of Poncin, the fanatical statistician of the late work, *L'Etonnante Aventure de la mission Barsac*. Parodying the activities of the Vernian *homo calculator*, he determines, for instance, that the tattoos of the local natives, put end to end, would trace one three hundred thousand, five hundred and twenty-eighth of the circumference of the earth. Computation is an exclusive vocation, entailing an oath of renunciation: 'Un statisticien digne de ce nom doit s'interdire de raisonner.'[145] Poncin is more than a humorous travesty of a Vernian type: he is the product of a sense of disillusionment with the ideal of mathesis. The disincarnate symbolism of mathematics, far from providing mimesis with an unshakeable foundation of objectivity, seems to encourage numerological fantasies. There are no such things in nature (if we exclude the God of Nicholas) as triangles, circles and spheres; but neither are there any numbers: numbers, as Russell points out, do not exist: they are convenient fictions. In Verne (as elsewhere in the nineteenth century), mathematics and reality diverge.[146]

In the symmetrical system of equal and opposite forces that informs the *Voyages*, the quest for the absolute interlocks at every point on its route with the anxiety of relativity. Thus, too, the taxonomic ordering of the world fails to yield the certitude and stability that would be its justification. *Vingt mille lieues sous les mers* enshrines the ambition to complete the textual account of the contents of the ocean; the *Nautilus* provides for the closure of marine lacunae in the epistemic grid. But the narrative journey also gives evidence, in alternately literal and figurative terms, of the phenomenon that Barthes calls 'drift': 'La dérive advient chaque fois que *je ne respecte pas* le tout, et qu'à force de paraître emporté ici et là au gré des illusions, séductions et intimidations du langage, tel un bouchon sur la vague, je reste immobile, pivotant sur la jouissance *intraitable* qui me lie au texte (au monde).'[147] It is no accident that this account parallels so closely the cycle of motion and arrest, of control and uncontrol, that characterizes the passage of the *Nautilus*. The submarine circumnavigation is at once an expedition through geographical space and a prolonged exposition of an ichthyological text; the manner of travelling corresponds to a mode of reading. Thus 'la dérive' also denotes the regular condition of the vessel's resident taxonomist. Conseil is affected by a species of linguistic fixation similar to that described by Barthes; like Barthes, Conseil is inordinately attached to the signifier; his systematic classifications are seen to become increasingly detached from the subjects they seek to anchor; his substantival framework, which does not respect 'le tout', has come adrift: 'Conseil, emporté dans les abîmes de la classification, sortait hors du monde réel.'[148] The function of taxonomy is to fill in the interstices of knowledge; but 'abîmes' indicates a parallel system of vacuities that doubles rather than solves the problem.

Like John Wilkins, in *An Essay towards a Real Character and a Philosophical Language* (who ingeniously elaborates a system of correspondences between letters, or sequences of letters, and divisions or subdivisions within forty classes of being which comprise the universe), Verne intermittently dreams that language might both acquire the rigour, precision, and logical necessity of mathematics, and exhaust the identity of a set of referents. Assigning to an object its scientific designation, and inserting it into a taxonomic schema, is the linguistic homologue, in Verne's writing, of the mathematical act of specifying its dimensions or numbers. Together, these complementary notations seek to give a definitive description of things; each proves unequal to its task.

The ideal of the Vernian savant is a stabilized corpus of knowledge; the essential condition of the processes (natural and linguistic) he aims to master is instability. Cyrus Smith, in *L'Ile mystérieuse*, perched on an island which is the transient remnant of a sunken continent, and lecturing on the perpetual displacement of land masses, their cyclical rise and fall, prophesies the transformation of the earth's surface, the rearrangement of land and ocean. *L'Eternel Adam* fulfils that prophecy, and recounts the sudden immersion of land in the sea (implying regression, since the world, in maturing, passes from the gaseous through the liquid, to the solid state). On a smaller scale, all elements are transitional. Verne's *en-soi*, like Sartre's *pour-soi*, is not what it is and is what it is not. The *être-là* of both natural and artificial objects is constantly in question; everything is infinitely transmutable; nothing is, without simultaneously becoming.[149]

The principle of equivalence, underlying both metaphor and mathematics, operates, in the *Voyages*, as the determinant of narrative structures: no longer is one thing simply qualified in terms of something else; it is capable, at any moment, of being physically changed into something else. Metaphor gives way to metamorphosis. Water, predicts Cyrus Smith, will be broken down into its constituents in order to solve (or postpone) any future limits-to-growth crisis: 'L'eau est le charbon de l'avenir.'[150] Meanwhile the magical art of eating is constantly transforming flora and fauna alike into fuel to feed man's insatiable internal combustion. The question asked of animals is not only *Ça se mange?* but also: *Ça se change?* Thus seals are transmogrified into bellows and candles, algae into nitroglycerine; their value is determined by their coefficient of convertibility: the quantity of distinct incarnations assumed, multiplied by the qualitative differences between them.

The common model of both macrocosmic and microcosmic instabilities is discernible in the outlines of Vernian cosmology. An expository passage in *De la terre à la lune* begins:

Un observateur doué d'une vue infiniment pénétrante, et placé à ce centre inconnu autour duquel gravite le monde, aurait vu des myriades d'atomes remplir l'espace à l'époque chaotique de l'univers.[151]

From his god-like, omniscient position, Verne's atemporal observer is enabled to perceive the (Laplacean) universe in its nascent phase, when it has already assumed the form of a sphere, with an unknown centre and an invisible circumference, but is permeated with randomness, its elementary particles still disconnected, devoid of logical relations. But the cosmos exists, even here, in a state of disposition or potential, available for reconstruction. The passage continues:

> Mais peu à peu, avec les siècles, un changement se produisit; une loi d'attraction se manifesta à laquelle obéirent les atomes errants jusqu'alors; ces atomes se combinèrent chimiquement suivant leurs affinités, se firent molécules et formèrent ces amas nébuleux dont sont parsemés les profondeurs du ciel.

Evolution involves a progressive, irresistible ordering of orderless material, a transition from chaos to organization, and from solitude to solidarity: lonely, wandering, rootless atoms are physically assembled by an inexorable law of attraction, and their union blessed by a chemical fusion.

Verne (in the person of his professorial narrator) then goes on to explain how an accelerating rotary movement produces first the 'étoile principale' of a galaxy, and, eventually, the 'étoiles secondaires' which split successively into planets and satellites. Two forces are at work in rotation: the centripetal, favouring condensation, which is overtaken by the centrifugal, favouring proliferation:

> Les molécules situées dans le plan de l'équateur (du soleil), s'échappant comme la pierre d'une fronde dont la corde vient à se briser subitement, auraient été former autour du soleil plusieurs anneaux concentriques semblables à celui de Saturne. A leur tour, ces anneaux de matière cosmique, pris d'un mouvement de rotation autour de la masse centrale, se seraient brisés et décomposés en nebulosités secondaires, c'est-à-dire en planètes.

There is no steady state in the Vernian universe; change is constant. What is peculiar to Verne's conception is that the very process of cosmic construction involves simultaneously both composition and decomposition. The formation of the smaller items depends directly on the disintegration of the larger ones; each individual unit is the fragment of some prior unit, since dissolved. And the same forces that generate a provisional unity also work towards the eventual breakdown of that unity. Construction and deconstruction, evolution and dissolution, are inseparable and even indistinguishable in Verne's paradoxical equation; the process of ordering generates renewed disorder.[152] Thus reversibility is built into the cosmos of the *Voyages*. History, correspondingly, is not simply a succession of metamorphoses: it is not modelled on the linear theory beloved of the Vernian savant; it is cyclical. The arrow of time points relentlessly forward into the distant past. Consequently, the end towards which the universe, like the narrative, moves, is identical with its chaotic genesis.

The world of the *Voyages* is not only disordered, labyrinthine, obscure; it tends to become more so, despite all efforts to reverse the trend. In a word, the closed system described by Verne, like that of thermodynamics, is afflicted with the condition of entropy. The earth is a remnant, a secondary nebulosity, a result of disintegration, like the asteroids one of the 'débris errants d'un astre brisé en plusieurs milliers de morceaux';[153] but that process of which it is the product threatens to reduce it to still more elementary particles.[154] And on Verne's fissiparous earth, things fall apart. It is the appointed task of Verne's epistemic guardians to articulate their environment in both the senses of the verb: at once to enumerate its discrete components and to strive to relate them one to another. Their objective is to devise a coherent framework, a grid, to envelop the globe, to counter its centrifugal force, and thus moderate its inherent tendency to fly apart.

L'Ile mystérieuse, a recapitulation of human evolution, also presents a model of the Vernian enterprise: to describe a hitherto unknown island which is, symbolically, a surrogate of the entire planet. The permanent preoccupation of the 'colonists', reflecting the denotative character of the discourse, is how to name the parts of their world. This compulsion to map out the island with language is an integral part of the project of colonization: names are potent word-magic: to name gives control over the thing named; to name is to strike a claim and appropriate. Names constitute a colonial cartography, an atlas of existence. In the course of the novel, all the techniques of measurement and analysis and classification are applied, and when, finally, the colonists discover (are allowed to discover) the hidden presence of the benevolent Nemo moored in a subterranean cavern, they seem to have conquered the island by exhausting its stock of secrets. But the empire of man is strictly provisional. *L'île Lincoln* is composed of such heterogeneous matter as to be intrinsically unstable, susceptible to disaggregation; on top of this, sitting in its midst, is an increasingly effervescent volcano. The devastating eruption that terminates the novel (inviting a *recommencement des choses* in Iowa), leaving nothing of the island intact except its map, affords an unsurpassable instance of a signifier bereft of signified.

The Vernian savant seeks to impose a condition of homoeostasis on his environment; but it seems as if the perpetual tension between the drive for stability and the rampant forces of instability has the effect of enhancing the inherent volatility and fragility of the world, of encouraging volcanoes. The book of knowledge impedes its own completion by reinforcing the book of nature's susceptibility to disintegration.

4.8 Explosions and exclamations

Verne is an avowed internationalist. His heroes are generally American or English. Even the specifically French *voyageurs* tend to mimic their Anglo-Saxon counterparts (thus Paganel sees himself and his compatriots with the eye of the Other: 'les Anglais nous appellent "mangeurs de grenouilles" ').[155]

Ardan, the lone French pilot of the lunar projectile, surpasses his American comrades in his possession of what Verne characterizes as a peculiarly American trait, 'l'instinct du big':[156]

Cet homme vivait dans une perpétuelle disposition à l'hyperbole et n'avait pas encore dépassé l'âge des superlatifs: les objets se peignaient sur la rétine de son œil avec des dimensions démesurées; de là une association d'idées gigantesques; il voyait tout en grand, sauf les difficultés et les hommes.[157]

The same description (minus the final exception) might be applied equally to the hyperbolic Verne. Verne's monsters amply justify their designation by being conspicuously monstrous; but that epithet (together with its synonyms: enormous, vast, colossal, etc.) is not monopolized by them: it is predicated at one time or another of most of the human and inhuman populace of the *Voyages*. Verne's creations are supremely tumescent entities: they appear so dangerously overinflated as to be on the verge of bursting apart under the strain of their internal expansion.

And, often enough, this is indeed precisely what occurs. *L'éclatement* is the premature fate that threatens to brutally cut short the existence of the brittle Vernian being or thing. The volcano, of course, has only to be sighted to be condemned to erupt sooner or later. But its function is essentially beneficent; it is a safety-valve without which the planet itself, like an over-heated boiler, would explode. Thus our stressful spheroid (itself the outcome of what seems to be a primordial 'big bang') remains temporarily intact; but the savant himself is no less susceptible to over-heating: he is as intensely combustible, as volcanic as the world he explores: 'sa pensée devait à tout prix se faire jour au-dehors, sous peine de faire éclater la machine . . . Ses yeux . . . sa bouche . . . étaient autant de soupapes de sûreté qui lui permettaient de donner passage à ce trop-plein de lui-même.'[158] Although the fissile condition due to a 'trop-plein' is common to many of Verne's most energetic travellers and inventors, none literally break up; some do, however, break down and, in emulation of their sinking sea-going vessels, decline into the depths of madness.

The *Voyages* enforce the analogy of character with ship or sub-marine, for the vehicle often stands as a surrogate self, an *alter ego*, a mechanical equivalent, to its pilot.[159] In the case of Phileas Fogg, machines are much less mechanical, more human, than their automatic passenger. While he remains impassive and intact, the boat on which he makes his Atlantic crossing is progressively demolished, or *dévoré*. Again, the nutritive metaphor is instructive: it is as if the decaying or exploding objects of Verne's imagination were chewed up by some invisible, impersonal force such as time, or speed, or gravity. It also explains why the terror of being devoured is so pervasive in the *Voyages*: it represents a double catastrophe, accomplishing in a single act the destructive effects of incarceration and entropy.

The submariner scooped off the *Nautilus* by a ravenous octopus is not swallowed alive, deposited intact, like Jonah, in the stomach of the beast: he is literally '*brisé* par les formidables bras du poulpe, *broyé* avec ses mandibules de fer' (my italics).[160] The destiny of dis-integration recurs in the fate devised by British imperialism for rebel natives (and invoked by the latter in reciprocal vengeance): 'Dix canons furent rangés sur le champ des manœuvres, un prison-nier attaché à chacune de leurs bouches, et cinq fois, les dix canons firent feu, en couvrant la plaine de débris informes, au milieu d'une atmosphère empestée par la chair brûlée.'[161] The mouths of the can-non dissect their victims instantly and visibly in an act of external mastication. The jaws of cannibals, perhaps more dreadful still than the mandibles of the octopus, effect a precisely similar result; thus the servants of a deceased tribal chief are efficiently atomized: 'En moins de temps qu'une plume rapide ne pourrait le retracer, les corps, encore fumants, furent déchirés, divisés, dépecés, mis, non pas en morceaux, mais en miettes.'[162] The multiplication of success-ive, virtually synonymous terms, the making of fine distinctions, indicate how analytically, how obsessively Verne traces the detailed effects of disintegration: the carefully rendered destruction of physical integrity, the brusque pluralization of the singular, the proliferation and scattering in space of suddenly disunified particles. This motif attracts a consistent vocabulary of disaggregation, the fragments of which can be found distributed at irregular intervals throughout Verne's *œuvre*, in the wake of ruined *châteaux*, shattered glass models of deceased divas (*Le Château des Carpathes*), self-detonating towns (*L'Etonnante Aventure de la mission Barsac*) and involuntarily exploding polar bears (*Les Aventures du capitaine Hatteras*).

But the explosion, the sudden destruction, even the act of cannibalism (at least among extremely ravenous or hasty cannibals), share a common defect: these events are too abrupt, too concise to permit a detailed exposition of the process of fragmentation. Not only is it the case that Verne tends to narrate *n* times an event occurring *n* times, but also that he prefers to determine the quantity of textual space allotted to that event in proportion to the period of time encompassed by it. This rule, matching narration to duration, prohibits him from dwelling upon momentary phenomena. ('En moins de temps qu'une plume rapide ne pourrait le retracer' registers the strain of reconciling a minimal occurrence and a maximal report.) So the extensive repertoire of idioms associated with the instant of disintegration requires, for its comprehensive performance, a more expansive, more protracted event than that constituted by mere explosion.

This requirement is met by the lingering, slow-motion dismantling of *L'Ile à hélice*. That automotive island is first figuratively – humanly and politically – split by schismatic factions within its floating community, an occurrence symbolized by the rupture of a marriage;[163] then literally fractured and disabled by the efforts of competing engineers, under the directions of the warring parties, to propel the island in opposite directions; and the process initiated by man is completed by nature when the island is at last finished off by a cyclone:

c'est un formidable météore qui va achever de l'anéantir . . . Un instant après, l'édifice entier n'est plus qu'un amas de débris . . . sa coque est perforée en mille endroits. Les joints craquent de toutes parts . . . la dislocation se propage . . . le parc se coupe . . . toute la population se disperse . . . un morceau d'un demi-mille carré vient de se détacher de Standard Island. C'est Tribord Harbour, ce sont ses fabriques, ses machines, ses magasins qui s'en vont à la dérive . . . Sa coque achève de se disloquer . . . Les compartiments se séparent.[164]

This encyclopedic catalogue of disaster, with both verbs and nouns playing virtuosically over the themes of detachment, dislocation, perforation, fragmentation, reads like a concentrated summation (another of Verne's microfigures) of the destructive conclusions of the Vernian text: the island, at once vehicle and domicile, which begins as a microcosm of the globe and model of the utopia of human and mechanical harmony, ends by recapitulating and amplifying the pervasive motif of partition. The causes assigned this gradual cataclysm, if not irrelevant to, are at least incommensurate with, their effects; the predominance of reflexive verbs evokes the spontaneous, autonomous quality of the transition from order to chaos. The final description of the atomized island seems to underscore this potential of all things to fall apart by elevating the particular catastrophe, via a cosmological analogy, to the status of an inexorable universal law:

A présent, de la merveilleuse Standard Island, il ne reste plus que des morceaux épars, semblables aux fragments sporadiques d'une comète brisée, qui flottent non dans l'espace, mais à la surface de l'immense Pacifique.[165]

The dénouement of the *Voyages* typically depicts an unknotting, the unravelling of a temporary unity.

The accumulation of *débâcles* in the *Voyages* has been predicated with the epithet 'apocalyptic'.[166] This description might be justified by reference to the coincidence of the diverse deaths of metal, machines, and men, with the ending of individual texts; this double terminus proposes a premonitory image of cessation symmetrically opposed to the prolific images of genesis that populate the novels. But if 'apocalyptic' implies 'an ordered series of events which end not in a great New Year, but in a final Sabbath',[167] then the application of the term to Verne is inappropriate. The apocalypse marks the end of an intelligible process; it proclaims the completion of history. The Vernian dénouement of physical degradation, by terminating an *histoire*, constitutes at once an allusion to, and a frustration of that historical closure, the termination of time which the anguish of mutability renders attractive to Verne's observers and travellers. Disintegration denotes the culmination of a crisis, not its resolution: it registers the incompleteness of the object or process which is its victim; it falsifies the expectation of an ending, disrupting the apocalyptic paradigm.

The clue to the understanding of the privileged if enigmatic status of fragmentation in the *Voyages* resides in the punctuation which is its symbolic counterpart: the exclamation mark. Before the advent of Céline, Verne could surely have had few rivals in the sheer prodigality with which he distributes exclamation marks. The title of Chapter 4 in *Hector Servadac*, 'Qui permet au lecteur de multiplier à l'infini les points d'exclamation et d'interrogation!', might apply to the *Voyages* as a whole. The exclamation mark has been the object of continual prohibitions or restrictions on its usage.[168] But judged by even the most permissive criteria,[169] Verne's proliferating exclamation marks, apt to accompany even the least exclamatory sentences, are liable to seem supernumerary. '!' is a performative device, akin to the *forte* of a musical score informing the interpreter how to play the phrase it accompanies, and denoting an otherwise imperceptible stress. It might be objected that the accumulation of such instructions, transferring to the reader the obligation to rectify textual deficiencies, is an indicator of the mediocrity of Verne's style, betraying its incapacity to give more articulate expression to complexity. But Verne was not indifferent to matters of style. In a letter to Hetzel, he writes of 'combien je cherche à devenir un styliste, mais sérieux: c'est l'idée de toute ma vie'.[170] His usage of the exclamation mark points to an awareness of the incapacity of language itself to measure up to his stated ideals of transparency and exhaustiveness.

The Vernian hero, faced with imminent death, sees his whole life pass in review before his mind's eye. The Vernian text, faced with an imminent ending, renarrates, in the form of a micronarrative, a retrospective résumé, all the events of the macronarrative, so that everything seems to happen twice over. The Vernian sentence also repeats itself in the punctuation at its close: the exclamation mark constitutes an encore. The *Voyages* abound in condensed, reflexive images such as the island or the unearthed (or de-sharked) document; the exclamation mark is more than one such microcosm: it is a microcosm of microcosms, the master key to the *Voyages*.

'!' is a composite notation which can be written, or read, in two separate ways, and is divisible into two separate characters. But its appearance is variable. According to typeface, its two components may resemble a straight line and a point, or an inverted triangle or cone suspended over a black circle or sphere. Taken together, these two possible representations of the exclamation mark comprise a compendium of the major figures of Verne's geometrical descriptions. Thus the exclamation mark is an encyclopedia of the Vernian imagination: it procures, for the attentive reader, an instantaneous and comprehensive voyage through the *Voyages*.[171]

But the exclamation mark has more than two constituent parts. It has three: a point (circle), a line (triangle), and a gap. The empty space dividing the outer components is an accomplice of those voids and discontinuities that proliferate in the *Voyages*, correlatives of the inarticulacy of surprise, horror, or ignorance. The exclamation mark is the snapshot of an explosive process whose participants seem to play out the quintessential Vernian drama of fragmentation. The exclamation mark is a potent, exorbitantly connotative notation: superficially effervescent, jovial,[172] it is also faintly but irrevocably tragic. Its closest partner among Verne's battery of stylistic devices is 'etc.'.

The etcetera is an incongruous yet indispensable entry in the Vernian inventory. In arithmetical terms, it is the equivalent of the letter 'r', standing for remainder. No matter how extended his sentences or densely packed his paragraphs, no matter how circumscribed the family of entities whose genealogy they pretend to exhaust, there subsists an unnamed or unnameable residuum unaccommodated by the page. 'Etc.' points beyond the page, assigning to the reader the responsibility for the indefinite extension of a transcendent taxonomy. In Verne, far from being (as it might be elsewhere) an ironic device insinuating the futility of expending further ink on a worthless subject,[173] the etcetera suggests rather the impracticability of completing a paradigm.[174] Thus the profusion of 'etc.'s betrays the interminability of the definitive aesthetic programme the *Voyages* undertake to complete: the totalization of knowledge.

In one respect at least, 'etc.' and '!' are quite antithetical in intention and effect. The anticipatory etcetera looks forward, falling over the edge of a sentence into an abyss of the unexpressed; it is a proleptic interpolation. The exclamation mark, on the other hand, is an analeptic interpolation: almost alone among punctuation marks, it looks backwards, forces on the reader a retrospective reassessment of the preceding sentence.[175] Both, however, are gestures of transcendence. 'Etc'. is a defensive manoeuvre, anticipating the objection that not everything that could be said has been said. '!', analogously, is an admission that something which cannot easily or reasonably be formulated needs to be added to a given statement. The exclamation mark is invariably in attendance on those frequent assertions (whose apparent insouciance it inevitably qualifies) of indescribability (*Quel spectacle indescriptible!*) adjoining Vernian descriptions. Elsewhere, the cadence of the exclamation mark serves as a reminiscence of those declarations of scriptural inadequacy: invested with a visual display of disaggregation, the punctuation par excellence of entropy, it evokes the inexhaustibility of the objects of scientific description. '!', like 'etc.', is, in short, an abbreviated form of the infinite.

Mathematically considered, the meaning of the exclamation mark in the *Voyages* is quite unequivocal. Verne's use of '!' duplicates its function in algebra, where it signifies a factorial operation, that is, the multiplication of the preceding number or quantity by every lesser integer (i.e. $n! = n(n-1)(n-2)\ldots 1$). Verne's proliferation of things and beings appears to be the product of a precisely identical operation, a process of multiple multiplication. This explosive propagation explains why Verne perceives the extension and accumulation of nominal inventories as finally unequal to the mission of exhaustive designation. While the signified conforms to the divine imperative to be fruitful and multiply, thus forming a geometrical progression, Verne's substantival signifier is confined to performing a series of additions, comprising a merely arithmetical progression. Thus the more numerous the names the writer enumerates, the further he is from completing his appointed task of enumeration.

If the fragmented exclamation mark is the pre-eminent punctuation of the *Voyages*, it is because it displays the incommensurability of monumental ends and inadequate means.

4.9 Anepistemophilia

The *Voyages* seek to construct an encyclopedia and an academy, a concordance of savants and their doctrines. But the *Académie* and the *Encyclopédie* were no longer, in the age of Verne, stable institutions.

On two consecutive occasions in 1809, the *Académie des Sciences* was obliged to terminate its sessions prematurely for want of further matter for discussion and speakers to provide it.[176] A commission, presided over by Cuvier, was appointed to determine the causes of this crisis and advise on possible remedies. In its report, the commission identified two major phenomena affecting the *Académie*. One: the proliferation of 'Sociétés savantes particulières', generating 'un auditoire plus approprié à des mémoires de détail'; two: the proliferation of specialized 'collections périodiques' in which the *Membres* were publishing their papers as soon as they were written. These two developments tended to deprive the *Académie* of a potential audience, and its annual and collective

Mémoires (which insisted on unpublished articles) of potential material.[177]

Cuvier's report ratified a transformation in the practice of science: the separation of disciplines was not of course new (although the way the disciplines were divided was indeed being constantly revised); what was new was the breakdown in communication between disciplines, the proliferating technical languages, each increasingly incomprehensible to anyone outside select coteries. Specialized modes of scientific discourse were becoming inaccessible not just to the intelligent amateur, but to the professionals.[178] The intellectual clerisy, thanks to its very success in disseminating information, was dissolving into mutually estranged clans. The scientific explosion had left the constituent particles of knowledge distributed more widely but also more remotely through space.

The *Encyclopédie* was constructed on the model of the *Académie*: assuming that individual omniscience was no longer feasible, it assembled a *pléiade de savants* to enunciate a body of knowledge beyond the compass of a single mind; but it remained an enormous collective mind, predicated on the fundamental kinship of the contributors and the verbal coherence of their contributions. The function of the *Encyclopédie*, as formulated by Diderot, was to 'exposer, autant qu'il est possible, l'ordre et l'enchaînement des connoissances humaines';[179] its ideal was an epistemic encirclement, a Vernian circumnavigation of the sphere of knowledge. The putative unity of the universe (in which 'tout [est] lié, contigu')[180] necessitated a unified map of knowledge. The essential criterion determining the validity of a statement was not its verifiability but its comprehensiveness and connectedness. Such was the cosmological theory of the authentic (philosophical) text: one either said everything or nothing.[181]

But with the turn of the century, the totality of knowledge had ceased to be conceivable as a unity; and with the definitive severing of science from philosophy, the business of constructing a *système*, the synthetic product of specious *a priori* reasoning, was thenceforward consigned, by the contemptuous scientist, to the metaphysician.[182] The encyclopedia would not cease to exist; but its status had irrevocably changed: from being the ultimate repository of knowledge, it had become, at best, a prolegomenon; at worst, it was an object of mockery or indifference, a joke. Chateaubriand denounced the *Encyclopédie* as the blasphemous contrivance of satanic atheists; but for Flaubert, it was much less the occasion of

scandal than of ridicule.[183] The condition of professional respect-
ability was no longer totalization but specialization. And the
respected medium of scientific discourse was increasingly the small-
scale, exclusive journal, not the intentionally all-inclusive book, as
commodious as the universe.[184] The book is condemned as unscientific.[185]

The various totalizing projects of the nineteenth century are gestures of nostalgia and conservatism; they mount a desperate
defence of a fortress already in ruins: the book as a unitary, systematic framework for the containment of information, equipped with
a natural or necessary language for its expression. Verne's nostalgic, reactionary novels constitute an attempt to reassemble the relatively unified classical discourse of the eighteenth century. The final
pages of *L'Ile à hélice*, following the destruction of the island, pose
the question: can it be reconstructed? – 'sera-t-il possible de réunir
des morceaux qui flottent isolément?'[186] Such is the central predicament, transposed from ark to archive, articulated in the *Voyages*,
and issuing in the *voyageur*'s enterprise of reunification.

This project, the essential vocation of Vernian man, can be discerned in Verne's heteroglot style: a discursive mosaic, a scrapbook
of verbal manners, a travel album of exotic linguistic snapshots,
juxtaposing miscellaneous souvenirs of archival journeying.[187]
Verne's polyglottal savants are located, by their ambition to
assemble all available information, at the intersection of disparate
idioms. The savant is, in effect, an interpreter, bestriding distant
disciplines. A doxographer, a mnemotechnician,[188] the sum of his
quotations, he is frequently compared to a book: he is a résumé of
the *Voyages*, a microtext, a single cell of a larger body containing,
in miniature, all the corporate characteristics: an encyclopedia, the
absolute book which the *Voyages* aspire to be, a compilation of all
other books, *une arche sainte*: 'un microcosme, un composé de toute
la science et de toute l'intelligence humaine'.[189] The erudite
voyageur is a writer as well as a reader, one capable (if only his
ceaseless travels allowed him the time) of writing the *Voyages*. His
authority, his right to write, resides in his all-encompassing knowledge. Only once he has travelled twenty thousand leagues beneath
the seas can Aronnax confidently assert: 'J'avais maintenant le droit
d'écrire le vrai livre de la mer.'[190] Since the distance he travels is a
guarantee of his learning, circumnavigation is the sufficient and
necessary condition of authorship. And the *Voyages*, equally, await
their justification in the completion of a global journey around the
scientific archive and the attainment of epistemic synthesis.

But if the Vernian savant-*voyageur* yearns for the physical stability and epistemic closure which would mark the end of his double journey through the world and the scientific archive, he simultaneously fears permanent immobility. Verne's ultimate hell, like Dante's, is not an inferno but a state of glaciation: the heat-death of the universe. Numerous Vernian prophets foretell the long-term doom awaiting the world: a gradual cooling, internally, in the earth's core, and, externally, in the sun, terminated by a condition of which the moon is already the symbolic victim: frozen senility. Perfect stasis, the thermodynamic fate inflicted by the conclusion of entropy, is a tomb.[191] Thus the utopia of rest and fixity is indistinguishable from the dystopia of fatal inertia.

The construction of the closed, confined, well-ordered space, the completion of the circle of knowledge and history, is alternately aspiration and affliction. Nemo, who constructs a submarine archive, is finally imprisoned within it: quadruply entombed, in bed, inside the *Nautilus*, which is trapped, in turn, inside the island, which sinks, after a volcanic convulsion, to the bottom of the ocean. Hence the ambiguity of the sealed area: it is at once refuge and coop, offering both the temptation of security and the threat of asphyxia. Vernian explosions, the product of overconsumption, condensed in their attendant punctuation of exclamation marks, and condensing the fractured narratives of the *Voyages*, project, no less than the disappointment of a frustrated design, the euphoria of release. In Verne's fiction, there is no space for the tranquil condition of physical stasis, epistemic synthesis, or historical closure. Thus the *Voyages* prolong indefinitely the anticipation of an end to travelling or writing.

Cyrus Smith's critique of Nemo is enigmatic: 'votre tort est d'avoir cru qu'on pouvait ressusciter le passé et vous avez lutté contre le progrès nécessaire'.[192] Nemo's sense of intellectual supremacy and the definitiveness of his library (an image of his mind externalized) depend on the closure of writing. His itinerant existence represents a flight from evolutionary humanity and a retreat into a timeless world secure against the incursions of the future into the present. Smith, on the other hand, admits that the library of knowledge contains many empty spaces (the spaces that are an integral feature of Verne's landscape of the partial void). The savant, tutored, like Nemo, in nothing less than everything, equally conversant in science and letters, an aristocratic amateur whose intellectual library is complete, belongs to the past: he is an extinct or obsolete animal, a fallen idol worshipped by an earlier and epistemologically more naive age. Cyrus Smith's judgement on Nemo, echoing Cuvier's requiem for the *Académie*, is a lament for the passing of the classical savant, who has been superseded by the *scientiste*.

In information theory, entropy represents a measure of the uncertainty of a message or the lack of information, in a word, of ignorance.[193] In the *Voyages*, the punctuation of entropy, the endemic '!'s and 'etc.'s are the signs of that ignorance, the verbal indicators of the amount of missing information. Information is the negative of entropy, or 'negentropy'. In these terms, the objective of the Vernian savant or *voyageur*, each of whom is a would-be disseminator of information, is the global maximization of negentropy, the abolition of entropy.[194] Hence the importance they attach to communication. Fluent communication is a prerequisite of community, the global village, the political and physical solidarity to which men and things spontaneously aspire; the *voyage*, in turn, seeks to accomplish the dream of timeless, spaceless, homogeneity.[195] But the disabling or disintegration of the Vernian vehicle, and the progressive multiplication and decomposition of objects in general, are pointers to the persistent attrition effected by entropy: the promotion of disunity.

The ubiquitous images of multiplication and division graphically narrate the fragmentation of the matter and media of science. Serres recalls that the clock was the 'modèle de tout le savoir neuf . . . à l'âge classique'.[196] The breakdown and falling-apart of the clocks constructed by Maître Zacharius, and the corresponding demise of the clockmaker,[197] he conjectures, signify the fragmentation of the classical configuration of the rational, Newtonian universe, encompassed by a unified framework of knowledge and accessible to the savant, conceived in turn as an *horloger*. More tangibly, the sheer profusion of the *Voyages*, mirrored in the individual text by its wayward distribution of disparate blocks of (narratively unjustifiable) information (occurring in the form of lectures, sermons, anecdotes, theories, recondite data), diverting the forward thrust of narrative into lateral digressions and detours, records the immense plurality of far-flung verbal islands that Verne proposed, heroically, to encompass and reunite in a single, discursive geography.

The first section devoted to Verne, while noting that a shark's stomach is opened up for inspection in *Les Enfants du capitaine Grant*, neglected to mention that the sailors' expectation of some surprising item among its contents is fulfilled by the discovery of a container. The container in turn divulges three documents: versions in three languages (English, French, and German) of a single text. But eroded by sea-water, and reduced to fragments, each is incomplete; decoding their common message depends on a synthesis: 'en rapprochant ces lambeaux de phrase, nous finirons par leur trouver un sens intelligible'.[198] However, even united, the documents leave important gaps. The decoders know that a shipwreck has occurred along a certain line of latitude, but they are forced to conjecture as to the longitude of the survivors. The novel traces the consequences of three successive interpretations of the fragmentary message, leading the would-be rescuers from Patagonia through Australia to New Zealand. Benign chance alone brings the *Duncan* to the island where the castaway Captain Grant, as author, delivers a fourth reading of the enigmatic text. He reveals that 'abor', which Paganel has obstinately assumed to be the beginning of the verb *aborder*, is in fact the end of the proper name of the island, Tabor, where the shipwrecked mariners had taken refuge.

The narrator points out a mitigating circumstance: 'Erreur difficile à éviter, cependant, puisque les planisphères du *Duncan* donnaient à cet îlot le nom de Marie-Thérésa.'[199] All the difficulties of the search-party arise from the fact that English and French give different names to the same island; a confusion of languages, of which the savant is no longer the master, is thus the occasion of a circumnavigation (with its attendant adventures) along the 37th parallel. The lack of a universal, unitary discourse, in which each thing would be endowed with its unique and necessary name, is the indispensable condition, in the *Voyages*, of travelling and writing.

The text is not only swallowed by the shark but 'rongé' by sea-water, gnawed away by erosion, and thereby reduced to fragments. These alimentary images recall the nutritive epistemology of the Vernian hero. The savant, like the writer, seeks to reunify the archive by assimilating everything, consuming all available literature; but to assimilate is to fragment. Throughout the *Voyages*, consumption is shown to comprise two antagonistic events: integration and disintegration. The commodity is typically subjected to a series of mutations and degradations, deprived of its original form in order to be digested (the sailor is 'brisé' by the octopus) or transformed (from a seal into a candle). Identical processes operate upon language: taxonomy disrupts geography: arranged into paradigmatic series, Verne's multiple terminologies are dislodged from their syntagmatic system: grammar gives way to the dominion of the noun.

There are no antitheses in the *Voyages*: entropy and negentropy, knowledge and ignorance, eating and being eaten are not opposite forces engaged in a conflict for pre-eminence; rather they constitute the twin aspects of a single reversible process. The function of the Vernian savant, as of the text, is to rectify a lack: but as he goes about filling in gaps he creates still more gaps waiting to be filled, enlarging the original lack. Eating generates appetite, eating away at the consumer ('rongé par la faim'); ordering generates disorder; the expansion of the book of knowledge entails the yet greater expansion of the book of ignorance.[200] If eating fragments, and fragmentation frustrates knowledge, then to the initial equation 'connaître, c'est manger' must be added its obverse: 'manger, c'est méconnaître'. Epistemophilia therefore implies anepistemophilia. The more the savant eats, says, or knows the more there is remaining to be eaten, said, or known.

Assimilation therefore contains a principle of proliferation. The centripetal theory of Verne's fiction is allied to a centrifugal practice: the cause of reintegration professed by the text, a consumer of language, produces an effect of disintegration. The multiplication of numbers and classifications does not tend towards a plenitude, but uncovers additional *abîmes*, deepens the 'vide sublime' of science:[201] science, as in Rabelais, is an abyss. In their assemblage of a Babel of codes and canons, the *Voyages* reproduce rather than rectify the decentralization undermining the authority of the academy and the encyclopedia.[202] Thus Verne stands as the titanic incarnation of the project of totalization and its most ironic commentator.

Jean Jules-Verne suggests that Verne sought to compensate for his medically prescribed dietary deprivation by inventing polyphagous adventures for his heroes, to assuage vicariously an appetite otherwise doomed to frustration. Yet, for all its prodigal nutrition, Verne's fiction does not satisfy but only perpetually overstimulates the demands of omnivoracity. In Verne's writing, increase of appetite grows by what it feeds on; but the language it feeds on also grows by being fed on.[203] Gastronomically, the world is at once insufficient to satiate an inexhaustible voracity and too abundant to be consumed. Epistemologically, the ultimate particles of Vernian matter elude quantification and designation. Aesthetically, the realist enterprise of definitive description is indefinitely postponed.

Verne is an ostentatiously intentionalist writer; but he is not reducible to the sum of his intentions. His primary ambition, perhaps the ambition of any writer, was to have nothing more to say, to retire from writing, his aesthetic task accomplished. He charged his *voyageurs* with the mission of putting an end to fiction by circumscribing all possible, partial statements within the limits of a complete and necessary discourse. But the *Voyages* (like the Bible, like Nicholas) only promise a final revelation which does not occur. Verne's fiction, tracing the obscure geometry of knowledge and ignorance through the reversible patterns of intentions and frustrations, constructions and destructions, beginnings and endings, explores the conditions of its own production and elusive completion.[204]

5

END

'and go till you come to the end; then stop'
(Lewis Carroll, *Alice's Adventures in Wonderland*)

The God of Revelation identifies himself as 'Alpha and Omega, the beginning (*archē*) and the end (*telos*), the first (*prōtos*) and the last (*eschatos*)' (22:13). The Book of Revelation (a late addition to the Biblical canon) identifies itself with God by seeking exemption from subtraction and addition, thereby constituting a textual incarnation of the divine minimum and maximum (and at the same time achieving the status of a perfect work of art, noted by Aristotle, such 'that you could not take from it nor add to it'):[1]

> For I testify unto every man that heareth the words of the prophecy of this book, If any man shall add unto these things, God shall add unto him the plagues that are written in this book: And if any man shall take away from the words of the book of this prophecy, God shall take away his part out of the book of life, and out of the holy city, and from the things which are written in this book. (22:18–19)

The Bible derives its authority from its integrity, rests its claim to be the word of God on its claim to pronounce the first and the last word on everything, to describe both the beginning and the end of Creation, genesis and apocalypse. But the Old Testament records a beginning where everything is already begun, while the New Testament only predicts an ending which is not yet.

Rousseau confessed: 'Je ne sais ni commencer ni finir.'[2] This inability to start or finish is not peculiar to Jean-Jacques, but rather the common predicament of the Bible and the other texts considered in this text, each of which (defying the curses of St John the Divine) adds to or subtracts from scripture, and is in turn added to or subtracted from. All the texts embody an aspiration to the condition of an origin or a terminus, prior or subsequent to writing, but which writing renders irrecoverable or unattainable. These two ideal moments, denoting either the absence or the presence of an archive, coincide with the epistemological vacuum and plenum of nescience and omniscience, each affording a privileged access to truths inaccessible to intermediate states.

Genesis initiates a *reshit* of pure ignorance, a *tabula rasa* whose human incarnation is twinned with a God endowed with knowledge of good and evil. The Renaissance reassigns the scriptural Fall to the Middle Ages, and seeks redemption by reconstructing the perfect wisdom of the classical library or relinquishing all literature. Rousseau postulates a pre-textual past and a post-textual future, a double golden age of reunification with nature or culture. Oriental-ism geographically relocates Rousseau's states or periods in the illit-erate barbarism of the East and the literate civilization of the West, constructing an archaeology to support a teleology of cultural trans-mission. Finally, the encyclopedic fiction of Jules Verne traces the transition from genesis to apocalypse, from an *archē* to a *telos* which marks the closure of history by the conclusion of an archive, thus doubly eradicating the novel.

Each of the texts, in short, invokes an antithesis, between Paradise and the Fall, *antiqua* and *moderna*, civilized and savage, Occident and Orient, science and literature, designed to order logi-cal, chronological, and epistemological priorities. But writing, mediating between extremes, enforcing a process of exchange on a relation of opposition, seems to be incapable of sustaining a stable duality. Each category affirms overtly the exclusion or annihilation of an opposite which it covertly assimilates. Thus the texts subtly sabotage the hierarchical models they aim to construct. Anepis-temology, prolonging an intermediate age between a lost plenitude and its reappropriation, prohibits the realization of the programme it articulates.

In Genesis, ignorance stands as an *ezer kenegdo* to divine knowl-edge, which it fulfils only by leaving it incomplete, while Adam, already fallen inside Eden, possesses knowledge even before acquiring it: thus God and man appear imperfect representatives of the perfections of omniscience and nescience. Renaissance writing, ineligible for the dignification of a *tabula rasa*, and discontinuous with the thesaurus of Antiquity, incapable of either transcending or reappropriating the past, duplicates the intermediary status of the Bible by relapsing into the Middle Age it condemns. Birth and rebirth recur as fictional moments, the one already over, the other still to come, in the work of Rousseau, which denounces as unknow-able the absence and the presence of knowledge. The theory, asserted by Hugo, of the dominion of an enlightened Occident over a benighted Orient is successively inverted by Napoleon's pragmatic substitution of Orientalization for Europeanization, and subverted by Chateaubriand's pathology of the sun, which not only implies the decay of the figural opposition between night and day, and hence between Orient and Occident, but deprives writing simultaneously of originality and finality. In Verne, the polarization between ignorance and knowledge evolves into a sequence of reversible adventures, whose heroes confidently anticipate but constantly postpone the omniscient climax of science.

Genesis records a sentence of exile. Each of the succeeding texts relates an exodus: an itinerary that is the subject and the condition of writing. Nicholas of Cusa and Erasmus set the soul in motion, vacillating between learning and illiteracy, folly and wisdom, earth and heaven, moon and sun; the text, its embodiment and counterpart, is condemned to be a discursive dog. Rousseau is a traveller who has long left behind his point of departure but is still short of a destination, while the Orientalists commute between, without ever attaining, the points of rest represented by the Orient and the Occident. Verne's *Voyages* translate travelling into the narrative metaphor of cognitive discovery; but the journey will not be completed so long as knowledge remains incomplete, so long as anything remains unsaid.

According to the doctrine propounded by the *Magasin d'éducation et de recréation*, the ideal text is a simple conduit of information; but according to information theory, literature is imperfect communication, a mere series of underoptimized messages distorted by noise. The problematic status of writing in the nineteenth century arose from the discrepancy between the normative prescription of what it should be and the negative description of what it was. The ambition to refashion literature on the pattern of science constituted an attempt to abolish a deviant mode of discourse, to bring it to an end: literature was the consequence of the Fall; it was a Middle Age awaiting its Renaissance; it was a savage which ought to be civilized; it was an Orient in need of colonization by a scientific Occident: it could only be redeemed by conforming to the privileged epistemological law it violated.

The realist text does not require the exhibition of a reliable scientific description, a neutral, objective, and exhaustive specification of the logos in which everything is assigned its proper name; sufficient to sustain its authority is the supposition that such a description should, in the last resort, exist or be capable of existing. The nineteenth-century novel is thus typically a system of allusion, paper currency whose nominal value relies for its confirmation on the gold standard of a treasury located elsewhere. Verne is the first among novelists to require the realist thesaurus of scientific discourse to honour its promises. What his fiction records is a condition of rampant inflation undermining the realist's credit.

The *Voyages* advertise a positivist conception of science as a container that can be filled, an ark preserving knowledge from liquid regression, a dictionary or encyclopedia destined to correlate the constituent facts of the universe in a singular, definitive discourse. Thus Lidenbrock asserts that 'la science est éminemment perfectible'; but he qualifies the view he articulates by adding: 'chaque théorie est incessamment détruite par une autre'.[3] The rule of reversibility governing the Vernian text entails a second conception of science, an inverted image of the first, overturning its naive certainties: science is a cracked vessel, an archive that sinks in the *abîmes* of its own classifications, a *vide* swallowing up or dispersing the vanishing particles of knowledge in its endless multiplication of discourses, a devalued, decentralized treasury.

Baudelaire (writing of Hugo) exclaims with relief: 'Ah! malgré Newton et malgré Laplace, la certitude astronomique n'est pas aujourd'hui même si grande que la rêverie ne puisse se loger dans les vastes lacunes non encore explorées de la science moderne.'[4] Science is proposed as the means of finishing off literature, but literature is summoned to supplement science by filling in the proliferating lacunae it generates. Scientific mathesis suffers from the very lack of epistemic completion for which it condemns literary mimesis. Thus the scientific foundation of fictional authority proves itself to be fictional.

The *Voyages* register the transition from the subordination of fiction to a scientific view of literature (as mimesis) to the subordination of physics to an aesthetic view of science (as imaginative construct). In Verne, the *roman scientifique* is usurped by the science fiction novel. And the point of intersection between science and fiction, their common denominator which is also the axis of the *Voyages*, is their ineradicable quota of ignorance. Kristeva observes that 'c'est donc au lieu de la rencontre de l'écriture avec la parole, de la science avec l'ignorance que le roman va naître, écho sensible de la théorie de la "Docte ignorance" dont Nicolas de Cues se fait l'apôtre'.[5] Thus Verne constitutes an exemplary case of the possibilities and limitations of fiction.

The Renaissance, Rousseau, Orientalism, Verne alternately desire and fear the completion of the book of knowledge which would forever close the book of nature. But in the *Voyages*, partial ignorance is installed as an absolute, as inexhaustible as the universe. Classical ignorance was a purely contingent, accidental state of affairs, a reminiscence of Eden; it was a benign malady susceptible to treatment and cure; it was venal, it was trivial, it was redeemable: it would disappear when the frontiers of science finally coincided with the circumference of the world. The dissolution of science into insular territories, ruled over by alternative languages, heralded the institutionalization of ignorance. Modern ignorance, fully conscious, expansive, and officially sanctified, at last accorded a *raison d'être*, by being a necessity has at the same time become a virtue, not merely inescapable but indispensable, an *ezer kenegdo* beneficial to the growth of knowledge. Knowledge and ignorance appear (already in Cuvier)[6] not mutually exclusive but inseparable and complementary, not enemies but allies. But the knowledge of ignorance is reversible and subversive because it implies the ignorance of knowledge.

Science is compelled to relinquish the ambition of omniscience; but if it cannot know everything, nor can it know anything incorrigibly.[7] Science is not a repository of truth but a structure of propositions always liable to revision or refutation. The intelligible turns out to be like the sensible: subject to mutability. Science, like literature, is suspended not merely between the limits of nescience and omniscience, but equally between the certainties of ignorance and knowledge: what looks like knowledge from the angle of ignorance looks more like ignorance from the angle of knowledge. Science is, in short, a *docta ignorantia* whose epistemological status is always in transition.

Bakhtin points out that

seul l'Adam mythique abordant avec sa première parole un monde pas encore mis en question, vierge, seul Adam-le-solitaire pouvait éviter totalement cette orientation dialogique sur l'objet avec la parole d'autrui.[8]

Science (the whore of science, Nicholas would say) aspires to that virginal state of language: the scientist characteristically conceives of himself as an 'éternel Adam'. Scientific knowledge is founded by reference to a state of ignorance, an epistemic point zero, a prediscursive phase of pure experience. Thus Claude Bernard opposes the *laboratoire*, the sanctum of experimental verities, an Archimedean point beyond discourse, to the *bibliothèque*, the domicile of unreliable opinion.[9] His scepticism about language is as mystical as the ascetic axiom of the Zen adept, that he who knows does not speak, and he who speaks does not know. In a similar vein, Thomas Sprat records that the members of the Royal Society have declared war on the duplicity of language, undertaken 'to separate the knowledge of Nature from the colours of *Rhetorick*, the device of *Fancy*, or the delightful deceit of *Fables*'. Rhetoric is the cause of ignorance: 'Who can behold, without indignation, how many mists and uncertainties, these specious *Tropes* and *Figures* have brought on our knowledge?'[10] Science perpetually dreams of dispensing with the library and confronting raw data, a transparent presence of nature that would make description superfluous. But, as Quine observes, 'the totality of our so-called knowledge or beliefs, from the most casual matters of geography and history to the profoundest laws of atomic physics or even of pure mathematics and logic, is a man-made fabric which impinges on experience only along the edges'.[11] The laboratory cannot abolish the library and scientific argumentation continues to resort to a variety of rhetorical devices,[12] one of which is the rejection of rhetoric. Science can never wholly transcend *maya*, *doxa*; scientists too are *logodaedali*. Proceeding from a textbook and issuing in a paper, scientific research inevitably encounters a conceptually constituted world. The pre-existence and the production of language are no less necessary conditions of the formulation of scientific theory than they are of a novel.

Nicholas of Cusa remarked that 'when there is comparatively little distance from the object of enquiry back to the object regarded as certain, a judgement is easily formed; when many intermediaries (*multis mediis*) are required, the task becomes difficult'.[13] The task of science is difficult precisely because an original object of certainty is lacking, because *multa media* are indeed required. But science is not just mediated by discourse;[14] it is a discourse: in the terms of the later Wittgenstein, it constitutes a family of language-games, linked by resemblance but not interchangeable. But neither, on the other hand, is it trapped in a prison-house of language; it would only be restricted by the stabilization of a canonical notation, a univocal *characteristica universalis*: the instabilities of language are the precondition of its proliferation. Hence Feyerabend's remark that 'without a constant misuse of language there can not be any discovery, any progress'.[15] Moreover, as Verne demonstrates, the centripetal drive towards singularity itself generates a centrifugal effect of plurality.

The writer, in turn, may adopt an attitude either of negation or reaffirmation towards his ancestry. But not even the most revolutionary of literary inventions (as Chateaubriand confirms) can hope to secede entirely from the past; its very distinctiveness depends for its recognition on a contrast with those conventions it purports to subvert. Equally, the opposite ambition (asserted by the Renaissance) to duplicate a pre-existing corpus is bound to be frustrated, since even exact repetition, separated from its object by time and the gesture of identification, cannot absolve the text from an obligation to be different. Originality and imitation are symmetrical illusions: the intention to cut loose from the intellectual tradition to which the writer is ineluctably attached, to relinquish discourse, is unrealizable; no less inescapable is the writer's isolation. Thus there is no archive that does not contain its own negation, and no archival negation that does not contain an affirmation of that archive.[16] All writing is a rewriting, defining and deviating from a thesaurus, transgressing the laws it articulates.

Science, then, does not so much resemble literature as both resemble literary criticism. Thus in philosophy the dominion of epistemology has tended to be usurped by hermeneutics.[17] The ambition of literary criticism to be a science, to reconvert hermeneutics into epistemology, betrays a nostalgia for a lost paradise.

The claim to know (or the ideal of knowing) everything, made by theology in the Middle Ages and science in the nineteenth century, has been echoed in the twentieth by literary criticism. George Bernard Shaw alludes to this pretension when he writes in a critical article (under the name of Corno di Basetto) that:

I regret to have to announce that *The British Bandsman*, an excellent paper devoted to the interests of the brass banditi, has had the mad presumption to 'strongly suspect that I am deficient in knowledge of wind instruments'. This is true; but I am not going to be told so by any British bandsman alive. How am I to make myself respected as a critic if the public for a moment suspects that there is anything I don't know?[18]

If, as C. S. Peirce's semiotic theory holds, the meaning of a sign (determined by reference to an 'interpretant' which is itself a sign)[19] must be deferred to the end of a potentially infinite series of operations, then the content of even a single term is equivalent to an encyclopedia. Since the interpretation of a text, a system of signs, therefore depends on its location within an indeterminate network of other texts, a multiplicity of encyclopedias, the critic is bound to be tempted by the prospect of omniscience.

This theological teleology underlies the intention expressed by Serres to complete an exhaustive description of the Vernian text;

and it recurs in Macherey's specification of the ideological blueprint of Verne's fiction, his aesthetic DNA, and in Vierne's reduction of the *Voyages* to the avatars of an initiatory archetype. Each of these critics, separately proclaiming a structuralist totalization, is a descendant of Emile Hennequin, whose *Critique scientifique*, appearing contemporaneously with the *Voyages*, elaborates an *esthopsychologie* designed to conclude a quest for unassailable validity and definitiveness in statements about literature (exempt from journalistic *opinion*), which echoes both the Vernian savant's search for unattainable stability and the Bernardian suspicion of the *bibliothèque*.[20]

Thus the *Voyages* constitute an encyclopedia not only of nineteenth-century codes of writing, but also, in their attendant decodings, of twentieth-century codes of reading. But the critic's convenient fictions of comprehensiveness, exclusivity, and adequacy, deriving from a mythical model of omniscient science, ignore the demytholigizing implications of Verne's writing: that the text, like the world, is not a problem with a unique solution and cannot be represented mathematically or eternally; that it can therefore sustain an indefinite number of possible descriptions, none of which is necessary; and that those descriptions, adding to or subtracting from the text, only endlessly multiply (without totalizing) its meanings.

Literature and science, obviating the classical distinction between the active and the contemplative, the creative and the critical, language and meta-language, rejoin the continuum of the interpretative enterprise. And the condition that makes interpretation necessary, the recalcitrance of meaning, also makes the completion of that task impossible. Criticism is obliged to leave its job undone, never to finish an undertaking which it does not begin. Thus the critic, unwilling to say nothing, incapable of saying everything, like the novelist, like the savant, requires an aesthetics of omission, of incompleteness, of partiality. Omniscience is incompatible no less with reading than with writing; as Gadamer points out, 'the universality of the hermeneutical experience would not be available to an infinite mind, for it develops out of itself all meaning, all noeton, and thinks all that can be thought in the perfect contemplation of itself'.[21] Plato places the sun of knowledge outside the cave of ignorance; but in Vernian science, the sun (of an underground aurora) is inside the cave (the inverted cosmos at the centre of the world). In the terms of Paul de Man, blindness is a prerequisite of insight.

Criticism is not alone in being in the middle of the way. This study has tried to show what is obvious, that it is difficult to have the first or last word. But the indispensable virtue of the book is its refutation of this thesis. Every book is a Bible, a textual theology equipped with a beginning and an end: an *archē* that is the first page, and a *telos* that is the last. The book is a tangible metaphor incorporating the birth and death that lie outside life, the *tabula rasa* and the thesaurus, a point of departure and a destination. As a medieval copyist concludes: 'And so the sailor is not more glad to reach harbour than the weary scribe to arrive at the last line of his manuscript.'[22] Writing frustrates the ambition it inspires of recovering an intransitive origin or attaining a definitive completion. But every text compensates for that prohibition by providing a transitive beginning and a transitory ending, affording to the writer, as to the reader, the temporary satisfaction of reaching if not the end, then at least an end.

NOTES

Preface

1 *The Real Life of Sebastian Knight*, p. 30.
2 *De l'esprit des lois*, Book XI, Chapter 20.

1 Beginning

1 A similar narrative structure can be discerned in, for instance, positivist, linguistic, and phenomenological descriptions, which typically recall states preceding description, defined, respectively, by data, *parole*, or consciousness.
2 Hippias informed Socrates that the Spartans were particularly fond of hearing about anything to do with *archaiologia* (*Greater Hippias*, 285D). This passage is cited by Groningen (*In the Grip of the Past*, p. 47), who makes a distinction between 'mythical' and 'historical' time in Greek thought ('Two conceptions of the past', Chapter 8, *ibid.*).
3 *Paradise Lost*, VIII, 250–1.
4 *The Pentateuch and Rashi's Commentary*, I, p. 2.
5 Heidel notes such parallels in *The Babylonian Genesis*.
6 *Other Inquisitions*, p. 24.
7 *Pentateuch*, I, p. 1. Hirsch has many supporters. Cassuto, for example (in *A Commentary on the Book of Genesis*), contests Rashi's view on the basis of the grammar of verse 2, which like verse 1, he reads as an independent sentence. But his inconclusive argument seems, like Hirsch's to be preceded by, rather than to justify, the requirement that Creation should constitute the beginning of time (I, pp. 19–20).
8 See André Caquot, 'Brèves remarques exégétiques sur Genèse I, 1–2', *In Principio*, pp. 9–21. Russell discusses the parallel case of a human author who can legitimately claim only an indefinite article: 'No proposition containing *the* (in the singular) can be strictly proved by empirical evidence. We do not know that Scott was *the* author of *Waverley*; what we know is that he was *an* author of *Waverley*. For aught we know, somebody in Mars may have also written *Waverley*. To prove that Scott was *the* author, we should have to survey the universe and find that everything in it either did not write *Waverley* or was Scott.

This is beyond our powers' (*An Inquiry into Meaning and Truth*, p.44). Thus the equivocal article of the first verse of Genesis may reflect the polytheistic disposition of its Babylonian sources. Needless to add, in the pre-Masoretic, pre-vocalized text, the meaning of the passage is still harder to determine. The Masoretic text represents an interpretation of an ambiguity which it does not resolve.

9 *Metaphysics*, 1013a.

10 *Ibid.*, 1076a. I am indebted on this point to Lloyd, *Polarity and Analogy*, pp. 231–2.

11 'Réflexions sur quelques-uns de mes contemporains', *Œuvres complètes*, p. 482.

12 Clearly, the concerns of this essay are not indifferent to those of scepticism. The sceptical and the anepistemological may be juxtaposed in a single text; but the two can nevertheless be distinguished. Scepticism asserts the ignorance to which anepistemology merely aspires. For scepticism, ignorance is an end; for anepistemology, it is a means, a prelude to the conclusion of knowledge. It would suffice to refute scepticism to show (as for example, Rescher does in *Scepticism*) that we can be said to have knowledge of something; anepistemology requires that we should know everything or nothing, not just anything. Scepticism claims to know ignorance; for anepistemology, the knowledge of ignorance is a distant goal. Thus anepistemology stands as a critique of scepticism.

13 I foresee that the section on the Renaissance, by saying so little about so much, is liable to cause maximum annoyance. This annoyance may be minimized by the consideration that I am not so much concerned with the period designated 'Renaissance' as with the concept of a rebirth, a repeat genesis, of which that period happens to be a prolific exponent.

14 Derrida calls the chiasmus 'le dessein thématique de la dissémination' (*La Dissémination*, p. 52).

15 Such is the fate, according to Genette, of all criticism (*Figures I*, p. 147).

16 'A Note on (towards) Bernard Shaw', *Labyrinths*, pp. 248–9.

17 In the preface or 'hors livre' to *La Dissémination*.

18 *A la recherche du temps perdu*, I, p. 482.

2 Nescience and omniscience

1 *Pensées*, Brunschvicg no. 339.

2 I follow here the conventional, if aleatory, expansion of the original consonants of the Tetragrammaton, in preference to 'Jehovah', which assimilates the vowels from *adonay* (Lord).

3 For convenience I use the King James translation throughout; transliteration of the Hebrew adheres to the conventions outlined in the *Encyclopedia Judaica*, Index Volume, p. 90.

4 *Genesis: A Commentary*, p. 78.

5 The schematic rigidity of Wellhausen's 'Documentary Hypothesis', which invokes a succession of sources (the original trio of J, E, and P has since multiplied), crudely collated by an incompetent editor, has been at least partially discredited. Cassuto in particular has demonstrated the hermeneutical value of refraining from disassembling the text into discrete and incompatible sub-texts (see *A Commentary on the Book of Genesis* and *The Documentary Hypothesis*). However, while allowing a multiplicity of sources, he seems to revert to the dogma of a homogeneously unified text whose kerygmatic singularity attests to its divine authority. But Genesis, if not a crude compilation, remains composite: like all texts, the meeting point of innumerable other texts. Alter's *The Art of Biblical Narrative* gives a persuasive account of the relevance to a reading of the Old Testament of its apparent anomalies and discrepancies. He thus provides a framework for the kind of synchronic analysis, transcending a purely archaeological description, recommended by Fokkelman in *Narrative Art in Genesis*.

6 *La divina commedia, Inferno*, V, 122–3.

7 The former view is held by, for example, Abraham ibn Ezra, who maintains that before eating of the Tree of Knowledge, man 'merely lacked the knowledge of good and evil in one respect (viz, sexual passion)' (cited in *The Soncino Chumash Bible*, ed. Cohen, p. 11). The latter view is expressed by Hertz: what he calls the 'dietary law' was designed to 'test the use [man] would make of his freedom' (*The Pentateuch and the Haftorahs*, I, p. 21).

8 Similarly, the Babylonian Adapa legend relates that 'He [Ea, the Creator] had given him [man] wisdom, (but) he had not given him eternal life' (see Heidel, *The Babylonian Genesis*, p. 126). Again, an Assyrian counterpart depicts a god instructing man in his duties as follows: 'In thy knowledge and afterwards in the tablet's (writing) . . . worship and goodness shall be raised' (cited in Smith, *The Chaldean Account of Genesis*, p. 79).

9 *Mimesis*, p. 11.

10 Leach writes that, '[a] noticeable characteristic of mythical stories is their markedly binary aspect; myth is constantly setting up opposing categories' (*Genesis as Myth*, p. 8).

11 Cassuto, *A Commentary*, I, p. 69.

12 Transformation tends to be exegetically subsumed under the generative. But if creation consists in rearranging a pre-existing universe, then the generative would tend to be subsumed under the transformational. Light would then be a metamorphosis of darkness, the firmament a modulation of earth and water.

13 Thus, in Jakobson's use of the terms, Creation is 'metaphoric' rather than 'metonymic': made up of independent units that are nevertheless not just contiguous but permeated by similarities and contrasts.

14 'It is a fundamental rule of Biblical narrative style that verbs describing

acts that took place in sequence should head their respective clauses, and take the form of the *imperfect* with consecutive *Wāw* [and]' (Cassuto, *A Commentary*, I, p. 27). Thus one of the recurrent rhetorical features of the Bible is, as Alter points out (pp. 76, 142), parataxis.

15 'A creature where the divine, the heavenly, is joined to the earthly, the spiritual to the material, the immortal to the mortal' (Hirsch, *Pentateuch*, I, p. 57). The twin elements of his microcosmic constitution, dust and divine breath, are members of antithetical connotative groups. On the one hand, dust points backwards to the earth from which man springs, to his original harmony with nature, and forwards to the dust to which he is doomed to return by his mortality, to the ground which he will be forced to work and eat in sorrow (*adam*, man, is twinned with *adamah*, earth); dust suggests an affinity with the serpent (who will eat dust), to other beasts of the field, and to Cain (a tiller of the ground); dust is inert, passive, dull. Breath, in contrast, of divine origin, is air, spirit, life; breath is dynamic, endlessly in motion, inexhaustible, mercurial; breath stresses man's kinship with Yahweh and with heaven.

16 Leach states that 'the "knowledge of good and evil" . . . means the knowledge of sexual difference' (p. 14). But Cassuto presents two decisive objections to the reduction of knowledge to carnal knowledge: (1) when the epistemological prohibition was pronounced, no woman existed; (2) the same knowledge is attributed to God. The *Lexicon* of Brown, Driver, and Briggs suffices to eliminate the equation with moral discrimination: it shows that in, for example, 2 Samuel 19:35 ('can I discern between god and evil?'), *yada* in the sense of discernment takes *beyn* (between) (BDB, p. 393). Hertz points out that 'good and evil' is a Hebrew idiom for 'all things', and therefore argues that 'knowledge of good and evil' may be taken to mean 'knowledge of all things, i.e. omniscience' (pp. 26, 19). Cassuto makes the phrase synonymous with the wisdom of the angel of God as expressed in 2 Samuel 14:20: 'to know all things that are in the earth' (*A Commentary*, I, p. 113).

17 'Une Idée fondamentale de la phénoménologie de Husserl: l'intentionnalité', *Situations I*, p. 29.

18 If all knowledge is, in some degree, carnal, then ignorance alone is a purely spiritual benison. Mary's affirmation, 'I know not a man' (Luke 1:34), indicates that virginity is the carnal counterpart to nescience. While sexuality entails a broadening of consciousness, chastity, a voluntary abstention from the pursuit of secular knowledge, effects a reversion to the *status ante lapsum*: it is an attempt to recover the intimacy of our Edenic ancestors' relationship with God.

19 Graves and Patai suggest that omniscience is a delusion, generated by hallucinogenetic mushrooms (*Hebrew Myths*, p. 81).

20 Hirsch notes that *ezer* is cognate with contradictory terms 'which all have the underlying conception of restricting, confining, limiting'; he

argues that it therefore designates 'that kind of help which relieves the other from a part of his obligations, allowing him thereby to concentrate his efforts to a smaller sphere of activity, and so to accomplish what is left to him in a more complete and perfect manner. It is a help by limiting and thus concentrating' (I, p. 65). *Kenegdo*, as Hertz points out, may mean either 'at his side' or 'as over against him' (p. 22); BDB, while translating 'corresponding to', also notes that its cognate is used in the idea of joining battle. Thus Rashi's comment: 'If he is worthy she shall be a help to him; if he is unworthy she shall be opposed to him, to fight him' (p. 11). The *ezer kenegdo*, in short, appears to fulfil by restricting, to support by opposing. The *Midrash Rabbah* aptly translates 2:18 as 'I will make him a *help against him*' (I, p. 133). This ambiguity is incidentally illustrated by Graves's view that the account of Eve's creation by way of the extraction of a rib from Adam derives from a misreading of an icon representing the insertion of a curved knife into his flank (*Adam's Rib*, p. 2).

21 Rashi (I, p. 12) suggests that the words emanate from the Holy Spirit.

22 The existence of this legislative ruling that governs even the legislator offers the solution to a classic textual crux. It is probable, in the light of this law of complementarity, that Yahweh's use of the plural personal pronoun in 1:26 and 3:22, 'Let us make man' and 'the man is become as one of us', is neither, as has been conjectured, a mere rhetorical gesture, nor a reminiscence of polytheistic source material, nor an allusion to otherwise absent members of a heavenly court: it is an evocation and anticipation (like the nominative plural, *Elohim* – Gods – of the opening verse) of the ubiquitous bias in favour of the pluralization of the singular, and a reminder that even in a monotheistic universe, God is compelled to couple.

23 *Collected Works*, XI, p. 394.

24 Auerbach asserts, rather dogmatically, that the character of Yahweh is determined by Hebraic descriptive technique, which is peculiarly elliptical: 'The concept of God held by the Jews is less a cause than a symptom of their manner of comprehending and representing things' (p. 8). The relation of cause and effect is, of course, impossible to determine; but it is clear that Auerbach's thesis neglects the kinship between the reversible structures of divine psychology and Biblical narrative. There is a further affinity: although prophecy is integral to the Old Testament, individual narratives are constructed sequentially so that the dénouement, when it occurs, is a genuine revelation, a surprise: the reader is invited to suspend his prior knowledge of the outcome. In this respect, he resembles Yahweh, who is ultimately the author of the narrative in which he appears as an unwitting character.

25 *Works*, XI, p. 394.

26 Cassuto notes that 'YHWH appears when the Bible presents the Deity to us in His personal character, and in direct relationship to human beings or to nature; whereas *Elohim* occurs when Holy Writ speaks of

God as a Transcendental Being, who stands entirely outside nature, and above it' (*A Commentary*, I, p. 87).

27 This analysis, based on textual evidence alone, does not presume to conclude whether God must or must not know this or that; no affiliation is proposed to any particular philosophical or theological tradition. Nevertheless, the view propounded by Levi ben Gershom (Gersonides) that God entertains only universal laws, not singular propositions, general categories not the contingent, and that 'un véritable acte de liberté étant totalement imprévisible, il ne peut être connu de Dieu' (see Touati, *La Pensée philosophique et théologique de Gersonide*, p. 144), seems to find support in 2:19: 'the Lord God . . . brought [beast and fowl] unto Adam to see what he would call them'. But Gersonides also argues that since the accidental is unreal, God's knowledge of reality remains unimpaired, still obedient to the unifying principle of *shelemut* or *temimut* (which Touati, p. 131, translates by *perfection* or *complétude*). Jung, in contrast, allows a principle of 'metaphysical disunity' (XI, p. 392). Nicholas of Cusa suggests that divine ignorance is a matter of indifference rather than incapacity: 'God could have foreseen much that He has not foreseen nor will foresee' (*De docta ignorantia*, Book I, Chapter 22, p. 49 in the Heron translation; p. 44 in the Leipzig edition).

28 Rashi, I, p. 17.

29 Cited in Cohen, p. 11. Alonso-Schökel suggests that 'la ciencia de Adán, anterior al pecado, es solamente ciencia del bien, de las cosas buenas que Dios ha creado y le va trayendo; después del pecado, la ciencia comienza a ser de bien y de mal' ('Motivos sapienciales y de alianza en Gn 2–3', p. 302). To judge by his public statements, the same might more confidently be asserted of God.

30 But the *tohu-wabohu* precedes the Word. The Word is not absolutely constitutive: the logos and the universe do not coincide.

31 *The Problems of Philosophy*, p. 26.

32 *Phaedrus*, 275E–276A.

33 *The Republic*, X, 598D. Mimesis is, specifically, at three removes from the original: the ideal issues in the real which yields an appearance which permits of representation (597E–598B).

34 A view upheld by Curtius, in *European Literature and the Latin Middle Ages*.

35 See Curtius, pp. 217–18, 223–5.

36 Thus Dante is the figurehead of the literary revival, elected by Boccaccio and Bruni among others.

37 In connection with later humanism, Bolgar cites Budé: 'Les lettres sont les escrains et aulmoires esquelz la science et la sapience a tousiours esté gardee et enclose' ('Humanism as a Value System', in *Humanism in France*, ed. Levi, p. 202).

38 Gilson notes that an 'opposition juridique et politique' (between Italy

and other countries) 's'est étendue chez Pétrarque au domaine du savoir' (*La Philosophie au moyen-âge*, p. 726).

39 An account of the humanist redefinition of the encyclopedia is given by Levi, and Simone, in *French Renaissance Studies 1540–70: Humanism and the Encyclopedia*, ed. Sharratt.

40 Simone demonstrates the persistence of this historical schematization in *Per una storia della storiografia letteraria francese* and *The French Renaissance*.

41 Vasoli remarks that 'on voit vite se profiler une nouvelle région, un autre âge de l'histoire humaine qui bien que continuant la bataille humaniste contre la "barbarie de l'âge du milieu", n'est pas moins consciente de son éloignement par rapport au monde ancien, reconnu désormais dans ses dimensions historiques plus réelles' ('La Première Querelle des "anciens" et des "modernes" aux origines de la Renaissance', *Classical Influences on European Culture*, ed. Bolgar, p. 69).

42 The Middle Ages justified editorial rectification of the past by analogy with the firm treatment meted out by the Jew to the foreign female captive he claims for a wife, as prescribed by Deuteronomy 21:10–13.

43 Petrarch and Bruni invoke the names of Augustine and St Basil to buttress the claims of antiquity, but discard their rule of qualification for inclusion in the classical thesaurus: that literature should be morally edifying (see, notably, St Basil's 'Address to Young Men on Reading Greek Literature', *Letters*, IV). Erasmus tries to restore the principle of *pietas litterata* (see Bolgar, *The Classical Heritage and its Beneficiaries*, p. 340ff), but his practice runs counter to his theory.

44 Bolgar has pointed out the indispensability to the Renaissance of the notebook method advocated by Erasmus (*The Classical Heritage*, pp. 272–5). The theory is re-examined by Cave in *The Cornucopian Text*.

45 'It was the renunciation of previous attempts to unite all knowledge and belief within a single system which marks the beginning of the dissolution of the medieval world outlook' (Leff, *The Dissolution of the Medieval Outlook*, p. 145).

46 *Renaissance France*, p. 10.

47 Haydn's *The Counter-Renaissance* postulates an anti-intellectual reaction succeeding the early humanist programmes. Defaux, in *Le Curieux, le glorieux et la sagesse du monde dans la première moitié du XVIᵉ siècle*, discerns two discourses, the one pro-, the other anti-*curiosité* (which he proceeds to trace in Rabelais). Such divisions inhere in the very concept of a renascence: humanism is invariably ambivalent about its own professed ideals.

48 Plato's philosophy would account for the disobedience related by Genesis. If moral behaviour, obedience to law, is conditional upon the acquisition of knowledge, then God's epistemic prohibition requires, in order to be obeyed, that it should first be contravened. A prohibition of knowledge is inherently unobeyable.

49 Thus Ecclesiastes says that 'God giveth to a man that is good in his sight wisdom, and knowledge, and joy' (2:26).

50 This conjunction is not of course new, but only renewed in the Renaissance. It is already present in Plato, whose work displays an ambivalence analogous to that discerned in the Bible. For Plato, the sensible is deficient in that it discloses reality only partially. The function of the *eidē* is to permit an encounter with pure being, uncorrupted by negation, in which knowledge would be complete. *Doxa* results from forgetting the truth, but *anamnēsis* (of the intelligible) also entails a selective amnesia, a forgetting (of the sensible). But it seems, then, that knowledge is complete only at the cost of exclusion: knowledge exists side by side with ignorance. The Forms are accordingly expanded to accommodate the multiplicity of things. But if they leave nothing out then they include incompleteness, becoming afflicted (as attested in the *Parmenides*) with the contingency affecting the sensible. Thus Gadamer points to 'the essential incompleteness of the dialectical endeavour' (*Dialogue and Dialectic*, p. 154). *Philosophia* implies only a desire for *sophia*, not its satisfaction.

51 *Microcosme*, I, 237–8; I, 365–8. Both passages are cited by Staub, *Le Curieux Désir*, p. 113.

52 Defaux has shown, in *Pantagruel et les sophistes*, that Gargantua's programme is wholly in accordance with medieval pedagogical theories (pp. 59–68).

53 *Pantagruel, Œuvres complètes*, pp. 205–6.

54 Brault, who considers the letter parodic from start to finish, examines some of the alternative implications of the phrase in ' "Ung abysme de science": On the Interpretation of Gargantua's Letter to Pantagruel', *Bibliothèque d'humanisme et de Renaissance* 28. He draws attention to the ironic use of the phrase 'le vrays puys et abisme de encyclopédie' in Thaumaste's praise of Panurge's supposed erudition (pp. 628–9; the passage cited occurs on p. 258 of the *Œuvres complètes*, Chapter XX).

55 Thus Nicholas conforms to Barthes's programme: 'Econduire le système comme appareil, accepter le systématique comme écriture' (*Barthes par Barthes*, p. 175). As Jaspers notes, 'it is impossible to expound his works in an internally consistent system' (*Anselm and Nicholas of Cusa*, p. 167).

56 Contrasted with the 'métonymique' of narrative forms and the 'métaphorique' of lyric poetry in 'Introduction à l'analyse des récits', *Communications* 8.

57 Aristotle describes the enthymeme as a 'rhetorical syllogism' whose premises may sometimes (and therefore only accidentally) be deficient in number but whose defining characteristic is to be probable rather than necessary, not of the order of *tekmēria* (*The Art of Rhetoric*, 1356b–1357c).

58 A frustration perhaps reflecting Nicholas's own: 'For I have not yet

been given the taste of how friendly the Lord is' (cited, from a letter, by Jaspers, p. 49).

59 Hirsch, commenting on Genesis 1:31, observes that the Hebrew word for 'everything' (*kol*) is cognate with terms meaning ring, hoop, crown, circle, and adds: 'all the expressions for the conception of completion and perfection are related in Hebrew to the word "circle" ' (I, p. 38).

60 *The Individual and the Cosmos in Renaissance Philosophy*, Chapter 1.

61 *The Vision of God*, trans. Salter, p. 59. This passage can be compared with San Juan's union of the 'gloomy night (*noche oscura*)' and the 'light . . . [that] lit and led me through / More certain than the light of noonday clear (*luz . . . Aquesta me guiaba / Más cierto que la luz del mediodía*)' (*The Poems of Saint John of the Cross*, pp. 10–11).

62 'By definition the minimum is that which cannot be less than it is; and since this is also true of the maximum, it is evident that the minimum is identified with the maximum (*manifestum est minimum maximo coincidere*)' (I, iv, p. 12; p. 10). Bett condemns this equation, naively, as a 'naive argument' (*Nicholas of Cusa*, p. 129).

63 The unfolding (*explicatio*) of God in the world guarantees the peripheral participation of our conjectures in truth. Jaspers comments that 'the conjectural character of the human mind is not to be confused with arbitrary conjecture, or scepticism in the sense of universal doubt' (p. 14).

64 *Etudes d'histoire de la pensée scientifique*, p. 20.

65 *Praisers of Folly*, p. 22.

66 'The *Praise of Folly* and its Background', *Twentieth-Century Interpretations of the 'Praise of Folly'*, ed. Williams, pp. 40–60 (p. 41).

67 According to Sartre, sincerity is 'une tâche impossible à remplir' (*L'Etre et le néant*, p. 98). Barthes (*S/Z*, p. 51) denounces the 'classic' text for signposting ironic statements with the effect that they are covertly marked as quotations; he demands of the multivalent text that it banish such invisible but perceptible *guillemets*. In Erasmus, the *guillemets* are visible but his attitude imperceptible.

68 Also adopted, in part, by Screech in *Ecstasy and the 'Praise of Folly'*. Unfortunately, Screech confers seriousness on only one short section of the text, the closing pages, which all the preceding pages are seen as playfully postponing. Screech asserts that 'Erasmus had a message to preach. He preached it untiringly' (p. 106). But if that is so, it seems implausible that he should waste so much time on, in Screech's reckoning, mere banter, before proceeding to sermonize. Screech's razor cuts out what is unnecessary to his (not Erasmus's) argument.

69 There is a plethora of translations of the *Praise of Folly*; Miller's seems to me the most accurate among the modern versions, adhering closely to the sinuosities of Erasmus's prose.

70 The Silenus figurine (the subject of a long passage in the *Praise of Folly* and of one of the longer essays of the *Adages*), contrasting an outer

(profane) appearance with an inner (sacred) reality, is sometimes advanced as the model of Erasmus's procedure and of the correct approach to the text, revealing a covert wisdom beneath the surface folly. But the simple dualism it embodies is inconsistent with the complexity of the *Praise of Folly*.

71 Erasmus's account of the Golden Age recalls Plato's mythical history, in the *Phaedrus*, of the invention of writing and the sciences by the Egyptian god Thoth. It is susceptible to the same sceptical analysis Derrida applies to Plato's text, showing that primordial speech is already contaminated with the maladies diagnosed by Thamus in Thoth's writing ('La Pharmacie de Platon', *La Dissémination*).

72 I use the word mainly in the linguistic sense defined by Jespersen: a word 'whose meaning differs according to the situation' (*Language, its Nature, Development and Origin*, p. 123). Jakobson has pointed out that the shifter nevertheless retains a fixed function: to refer back to the message of which it is part (*Essais de linguistique générale*, p. 179).

73 Leyden edition, V, p. 341AB, cited by Screech, p. 104, whose translation this is.

74 Introduction to *The Praise of Folie*, p. 4.

75 Thus, for example, the sceptical argument, as in Montaigne, is itself placed in parenthesis, barely articulated before being retracted. Popkin (*The History of Scepticism from Erasmus to Descartes*, p. 5) refers to the passage which runs: 'human affairs are so manifold and obscure that nothing can be clearly known' (p. 71, p. 130). But this immediately gives way to a qualification: 'Or, if anything can be known, it often detracts from the pleasures of life.'

76 *Excitationum* V, *Opera* (Basel), p. 473, cited by Jaspers, p. 112.

77 *Vision*, p. 110.

78 A similar approach might be made to the imaginary journeys of Rabelaisian travellers, reading them as parodic images of a cognitive quest. This avenue is partially explored by Chesney in *The Counter-voyage of Rabelais and Ariosto*. The self-analytical Montaigne remarks that 'mon stile et mon esprit vont vagabondant de mesme' (*Essais*, III, ix, p. 966). Like Rabelais, he adds a further connotation to motion: 'Ce sont icy, un peu plus civilement, des excremens d'un vieil esprit, dur tantost, tantost lache, et tousjour indigeste' (*ibid.*, p. 915). Thibaudet has noted that one of the most frequent images in Montaigne is that of movement: 'Le mouvement du corps lui fournit spontanément des façons d'exprimer la mobilité de ses idées' (*Montaigne*, p. 531). This point is developed by Starobinski in *Montaigne en mouvement*, esp. pp. 267–85.

79 D. T. Suzuki has written that '*Wu-hsin* or *wu-nien* is one of the most important ideas in Zen. It corresponds to the state of innocence enjoyed by the first inhabitants of the Garden of Eden, or even to the mind of God when he was about to utter his fiat "Let there be light" ' (*Zen and Japanese Culture*, p. 111). Literally, *wu-hsin* is usually trans-

lated as 'no-mind', while its virtually synonymous counterpart, *wu-nien*, is rendered as 'no-thought' (see Suzuki, *The Zen Doctrine of No-Mind, passim*). Because *hsin* enjoys a wider spectrum of connotation than 'mind', encompassing passion as well as reason, and implicating 'the totality of our psychic functioning' (Watts, *The Way of Zen*, p. 44), *wu-hsin* has also been assimilated to Jung's unconscious and T. S. Eliot's conscious unconsciousness (in which, according to 'East Coker', 'the mind is conscious but conscious of nothing').

80 Cited in Watts, p. 12.

81 *Essays in Zen Buddhism*, p. 104.

82 This analysis would require a qualification of Barthes's view of *jouissance* that 'rien ne la sépare du satori' (*Le Plaisir du texte*, p. 57).

83 If this study were, *per impossibile*, to propose a sufficient history of all the writing relevant to the problematic only adumbrated here, it would be indispensable to consider at length the work of Descartes and Pascal (and others). The methodological doubt advocated by Descartes invokes an anepistemological strategy (thus the *Discours de la méthode* begins by relating how the author gave up the study of books in favour of studying the book of the world) only as a prelude to the reconstruction of a purified, fortified, encyclopedic epistemology on the unshakeable foundation of the *cogito*. Once something is known and scepticism is thus vanquished, it becomes possible to proceed to know everything. But Pascal's notion that in order to know anything it is necessary (but impossible) to know everything deprives the Cartesian reconstruction even of its origin in the ego. If it is impossible to know the parts without knowing the whole (see *Pensées*, Brunschvicg no. 72), then not only the universe but the *Je* too is afflicted with the condition of unknowability. Thus Pascal perceives himself 'abîmé dans l'infinie immensité des espaces que j'ignore et qui m'ignorent' (*ibid.*, no. 205). (Poulet comments: 'la connaissance de l'univers n'est plus ici la seconde partie d'un traité de métaphysique, intitulée "Connaissance de la Nature", supplément à la connaissance de soi; elle est la condition *sine qua non* de celle-ci' (*Les Métamorphoses du cercle*, p. 53).) Rousseau is a convenient locus for the examination of each of the Cartesian and Pascalian alternatives, since he both affirms reflexive consciousness as the paradigm for knowledge about the world and denies the certainty of self-knowledge.

84 Thus the account of his initiation into literature records a personal tragedy: 'Dès cet instant je fus perdu' (*Œuvres complètes*, I, p. 351).

85 In the sixth of his *Lettres écrites de la montagne*, he inquires: 'Concevez-vous qu'on ait à se justifier d'un crime qu'on ignore, et qu'il faille se défendre sans savoir de quoi l'on est accusé?' and adds: 'C'est pourtant ce que j'ai à faire' (III, p. 804).

86 The *Lettres à Malesherbes* are the model on which Rousseau will pattern his later writing; his purpose, he declares, is to present a veracious self-portrait because 'je vois par la maniere dont ceux qui

pensent me connoître, interpretent mes actions, et ma conduite qu'ils n'y connoissent rien. Personne au monde ne me connoit que moi seul' (I, p. 1133). It will be obvious what this argument owes to Starobinski, who points out that 'la seule chose qui semble importer à l'auteur des *Dialogues* et des *Rêveries*, ce n'est pas que l'humanité future réforme ses lois, mais qu'elle change d'attitude à l'égard de Jean-Jacques' (*Jean-Jacques Rousseau: la transparence et l'obstacle*, p. 63).

87 Tanner comments on this passage that Saint-Preux 'epitomizes the man who is forced to deflect and pervert his feelings into writing' (*Adultery in the Novel*, p. 122).

88 The Pléiade edition shifts the 'Seconde Préface' back to the beginning; the Garnier edition keeps it in place at the end.

89 Rousseau's method recalls Saint Augustine's: the latter 'recommande de rassembler dans un seul ouvrage toutes les connaissances nécessaires à son interprétation' (Gilson, p. 178).

90 Rousseau recognizes that he can only furnish the reader with the fragments of a life: 'C'est à lui d'assembler ces élémens et de déterminer l'être qu'ils composent; le résultat doit être son ouvrage, et s'il se trompe alors, toute l'erreur sera de son fait' (I, p. 175).

91 Two recent restatements of the primitivist reading of Rousseau occur in Harbison (*Deliberate Regression*) and Terrasse (*Jean-Jacques Rousseau et la quête de l'âge d'or*). The classic critiques of this interpretation by Lovejoy ('The Supposed Primitivism of Rousseau's *Discourse on Inequality*') and Cassirer (*The Question of Jean-Jacques Rousseau*) only invert the perspective they condemn by turning the primitivist into a (scarcely less naive) progressivist, projecting celebration of the past into a blueprint for the future. Derrida (in *De la grammatologie*) has emphasized the interplay between the contradictory implications of Rousseau's account of language. But de Man has shown (in *Blindness and Insight* and *Allegories of Reading*) that Derrida's methodology is too intentionalist in attributing a logocentric doctrine to the writer which his writing subverts. Derrida's deconstructionist strategy depends on the deconstruction already effected by Rousseau. My own approach to Rousseau roughly corresponds to the Tlönian view that 'a book which does not contain its counterbook is . . . incomplete' (Borges, *Labyrinths*, p. 37).

92 *La Transparence*, pp. 339–40.

93 The text is oblique, the attitude of the author necessarily elusive. But in a note at the end (one of a series balancing the multiple prefaces at the beginning) Rousseau writes (referring specifically to the concept of an 'institution des langues'): 'ce n'est pas à moi qu'on permet d'attaquer les erreurs vulgaires, et le peuple lettré respecte trop ses préjugés pour supporter patiemment mes prétendus paradoxes' (III, p. 219). This suggests that the text can be read as both the restatement and the interrogation of an idea, already ancient (which may be one of the 'erreurs vulgaires').

94 *Allegories*, p. 146. My reading of the text at this point (and as a whole) owes much to my reading of de Man (and to his criticism of an earlier draft of this study).

95 My reading here owes something to Napoleon. In his 'Notes sur le *Discours*', Napoleon interprets *l'homme sauvage* as being not very different from *l'homme civil*: he is always a social being in whom *sentiment* and *raison* are inherent (*Napoléon inconnu*, ed. Masson and Biagi, II, p. 286). Starobinski notes but declines to draw the conclusion from the collapse of the hypothesis of an inventor of languages that the writer is obliged to 'renoncer à la notion même de l'homme sauvage, à toute l'histoire pré-sociale, et ruiner toute la construction théorique du *Discours*' (Rousseau, III, p. 1328).

96 The *Essai sur l'origine des langues* follows the same itinerary: the analysis of *écriture* folds back upon and envelops the analysis of *parole*, undercutting the logocentric priority of speech over writing.

97 Again, the *Essai* mirrors the *Discours*: it concludes by depicting a final form of society, a repetition of the primitive state, now controlled by 'canons' and 'écus', in which 'on n'a plus rien à dire au peuple sinon, *donnez de l'argent*' (pp. 198–9).

98 Hence Derrida's comment: 'le signe est toujours signe de la chute' (*Grammatologie*, p. 401). His analysis of the *Essai* stands as a summary of the *Discours*: 'le supplément est toujours le supplément d'un supplément. On veut remonter du supplément à la source: on doit reconnaître qu'il y a du supplément à la source' (*ibid.*, p. 429).

99 'Puisque la contradictoire de chaque proposition fausse est une vérité, le nombre des vérités est inépuisable comme celui des erreurs'(*Emile*, IV, p. 428).

100 *Grammatologie*, p. 291.

101 Rousseau explains why the programme he proposes is a chimera: if the 'objet particulier' is outside the state then the *volonté* is not *générale*; if it is inside then it is part of the whole, but 'alors il se forme entre le tout et sa partie une rélation qui en fait deux êtres séparés, dont la partie est l'un, et le tout moins cette même partie est l'autre. Mais le tout moins une partie n'est point le tout, et tant que ce rapport subsiste il n'y a plus de tout mais deux parties inégales' (III, pp. 378–9).

102 *La Transparence*, p. 109.

103 Introduction to *Rousseau juge de Jean-Jacques*, p. x.

104 *Histoire de la littérature française*, p. 4.

105 The words are usually attributed to Couffinhal: see, for instance, Grimaux, *Lavoisier*, p. 363.

106 Curtius, *European Literature*, p. 265.

3 The Occidental Orient

1 *Of Learned Ignorance*, II, xii, p. 111; pp. 103–4.

2 'Reason in philosophy', *Twilight of the Idols*, p. 37.

3 The Orient is not so much a fixed place as a scene whose boundaries are shifting and imaginary: it extends (at least) from Spain to Japan. In this text, which is, in contrast, circumscribed by spatial limits, I tend to equate the Orient with the Middle East, the lands around the eastern end of the Mediterranean, roughly the area referred to by C. Bradford Welles as 'The Hellenistic Orient' (in *The Idea of History in the Ancient Near East*, ed. Dentan, pp. 135–67).

4 'Mardoche', *Premières poésies*, p. 66.

5 '[Hugo] s'étendait sous l'énorme éventail [de la *Butte au Moulin*] et aspirait les bouffées d'air en regardant le crépuscule éteindre l'horizon et en se livrant à ses rêveries qui devinrent les *Soleils couchants* des *Feuilles d'automne*' (*Victor Hugo raconté*, II, p. 237).

6 *La Fantaisie de Victor Hugo*, I, pp. 122–3.

7 The *Grand Larousse de la langue française* declares, under the heading of *soleil* and the subheading *fig.*: 'symbolise ce qui, personne ou chose, a un grand éclat, du prestige'; it mentions God, power, liberty, youth, kings. Christine Brooke-Rose offers an example from *Troilus and Criseyde* in which the 'sonne of alle blisse' is identified with the heroine. She adds that the metaphor attracts a typically genitival construction: *le soleil de* etc. (*A Grammar of Metaphor*, p. 152).

8 The sun is 'the offspring of the good (*agathou*) which the good begot to stand in a proportion (*analogon*) with itself: as the good is in the intelligible region to reason (*noun*) and the objects of reason (*nooumena*), so is this in the visible world to vision and the objects of vision' (*The Republic*, VI, 508C).

9 Cited in Cave, *The Cornucopian Text*, frontispiece.

10 *Marges de la philosophie*, p. 295. Cf. Baudelaire, who names the sun as 'ce père nourricier' ('Le Soleil', *Œuvres complètes*, p. 95).

11 Thus Hegel writes: 'the external and physical sun rises (in the east), and it sets in the west: but it is in the west that the inner sun of self-consciousness, which emits a higher radiance, makes its further ascent' (*Reason in History*, p. 197; referred to by Derrida, *Marges*, p. 321).

12 *Répertoire II*, p. 182.

13 Curtius notes that Silvestris glosses a line from Virgil by equating *Noctes* with 'ignorance' and *Dies* with 'science' (*European Literature*, p. 353).

14 Quoted in Chateaubriand, *Mémoires d'outre-tombe*, I, 2, p. 240.

15 Daniel, in *Islam and the West* and *The Arabs and Medieval Europe*, traces the early history of the representations and misrepresentations of Islam in the Christian West.

16 *Voyage*, p. 372.

17 *Ibid.*, p. 117.

18 *Ibid.*, p. 390.

19 Schwab, *La Renaissance orientale*, p. 12.

20 The argument so far is consistent with Said's thesis, in *Orientalism*, that Europe in general, and France in particular, has constantly sought

to dominate (exploit, expropriate, colonize) the Orient. But Said's broad perspective and polemical commitment induce in him an attitude to the text not dissimilar to the Occidental attitude towards the Orient: his thesis is an empire to which all writers are enslaved. The texts which I shall consider here perpetuate but also deviate from the imperialist discourse denounced by Said.

21 Cf. Hegel: 'World history travels from east to west; for Europe is the absolute end of history, just as Asia is the beginning' (p. 197).

22 I derive these terms from Bachelard in *La Poétique de l'espace* (see, in particular, p. 12).

23 Musset's *Lettres de Dupuis et Cotonet* affirms that 'le Romantisme, c'est . . . l'oriental' (*Œuvres complètes en prose*, p. 830). Schwab recalls Schlegel's influential statement: 'C'est en Orient que nous devons chercher le suprême romantisme' (p. 20).

24 *Voyages en Orient*, p. 304.

25 *Mémoires et œuvres de Napoléon*, ed. Martel, p. xvi.

26 *Le Classicisme des romantiques* by Moreau and *Le Romantisme des classiques* by Deschanel indicate that these terms, Romantic and Classical, should be understood as designating not so much separate historical periods as alternative potential dispositions inherent in all writing.

27 Canat, asserting the contemporaneous occurrence of a 'Renaissance grecque', comments that 'ces lignes ne sont déjà plus au point'; he argues that 'un orientalisme sincère doit pousser jusqu'à l'hellénisme' (*L'Hellénisme des romantiques*, II, pp. 80, 84). But the philhellenism evident in *Les Orientales* (composed in the wake of the Greek War of Independence) does not entail hellenism. As Canat himself observes in an earlier work, for many Romantic writers (whether or not of the armchair variety) 'la Grèce n'était pas le but de leur voyage. Ce qu'ils allaient chercher c'était l'orient. On prend la Grèce parce qu'elle est sur la route de l'Asie, puis de l'Egypte. Mais on ne s'y arrête pas' (*La Renaissance de la Grèce antique*, p. 138). Thus the full title of Chateaubriand's *Itinéraire de Paris à Jérusalem* includes the phrase 'en allant par la Grèce': Greece is only an incidental station along the way. Chateaubriand's journey through space is also a journey backwards in time: the greater the distance to the East, the greater is its antiquity, its priority.

28 Richard, *Etudes sur le romantisme*, p. 195.

29 Gaudon refers to 'le goût immodéré de Hugo pour l'antithèse' (*Le Temps de la contemplation*, p. 392). The poem 'Dieu éclaboussé par Zoïle' contains what Lejeune calls 'une indirecte et savoureuse satire de Hugo par lui-même' (*L'Ombre et la lumière dans 'Les Contemplations' de Victor Hugo*, p. 68):

> Dieu ne fait de l'effet qu'en forçant les contrastes.
> Son univers, malgré des détails assez vastes,
> N'est qu'un long cliquetis au fond très puéril;

Le blanc, le noir, le jour, la nuit; décembre, avril.

. . .

Je voudrais bien le voir sortir de l'antithèse,
On sourit dès qu'on met à nu le procédé.

(*Œuvres complètes*, X, p. 747)

30 Guimbaud states that 'dès sa vingt-deuxième année et à la faveur d'une de ses plus charmantes inspirations, il avait nettement séparé et opposé "les deux mondes", l'occidental et l'oriental' (*'Les Orientales' de Victor Hugo*, p. 65).

31 The persistence of this antimony in Hugo's work is confirmed by Gregh: 'il mourait, ayant encore murmuré dans son agonie un dernier vers: "C'est ici le combat du jour et de la nuit" ' (*Victor Hugo: sa vie, son œuvre*, p. 113).

32 Baudouin's *Psychanalyse de Victor Hugo* contains a statistical analysis of the antitheses in *Les Contemplations* and *La Légende des siècles* which attributes the highest frequency to the case of *lumière/ombre*. Second comes *bien/mal*. Lejeune has outlined the range of connotations attributed to *lumière* and *ombre*, including, with regard to the former, *être*, *vie*, *esprit*, *bien*, *vérité*, *paradis*, and to the latter, *néant*, *mort*, *matière*, *mal*, *erreur*, *enfer* (p. 47).

33 The Spanish woman represents an ambiguous case in herself: she appears alternately European and Oriental, white- and dark-skinned. Spain enacts internally (see, for example, 'Romance mauresque') the conflict being played out between East and West.

34 Taken from *Le Globe* and *La Revue française* (cited, *Œuvres poétiques*, I, p. 1291).

35 Musset, *Œuvres complètes*, p. 836.

36 *La Fantaisie*, I, p. 126.

37 'En relisant *Les Orientales*', *Essais de stylistique structurale*, pp. 242–58; see, for example, pp. 243–4 for comment on Barrère. Riffaterre ascribes the stress on Oriental obscurity to a merely idiosyncratic Hugolian symbology.

38 This action is concisely evoked in 'Sara la baigneuse': 'On voit tout ce que dérobe / Voile ou robe' (I, p. 630). An aural equivalent of this visual episode occurs in the Doppler effect of 'Les Djinns'.

39 *Etudes*, p. 192.

40 Including hyperbole, the multiplication of synonyms, the pleonastic epithet (parodied by Musset – Romanticism, he concludes, consists in the excessive use of the epithet).

41 Barrère points out that 'Hugo ne cache donc pas ses sources, il les revendique, au contraire' (I, p. 119).

42 *Essais de linguistique générale*, p. 222.

43 *Etudes*, p. 191.

44 *Poetics*, 1459A.

45 *Œuvres poétiques*, II, p. 829. Hugo's most concentrated, encyclopedic vision of the 'tout' occurs in 'La Pente de la rêverie':

Ainsi j'embrassais tout, et la terre, et Cybèle;
La face antique auprès de la face nouvelle;
Le passé, le présent; les vivants et les morts. (I, p. 773)
Guyon observes that 'le poète selon Hugo, sera donc totalitaire' (*La Vocation poétique de Victor Hugo*, p. 41).

46 What the 'esprit' discovers at the bottom of 'La Pente de la rêverie' is 'l'éternité' (I, p. 774).

47 Villiers comments that according to Hugo's metaphysic 'toute âme est capable de savoir tout ce que sait Dieu' (*L'Univers métaphysique de Victor Hugo*, p. 280). But the Oriental does not consult even his potential for omniscience.

48 Schwab stresses this particular connotation assigned by Hugo (in contrast to Lamartine, Michelet, Goethe) to the 'immensités asiatiques': 'il ne les voit d'habitude ni en images de plaines libératrices ni en images de sommets exaltants, mais en images d'abîmes sombres et vertigineux' (p. 385).

49 Quoted in Mme de Rémusat, *Mémoires*, I, p. 274.

50 'On Truth and Falsity in their Ultramoral Sense', *Early Greek Philosophy and Other Essays, Complete Works*, II, p. 180.

51 *Ibid.*, p. 184.

52 *Le Moniteur* (11 *germinal*, 1798) records that 'il se prépare une expédition à la fois militaire et savante, dont la destination est pour une autre partie du monde' (cited in Belliard, *Histoire scientifique et militaire de l'expédition française en Egypte*, III, p. 37). *La Décade égyptienne*, published in Cairo under the ultimate direction of Napoleon, conflates these two aspects in an allusion to 'la sagesse armée' of the French contingent (facsimile edition in *The Journals of Bonaparte in Egypt 1798–1801*, ed. Boustany, I, p. 15).

53 *Works*, XI, p. 184.

54 Cited in Périvier, *Napoléon journaliste*, p. 7. Cf. Martel: 'Napoléon écrivain prend place parmi les maîtres originaux de notre littérature, les créateurs . . . [c'est] un rêveur, un poète, en même temps qu'un homme d'action' (*Mémoires et œuvres de Napoléon*, p. ix). He is not only a great writer but also, according to Sainte-Beuve, 'un grand critique à ses heures perdues' (*Nouveaux lundis*, VII, p. 261). Here is one example of his decisiveness: 'Sa Majesté lit Milton, le critique, l'abandonne' (Gourgaud, *Sainte-Hélène: Journal inédit*, I, p. 434); and another of his thoroughness: 'Sa Majesté demande *Zaïre*, critique chaque vers, et rentre à 10 heures' (*ibid.*, II, p. 183). In *The Myth of Napoleon* (*Yale French Studies*, 26), an article whose title translates Sainte-Beuve's judgement (pp. 119–27) offers further examples.

55 Tomiche, *Napoléon écrivain*, p. 147.

56 The numerous political and economic factors contributing to Napoleon's invasion have been enumerated by Napoleon and other historians; they include the contraction of the Ottoman Empire, the

demand to replace lost French colonies in the West, the desire to strike an indirect blow at the British Empire by threatening further expansion eastwards. But it seems likely that the immediate determinant of the Egyptian adventure was the state of relations between Napoleon and the Directory. The Directory feared the growing power and popularity of the youthful general, and sought a distant foreign area for his activities in which he might meet with defeat; while Napoleon conceived an Egyptian campaign as an expedient postponement and practical rehearsal of his intended challenge to the government at home.

57 His portable library expands to a thousand volumes strong during his career; see *Mémoires et œuvres*, p. 318.

58 *Journals*, I, p. 6. In the course of the Spanish expedition, in contrast, he advocates a more active programme of 'regeneration': 'Votre monarchie est vieille: ma mission est de la rajeunir. J'améliorerai toutes vos institutions . . . je veux que vos derniers neveux conservent mon souvenir et disent: Il est le régénérateur de notre patrie!' (XVII, p. 203). But there are close parallels between the two invasions: Spain is part of the Orient for Napoleon, as for Hugo; thus he remarks: 'The Spanish people is vile and cowardly, about the same as I found the Arabs to be' (cited by Herold, *The Age of Napoleon*, p. 214).

59 The theory of the inexorable expansion of an intellectual empire is anticipated in the eighteenth century by Condorcet in his *Esquisse d'un tableau historique des progrès de l'esprit humain*: once ignorance is banished from France, France has the duty to banish ignorance elsewhere; nowhere is inaccessible to the spread of *lumières*. Thus according to J.-B.-H. Fourier (and others), Egypt invites or demands the intervention of the West as the repository of enlightenment: 'Le propre de ce pays est d'appeler l'attention des princes illustres' (*Description de l'Egypte*, I, p. i). The Orient asks to be annexed.

60 *Napoléon inconnu*, ed. Masson and Biagi (henceforth, Masson), II, p. 17. Another version of this story is related by Borges, 'The Masked Dyer, Hakim of Merv' (*Borges: A Reader*, ed. Monegal and Reid, pp. 60–3).

61 At the head of numerous *ordres*, *proclamations* etc. (IV, p. 191 and elsewhere).

62 The phrase is Sainte-Beuve's (*Causeries du lundi*, I, p. 188).

63 Masson, II, p. 316.

64 *Mémoires*, I, pp. 102–3.

65 In 1789, Napoleon sent a text to Dupuy, one of his former masters, for correction, and received the following critique: 'j'en ai trouvé le fond excellent; mais il y a plusieurs mots impropres, mal assortis, répétés près l'un de l'autre, ou dissonants, des réflexions qui me paraissent inutiles ou trop hardies, ou capables d'arrêter la narration et de la faire languir, des retranchements, des additions et quelques changements à faire dans certains endroits' (cited in Masson, II, p. 66). His earlier

Italianate style gives way to a more laconic manner which he seeks to impose universally: see n. 107.

66 Thiry gives a detailed breakdown of its members (*Bonaparte en Egypte*, p. 40), who include musicians and artists as well as engineers and mathematicians. Herold, who ignores the symbolic, expresses bafflement regarding the participation of artists in the expedition (*Bonaparte in Egypt*, p. 30).

67 Thus they occupy an ambiguous position within the ranks of the army: at once unmilitary, and militant culture mongers. Barthélemy and Méry refer to them as 'les sages de l'armée . . . soldats inoffensifs . . . cortège pacifique . . . doctes voyageurs, modestes conquérans' (*Napoléon en Egypte*, pp. 99–100).

68 Martel describes the genre of the Napoleonic proclamation as 'l'une des plus belles formes de l'éloquence: cette chose grave, enthousiaste, entraînante, lyrique comme une ode, bruyante comme une sonnerie de clairon, véritable poème en prose dont la lecture enflammait des coeurs' (*Mémoires et œuvres*, p. xxii). Sir Walter Scott, on the other hand, refers to them as 'those singular harangues, which evince such a mixture of talent and energy with bad taste and bombast' (*The Life of Napoleon Buonaparte*, IV, p. 60).

69 The first is noted by Tomiche, p. 45; the second is recorded by Bourrienne, with reference to Josephine and extra-marital adventures (*Mémoires sur Napoleon, le directoire, le consulat, l'empire et la restauration*, II, p. 212).

70 Published in twenty-three massive volumes between 1809 and 1828. Said refers to it as 'that great collective appropriation of one country by another' and observes that 'each page is a square metre in size as if the project and the size of the page had been thought of as possessing comparable scale' (*Orientalism*, pp. 84, 85). Fourier, in his 'préface historique', stresses the principle of a totalization of knowledge embodied in the person of the Emperor: 'Loin d'admettre dans les sciences une distinction qui ne s'accordait point avec l'élévation de ses vues, celui qui les associait à son triomphe les considérait toutes comme ne formant qu'une seule famille' (*Description*, I, p. xxxviii).

71 *Œuvres poétiques*, I, p. 682.

72 Arabs are 'les plus grands voleurs, et les plus grands scélérats de la terre' (IV, p. 253). Egypt, on the other hand, is 'la plus belle partie du monde' (IV, p. 191), so that 'la République ne peut pas avoir une colonie plus à sa portée ou d'un sol plus riche' (IV, p. 253).

73 'Il est difficile de voir . . . un peuple plus misérable, plus ignorant, et plus abruti' (IV, p. 252).

74 Napoleon is a keen reader of Plato's *Republic*. Masson and Biagi (I, p. 281) cite Mme de Rémusat's remark (in her *Lettres*, I, p. 351) that she is planning to read Plato: 'Oui, mon ami, Platon, dont j'étais, comme vous savez, si tentée depuis que j'en entendais tant parler à l'Empereur.'

75 On the voyage over, a discussion group headed by Napoleon is alleged to have engaged in a three-day debate following a reading of Rousseau's *Discours sur l'origine de l'inégalité*. Napoleon's letter to his brother, Joseph, on the subject of Arabs, contains a critical allusion to the text: 'Ce sont des sauvages horribles . . . Oh, Jean-Jacques, que ne peut-il voir ces hommes, qu'il appelle "les hommes de la nature!" il frémiroit de honte et de surprise d'avoir pu les admirer' (*Lettres originales de l'armée française en Egypte interceptées par l'escadron de Nelson, Journals*, X, pp. 18–19).

76 Napoleon argues, in his address to the *Institut*, that 'les vraies conquêtes, les seules qui ne donnent aucun regret, sont celles que l'on fait sur l'ignorance' (*Mémoires et œuvres*, p. 378). After initial reluctance, Monge yields to Napoleon's persuasion (or coercion) to join the *Commission*: 'me voilà donc transformé en argonaute. C'est un miracle de notre nouveau Jason qui ne va pas fatiguer les mers pour la conquête d'une toison dont la matière ne pourra pas beaucoup augmenter le prix, mais qui va porter le flambeau de la raison dans un pays où depuis bien longtemps sa lumière ne passait plus, qui va étendre le domaine de la philosophie et porter plus loin la gloire nationale' (Thiry, p. 40). The more sceptical Hazlitt tells the story of Napoleon asking Sheikh El-Mondi: 'What is the most useful thing I have taught you in the six months I have been among you?', to which the Sheikh replies: 'The most useful thing you have taught me is to drink at my meals' (*The Life of Napoleon Buonaparte*, II, p. 198).

77 Masson, II, p. 497.

78 Bourrienne's account of Cafferelli's death omits any mention of this speech (*Mémoires sur Napoléon, le directoire, le consulat, l'empire et la restauration*, II, p. 234).

79 Curl's *The Egyptian Revival* shows that this process of exchange is a recurrent event in the history of culture. But although interest in Egypt preceded Napoleon, nevertheless the expedition that closed the eighteenth century provided the scholarly basis for the Egyptomania of the nineteenth.

80 Chateaubriand, in the conclusion to his *Mémoires d'outre-tombe*, refers to a 'vase' containing the 'liqueur' of 'civilisation' whose function (hitherto unaccomplished, laments Chateaubriand) is to 'verser la liqueur dans un autre vase' (II, 4, p. 581).

81 Volney says the process will take 'des siècles' (p. 394).

82 Fourier comments on Egypt's passage from civilization to barbarism that it seems as if 'ce pays était destiné à connaître les états les plus contraires de la société humaine (*Description*, I, p. iii).

83 Scott, IV, p. 52.

84 *Journals*, VI, p. 3.

85 *Description*, I, p. xxxviii.

86 *La Comédie humaine*, ed. Bouteron and Longnon, XXIV, p. 173.

Cited in *L'Histoire de Napoléon racontée par les grands écrivains*, ed. Burnaud and Boucher, p. 17.

87 It is useful to recall that on the following day a letter signed by this same Napoleon is received by General Fagière, expressing the hope that 'à l'heure qu'il est . . . vous aurez, de concert avec le général Duqua, soumis le village de Soubat et exterminé ces coquins d'Arabes' (IV, p. 489).

88 Masson, II, p. 17.

89 From a letter to Joséphine, *Mémoires et œuvres*, p. 55.

90 In conversation with Las Cases, *Le Mémorial de Sainte-Hélène*, I, p. 1106. The full text reads: 'J'étais le soleil qui parcourt l'écliptique en traversant l'équateur. A mesure que j'arrivais dans le climat de chacun, toutes les espérances s'ouvraient, on me bénissait, on m'adorait; mais dès que j'en sortais, quand on ne me comprenait plus, venaient alors les sentiments contraires, etc.'

91 As reported by Las Cases, I, p. 1108. The medical trope occurs frequently in Napoleonic rhetoric: see, for example, his proclamation to the Spanish: 'après une longue agonie, votre nation périssait. J'ai vu vos maux; je vais y porter remède' (XVII, p. 203).

92 Las Cases, I, p. 1109.

93 The abortion of the Egyptian project is mirrored in the admitted incompleteness of the *Description de l'Egypte*: Fourier observes that 'dans les mémoires qui font partie de la collection, on s'est proposé de compléter la description de l'Egypte', but has to concede that 'on ne peut point, en effet, borner les recherches sur l'Egypte; aucun sujet de littérature n'est plus fécond et vaste, et ce serait en méconnaître l'étendue que de vouloir l'épuiser' (I, pp. lxxxiii–lxxxiv) – although he adds: 'on peut assurer qu'il y a peu d'omissions, ou qu'elles ne sont point importantes' (I, p. lxxxvi).

94 *Ibid.*, I, p. xxxiv.

95 Masson, I, pp. 141–4; II, pp. 462–9.

96 *Ibid.*, 'Position politique', II, p. 469.

97 *Causeries*, I, p. 179. In 'Sur le suicide', Napoleon acknowledges the distance between himself and the French natives: he contemplates suicide because 'les hommes avec qui je vis et vivrai probablement toujours ont des mœurs aussi éloignées des miennes que la clarté de la lune diffère de celle du soleil' (Masson, I, p. 146). This passage shows two things: (1) Napoleon had no intention of doing away with himself: the verb of living is in the future tense ('vivrai'); (2) from his earliest texts, he freely identified himself with the sun – others are lunatics.

98 *Mémoires*, I, pp. 115, 104.

99 Las Cases, I, p. 505. For 'prendre à revers', the English translation, inverting the disposition of forces, gives: 'I should have turned my back on Europe' (*Memorial*, II, p. 88).

100 Las Cases, I, p. 504.

Notes

101 This elusiveness, recognized by Talleyrand ('Ses passions nous échappent; car il trouve encore le moyen de les feindre quoi qu'elles existent réellement' (Rémusat, *Mémoires*, I, pp. 117–18)), is deliberately cultivated by Napoleon: 'j'ai dans mon caractère tout ce qui peut contribuer à affermir le pouvoir, et à tromper ceux qui prétendent me connaître (*ibid.*, I, p. 108). Absolute power mystifies absolutely. Those who offer 'affirmations positives' about him, he says to Las Cases, 'se montreraient plus habiles que moi, qui, très souvent, aurais été embarrassé d'affirmer avec vérité toute ma pleine et entière pensée' (Las Cases, II, pp. 375–6).

102 Rémusat, *Mémoires*, I, p. 268. Napoleon's attitude towards literature may have been similar: according to Arnault, 'les productions des arts comme les découvertes des sciences, ne lui plaisaient entièrement qu'autant qu'elles étaient d'application utile à ses besoins présents' (*Souvenirs d'un sexagénaire*, II, 4, pp. 8–9; cited in Healey, *The Literary Culture of Napoleon*, p. 51).

103 *L'Ame de Napoléon*, p. 14.

104 For Napoleon, historical truth is mostly just 'une fable convenue' (Las Cases, II, p. 373).

105 Gourgaud, I, p. 457.

106 'Ce qui est supérieur en Mahomet, c'est qu'en dix ans, il a conquis la moitié du globe, tandis qu'il a fallu trois cents ans au christianisme pour s'établir' (Gourgaud, II, p. 77).

107 Napoleon's reader's digestive theory of literature is outlined in Las Cases, I, p. 317: 'Ce serait un travail bien précieux et bien goûté sans doute, que de se dévouer à réduire, avec goût et discernement, les principaux ouvrages de notre langue. Je ne connais guère que Montesquieu qui pût échapper à ces réductions.' The example of his surgical approach to Rousseau is given by Reverdin, 'Napoléon, correcteur de style de Rousseau', *Annales de la Société Jean-Jacques Rousseau*, XXX, pp. 143–8.

108 *Journals*, I, pp. 85–6.

109 Thus Fourier: 'La lumière des arts y avait brillé quelques instants; mais [ce pays] devait encore devenir la proie de la barbarie dont les armes françaises l'avaient délivré' (*Description*, I, p. lxxiv).

110 *Œuvres poétiques*, I, p. 684.

111 Las Cases, II, p. 648. Jean-Baptiste Pérès, in his *Grand Erratum, source d'un nombre infini d'errata à noter dans l'histoire du XIXe siècle*, takes the analogy a stage further, asserting that Napoleon never existed and was nothing more than a poetic personification of the sun. He notes the resemblance of *Napoléon* and *Apollon*, decodes *Bonaparte* as 'light', and argues that Napoleon's career imitates precisely the course of the sun: just as the sun rises out of the east to set in the west, so Napoleon returns from his Egyptian campaign to reign over France (for 12 years, equivalent to the 12 hours of the day) before sinking into oblivion in the western reaches of the South Atlantic, on

Saint Helena. (Albert Sonnenfield gives an account of this text and its satirical purpose in 'Napoleon as Sun Myth', *The Myth of Napoleon*, *Yale French Studies*, 26, pp. 32–6.) Napoleon at least admits to being an idolator of the sun: 'Si j'avais à avoir une religion, j'adorerais le soleil, car c'est lui qui féconde tout, c'est le vrai Dieu de la terre' (Gourgaud, I, p. 434).

112 Whose anti-hero appears successively, but monotonously, as Borgia, Attila, Nero.

113 Hence this remark in the *Mémoires*: 'En osant quitter Bonaparte, je m'étais placé à son niveau' (I, 2, p. 135). Descotes gives numerous examples of Chateaubriand's self-elevation in *La Légende de Napoléon et les écrivains français du XIXe siècle*. Coelho, adopting Chateaubriand's Chateaubriand-centred view of history, comments that 'les premières ambitions de Napoléon furent littéraires, celles de Chateaubriand militaires et politiques. Une partie du siècle réside dans le chassé-croisé, dont le risque est mortel, de ces deux prodigieux destins, leurs haines, leurs affinités . . . leur étrange fidélité' (Introduction to Chateaubriand's *Pensées et premières poésies*, p, 9).

114 References to this edition henceforward in parentheses.

115 *Mémoires*, I, 2, p. 347.

116 It is clear that additional reading may have taken place in the intervening years between the journey and the final publication of the *Itinéraire*; Chateaubriand's anxiety bridges the phases of travelling and writing.

117 *Chateaubriand, l'homme et l'œuvre*, p. 173.

118 Cf. Bassan: 'Chateaubriand nous présente une bibliographie critique et raisonnée sur la Terre-Sainte' (*Chateaubriand et la Terre-Sainte*, p. 140).

119 Thibaudet seeks the explanation for his 'volonté de décor, cette tension d'un dedans vers un dehors' (*Histoire*, p. 30) in the Revolution, which gives rise to a generation of exiles. Schwab associates it with the disenchanted intellectual's search for *autre chose* (*Renaissance*, p. 502). Sainte-Beuve's comment that the *déracinement* enforced by events produced conditions in which originality could flourish (cited by Thibaudet) unites these views.

120 Richard notes, more generally, that Chateaubriand's *élan* meets with 'l'insuffisante opposition des choses' (*Paysage de Chateaubriand*, p. 8).

121 According to Bassan, 'Chateaubriand crée le type de l'écrivain-voyageur' (p. 230).

122 Or amorous: Natalie de Noailles is proposed (by Bassan and others) as the 'houri' who seems to have imposed the Oriental journey on Chateaubriand as a challenge or initiation (see *Mémoires*, I, 2, pp. 196–7n). Thus Chateaubriand speaks of his journey as a quest for 'de la gloire pour me faire aimer' (II, 4, p. 407n).

123 The first sentence of the *Essai sur les révolutions* does not concern revolutions; it asks: 'Qui suis-je?'

124 Lévi-Strauss, *Tristes tropiques*, p. 147.

125 This relation has been examined in part by Grevlund, who writes that 'le paysage "intérieur" et le paysage "extérieur" se doivent mutuellement leur existence' (*Paysage intérieur et paysage extérieur dans les 'Mémoires d'outre-tombe'*, p. 16). The principle that informs Chateaubriand's practice is formulated by Lamartine: 'Il y a des harmonies entre tous les éléments comme il y a une générale entre la nature matérielle et la nature intellectuelle. Chaque pensée a son reflet dans un objet créé qui la répète, la réfléchit et la rend avec une complète et admirable analogie' (*Voyages*, p. 199). The business of art, adds Lamartine, is to discover 'quelques mots de cette langue universelle des analogies'. Hence Chateaubriand's aesthetic horror at disharmony, the lack of analogy.

126 Curiously, palm-trees invariably make Chateaubriand think of home: this may be because one of the redemptive gestures of the French army (recorded in *Description de l'Egypte*, I, p. lxxiv, and *Mémoires*, I, 2, p. 340) was to have demolished numerous unsightly buildings (occupied by Arabs) and planted palm-trees in their place.

127 Only the already decaying, irreversibly corrupted society of the North American Indians is held to enjoy, or rather, have recently enjoyed, the state of infancy.

128 For a more detailed elaboration of this taxonomy of deficiencies, see II, pp. 1068–9.

129 Thus Richard argues that the *ruine* is the mimetic equivalent of the authorial self: 'Le moi chateaubrianesque n'est-il pas cette tour délabrée, dressée parmi un désert d'hommes, cet être menacé de mort?' (*Paysage*, p. 71); Chateaubriand confirms the connection: 'Les hommes ne ressemblent pas mal aussi à ces ruines qui viennent tour à tour joncher la terre'; 'l'homme . . . va méditer sur les ruines des empires, il oublie qu'il est lui-même une ruine encore plus chancelante, et qu'il sera tombé avant ces débris' (*Voyage en Italie*, II, pp. 1445, 1484).

130 *Paysage*, p. 29.

131 *Mémoires*, I, 2, pp. 240–1.

132 Chateaubriand's short biography of these metamorphosed Frenchmen issues in a generalization equally applicable to himself: 'Nous sommes dans le siècle des merveilles; chaque Français semble être appelé aujourd'hui à jouer un rôle extraordinaire: cinq soldats, tirés des rangs de notre armée, se trouvaient, en 1806, à peu près les maîtres au Caire' (II, p. 1145).

133 *Mémoires*, I, 1, pp. 468–9.

134 *Histoire*, p. 34, and *Répertoire II*, p. 152.

135 The textual content of ruin and desert recur in Chateaubriand's comments on Pascal in *Génie du christianisme*: 'Il y a un monument curieux de la philosophie chrétienne, et de la philosophie du jour: ce sont les *Pensées* de Pascal, commentées par les éditeurs. On croit voir les

ruines de Palmyre, restes superbes du génie et du temps, au pied desquelles l'Arabe du désert a bâti sa misérable hutte' (p. 825). In the same section, Chateaubriand quotes approvingly Pascal's notion of 'une ignorance savante' joining the extremes of ignorance and knowledge (Brunschvicg no. 327).

136 See *Génie du christianisme*, p. 473; the 'désert' comprises both 'plaine' and 'forêt'. Again, in *Essai sur les révolutions*, p. 82, he seems to include a forest *within* the desert: 'Celui qui lit l'histoire ressemble à un homme voyageant dans le désert, à travers ces bois fabuleux de l'antiquité qui prédisaient.' Porter notes 'the visual conundrum posed by *désert-bois fabuleux*' (*Chateaubriand, Composition, Imagination, and Poetry*, p. 39).

137 *Répertoire II*, p. 182.

138 The Atlantic of the Brittany coast, which Chateaubriand regards as his *patrie*, is also 'ce désert d'océan' (I, p. 667).

139 This language is at once figurative and nominative. Chateaubriand follows Rousseau by associating the Orient with figurative language (see *Essai sur l'origine des langues*). But if metaphor is original then it is also referential: it names. The power to name signifies for Chateaubriand the lordship and mastery (a reflection of divine authority) of the namer over the named. To write about the Orient is at once to name it, to dominate it, and to leave one's name indelibly inscribed upon its surface (as upon the pyramid whereon, prevented from reaching it himself due to the Nile being in flood, he charges M. Caffe to engrave his name).

140 Said observes that the Orient 'alternated in the mind's geography between being an Old World to which one returned, as to Eden or Paradise, there to set up a new version of the old, and being a wholly new place to which one came as Columbus came to America, in order to set up a New World (although, ironically, Columbus, himself thought that he discovered a new part of the Old World)' (*Orientalism*, p. 58).

141 *Mémoires*, II, 3, p. 678.

142 *Figures II*, p. 105.

143 *Ibid.*, p. 103.

144 Cited, *ibid.*, p. 106. A point anticipated by Saint Augustine: 'nox ad diem pertinet' (*De Genesi ad litteram*, IV, 25, 42 (cited by Solignac, *In Principio*, p. 167)).

145 Derrida recalls that Thoth, the Egyptian god of writing, anathematized by Plato, is intimately associated with the moon (*La Dissémination*, p. 100).

146 Thus Harbison writes: 'the desert in Chateaubriand is the most gigantic of tombs' (*Deliberate Regression*, pp. 126–7).

147 *Mémoires*, I, 1, p. 15.

148 'En effet, mon *Itinéraire* fut à peine publié, qu'il servit de guide à une foule de voyageurs' (II, p. 695).

149 This and following quotations: *Génie*, pp. 555–6.

150 Chateaubriand's theory might be compared to Russell's hypothesis that it is not impossible that the world sprang into being five minutes ago, exactly as it then was, with a population that 'remembered a wholly unreal past' (*The Analysis of Mind*, p. 159).

151 The *Essai sur les révolutions* employs the same argument to banish Genesis altogether: 'Qu'apercevons-nous donc au moment où l'histoire s'ouvre? De grandes nations déjà sur leur déclin, des mœurs corrompues, un luxe effroyable, des sciences abstraites, telle que l'astronomie, l'écriture et la métaphysique des langues, arts dont l'achèvement semble demander la durée d'un monde' (p. 52).

152 *Renaissance*, p. 497. Zeldin points out that '*civilisation* (like *nation*) was a new word, first used in 1766, and admitted into the dictionary of the French Academy only in 1798 (the year in which the word *nationalism* was first used in France)', and recalls Guizot's assertion (in 1828) that 'one can say, without flattery, that France has been the centre, the home of civilization in Europe' (*France*, II, pp. 6–7).

153 In the terms of the *Description de l'Egypte*, I, p. iii.

154 Cf. Simon Pelloutier's view that 'l'ignorance et le mépris des lettres sont la véritable origine de la poésie' (cited in van Tieghem, *Le Préromantisme*, I, p. 38).

155 Even where the native American is not already degraded by European vices, he participates, in any case, in an advanced indigenous society. Butor comments: 'Chateaubriand s'aperçoit en Amérique que le Sauvage qu'il étudie n'est nullement un regard tout simple et tout pur capable de nous débarrasser par sa naïveté de tous nos préjugés et superstitions, qu'il est civilisé autrement mais indubitablement, et qu'il voit le monde, lui aussi, par l'intermédiaire d'une mythologie fort savante' (*Répertoire II*, p. 176).

156 *Mémoires*, II, 4, p. 581. This seems to be the answer to the question asked earlier in the text: 'Avons-nous porté la civilisation au dehors, ou avons-nous amené la barbarie dans l'intérieur de la chrétienté?' (I, 2, p. 242). This answer is perhaps prefigured in a letter written during his trip to Italy: 'Je commence à croire que cette France si policée est un peu barbare' (*Correspondance générale*, I, p. 108).

157 Cf. Lévi-Strauss: 'L'Islam, c'est l'Occident de l'Orient' (*Tristes tropiques*, p. 468).

158 It is in the light of this reorientation that it would be possible to study the French interest in the Orient of the later nineteenth century.

159 Derrida argues that 'chaque fois qu'il y a une métaphore, il y a sans doute du soleil quelque part; mais chaque fois qu'il y a du soleil, la métaphore a commencé' (*Marges*, p. 300).

160 'L'homme sauvage est un chien', asserts Napoleon, thus refuting Rousseau, according to a conversation recalled by Roederer, *Journal*, p. 165.

161 *Mémoires*, I, 1, p. 5.

162 *Ibid.*, II, 4, p. 606. Levaillant points out (in an appendix, II, 4, pp. 786–8) that it is impossible that, on the date given (16 November 1841), moon and sun should both be in the sky at the same time, and suggests (following Danjon) correcting the date to the first of the month. Less literally, the conjunction of the two appears automatic in Chateaubriand's firmament. By the second paragraph of Book 3 (I, 1), the sun is still only setting: 'Le livre précédent fut écrit sous la tyrannie expirante de Bonaparte et à la lueur des derniers éclairs de sa gloire.'

163 Cf. Lévi-Strauss: 'Pour les savants, l'aube et le crépuscule sont un seul phénomène' (*Tristes tropiques*, p. 68).

164 *Mémoires*, II, 4, p. 605.

165 The same sense of a truant sun appears in Hugo: 'Le soleil qu'on espère est un soleil couché' (*Œuvres poétiques*, I, p. 831).

166 *Post-scriptum de ma vie*, p. 42.

167 This structure often receives metaphorical elaboration. Thus, in *Génie*, 'l'homme est suspendu dans le présent, entre le passé et l'avenir, comme sur un rocher entre deux gouffres' (p. 546), while the *Mémoires* summarize the position of their author as follows: 'Je me suis rencontré entre deux siècles, comme au confluent de deux fleuves; j'ai plongé dans leur eaux troublées, m'éloignant à regret du vieux rivage où j'étais né, nageant avec espérance vers une rive inconnue' (II, 4, p. 602).

168 As the recent proliferation of Vernian studies abroad has testified, Verne is more various than the legendary Jules, the naive product and exponent of Second Empire positivism, the prolific but obsolete prophet of juvenile technological utopias. But Verne's *Voyages extraordinaires*, projecting their internal structures upon the narrative surface, represent the Beaubourg of literary architecture: thus ingenious exegeses invoking mythic archetypes (Vierne), psychoanalytical arcana (Moré), and Marxist contradictions (Macherey) may misconstrue the Vernian text by neglecting the superficial and the obvious. What follows is an attempt to rectify this deficiency. My forthcoming critical study of Verne will seek to show that he is more (in Barthes's terms) an *écrivain* than a mere *écrivant*.

169 This state of affairs is noted by the Goncourts: 'Quelque chose que la critique n'a pas vu, un monde littéraire nouveau, les signes de la littérature du XX\ siècle. Le miraculeux scientifique, la fable par A + B; une littérature maladive et lucide. Plus de poésie; de l'imagination à coups d'analyse . . . Les choses ayant plus de rôle que les hommes; l'amour cédant la place aux déductions et à d'autres sources d'idées, de phrases, de récit et d'intérêt; la base du roman transportée du coeur à la tête et de la passion à l'idée; du drame à la solution' (*Journal*, III, pp. 17–18).

Notes

4 The scientific fictions of Jules Verne

1 One exemplary case would be Plato's *Symposium*.

2 Lévi-Strauss (in *Le Cru et le cuit* and *L'Origine des manières de table*) has correlated language and cuisine: 'la cuisine d'une société est un langage dans lequel elle traduit inconsciemment sa structure, à moins que, sans le savoir davantage, elle ne se résigne à y dévoiler ses contradictions' (*L'Origine*, p. 411). Barthes has pointed out that the pattern of courses and the alternatives within each course as set out, vertically and horizontally, in a menu, correspond to the syntagmatic and paradigmatic axes of language (*Eléments de la sémiologie*, p. 135). In the terms of that analogy: paradigmatically, Rabelais tends towards infinity, Flaubert towards zero; syntagmatically, Rabelais is anarchic, Flaubert, well-governed. Richard's observation that 'on mange beaucoup dans les romans de Flaubert' (*Littérature et sensation*, p. 119) needs to be qualified by including a recognition of fastidiousness, an ascetic selectivity in the midst of plenty. Saint Antoine enacts the Flaubertian aesthetic by conjuring up and resisting the temptation of a Rabelaisian feast.

3 *Les Enfants du capitaine Grant*, Part I, Chapter i, p. 3 (subsequent references to other volumes of the *Voyages extraordinaires* – only some with distinct parts – given in the same sequence and numeration).

4 Pierre Dumonceaux, 'Les Dépaysements culinaires dans l'œuvre de Verne': paper originally given at the 'Colloque de Nantes: Jules Verne et le roman', published as 'Cuisine et dépaysement dans l'œuvre de Jules Verne', *Europe*, 595.

5 But the wholesome fare served, for example, in the Lidenbrock household, is by no means rudimentary: 'Une soupe au persil, une omelette au jambon relevé de veau à la compote de prunes, et, pour dessert, des crevettes au sucre, le tout arrosé d'un joli vin de la Moselle' (*Voyage au centre de la terre*, ii, p. 10). The construction (noun phrase) à/au/à la (noun phrases) – in principle, indefinitely extendible, as : 'une omelette au jambon relevé d'oseille à la muscade . . . ' – is at once a coefficient of the complexity of the standard menu and a product of the Vernian fondness for the accumulation of detail.

6 An obvious example of this arrangement is provided by the submarine parody of an on-shore meal served aboard the *Nautilus*: 'filet de tortue de mer . . . foies de dauphin . . . une conserve d'holothuries . . . une crème dont le lait a été fourni par la mamelle des cétacés, et le sucre par les grands fucus de la mer du Nord . . . des confitures d'anémones' (*Vingt milles lieues sous les mers*, I, x, pp. 93–4).

7 Brillat-Savarin, *Physiologie du goût*, I, pp. 101–2.

8 Similarly, the transition from nature to culture, in Lévi-Strauss's terms, is registered in the passage from *le cru* to *le cuit*.

9 *Physiologie*, I, p. 86.

10 Brillat-Savarin's 'Aphorisme IV', 'Dis-moi ce que tu manges, je te

216

dirai ce que tu es' (*Physiologie*, I, p. viii), is implicit in Verne's descriptions of indigenous peoples. Rousseau's Saint-Preux traces connections between diet, character, sex, and nationality: women drink milk while men prefer stronger liquors; the effeminate Italians favour vegetables; the barbaric English eat too much red meat (*La Nouvelle Héloïse, Œuvres complètes*, II, pp. 452–3). More prosaically, Verne notes (in *Voyage au centre de la terre*) that the ichthyophagous Greenlander smells distinctly fishy.

11 He is a more gastronomically dedicated reincarnation of the French type sketched by Saint-Preux, who 'souple et changeant, vit de tous les mets et se plie à tous les caractères' (Rousseau, *Œuvres*, II, p. 453). He exhibits the same 'grim determination' ascribed by Emerson to Margaret Fuller, 'to eat this huge universe' (cited by Lovejoy, *The Great Chain of Being*, p. 310).

12 Cf. Michaux, *Un Barbare en Asie*, p. 129: 'Car il [Thomas Cook] considère que sans un grand appétit, personne ne se mettrait en route.'

13 *Les Aventures du capitaine Hatteras*, II, viii, p. 324.

14 *Les Enfants du capitaine Grant*, I, xx, p. 137.

15 *Figures III*, p. 146.

16 *Les Aventures du capitaine Hatteras*, II, viii, p. 324.

17 *Voyage au centre de la terre*, xv, p. 87.

18 *Les Enfants du capitaine Grant*, III, vi, p. 424.

19 *Les Aventures du capitaine Hatteras*, II, xvii, p. 405.

20 To which may of course be added the Napoleonic law: 'il vaut mieux être mangeur que mangé' (Masson, II, p. 469).

21 *Le Chancellor*, liv, p. 191.

22 The chapter in *Les Enfants du capitaine Grant* entitled 'Où le cannibalisme est traité théoriquement' gives a detailed account of the logic of anthropophagy in New Zealand: religion and ritual only consecrate a custom that hunger has necessitated and taste perpetuated. Even Ned Land (in *Vingt mille lieues sous les mers*), deprived of victuals, entertains the notion of cooking his companions.

23 Lévi-Strauss distinguishes between an *endo-cuisine*, 'déstinée à un petit groupe clos', and an *exo-cuisine*, 'celle que l'on offre à des invités'. Cannibalism, in these terms, 'par définition, est une endo-cuisine par rapport à l'espèce humaine' ('Le Triangle culinaire', pp. 22–3). It therefore conflicts with Verne's exo-cuisinic conception of the world as a feast to which all are invited.

24 Whereas in the fantastic but materialist nutrition of Rabelais abundant assimilation is causally connected to no less plentiful elimination, in Verne's pseudo-positivist and idealist system not even the lower orders in the hierarchy of characters, the domestic, the clown, the negro, the orang-outang, to whom most of the routine and disagreeable functions are consigned, ever stoop to excretion. Lévi-Strauss relates myths involving 'personnages sans anus' who are constrained to feed on the fragrance of flowers (*L'Origine*, pp. 393ff). But in Verne food never

generates fat: obesity is not a problem for Vernian man (although he may be pre-narratively equipped with an ample girth, an amiable rotundity).

25 *Physiologie*, I, p. 107.

26 *Jules Verne*, pp. 16–18.

27 *Situations, I*, p. 29.

28 *Autour de la lune*, viii, p. 81.

29 *Les Aventures du capitaine Hatteras*, I, v, p. 39.

30 I. O. Evans has written of Verne's writing: 'it is certainly well that there is a complete absence of lust' (*Jules Verne and his Work*, p. 160). Certainly there is an absence of sex, and a scarcity of women: William Golding observes, in connection with *Le Tour du monde en quatre-vingts jours*, that Verne must be the only French writer who could get his hero right round the globe without his meeting more than one woman en route ('Astronaut by Gaslight', p. 841). But there is no lack of desire in the *Voyages*. Sexual energy has not been eliminated, only displaced, rerouted into geographical grappling with the earth-mother. The *voyageurs* do not mate: they sublimate. Psychoanalytically considered, Verne's heroes are exemplary cases of 'epistemophilia'. Freud's analysis locates the origin of this 'instinct for knowledge or research' in a pre-genital phase and links its subsequent obsessional manifestations with a repressed desire for sexual mastery ('Three Essays on Sexuality', *Standard Edition*, VII, pp. 194ff; also 'The Origins of Compulsion and Doubt', X, pp. 245ff, *Introductory Lectures on Psychoanalysis*, XVI, pp. 327ff).

31 *Les Enfants du capitaine Grant*, III, vi, p. 423.

32 *Voyage au centre de la terre*, i, p. 6.

33 *Autour de la lune*, iv, p. 41.

34 Curtius notes that alimentary metaphors 'are not unknown to Antiquity. Pindar praises his poetry as furnishing something to eat' (*European Literature*, p. 134).

35 *L'Ile à hélice*, I, vii, p. 116.

36 Job 38:16, 18.

37 *La Tentation de Saint Antoine* (1849), p. 350.

38 *Maître Zacharius* (with *Mistress Branican*), v, pp. 510, 511.

39 According to family legend: see, in particular, Soriano, *Jules Verne*, pp. 25–8.

40 *Maître Zacharius*, v, p. 512.

41 Hertz remarks that 'garden', equivalent to the Persian 'paradise', signifies enclosure (*Pentateuch*, p. 19); Hirsch glosses: 'a fenced-in place, enclosed for human purposes', and notes that it is cognate with guard, protect (*Pentateuch*, I, p. 57).

42 Bell calls this work 'perhaps literature's outstanding example of an attempt at the impossible'. But he also recalls that Dumas conceived of two ways of approaching a history of the world: ' "either to keep to Biblical tradition, which goes back only six or seven thousand years,

which would be too short; or else to follow science, which would be too long" '(*Alexandre Dumas*, p. 273). Dumas sticks mainly, however, to the former; Verne chooses the longer itinerary of science.

43 'Avertissement de l'éditeur', *Aventures du capitaine Hatteras*, p. 2.

44 *Jules Verne*, ed. Touttain, pp. 57–62 (p. 62). However, in an interview, Verne more confidently states that: 'It is my intention to complete, before my working days are done, a series which shall include, in story form, my whole survey of the world's surface and heavens; there are still left corners of the world to which my thoughts have not yet penetrated. As you know, I have dealt with the moon, but a great deal remains to be done, and if health and strength permit me, I hope to finish the task' (Belloc, 'Jules Verne at Home', p. 213).

45 *Les Enfants du capitaine Grant*, I, xx, p. 138.

46 According to the principle of sufficient reason, every true proposition is analytic since the predicate is in the subject. See, for example, Leibniz's 'Discourse on Metaphysics', *Philosophical Papers and Letters*, ed. Loemaker, pp. 307–8.

47 Foucault, 'L'Arrière-fable', *L'Arc*, 29, p. 9.

48 *Les Aventures du capitaine Hatteras*, II, xxi, pp. 443–4.

49 Recorded in an interview with Robert H. Sherard for *TP's Weekly*, 9 October 1903, reprinted as 'Jules Verne Revisited', in Haining (ed.), *The Jules Verne Companion*, pp. 58–61 (p. 60).

50 *Speculations*, p. 9.

51 'Jules Verne ou le récit en défaut', *Pour une théorie de la production littéraire*, p. 203.

52 Serres, *Jouvences sur Jules Verne*, p. 11.

53 *Of Learned Ignorance*, I, xiii–xv.

54 Barthes remarks that 'il faut attendre Balzac pour que le roman ne soit plus seulement l'espace de purs rapports humains, mais aussi de matières et d'usages appelés à jouer leur partie dans l'histoire des passions' ('Les Planches de l'*Encyclopédie*', *Nouveaux essais critiques*, p. 88). But we have to wait until Verne before matter is released from its subordination to the passions.

55 See *L'Etre et le néant*, pp. 32ff.

56 The absolute integrity of Vernian man implies that no art is needed to tell the mind's construction in his face: psychology and physiognomy are indistinguishable; a man's soul is instantly available to the casual observer for inspection and recognition: 'un homme de haute taille, dont la physionomie me frappa par des signes non équivoques d'une profonde duplicité' (*Une Ville flottante* (with *Une Capitaine de quinze ans*), ix, p. 412).

57 'Pierre absent hante ce café', *L'Etre et le néant*, p. 43.

58 *Voyage au centre de la terre*, iv, p. 18.

59 *Ibid.*, xxii, p. 123.

60 The moon is an older replica of the planet whose satellite it is: 'C'est donc une surface boursouflée, crevassée, une véritable écumoire,

digne de la qualification peu poétique que lui ont donnée les Anglais de "green cheese", c'est-à-dire, "fromage vert" ' (*Autour de la lune*, xi, p. 111).

61 *Voyage au centre de la terre*, x, p. 56.

62 The Orphic journey constitutes an initiation into manhood: it offers a rehearsal of the consummation promised to Axel by Graüben, his fiancée, on his return. Hence Axel's mingled terror and impatience, nostalgia and anticipation on the lip of the crater leading underground: 'un de mes souvenirs s'envola vers ma jolie Virlandaise, et je m'approchai de la cheminée centrale' (*ibid.*, xvii, p. 97).

63 Verne places decoding and digestion in a precise parallel: so long as the script remains undeciphered, the occupants of the Lidenbrock household, incarcerated by the monomaniacal professor, must go hungry, deprived at once of understanding and sustenance, the food of body and mind. Conversely, the discovery of the key to the code unlocks the house and allows access to provisions.

64 *Ibid.*, xlv, p. 251.

65 *Ibid.*, xx, p. 115.

66 *Ibid.*, xxx, p. 164.

67 *Ibid.*, xliii, pp. 238–9.

68 *Ibid.*, xx, p. 113.

69 *Ibid.*, xxx, p. 165.

70 *Ibid.*, xxxviii, p. 212.

71 *Ibid.*, viii, pp. 48–9.

72 *Jules Verne et les sciences humaines: colloque de Cerisy*, p. 314.

73 *Le Tour du monde en quatre-vingts jours*, xi, p. 57.

74 *Ibid.*, v, p. 26.

75 'Ce grand triangle renversé dont la base est au nord et la pointe au sud' (*ibid.*, x, p. 51).

76 *Jouvences*, p. 121.

77 *Le Tour du monde*, xx, p. 127.

78 *Voyage au centre de la terre*, xxiv, p. 132.

79 Hetzel is alleged to have said to Verne: 'Vous avez de la perpendiculaire' (quoted by Allotte de la Fuÿe, *Jules Verne: sa vie, son œuvre*, p. 232).

80 *Les Enfants du capitaine Grant*, II, xvi, p. 320.

81 *Le Chancellor*, xl, p. 143.

82 Axel's nightmare on the eve of departure envisages this eventuality: 'Je tombais au fond d'insondables précipices . . . Ma vie n'était plus qu'une chute interminable' (*Voyage au centre de la terre*, vii, p. 42).

83 Even his death will not prevent his attainment of a universal knowledge; rather, it will hasten that end by facilitating a Platonic ascent to omniscience: 'Dans l'autre vie, l'âme n'aura besoin, pour savoir, ni de machines ni d'engins! Elle s'identifiera avec l'éternelle sagesse' (*Autour de la lune*, xix, p. 195).

84 *Hier et demain* (with *Le Sphinx des glaces*), p. 544.

85 The text is a posthumously published *nouvelle*. Gondolo della Riva has attributed much or most of the final manuscript to Michel Verne ('A propos des œuvres posthumes de Jules Verne'). But while it is true that all the posthumous works must be regarded as in some measure collaborative, nevertheless, as Butcher points out, 'personne ne sait si Michel Verne n'a pas, par exemple, recopié une version antérieure, due à son père' ('Le Sens de *l'Eternel Adam*', p. 73). Manuscript evidence, in short, is not definitive; but it must be allowed that the corpus of writing I refer to as 'Verne' is, of its nature, a collective enterprise.

86 *Hier et demain*, p. 515.

87 *Ibid.*, p. 521.

88 *Ibid.*, p. 516.

89 *Ibid.*, pp. 526–7.

90 Although, as Butcher shows, 'un vestige de langage n'a jamais été perdu' ('Le Sens de *L'Eternel Adam*', p. 73).

91 *Hier et demain*, p. 540.

92 *Ibid.*, p. 544.

93 *Ibid.*, p. 530.

94 *L'Etre et le néant*, p. 576.

95 *Voyage au centre de la terre*, xxv, p. 134.

96 *Vingt mille lieues sous les mers*, II, xxii, p. 526. The fragile dinghy in which the narrator escapes from the doomed sub is only spared the same fate by the intervention of narrative magic: as the chapter ends, Aronnax loses consciousness, while the following chapter generously exempts him from accounting for his survival: 'Comment le canot échappa au formidable remous du Maelström . . . je ne saurai le dire' (xxiii, p. 527).

97 Cited by Hulme, *Speculations*, p. 35.

98 Cf. Butcher, who makes the point that 'si l'on regarde une hélice régulière d'en haut, elle semble circulaire' ('Le Sens de *L'Eternel Adam*', p. 78). He adds that 'si on la regarde de côté, elle semble former une série continue de courbes périodiques': the circle is implicit in the sine-curve.

99 Cited in Jean Jules-Verne, p. 112.

100 *Les Aventures du capitaine Hatteras*, II, xxx, pp. 479–80.

101 *Vingt mille lieues*, I, xiv, p. 134: 'On les classe en poissons qui se mangent et en poissons qui ne se mangent pas.'

102 *Ibid.*, I, ii, p. 9.

103 Verne's personnel are constants, the fixed-value capital of his fictional economy, thus validating the tautological statement, 'Nab était Nab' (*L'Ile mystérieuse*, I, xix, p. 150). They are frequently compared to machines (Ned Land is a telescope and a cannon) and like hardware, they rarely develop, only deteriorate. Their purely functional destiny is liable to be distorted by the presence of women, who must therefore be prohibited from the arena of animus: 'Love is an all-absorbing passion and leaves room for little else in the human breast; my heroes

need all their wits about them, and the presence of a charming young lady might now and again sadly interfere with what they have to do' (Belloc, p. 208).

104 *Vingt mille lieues*, I, iii, p. 18.

105 *Ibid.*, II, vi, p. 319.

106 *Ibid.*, II, iii, p. 288.

107 *Les Aventures du capitaine Hatteras*, II, xxi, pp. 443–4.

108 The corresponding sketch by Riou in the original edition shows an insubstantial craft crewed by frail human figures, hemmed in on all sides by a black bestiary of hypertrophied birds and fish, swooping and diving and threatening (it seems) to capsize the flimsy vessel.

109 Cf. Barthes's brief, dense essay, 'Nautilus et Bateau ivre', where he argues that the 'principe existentiel' of the *Voyages* is 'l'enfermement' (*Mythologies*, p. 80).

110 *Vingt mille lieues*, II, vii, p. 334.

111 Serres argues that 'en fait, le sous-marin plonge moins sous les eaux que le nautile n'indexe, par son mouvement vertical, toute l'épaisseur des classifications. L'immersion n'est qu'une lecture, verticale et de haut en bas, des rubriques du dictionnaire' (*Jouvences*, p. 152).

112 *Vingt mille lieues*, II, xvi, p. 451.

113 'C'était un monstre horrible . . . un calmar de dimensions colossales' (*ibid.*, II, xviii, p. 477). All Verne's imaginary beasts are monstrous, calling up a shoal of synonymous epithets: *énorme*, *immense*, *titanesque*, etc.

114 *Ibid.*, II, xxii, p. 402.

115 *Ibid.*, I, xiv, p. 133.

116 *Pensées*, Brunschvicg no. 139.

117 So Fogg – just as Des Esseintes, the hero of Huysmans's *A Rebours*, consigns mere living to his servants – leaves touristic sightseeing to his menial, Passepartout. The *voyageur* is not generally concerned with the maximization of speed: his ideal is the snail, who carries his home on his back: 'Voyager dans sa maison, une maison roulante, ce sera probablement le dernier mot du progrès en matière de voyage' (*La Maison à vapeur*, ii, p. 18).

118 *Vingt mille lieues*, I, xxiii, p. 229.

119 *Ibid.*, I, xi, p. 98. Revealingly, 'ouvrages d'économie politique' are therefore 'proscrits'.

120 *Ibid.*, I, xi, pp. 99–100.

121 Whatever the size of his accommodation, the Vernian traveller habitually transforms it into a museum: 'le docteur se donnait un plaisir de savant ou d'enfant à mettre en ordre son bagage scientifique . . . Tout cela se classait avec un ordre qui eût fait honte au British Museum' (*Les Aventures du capitaine Hatteras*, I, iv, p. 25).

122 The nineteenth century, of which Verne is in many respects the culminating expression and index, testifies to the persistence of the Napoleonic theory of the *mission*. Thus the Vernian *voyage* is typically

assigned the task of intellectual colonization; the objective of the moon journey is exemplary: 'Pour coloniser les régions lunaires, pour les cultiver, pour les peupler, pour y transporter tous les prodiges de l'art, de la science, et de l'industrie. Pour civiliser les Sélénites' (*Autour de la lune*, vii, p. 79).

123 *Vingt mille lieues*, I, xi, p. 98.

124 *Ibid.*, I, x, pp. 93–4.

125 *Le Château des Carpathes*, i, pp. 1–2.

126 *L'Ile à hélice*, I, vii, p. 113.

127 In *Balzac: Fiction and Melodrama*, Prendergast maintains that the ubiquitous aphorism of the *Comédie humaine* testifies, by virtue of its very explicitness, to the withering away of the authority of a body of social wisdom to which Balzac alludes (or contributes). The nineteenth century's consent to the seduction of science is implicit in Gautier's review of *Les Aventures du capitaine Hatteras*: 'la technicité maritime, mathématique et scientifique employée à propos et sobrement imprime un tel cachet de vérité à ce fantastique *Forward* qu'on ne peut se persuader qu'il n'a pas accompli son voyage d'exploration' ('Voyages imaginaires', Touttain, pp. 85–7 (p. 87)).

128 *Jules Verne*, p. 87.

129 *Vingt mille lieues*, I, xi, p. 104.

130 *Ibid.*, II, xvii, p. 464.

131 *Répertoire [I]*, p. 187.

132 Suvin distinguishes science fiction from both naturalism and fantasy by defining it as the 'literature of cognitive estrangement' (*Metamorphoses of Science Fiction*, p. 4). The *Voyages* are deemed minimalist science fiction since, although they have recourse to occasional 'nova' (Suvin's term for technological or theoretical innovations), they seek to minimize or gloss over deviations from a received paradigm of persons and things and places.

133 'Jules Verne Revisited', Haining, pp. 59–60. For Verne's views on Poe, see 'Edgar Poe et ses œuvres', *Musée des familles*, pp. 193–208.

134 *Le Château des Carpathes*, i, p. 2.

135 *Vingt mille lieues*, II, xix, p. 483.

136 *Autour de la lune*, xv, p. 156.

137 Cf. Barthes's comment on *L'Ile mystérieuse*, the prototypical novel of the *Voyages*: '[c'est] le contraire même d'un roman d'anticipation, c'est un roman de l'extrême passé, des premières productions de l'outil' ('Par où commencer?', p. 5). Verne is a most reactionary futurist. Characteristically, in a speech to a girls' school, he delivers a spirited denunciation of the bicycle (*Discours*, p. 11). Again, the museum on broad the 'propeller-island' is determinedly conservative: 'Ce qu'il convient d'observer, c'est que les impressionistes, les angoissés, les futuristes, n'ont pas encombré ce musée' (*L'Ile à hélice*, I, vii, p. 113).

138 Cf. Suvin, who writes that Verne's *œuvre* 'is more interpolated into

than extrapolated from the imaginative space of exotic geography, zoology, mineralogy and similar' (p. 150).

139 Borges, 'Notes on Walt Whitman', *Other Inquisitions*, p. 66.

140 Borges, 'La biblioteca de Babel', *Obras completas*, p. 469. Cf. also Derrida: 'la forme idéale [des livres] sera un livre de science totale, livre de savoir absolu résumant, récitant, ordonnant substantiellement tous les livres et parcourant le cycle de la connaissance' (*La Dissémination*, p. 54).

141 *Voyage au centre de la terre*, xiv, p. 84.

142 The geometrical configuration of underground caverns and ice-fields (picked up by Butor in his essay on Verne in *Répertoire*) attracts Verne's attention precisely because it constitutes a deviation from an ungeometrical norm.

143 Cf. Nicholas: 'Even the earth is not a sphere as some have maintained, though it is inclined to sphericity' (*Of Learned Ignorance*, II, xii, p. 111; p. 104). As Verne replaces 'sphere' by 'spheroid', so too Russell proposes that the opinion 'There is a dog' should be replaced by 'I see a canoid patch of colour' (*An Inquiry into Meaning and Truth*, p.19). Descriptive exactness leads to imprecision.

144 *De la terre à la lune*, i, p. 3.

145 *L'Etonnante Aventure de la mission Barsac*, II, iv, p. 276.

146 An account of their divergence is given by Kline in *Mathematics: The Loss of Certainty*, Chapter 13.

147 *Le Plaisir du texte*, pp. 32–3.

148 *Vingt mille lieues*, II, x, p. 368. As Borges concludes at the end of an examination of classificatory systems, real (Wilkins) and imaginary (the 'Celestial Emporium of Benevolent Knowledge'), 'obviously there is no classification of the universe that is not arbitrary and conjectural' ('The Analytical Language of John Wilkins', *Other Inquisitions*, p. 104).

149 The volcano looms over the *Voyages* as a symbol of transformation. Rock is liable to be liquefied in the shape of volcanic magma, while solids are vaporized by the viscous fire of lava which, on cooling, stiffens and solidifies. The multivalent image of the volcano refutes Bachelard's assertion that 'aucune image ne peut recevoir les quatre éléments' (*L'Eau et les rêves*, p. 96).

150 *L'Ile mystérieuse*, II, xi, p. 278.

151 This and following passages, *De la terre à la lune*, v, pp. 27–8.

152 Serres writes that 'depuis Laplace, l'homme de la clôture, le monde est un système stable où toute variation revient à l'invariant, sous la législature du cercle. Verne trace naïvement les routes de Laplace' (*Jouvences*, p. 97). In fact, on the contrary, Verne introduces a principle of ubiquitous instability into the stable Laplacean universe: he disrupts the inherited paradigm of the *Exposition du système du monde*.

153 *De la terre à la lune*, v, p. 28.

154 The eighteenth-century 'chain of being' and the organic unity postulated by Comte and Hegel have been dissolved, replaced by a system which has less in common with Eddington's 'table of common-sense' than with his 'table of physics', and consists mostly of empty space presided over by a few stray molecules.

155 *Les Enfants du capitaine Grant*, II, iv, p. 224.

156 *L'Ile à hélice*, I, v, p. 70.

157 *De la terre à la lune*, xviii, p. 111.

158 *Les Aventures du capitaine Hatteras*, I, iii, p. 20. Similarly, the highly-strung Hatteras exclaims: 'Oh! laissez mon coeur faire explosion entre vos mains!' (*ibid.*, II, xxv, p. 477).

159 Both Macherey and Suvin dwell on this affinity of Vernian man and his machine.

160 *Vingt mille lieues*, II, xix, p. 483.

161 *La Maison à vapeur*, I, iii, p. 29.

162 *Les Enfants du capitaine Grant*, III, xii, p. 472.

163 The Rousseauiste ideal of solidarity recurs in Verne, and is similarly frustrated by the propensity of society to dissolve into violent anarchy.

164 *L'Ile à hélice*, II, xiii, pp. 485–9.

165 *Ibid.*, II, xiii, p. 490.

166 By Vierne, Moré, and others.

167 Kermode, *The Sense of an Ending*, p. 5.

168 Typically enunciated in the eighteenth century by Joseph Robertson: 'it may not be improper to caution the young and inexperienced writer against the immoderate use of exclamations. Whenever we see a page in prose, profusely interspersed with points of admiration, we generally find it full of unnatural reveries, rank and bombast' (*An Essay on Punctuation*, p. 113). Exclamation marks run the risk of inflationary devaluation: the more there are, the less any of them is worth.

169 See, for example, *Le Grand Dictionnaire universel du XIXe siècle*, art. 'Exclamation': 'Le point exclamatif se met encore après toute phrase ou toute partie de phrase exprimant la surprise, l'admiration, l'effroi devant être prononcée d'un ton propre à évoquer les mêmes sentiments.'

170 Cited in Jean Jules-Verne, p. 114.

171 Like the symbols of a choreographic script, it duplicates, in the juxtaposition of a cone and a globe, the relation of the lunar capsule and the earth (the projectile might be pointing towards and thus returning to its home planet). The Spanish edition of the *Voyages* doubles the number of exclamation marks but inverts half of that grand total: sentences are not merely suffixed by '!' but prefixed by '¡'. In this latter case it appears that a globule has emerged from a cone, allowing or encouraging the reader to perceive therein the expulsive action of a cannon or a volcano. Conversely, '!' is an inverted volcano in eruption.

172 T. F. and M. F. A. Husband conjecture that 'this mark was originally *Io*, the Latin exclamation of joy, written so: $\frac{I}{o}$. The form of *I* became

obscured and the *o* filled up' (*Punctuation: Its Principles and Practice*, p. 39n). Partridge attributes this derivation to Bilderdijk, but prefers the hypothesis that the upper stem of '!' represents 'probably a pointer, perhaps a dagger' (*You Have a Point There*, p. 79).

173 Winifred Nowottny offers as an example of the derisive use of the abbreviation the opening line of Canto III of Byron's *Don Juan*: 'Hail, Muse! *et caetera* – We left Juan sleeping' (*The Language Poets Use*, p. 30). The conjunction of '!' and 'etc.' seems to afford an instance of the redundancy to which Byron ironically alludes.

174 Verne's etceteras might be compared to the huge hand-drawn 'ETC.' that fills the closing page of Kurt Vonnegut's *Breakfast of Champions*. The ending, the etcetera implies, is a convenient artifice or fictional necessity, to which nothing in non-fictive life corresponds: the reader is invited to extrapolate the closed narrative into the open space of experience. Similarly, in the *Voyages*, the conclusion of the inventorial sentence is often imposed by considerations (excessively protracted suspension of narrative, the risk of tedium, etc.) quite other than the actual exhaustion of an inventory.

175 The Spanish strategy of introducing an anticipatory inverted exclamation mark at the beginning of the sentence rationally relocates a call to attention, irrationally postponed in Verne's original until the end of that to which it is proposed to call attention. Thus the reader is alerted at the proper moment, not almost as an afterthought. In this arrangement something is gained in convenience and symmetry; but something is also lost: a quality of surprise.

176 Hahn, *The Anatomy of a Scientific Institution*, gives a history of the *Académie des Sciences*, including a reference to this episode (pp. 306–7).

177 *Procès-verbaux de l'Académie des Sciences*, IV, pp. 227–8.

178 'L'homme le plus instruit n'entend plus ce qu'on dit' (*ibid.*). Gilpin characterizes the period by its 'institutional proliferation and intellectual fragmentation' (*France in the Age of the Scientific State*, p. 81). See also Zeldin, II, p. 576, who places the rise of mutual incomprehension around the middle of the nineteenth century.

179 *Encyclopédie*, I, p. i.

180 Diderot, *Œuvres philosophiques*, p. 316.

181 Thus Diderot maintains that 'l'indépendance absolue d'un seul fait est incompatible avec l'idée de tout, et sans l'idée de tout, plus de philosophie' (*ibid.*, p. 186).

182 Notably by Bernard in *Introduction à l'étude de la médecine expérimentale*, where he confirms and advocates the extension of the 'fractionnement' or 'morcellement' of the 'domaine expérimental' (p. 46).

183 Thus the *Dictionnaire des idées reçues* notes, under the heading 'Encyclopédie': 'En rire de pitié' (*Bouvard et Pécuchet*, II, p. 247). *Bouvard et Pécuchet* satirizes the totalizing text. Its heroes are launched on a circular and futile odyssey around the intellectual globe.

The absurdity of the pair's undertaking is located less in their consideration (however fallible) of particular matters than, less tangibly, in the phantasmal outline of encyclopedic totality that haunts their collective efforts. Their garden at Chavignolles, counterpointing the ambition of synthesis with the achievement of fearful, unmitigated heterogeneity, is the horticultural equivalent of the *Encyclopédie*. The *Encyclopédistes* held that one must either know everything or nothing; the adventures of Bouvard and Pécuchet suggest, inversely, that to attempt (vainly) to know everything is to know precisely nothing.

184 Pasteur dreams nostalgically of a text that will reunite within a single volume the scattered pages of his work. In the preface to *Etudes de chimie moléculaire*, he insists that his 'divers mémoires . . . quoique distribués dans un certain nombre d'années . . . forment une suite non-interrompue, et je les présente ici comme les divers chapitres d'un même travail' (*Œuvres complètes*, I, p. 391). This book was never written: only a preface and introduction remain.

185 Kuhn suggests that 'the scientist who writes [a book] is more likely to find his reputation impaired than enhanced' (*The Structure of Scientific Revolutions*, p. 20).

186 *L'Ile à hélice*, II, xiv, p. 495.

187 Its heterogeneous elements have been inventoried by Robin: 'Combinaison de prose et de vers, amalgames de toutes sortes d'idiomes, réunies d'horizons et d'époques différentes – latin sacré, latin profane, latin de cuisine, français classique, yankee, pseudo-islandais, italien de bel canto, argot estudiantin, balbutiements indigènes réputés cocasses etc. . . . onomastique extravagante, création verbale riche en monstres linguistiques – "surtarbrandur", "aviés", "philanthropophages" – ou en néologismes, apports de multiples langues techniques et scientifiques, ce sont là autant de caractéristiques qui contribuent à faire de la langue vernienne un ensemble délibérément composite' (*Un Monde connu et inconnu: Jules Verne*, p. 233). The *Voyages* manifest, vertiginously, the 'plurilinguism' and 'plurivocality' that Bakhtin ascribes to the novel (see 'Du discours romanesque', *Esthétique et théorie du roman*, pp. 83–183).

188 The method of the savant consists in anamnesis; like the slave-boy in the *Meno*, whom Socrates shows to be innately capable of solving a geometrical problem, he is already equipped with all the answers: he has only to recollect the appropriate theory or fact. Unlike the Platonic recollector, however, he owes his knowledge not to unmediated access to suprasensory archetypes but to reading: 'je suis seulement un homme doué d'une bonne mémoire et qui a beaucoup lu' (*Les Aventures du capitaine Hatteras*, II, iv, p. 288).

189 *L'Ile mystérieuse*, I, ix, pp. 61–2.

190 *Vingt mille lieues*, II, xviii, p. 472.

191 Hence the terror of the 'point neutre', the point imagined by Verne where the opposite attractions of earth and moon cancel out: 'A ce

point, un corps n'ayant aucun principe de vitesse ou de déplacement en lui, y demeurerait éternellement immobile . . . suspendu à cette place comme le prétendu tombeau de Mahomet, entre le zénith et le nadir' (*Autour de la lune*, viii, p. 84).

192 *L'Ile mystérieuse*, III, xvi, p. 504. Moré and others have proposed that Nemo is castigated for wishing away imperialism, naively conceived of as a benign force of progress. But Smith's reproach seems to imply a broader critique of the savant in general.

193 The derivation of this avatar of the entropy of thermodynamics has been traced by Brillouin in *Science and Information Theory*.

194 Foucault similarly remarks that 'les romans de Jules Verne, c'est la négentropie du savoir' ('L'Arrière-fable', p. 11). But Foucault's argument reaches conclusions diametrically opposed to those obtained here (see below, n. 202).

195 Thus Ardan envisages the abolition of distance: 'Pour moi, le monde solaire est un corps solide, homogène; les planètes qui le composent se pressent, se touchent, adhèrent, et l'espace existant entre elles n'est que l'espace qui sépare les molécules du métal le plus compact, argent ou fer, or ou platine' (*De la terre à la lune*, xix, p. 117).

196 *Jouvences*, p. 162.

197 A theme anticipated by Poe: 'And the life of the ebony clock went out' ('Masque of the Red Death', *Collected Works*, II, p. 677).

198 *Les Enfants du capitaine Grant*, I, ii, p. 8.

199 *Ibid.*, III, xxi, p. 540. A further error occurs. In the English text, the fragment 'aland' leads Paganel to infer 'New Zealand' as the primal word of which it is the remnant. Captain Grant informs him that its French equivalent is 'à terre'. It was not beyond the ingenious Verne to insert deliberate errors; but it must be added that his texts abound in translations, not all of them reliable (thus justifying his anxiety regarding the confusion of tongues).

200 To Pencroff's assertion, 'Quel gros livre . . . on ferait avec tout ce qu'on sait!', Cyrus Smith replies, 'Et quel plus gros livre encore on ferait avec tout ce qu'on ne sait pas' (*L'Ile mystérieuse*, III, xiv, p. 482).

201 Against plunging into which Verne warns his schoolgirl audience in his *Discours*, p. 11.

202 The Tower of Babel is one of the recurring images that Verne elicits from his reading of Genesis. It constitutes, for example, the metaphorical centre of the dystopian city of Blackland (which is eventually detonated) in *L'Etonnante Aventure de la mission Barsac*. Popper asserts that 'if some day it should no longer be possible for scientific observers to reach agreement about basic statements this would amount to a failure of language as a means of universal communication. It would amount to a "new Babel of tongues"; scientific discovery would be reduced to absurdity. In this new Babel, the soaring edifice of science would soon lie in ruins' (*The Logic of Scientific Discovery*, p. 104). Verne records the collapse of precisely this obsolete

image of science as an edifice, an architecture with an unshakeable foundation. Foucault argues that Vernian science is articulated by a 'voix blanche' ('L'Arrière-fable', p. 11; see above, n. 194), a neutral, uniform, monotonous idiom, only disrupted by the insertion of disparate narrative forces. He thus inverts the central perception of the *Voyages*, namely, that entropy has penetrated the sanctum of scientific discourse.

203 Durkheim would convict the savant of *anomie*; he is guilty of 'la passion de l'infini' (*Le Suicide*, p. 282). But this is because the object of desire is infinite: discourse might be compared to the magic pudding (in the book of that name by Norman Lindsay) which, however much of it is consumed, remains undiminished.

204 It is hard to say where the *Voyages* begin and end, since the generic title is only imposed on the series after it has already begun, while Verne's *œuvre* culminates in a number of posthumous Vernian texts whose authorship is obscure. Thus the boundaries of the canon remain open.

5 End

1 *Nicomachean Ethics*, 1106b.
2 *Œuvres complètes*, I, p. 114.
3 *Voyage au centre de la terre*, vi, pp. 32–3.
4 'Réflexions sur quelques-uns de mes contemporains', *Œuvres complètes*, pp. 472–3.
5 *Le Texte du roman*, p. 141.
6 He derives from the observation that 'nous sommes dans l'ignorance la plus absolue' the promise of 'succès certains à tout observateur raisonnable' (*Rapport historique sur les progrès des sciences naturelles depuis 1789 et sur leur état actuel*, p. 10).
7 Rescher stresses the distinction between knowledge and absolute knowledge in *Scepticism*, pp. 138ff.
8 *Esthétique et théorie du roman*, p. 102.
9 *Introduction à l'étude de la médecine expérimentale*, pp. 248ff.
10 *History of the Royal Society*, pp. 62, 112.
11 'Two Dogmas of Empiricism', *From a Logical Point of View*, p. 42.
12 See Phillips, *Wittgenstein and Scientific Knowledge*, pp. 196ff.
13 *Of Learned Ignorance*, I, i, pp. 7–8; p. 5.
14 A view espoused by Bunge who asserts that 'science has a language but is not a language' (*Scientific Research*, I, p. 47).
15 *Against Method*, p. 27. Thus the dichotomy suggested by Barthes (in the *Essais Critiques*) between transitive and intransitive writing, the *écrivant* and the *écrivain*, the one concerned with pure observation, the other with pure verbal play (a distinction comparable to I. A. Richards's division between 'scientific' and 'emotive') appears misleadingly schematic (as Barthes himself seems to admit, in his refer-

ence to a 'type bâtard: l'écrivain-écrivant' (*ibid.*, p. 153), and in his article 'Science versus Literature', where the initial antithesis is dissolved: 'science will become literature, to the same extent that literature . . . already is and always has been a science' (*TLS*, 28 September 1967, p. 897).

16 This analysis suggests that Kuhn's account (in *The Structure of Scientific Revolutions*, comparable to Foucault's partition of history into a chain of distinctive *epistēmai* in *Les Mots et les choses*) of a 'paradigm' determining a code of scientific conduct and implying an opposition between 'normal science' and 'revolutionary science', and Feyerabend's anarchistic theory (in *Against Method*) that 'anything goes', implying permanent revolution, are respectively too prohibitive, exaggerating the closure of a system, and too permissive, exaggerating its openness: the one makes change, the other continuity, equally inconceivable. As T. S. Eliot argues (in 'Tradition and the Individual Talent'), the meaning of any discourse is determined by its relation to previous discourse, but the new constantly redefines our sense of the old.

17 A transition advocated by Gadamer (and reiterated by Rorty in *Philosophy and the Mirror of Nature*), who notes that the Renaissance image of the book of nature produced a correspondence between the self-descriptions of literary criticism and natural science, both of which were concerned with reading a text: 'to this extent scientific method is based on the model of literary criticism' (*Truth and Method*, p. 160).

18 *London Music in 1888–89*, p. 58.

19 See, for example, *Collected Papers*, IV, p. 132: 'The meaning of a sign is the sign it has to be translated into.' The encyclopedic implication of the theory is examined by Eco in *The Role of the Reader*, pp. 176ff.

20 I invite the reader to make up his or her own list of *bêtes noires* at this point.

21 *Truth and Method*, p. 442.

22 Cited in Wolff, *The Awakening of Europe*, p. 58.

TRANSLATIONS

The following translations make no pretence of being an adequate substitute for the passages cited. But they may nevertheless be of assistance. I have not translated certain brief quotations whose meaning is sufficiently self-evident or already glossed in the text.

p. ix *il ne faut* one must not always so exhaust a subject that one leaves nothing for the reader to do.

5 *tout poète* every poet . . . inevitably effects a return towards the lost Eden.

9 [*mon soupçon*] [my suspicion] was that (while each day I considered myself as if on the threshold of my life which was still intact and would not begin until the next morning) my existence had already begun, rather more, that what was due to follow would not be very different from what had gone before.

10 *je puis* I can well conceive of a man without hands, feet, head . . . But I cannot conceive of man without thought.

28 *Ensemble s'entr'aymant* Together loving one another, ignorant, they did not know by whom, to whom, why, and how they lived.

Ensemble dechassés Together banished from the delightful Paradise in which, in their innocence, divinely, they had of old named and known everything, now all uncertain in their naked memories.

Et quant à And as for the knowledge of the facts of nature, I wish that . . . nothing should be unknown to you.

Somme In short, let me see an abyss of science.

32 *la Docte* Learned Ignorance is learned far more than it is ignorance.

42 *généralement* generally, people who know little speak a lot and people who know a lot speak little.

je ferais I could carry on a quite lovely conversation by post.

43 *pourra me croire* could believe me a dishonest man deserves himself to be stifled.

Quel bonheur What bliss to have found ink and paper!

44 *n'a jamais* has never finished having his say; like a vigorous spring which flows without end and is never exhausted.

Encore une One more letter, Monsieur, and you are free of me.

On verra It will be seen in my third part if ever I have the strength to write it.

p. 44   *Je suis* I am, in recounting my journeys, as I was in making them; I cannot arrive.

46   *recompose* recomposes a philosophical Genesis lacking neither the garden of Eden, nor the transgression, nor the confusion of tongues.

version laïcisée secularized, 'demythified' rendering of the history of origins.

il est évident it is evident, from reading the Sacred Books, that the first man having received knowledge and precepts immediately from God was not himself in this state [of nature].

parloient spoke of savage man and depicted civil man.

Commençons Let us then begin by dismissing all the facts.

47   *la base* the unshakeable base on which it is erected.

c'est en un sens it is in a sense by dint of studying man that we have rendered ourselves incapable of knowing him.

si difficile so difficult to see . . . I have hazarded some conjectures less in the hope of resolving the question than with the intention of clarifying it and reducing it to its true state.

qui n'existe which no longer exists, which has perhaps not existed, which probably never will exist.

la paix peace and innocence escaped us for ever before we had tasted their delights; imperceptible to the stupid men of early times, eluding the enlightened men of later times, the happy life of the golden age was always a state foreign to the human race, as a result either of ignoring it when we could enjoy it, or of losing it when we might have known it.

48   *les instrumens* the instruments of tilling had fallen from the heavens into the hands of savages.

toutes choses all things . . . by the gods, for want of conceiving how they could have learned them by themselves.

En un mot In a word, how could this situation induce men to cultivate the earth, so long as it is not shared out among them, that is to say, so long as the state of nature is not annulled?

cette premiére difficulté this first difficulty overcome.

l'espace immense the immense space that must have existed between the pure state of nature and the need of languages.

49   *si les Hommes* if men needed speech to learn to think, they needed far more to be able to think to find the art of speech.

pour indiquer to indicate a new 'immense space' intervening between the 'need of languages' and languages being established.

la parole speech seems to have been most necessary to establish the practice of speech.

Si un Chêne If one oak was called *A*, another oak was called *B*.

des observations observations and definitions, that is, natural history and metaphysics, much more than the men of that time could have had.

les premiers the first inventors . . . our new grammarians.

p. 49 *ils avoient* they had at first gone too far in multiplying the names of individuals from ignorance of their genera and species.

ils firent they then made too few species and genera for want of considering beings in all their differences.

50 *Quant à moi* As for me, alarmed at the multiplying difficulties, and convinced of the all but proven impossibility of languages being born and established by purely human means, I leave, to whomsoever might wish to undertake it, the discussion of this difficult problem: which was the more necessary, the prior existence of society to the institution of languages, or the prior invention of languages to the establishment of society.

51 *C'est ici* Here is the ultimate limit of inequality, and the extreme point which closes the circle and touches the point from which we departed: it is here that all individuals become equal once more because they are nothing.

sitôt qu'il parle as soon as it speaks, there is neither probity nor duty to consult, and the blindest obedience is the sole virtue remaining to the slaves.

il faut it is therefore necessary to speak in order to have general ideas.

54 *jouis* enjoy simultaneously love and innocence.

sous le voile beneath the veil of pleasure or self-interest.

55 *le roman* the novel offers us the spectacle of a dialectic which issues in a synthesis.

Tu as voulu You tried to reconcile filial affection with untameable love; in giving yourself up to all your inclinations at once, you mix them up instead of harmonizing them, and become guilty through virtue.

il n'y a nothing is beautiful except what is not.

on jouït one enjoys less what one obtains than what one hopes for.

56 *il y a* there are lacunae and voids that I can only fill in with the aid of stories.

je n'ai I have only one thing to fear in this enterprise: not telling too much or telling lies, but rather not telling everything, and suppressing truths.

[il] commence [it] begins to die from the moment of its birth and carries within itself the causes of its destruction.

57 *Jean-Jacques* Jean-Jacques and he who believes him dishonest are knotted together in the same mortal embrace.

cumulant combining against me all imaginable accusations.

la proclamation the proclamation of the French Republic actually coincides with the abolition of the Republic of letters.

58 *la République* the Republic has no need of savants.

61 *d'une façon* in a ridiculous enough way, last summer, going to see the sun go down.

se couchait would retire precisely at the hour at which (when in fog the cat prowls and weeps) Monsieur Hugo goes to see Phoebus the fair retire.

p. 61   *Tout d'abord* First of all, it is and aims to be a challenge to good sense: space, he says, belongs to the poet who can dream of the Orient in Paris, but equally of the sun, without seeing it.

61   *L'Orient!* Orient! Orient! what do you see there poets? It is perhaps the evening that one takes for a dawn.

62   *toute entière* quite complete perfection which resides in the true knowledge of good letters and sciences.

le père the father of all figures. Everything turns around it, everything turns towards it.

à la fin at the end of the eighteenth century, the metaphor of day and night was very widespread: from the religious point of view, the day of Christianity was opposed to the night of paganism, from the aesthetic point of view, the golden age of the 'ancient' to the 'night' of the Middle Ages.

Je vois I already see the schism collapsing, the Orient and the Occident reuniting, and Asia seeing the rebirth of day after such a long night.

63   *Il faut* It has to be said: of all the men who have dared prescribe laws to peoples, none has been more ignorant than Mahomet; of all the absurd compositions of the human spirit, none is more wretched than his book.

Il suffit It suffices to observe that this ignorance permeating all classes, extends its effects to all types of moral and physical knowledge, to the sciences, to the fine arts, and even to the mechanical arts. The simplest of these are still in a sort of infancy there.

66   *Tout un monde* A whole world, distant, absent, almost dead.

moins heureux less fortunate and less wise awaited the uniform passage of the seasons within the same horizon, and like the green tree which from afar reproduces him in outline, at his door shedding his days like leaves, took root on the threshold of his house!

67   *Au siècle* In the age of Louis XIV people were Hellenists, now they are Orientalists.

pourquoi why could there not be a literature as a whole, and more particularly the work of a poet, akin to those beautiful old towns of Spain, for example, where you find everything.

la mosquée the Oriental mosque . . . at the other end of town . . . hidden in the sycomores and palm-trees.

68   *si on lui demandait* if one were to ask him what he wanted to do here, he would say that it is the mosque.

vive sympathie a poet's lively fellow-feeling . . . for the Oriental world.

dans l'arsenal in the arsenal of Hugolian figures, there is one however which dominates, in quantity as in importance, all the others: it is, as we know, antithesis.

69   *Jamais tant* Never have so many intelligences searched at the same

time this great abyss that is Asia. We have today a scholar stationed
in each of the languages of the Orient, from China to Egypt.

p. 70   *Choisis enfin* Choose finally, before your God arises, between Jesus
and Omar, the cross and the sword, the halo and the turban.

71   *Ces ponts* These bridges, these aqueducts, these arches, these round
towers, alarmed the eye lost in their profound sinuosities.

Elle va She walks, runs, stops, and flies.

Certes Of course, old Omer, pasha of Négrepont, would have given his
all for her.

73   *Garde-toi* Protect yourself from the sun which bronzes our dusky
brows, but burns a rosy complexion.

L'astre-roi The king-star was setting. Calm, sheltered from the wind,
the sea reflected this globe of living gold, this world, soul and torch
of our own, and in the reddish sky and in the vermilion waves, like
two friendly kings, could be seen two suns coming to meet one
another.

74   *déchire* cuts through the mist with its golden spires.

l'Egypte Egypt is aglow with the fire of his dawn.

75   *Telle en plein jour* As in broad daylight sometimes, beneath a fiery
sun, the moon, star of the dead, white against a blue sky, half shows
its nocturnal face.

Cachée Hidden from the bold gazes of the unbelievers and Albanians.

Déjà trois Already three times, out of their scabbards . . . the blades
of the daggers have shone.

76   *sur mes regards* over my eyes from which the light is going out a veil
of death is unfurling.

77   *immense entassement* boundless, veiled piling up of darkness.

chaque colonne each column burns and whirls like a great torch.

Prend feu Catches fire like a beacon.

Ainsi tout Thus all disappears beneath the dark whirlwind.

Sur leurs débris Over their extinguished remains extends a frozen
lake.

Eteint Extinguishes their flaming evenings and freezes their dawns.

plus d'ardente Gomorrhe no more blazing Gomorrah throwing a red
reflection on the dark facade of Babel.

quinze ans fifteen years old . . . the age at which the eye lights up and
shines.

78   *sans en faire* without making any, listen to stories.

l'œuvre poétique the poetic work must in reality be defined as a verbal
message in which the poetic function is dominant.

écrire to write, first of all, for [Hugo] is to bring chaos into being . . .
But it is also to dominate it scripturally, to control it by the very act
of naming . . . Language offers itself . . . as chaos . . . but also as the
space wherein man makes himself master, or at least signifier of his
chaos.

p. 79 *le grand œil* the great fixed eye looking out on the great all.

   yeux eyes plunged further than the real world.

80 *J'aime* I love those dark and heavy wagons which, at night, trundling noisily past the farms' front gates, make the dogs bark in the darkness.

  Là, en effet There, indeed, all is grand, rich, fecund, as in the Middle Ages, that other sea of poetry.

81 *en Egypte* in Egypt . . . I dreamed of all things.

  je voyais I saw the means of executing all that I had dreamed.

82 *Napoléon* Napoleon is the greatest man of his century, we are agreed, but he is also the greatest writer.

  peu d'hommes few men have written as much.

83 *la première ville* the first town that we are going to meet was built by Alexander. We will find at each step memories worthy of exciting emulation by Frenchmen.

  Nous ne vivons We no longer live in those times when conquerors knew only how to destroy wherever they carried their arms: the thirst for gold governed their actions; devastation, persecutions, intolerance accompanied them everywhere. Today, on the contrary, the Frenchman respects not only the laws, customs, habits, but even the prejudices of the peoples whose territory he occupies. He leaves it to time, reason, and education to effect the changes that philosophy and the accumulated knowledge of the centuries have prepared, and whose application becomes more imminent every day.

84 *ce prince* this prince, great, generous, enlightened, magnanimous, saw the Arab empire flourish in the bosom of peace. Feared and respected by his neighbours, he was attending to the task of encouraging the growth and advance of the sciences, when the peace was disturbed by Hakem, who, coming out of the heart of the Khorasan, began to gather followers around him in all parts of the empire.

86 *tous les hommes* all men are equal before God; wisdom, abilities, and virtues alone place differences between them. Now what wisdom, what abilities, what virtues so distinguish the Mamelukes that they and they alone should get everything that goes to make life pleasant and sweet?

  Tous les Egyptiens All Egyptians will be called upon to manage all positions: the wisest, the most highly educated, the most virtuous will govern, and the people will be happy.

  Je pourrais demander I could bring you all to book for the most secret sentiments of the heart, for I know everything, even what you have never said to anyone; but a day will come when everyone will clearly see that I am guided by orders from above and that all the efforts of men can have no effect on me.

87 *la religion chrétienne* the Christian religion is that of a very civilized

people. It elevates man; it proclaims the superiority of mind over matter, of the soul over the body.

p. 88   *Il s'adressait* He was addressing savage, impoverished peoples, lacking everything, quite ignorant; if he had spoken to their intellects, he would not have been understood.

89   [*il*] *avait* [he] had many doubts to express, and I many interesting truths to teach him.

il périt he perished gloriously at the siege of Saint-Jean d'Acre, delivering on his death-bed a very eloquent speech on public education.

90   *il avait* he had returned the arts and sciences to their cradle.

91   *Le succès* The success obtained in this matter by Bonaparte proves that all men, even the least educated, and consequently the most liable to prejudice and bias, are never insensitive to the language of sweetness and light, especially when it comes from the mouth of someone who has force and power in his hands.

l'Egypte Egypt could quickly become not just a colony, but in some way a French province, and offer to its new inhabitants the image of their own homeland.

Mes enfants Lads, the countries you are about to conquer are attached to a bunch of gods that you are going to respect because the Frenchman must be everyone's friend, and defeat people without upsetting them. Get it into your heads not to touch anything at first, because you will have everything later! March!

92   *depuis que* since the world was world, it was written that after destroying the enemies of Islam, and bringing down the crosses, I would come out of the West to fulfil the task laid upon me . . . in the holy book of the Koran, in more than twenty passages, what is happening was foreseen, and what will happen is similarly explained.

nous ne sommes we are no longer those infidels of barbarous times who came to fight your faith; we recognize it as sublime, we support it, and the moment has arrived when all regenerated French people will also become true believers.

empêcher prevent mankind from being blinded by the light which shone from his face.

93   *fluide magique* magic fluid [which] hides from us the things that it is most important we know.

Sa personne His person was henceforth as superfluous in the East as it was indispensable in the West: everything announced to him that the moment designated by destiny had arrived.

[*il*] *passa* [he] spent the night in his tent devouring these papers, and resolved there and then to return to Europe in order to remedy, if there was still time, the ills of the homeland and save its life.

renfermé shut up for the greater part of the day in his room, where he read, says Genteaume, now the Bible, now the Koran.

p. 95   *une population* a very hostile population, yearning for the chance to slaughter all Frenchmen.

       l'Egypte Egypt is useful not only for what she possesses, but even more so for what she lacks.

96   *Il faut* You have to be on one side or the other: as well be on the side of the winners, those who devastate, pillage, burn; given the choice, it is better to be the eater than the eaten.

       [*est*] *sorti* emerged from a half-savage island.

       Il ne sait He knows neither how to enter nor how to leave a room; he is ignorant of how to greet, how to rise or to sit.

       ils ne connaissent they have never even heard of a pair of scissors . . . they are ignorant of the use of windmills.

       il fallait we had to re-embark or reconcile ourselves to the religious ideas and escape the anathemas of Islam.

97   *Je prenais* I would have taken Europe from the rear, the old European civilization would have remained encircled, and who would then have dreamed of disturbing the course of French destiny or of the regeneration of the century!

       J'étudiai I studied history less than I conquered it; that is, I wanted of it and retained only what could give me new ideas, disdaining the superfluous, capturing only certain results.

       il fallait we had to persuade the muftis, the ulemas, the princes, the imams, to interpret the Koran in favour of the army.

       Vous savez You know how much effect words have on soldiers.

98   *La langue française* The French language is not a well-made language . . . I really ought to have codified it.

99   *Enfin* At last we see the dawn of happiness shine upon us: the time determined by God has arrived; an atmosphere of felicity surrounds us; the brilliant star of victory which leads the French warriors has shed upon us its radiant light.

       assez heureuse fortunate enough to enjoy, for ten years of peace, the benefits of French administration.

       la civilisation civilization would have spread into the interior of Africa by way of Sennar, Abyssinia, Darfour, Fezzan; several great nations would have been called upon to enjoy the benefits of the arts, the sciences, the religion of the true God, for it is through Egypt that the peoples of the centre of Africa must receive light and happiness.

       Tels les derniers Just as the last rays of the sun setting behind the immensity of the ocean illuminate the sky, so the thought of Napoleon I illuminates the future.

       C'est le 5 mai It was the fifth of May, at about six p.m., at the very instant when the cannon announced sunset, that his great soul departed this earth.

100   *Il s'agissait* It was a matter not only of delivering the sacred tomb, but also of determining which should triumph on earth, a cult hostile to civilization, systematically favourable to ignorance, despotism,

slavery, or a religion which had revived in the moderns the genius of learned antiquity, and abolished servitude . . . The spirit of Mohammedanism is persecution and conquest; the Gospel, on the contrary, preaches only tolerance and peace.

p. 101   *la patience* the patience to read about two hundred modern accounts of the Holy Land, the Rabbinic compilations, and the passages of the ancients on Judaea.

102   *je vois* I see that all the epic poets were very learned men: they were especially nourished by the works of those who had preceded them in the path of the epic: Virgil translated Homer; in each stanza, Tasso imitates some passage of Homer, Virgil, Lucian, Statius; Milton takes from everywhere, and adds to his own treasures the treasures of his predecessors.

il me suffit it suffices me to be sheltered beneath their authority; I consent to being wrong with them.

Que dirait-on What would one say of a man who, travelling through Greece and Italy, took as his sole task to contradict Homer and Virgil?

c'est en effet it is indeed with the Bible and the Gospel in one's hand that one must travel the Holy Land.

103   *La plume* The pen falls from my grip: one is ashamed to be still blackening paper after a man has written such verses.

Que dirais-je What could I say of Egypt? Who has not seen it today? The *Voyage* of M. de Volney in Egypt is a genuine masterpiece in every respect other than erudition: erudition has been exhausted by Sicard, Norden, Pococke, Shaw, Niebhur and a few others . . . I myself have already said elsewhere all that I had to say on Egypt.

104   *Ici j'éprouve* Here I encounter a genuine difficulty. Must I offer an exact portrayal of the Holy Places? But then I can only repeat what others have said before me: never was a subject less known to modern readers, and yet never was a subject so completely exhausted.

Si la multitude If the multitude of accounts wearies the writer who wishes to speak today of Egypt and Judaea, he experiences, when it comes to the antiquities of Africa, a quite contrary difficulty owing to the dearth of documents.

On peut One can therefore say that the subject that I am about to consider is new; I will show the way: the clever will come after me.

105   *Christophe Colomb* Christopher Columbus must have felt something of that feeling Scripture attributes to the Creator when after producing the earth out of nothingness, he saw that his work was good: *and God saw that it was good.* Columbus created a world.

Je viens I come to join the crowd of obscure travellers who have seen only what everyone has seen, who have not advanced the sciences an inch, who have added nothing to the treasure of human knowledge.

106   *un grand nombre* a great number of the pages of my books have been written beneath a tent, in deserts, at sea; I have often held the pen

without knowing how I would prolong my existence for a few moments more.

p. 106   *Asie* Asia, a part of the world which had not yet seen the trace of my steps, alas! nor those sorrows that I share with all men.

107   *j'allais* I went in search of some images, that's all.

revient returns to his home with a few new images in his head and a few more feelings in his heart.

le survol flying over Arabia offers a series of variations on a single theme: the desert.

108   *quand on songe* when one thinks that once these lands were inhabited only by Greeks of the late Empire, and that they are occupied today by Turks, one is shocked at the contrast between the peoples and the places; it seems that such vile slaves and such cruel tyrants should never have disgraced such a magnificent abode.

Les palmiers The palm-trees appeared aligned on the bank like those avenues with which the *châteaux* of France are decorated; nature is thus pleased to recall the ideas of civilization, in the country where this civilization had its birth and where today ignorance and barbarity reign.

109   *Nous passâmes* We passed through the Menouf canal, which prevented me from seeing the beautiful wood of palm-trees that is situated on the main western branch; but the Arabs were then infesting the western bank of this branch which borders the Libyan desert.

j'avais I had under my gaze the descendants of the primitive race of men, I saw them with the same manners they have preserved since the days of Agar and Ismaël: I saw them in the same desert which was assigned to them by God as their heritage . . . the Arab, thrust, so to speak, onto the great highway of the world, between Africa and Asia, wanders in the shimmering regions of the dawn, on a ground devoid of trees and water.

110   *une religion* a religion which razed the library of Alexandria, which prides itself on its supreme contempt for literature and the arts.

il n'y a in Mahomet's book there is neither a principle of civilization, nor a precept capable of elevating the character: this book preaches neither the hatred of tyranny nor the love of liberty.

112   *l'imagination* Chateaubriand's imagination abandons itself to a great dramatization of absence. It extends around the self a desert of negativity.

Je n'ai I have before my eyes, of the sites of Syria, Egypt, and the Punic country, only the places having an affinity with my solitary nature; they please me independently of antiquity, art, or history.

Les pyramides The pyramids struck me less by their size than by the desert they were set against.

113   *peut-être* perhaps the genius of nations can be exhausted; and when it has produced everything, travelled everywhere, tasted everything,

sated with its own masterpieces, and incapable of producing new ones, it becomes mindless and reverts to purely physical sensations.

p. 113   *naturellement* naturally on the savage side, it was not what is called society that I came to seek in the Orient: I was impatient to see camels and to hear the cry of the elephant driver.

L'Egypte Egypt seemed to me the most beautiful country on earth: I love even the deserts which surround it and which open up to the imagination the fields of immensity.

114   *je commençais* then I was beginning the journey, and now I am finishing it. The world, at these two periods of my life, presented itself to me precisely in the form of these two deserts where I saw two types of tomb: cheerful solitudes and arid sands.

l'equivalent the equivalent of the English *wilderness*. It in no way evokes sterility, the Sahara; on the contrary, this desert is characterized by the splendour of its flora. It signifies a place left intact by human society.

115   *Où y a-t-il* Where is there something new? Is it in the East? . . . Let us go there.

puisque since we are seeking new suns, I will rush before their splendour and will no longer await the natural appearance of the dawn.

c'est dans it is in those nights that an unknown muse appeared to me.

l'imagination the poetic imagination is more interested in night than day.

un choix a guilty choice, a bias in favour of the forbidden, a transgression.

la relation the relation between day and night is not only one of opposition, and thus of mutual exclusion, but also of inclusion: in one of its senses, day excludes night, in the other, it contains it.

découvrir reveal in your light the delightful secrets of these deserts.

116   *je passerai* I will pass away in my turn: other men as evanescent as I will come to make the same reflections on the same ruins.

117   *Dieu* God must have created, and undoubtedly did create the world with all the marks of old age and complementarity that we see in it.

la nature nature, in its innocence, would have been less beautiful than it is today in its corruption.

cette autobiographie this gigantic autobiography . . . that the West of the nineteenth century began to entitle 'civilization'.

118   *la civilisation* the present-day decomposed civilization does not pass through barbarous countries; it is lost within itself; the vessel containing it has not poured the liquor into another vessel; rather the vessel is smashed and the liquor spilt.

119   *les rayons* the rays of my sun, from sunrise to sunset.

pâle reflet pale reflection . . . of an immense light.

Je vois I see the reflections of a dawn when I will not see the sun rise.

Tu contiens You contain in your eye sunset and sunrise.

p. 119   *la distance* the distance of these stars is so great that their light can only reach the contemplating eye when these stars are already extinguished, the source before the ray.

il ne fait it is not day, during the day, nor night at night.

122   *L'univers* The universe is equal to his vast appetite.

il faut we must . . . eat too much.

123   *il est* it is customary on board every ship to carefully inspect the stomach of a shark. Sailors, knowing its indiscriminate voracity, expect some surprise; and they are not always disappointed.

124   *un festin* a skilfully organized feast is like an abbreviation of the world.

125   *dans les régions* in the Arctic regions you have to eat plenty; it is one of the prerequisites not only of strength but of life itself.

En manger To eat of them in moderation would show ingratitude towards Providence; we must eat too much.

très schématiquement very schematically, one can say that a narrative, of any kind, can recount once what happened once, *n* times what happened *n* times, *n* times what happened once, and once what happened *n* times.

dans les récits in the narratives of Arctic travellers, meals [are] constantly being discussed.

126   *la nécessité* the necessity for the carnivore of restoring his flesh and blood with the nitrogen stored in animal matter.

leurs lèvres their lips thrust forwards, their bared teeth, ready for violent snatching, will tear like the teeth of flesh-eaters, with the brutal voracity of beasts.

128   *Le mouvement* Motion and life cause a continual loss of substance in the living body; and the human body, that most complicated of machines, would soon break down if Providence had not provided it with a spring which gives warning of the moment when its forces are no longer commensurate with its needs. This early-warning device is the appetite.

129   *Tout en lui* Everything in him, stomach and brain, was overexcited to the highest degree.

il leur fallait they needed a substantial food, for one can say that they have their hearts in their bellies.

On hérite One thus inherits his soul, his strength, his value, all of which are stored, in particular, in the brain.

J'avouerai I will admit that I bit with appetite into the geological sciences; I had mineralogist's blood in my veins.

130   *distraire* distract for a moment, addressing the mind . . . and even the stomach.

131   *Aussi* And so, to that question posed six thousand years ago by Ecclesiastes: 'Who has ever been able to plumb the depths of the abyss?', two men out of all men now have the right to reply. Captain Nemo and I.

p. 131   *Je veux* I want to know everything, I want to go right down into the core of the planet, I want to walk along the ocean floor, I want to run across the sky, clinging onto comets' tails. Oh! I would like to go to the moon to hear the silvery snow of its shores crunch beneath my feet and to descend its underground crevasses.

     Il faut You must eat the fruits of the tree of science. Man can become the equal of God.

     Qui tentera Whosoever attempts to become the equal of God will be *damned* for all eternity.

133   *résumer* recapitulate all the knowledge, *geographical, geological physical*, and *astronomical* amassed by modern science, and to rewrite, in the attractive and picturesque form which is his own, the history of the universe.

     peindre describe the entire earth, the whole world, in the form of the novel.

     Ah, Robert Ah, Robert, simile, do you see, is the most dangerous rhetorical figure I know. Beware of it all your life; and only use it as a last resort.

134   *méduses* microscopic jellyfish observed by Scoresby in the seas off Greenland, and which this navigator numbers at twenty-three trillion eight hundred and eighty-eight thousand billion millions in a space of two square miles.

     Ce nombre This number being beyond our powers of comprehension, the English whaler, in order to make it more comprehensible, said that to count it eighty thousand people would have been occupied day and night since the creation of the world.

137   *toutes ces pierres* all those hollow stones within which stirred small crystals.

139   *je crois* I believe and always will believe in a molten centre; but I admit that certain ill-defined circumstances can modify this law under the action of natural phenomena.

     Toute l'histoire The entire history of the carboniferous period was written on these sombre walls, and a geologist could easily follow its various phases.

     Je mettais Unhesitatingly I put a name to these gigantic bones.

140   *A une certaine* At a certain period, the earth was formed of an elastic crust, subject to alternating highs and lows by virtue of the laws of attraction. It is probable that subsidences of the earth took place and that a part of the sedimentary formations was dragged down into the depths of the suddenly created chasms.

141   *des cassures* fractures, crevices, faults, where a part of the higher ground very likely slipped down.

142   *Il ne voyageait* He no longer travelled, he described a circumference. He was a heavy body, travelling on an orbit of the terrestrial globe, according to the rational laws of mechanics.

144   *pestait* railed against horizontality, he, 'the man of verticals'.

p. 145   *Entre la brute* Between the brute beast and the Australian exists the unbridgeable abyss separating genera.

       C'est un It is a bestial instinct which impels us and which none can repress. It seems, at this moment, that we no longer have anything human about us.

146   *Mais le jour* But would the day ever come when the insatiable desire of man would be satisfied? Would the day ever come when, having completed his ascent of the slope, man could rest on the finally conquered summit?

147   *débute* commences by the most simple forms, and becomes increasingly complex before issuing finally in man, its final and most perfect expression. Man, scarcely having appeared on earth, immediately begins and unceasingly continues his ascent. Slowly but surely, he approaches his end, which is the perfect knowledge and absolute domination of the universe.

       ignoraient were still ignorant of the telephone and the electric light.

       On s'accorda It was agreed that humanity had attained an intellectual level unknown before our own era, and which justified us in believing in its definitive victory over nature.

148   *Ce fut* It was at that exact moment that the cataclysm occurred.

       notre vie our cerebral life is over. Eating, and more eating, such is our perpetual goal, our exclusive preoccupation.

       [il] acquérait [he] was acquiring, slowly and painfully, an intimate conviction of the eternal return of things.

149   *nous descendions* we were going down a sort of spiralling screw.

       il décrivait it described a spiral whose radius was ever diminishing.

150   *Les rochers* The rocks clinging to each other were only held in position by a miracle of equilibrium. The mountain was, in truth, only an agglomeration of stones fallen from above . . . This island . . . was due only to the cumulative aggregation of volcanic dejects.

151   *Je m'occupais* So I was busying myself meanwhile with classifying my mineralogical, botanical, and zoological treasures, when the incident of the *Scotia* occurred.

152   *le rangeait* classed it, not without good reason, in the class of the cartilaginous, order of the chondropterygians with fixed gills, family of selatians, genus of squali.

       Les oiseaux Birds flew in innumerable flocks, like huge, dense storm clouds . . . all the specimens of the great aquatic family . . . with gigantic proportions . . . these aerial monsters.

       cet élément this element ploughed by all species . . . the marine monsters.

153   *ceux que* those that the speed of the *Nautilus* hid from my eyes.

       Il me semblait I felt as though I were trapped between some monster's great jaws which were irresistibly closing.

154   *nous regardions* we were looking out as if this pure crystal had been the glass of an immense aquarium.

p. 154   *tout ce que* all the finest works humanity has produced in history, poetry, fiction and science.

un musée a museum in which an intelligent and prodigal hand had joined all the treasures of nature and art.

155   *Je veux* I want to believe that humanity has neither thought nor written any more.

Mon cuisinier My cook is a skilled preparer of foods . . . who excels in preserving these varied products of the ocean . . . Here is a preserve of holothurians.

Nous sommes We belong to a time when everything happens – one almost has the right to say when everything has already happened.

Afin de To assure them eternal life, these pictures are placed inside glass cabinets where a vacuum has previously been created . . . Thanks to this climate without rain or fog, groups, statues, busts, can with impunity resist the ravages of time.

158   *Si notre récit* If our story is not probable today, it might be so tomorrow thanks to the scientific resources of the future.

J'en ai revu I have reread the account of it. I read it to Conseil and the Canadian. They found it accurate as regards fact, but inadequate as regards effect. To paint such pictures would require the pen of the most illustrious of our poets.

160   *Assez* Enough. When science has pronounced, one can only remain silent.

161   *Qu'ajouter* What to add to these numbers so eloquent in themselves? . . . Nothing.

Un statisticien A statistician worthy of the name must forbid himself reasoning.

162   *La dérive* Drift occurs each time that *I do not respect* the whole, and that as a result of seeming transported hither and thither at the whim of the illusions, seductions and intimidations of language, like a cork on the waves, I remain stationary, pivoting on the *inflexible* bliss which links me to the text (to the world).

Conseil Conseil, carried away into the abysses of classification, left behind the real world.

163   *Un observateur* An observer endowed with an infinite range of vision, and placed at that unknown centre around which the world revolves, might have seen myriads of atoms filling all space during the chaotic period of the universe.

164   *Mais peu* But gradually, over the centuries, a change took place; a law of attraction manifested itself, to which the hitherto errant atoms became obedient; these atoms combined together chemically according to their affinities, formed themselves into molecules and composed those nebulous clusters which stud the furthest reaches of the sky.

Les molécules The molecules situated on the plane of the (sun's) equator, escaping like the stone from a sling whose cord has suddenly snapped, would have formed around the sun several concentric rings similar to that of Saturn. In their turn, these rings of cosmic matter, propelled by a rotary motion round the central mass, would have been smashed and decomposed into secondary nebulosities, that is, into planets.

p. 165   *débris errants* errant debris of a star shattered into several thousands of pieces.

166   *Cet homme* This man lived his life perpetually prone to hyperbole and had not yet passed the age of superlatives: objects were depicted on the retina of his eye with enormous dimensions; hence an association of gigantic ideas; he saw everything enlarged, excepting difficulties and men.

167   *sa pensée* his thought had at all costs to find an outlet, without which it would cause the machine to explode . . . His eyes . . . his mouth . . . were so many safety valves which allowed him to give vent to this overflow of himself.

  brisé smashed by the great arms of the octopus, ground by his iron mandibles.

  dix canons ten cannons were drawn up on the parade ground, a prisoner fixed to each of their mouths, and five times the ten cannons gave fire, covering the plain with formless debris in an atmosphere tainted with the smell of burnt flesh.

  En moins de In less time than a swift pen could record it, the bodies, still smoking, were torn apart, divided, dismembered, chopped not into pieces but into crumbs.

168   *c'est* it is a great cyclone which will complete its destruction . . . An instant later, the entire edifice is no more than a mass of debris . . . its hull is perforated in a thousand places . . . The welds are cracking everywhere . . . the disintegration is spreading . . . the park is cut in two . . . the whole population is dispersing . . . a half-mile square piece has just split apart from Standard Island. It is Starboard Harbour, its factories, its machines, its shops drifting away . . . Its hull is finally breaking up . . . The compartments are separating.

169   *A présent* At present, all that is left of the marvellous Standard Island is a few scattered remnants, like the sporadic fragments of a smashed-up comet, which float not in space but on the surface of the immense Pacific.

170   *Qui permet* Which allows the reader to multiply exclamation and question marks to infinity!

173   *exposer* reveal, as far as possible, the order and coherence of human knowledge.

174   *sera-t-il* will it be possible to reunite the separately floating pieces?

  un microcosme a microcosm, a composite of all science and all human intelligence.

  J'avais I now had the right to write the true book of the sea.

p. 175   *votre tort* your fault is to have believed that the past could be brought
back to life and to have struggled against inexorable progress.

177   *Erreur* An error difficult to avoid, however, since the planispheres of
the *Duncan* gave the name of Marie-Thérésa to this little island.

183   *la science* science is eminently perfectible . . . each theory is incessantly destroyed by another.

Ah! malgré Ah! Despite Newton and Laplace, astronomical certitude is not so great today that the imagination cannot find a place in
the vast and as yet unexplored lacunae of modern science.

c'est donc it is therefore at the intersection of writing with the
spoken word, of science with ignorance that the novel will be born,
a perceptible echo of the 'Learned Ignorance' of which Nicholas of
Cusa became the apostle.

184   *seul l'Adam* only the mythical Adam, in his first words, approaching
a world not yet put in question, still virgin, only Adam-the-solitary
could wholly avoid this dialogic relationship in respect of the object
with the words of other people.

BIBLIOGRAPHY

This bibliography simply lists the books cited in the text. It omits reference to standard Biblical and classical works. Where no place of publication is given, English titles were published in London, French titles in Paris.

Allotte de la Fuÿe, Marguerite. *Jules Verne: sa vie, son œuvre*, 1928

Alonso-Schökel, L. 'Motivos sapienciales y de alianza en Gn 2–3', *Biblica*, 43 (1962), 295–316

Alter, Robert. *The Art of Biblical Narrative*, New York, 1981

Arnault, Antoine Vincent. *Souvenirs d'un sexagénaire*, 4 vols. in 2, 1833

Auerbach, Erich. *Mimesis: The Representation of Reality in Western Literature*, trans. Willard K. Trask, Princeton, 1953

Bachelard, Gaston. *L'Eau et les rêves*, 1942

    La Poétique de l'espace, 1964

Bakhtin, Mikhail. *Esthétique et théorie du roman*, trans. D. Oliver, 1978

Balzac, Honoré de. *La Comédie humaine*, ed. Marcel Bouteron and Henri Longnon, 21 vols., 1926–63

Barrère, Jean-Bertrand. *La Fantaisie de Victor Hugo*, 3 vols., 1949–60

Barthélemy, Auguste, and Méry, Joseph. *Napoléon en Egypte*, 1835

Barthes, Roland. *Barthes par Barthes*, 1975

    Eléments de la sémiologie (with *Le Degré zéro de l'écriture*), 1968

    Essais critiques, 1964

    'Introduction à l'analyse des récits', *Communications*, 8 (1966), 1–27

    Mythologies, 1957

    Nouveaux essais critiques (with *Le Degré zéro de l'écriture*), 1972

    'Par où commencer?', *Poétique*, 1 (1970), 3–9

    Le Plaisir du texte, 1973

    'Science and Literature', *TLS*, 28 September 1967, pp. 897–8

    S/Z, 1970

Basil, Saint. *The Letters*, trans. R. J. Defferai and M. R. P. McGuire, 4 vols., 1934

Bassan, Fernande. *Chateaubriand et la Terre-Sainte*, 1959

Baudelaire, Charles. *Œuvres complètes*, ed. M. A. Ruff, 1968

Baudouin, Charles. *Psychanalyse de Victor Hugo*, Geneva, 1943

Bibliography

Beauchamp, Paul. *Création et séparation: étude exégétique du chapitre premier de la Genèse*, Bruges, 1969

Bell, A. Craig. *Alexandre Dumas: A Biography and Study*, 1950

Belliard, Augustin Daniel, Comte, and others. *Histoire scientifique et militaire de l'expédition française en Egypte*, 10 vols., 1830–6

Belloc, Marie A. 'Jules Verne at Home', *Strand Magazine* (Jan.–June 1895), 206–13

Bernard, Claude. *Introduction à l'étude de la médecine expérimentale*, 1865

Bett, Henry. *Nicholas of Cusa*, 1932

Bloy, Léon. *L'Ame de Napoléon*, 1920

Bolgar, R. R. *The Classical Heritage and its Beneficiaries*, 1954
(ed.) *Classical Influences on European Culture AD 1500–1700*, Cambridge, 1976

Bonaparte, Napoléon. *Correspondance*, 32 vols., 1858–70
The Journals of Napoleon in Egypt 1798–1801, ed. Saladin Boustany, 10 vols., Cairo, 1971
Mémoires et œuvres de Napoléon, ed. (with an 'étude littéraire') Tancrède Martel
Napoléon inconnu, papiers inédits (1786–1793), ed. Frédéric Masson and Guido Biagi, 2 vols., 1895

Borges, Jorge Luis. *Borges: A Reader*, ed. Emir Rodriguez Monegal and Alastair Reid, New York, 1981
Labyrinths, ed. D. A. Yates and J. E. Irby, Harmondsworth, 1970
Obras completas, 1923–1972, Buenos Aires, 1974
Other Inquisitions, trans. Ruth L. C. Simms, 1973

Bourrienne, Antoine Fauvelet de. *Mémoires sur Napoléon, le directoire, le consulat, l'empire et la restauration*, 2 vols., 1829

Boustany (ed.), see under Bonaparte

Brault, Gérard S. ' "Ung abysme de science": On the Interpretation of Gargantua's Letter to Pantagruel', *Bibliothèque d'humanisme et de Renaissance*, 28, Geneva (1966), 615–32

Brillat-Savarin, Anthelme. *Physiologie du goût, ou méditations de gastronomie transcendante*, 2 vols., 1826

Brillouin, Leon. *Science and Information Theory*, New York, 1962

Brooke-Rose, Christine. *A Grammar of Metaphor*, 1958

Brown, F., Driver, S. R., Briggs, C. A. *A Hebrew and English Lexicon of the Old Testament*, Oxford, 1959

Bunge, Mario. *Scientific Research*, 2 vols., Berlin, 1967

Burnaud, R. and Boucher, F. *L'Histoire de Napoléon racontée par les grands écrivains*, 1921

Butcher, William. 'Le Sens de *l'Eternel Adam*', *Bulletin de la Société Jules Verne*, 58 (1981), 73–81

Butor, Michel. *Répertoire [I]*, 1960
Répertoire II, 1964

Canat, René. *L'Hellénisme des romantiques*, 3 vols., 1951–5
La Renaissance de la Grèce antique, 1911

Bibliography

Caquot, see under *In Principio*

Cassirer, Ernst. *The Individual and the Cosmos in Renaissance Philosophy*, trans. M. Domandi, Oxford, 1963

 The Question of Jean-Jacques Rousseau, ed. and trans. Peter Gay, Bloomington and London, 1963

Cassuto, Umberto. *A Commentary on the Book of Genesis*, trans. I. Abrahams, 2 vols., Jerusalem, 1961

 The Documentary Hypothesis, trans. I. Abrahams, Jerusalem, 1961

Cave, Terence. *The Cornucopian Text*, Oxford, 1979

Chateaubriand, François René, vicomte de. *De Buonaparté et des Bourbons, et de la nécessité de se rallier à nos princes légitimes pour le bonheur de la France et celui de l'Europe*, London, 1814

 Correspondance générale, ed. Louis Thomas, 5 vols., 1912–14

 Essai sur les révolutions and *Génie du christianisme*, ed. Maurice Regard, 1978

 Mémoires d'outre-tombe, ed. Maurice Levaillant, 4 vols. in 2, 1949

 Œuvres romanesques et voyages, ed. Maurice Regard, 2 vols., 1969

 Pensées et premières poésies, with an introduction by Alain Coelho, Nantes, 1980

Chauvier, J. H. *A Treatise on Punctuation*, trans. J. B. Huntingdon, 1849

Chesney, Elizabeth A. *The Countervoyage of Rabelais and Ariosto*, 1982

Cohen, A. (ed.) *The Soncino Chumash Bible*, 1947

Condorcet, Marquis de. *Esquisse d'un tableau historique des progrès de l'esprit humain*, ed. O. H. Prior, 1933

Curl, James Stevens. *The Egyptian Revival*, 1982

Curtius, Ernst Robert. *European Literature and the Latin Middle Ages*, trans. Willard R. Trask, 1953

Cuvier, Georges. *Rapport historique sur les progrès des sciences naturelles depuis 1789 et sur leur état actuel*, 1809

Daniel, Norman. *Islam and the West: The Making of an Image*, Edinburgh, 1960

 The Arabs and Medieval Europe, London and Beirut, 1975

Defaux, Gérard. *Le Curieux, le glorieux et la sagesse du monde dans la première moitié du XVIe siècle: l'exemple de Panurge (Ulysse, Démosthène, Empédocle)*, Lexington, 1982

 Patagruel et les sophistes: contribution à l'histoire de l'humanisme chrétien au XVIe siècle, The Hague, 1973

de Man, Paul. *Allegories of Reading: Figural Language in Rousseau, Nietzsche, Rilke and Proust*, New Haven and London, 1979

 Blindness and Insight: Essays in the Rhetoric of Contemporary Criticism, New York, 1971

Dentan, Robert C. (ed.) *The Idea of History in the Ancient Near East*, New Haven, 1955

Derrida, Jacques. *La Dissémination*, 1972

 De la grammatologie, 1957

 Marges de la philosophie, 1972

Bibliography

Deschanel, Emile. *Le Romantisme des classiques*, 1883

Descotes, Maurice. *La Légende de Napoléon et les écrivains français du XIXe siècle*, 1967

Description de l'Egypte, ou recueil des observations et des recherches qui ont été faites en Egypte pendant l'expédition de l'armée française, publié par les ordres de sa majesté l'empereur Napoléon le grand, 23 vols., 1809–28

Diderot, Denis. *Œuvres philosophiques*, ed. Paul Vernière, 1956

Dumonceaux, Pierre, 'Cuisine et dépaysement dans l'œuvre de Jules Verne', *Europe*, 595–6 (nov–dec. 1978), 127–37

Durkheim, Emile. *Le Suicide: étude de sociologie*, 1930

Eco, Umberto. *The Role of the Reader: Explorations in the Semiotics of Texts*, Bloomington, 1979

Encyclopedia Judaica, ed. C. Roth, 16 vols., Jerusalem, 1971–2

Encyclopédie ou Dictionnaire raisonné des sciences, des arts, et des métiers, par une société de gens de lettres. Mis en ordre et publié par M. Diderot, et quant à la partie mathématique, par M. d'Alembert, 17 vols., 1751–65

Erasmus. *Opera omnia*, Vol. I–, Amsterdam, 1969–

    Opera omnia, 11 vols., Leyden, 1703–6 (republished London, 1962)

    The Praise of Folie, trans. E. Chaloner, Oxford, 1965

    Praise of Folly, trans. Clarence I. Miller, New Haven and London, 1979

Evans, I. O. *Jules Verne and his Work*, 1966

Feyerabend, Paul. *Against Method: Outline of an Anarchistic Theory of Knowledge*, 1976

Flaubert, Gustave. *Bouvard et Pécuchet* and *Dictionnaire des idées reçues*, ed. René Dumesnil, 2 vols., 1945

    La Tentation de Saint Antoine, ed. Conard, 1902

Fokkelman, J. P. *Narrative Art in Genesis: Specimens of Stylistic and Structural Analysis*, Amsterdam, 1975

Foucault, Michel. 'L'Arrière-fable', *L'Arc*, 29, Aix-en-Provence (1966), 5–13

    Les Mots et les choses, 1966

Fourier, see under *Description*

Freud, Sigmund. *Standard Edition of the Complete Psychological Works*, ed. James Strachey, 24 vols., 1953–73

Gadamer, Hans-Georg. *Dialogue and Dialectic*, trans. P. Christopher Smith, New Haven and London, 1980

    Truth and Method, trans. P. Christopher Smith, New York, 1975

Gaudon, Jean. *Le Temps de la contemplation*, 1969

Genette, Gérard. *Figures, I, II, III*, 1966–72

Gilpin, R. *France in the Age of the Scientific State*, Princeton, 1968

Gilson, Etienne. *La Philosophie au moyen-âge*, 1942

Golding, William. 'Astronaut by Gaslight', *The Spectator*, 9 June 1961

Goncourt, Edmond and Jules de. *Journal: mémoires de la vie littéraire*, ed. Robert Ricatte, 22 vols., Monaco, 1956

Bibliography

Gondolo della Riva, Piero. 'A propos des œuvres posthumes de Jules Verne', *Europe*, 595–6 (nov.–dec. 1978), 73–82

Gourgaud, Général Baron. *Sainte-Hélène: Journal inédit de 1815 à 1818*, 2 vols., 1899

Le Grand Dictionnaire universel du XIXᵉ siècle, 1870

Graves, Robert. *Adam's Rib and Other Anomalous Elements in the Hebrew Creation Myth: A New View*, 1955

Graves, Robert, and Patai, Raphael. *Hebrew Myths*, 1963

Gregh, Fernand. *Victor Hugo: sa vie, son œuvre*, 1954

Grevlund, M. *Paysage intérieur et paysage extérieur dans les 'Mémoires d'outre-tombe'*, 1968

Grimaux, Edouard. *Lavoisier 1743–1794*, 1888

Groningen, B. A. van. *In the Grip of the Past; Essay on an Aspect of Greek Thought*, Leyden, 1963

Guimbaud, Louis. *'Les Orientales' de Victor Hugo*, Amiens, 1928

Guyon, Bernard. *La Vocation poétique de Victor Hugo: essai sur la signification spirituelle des 'Odes et Ballades' et des 'Orientales'*, 1954

Hahn, Roger. *The Anatomy of a Scientific Institution: the Paris Academy of Sciences, 1666–1803*, Berkeley, 1971

Haining, Peter (ed.) *The Jules Verne Companion*, 1978

Harbison, Robert. *Deliberate Regression*, 1980

Haydn, Hiram C. *The Counter-Renaissance*, New York, 1950

Hazlitt, William. *The Life of Napoleon Buonaparte*, 4 vols., 1818

Healey, F. G. *The Literary Culture of Napoleon*, Geneva, 1959

Hegel, G. W. F. *Reason in History: Lectures on the Philosophy of World History*, trans. H. B. Nisbet, Cambridge, 1965

Heidel, Alexander. *The Babylonian Genesis*, Chicago, 1942

Hennequin, Emile. *La Critique scientifique*, 1888

Herold, Jean Christopher. *The Age of Napoleon*, Harmondsworth, 1969
Bonaparte in Egypt, 1962

Hertz, Joseph H. (ed.) *The Pentateuch and the Haftorahs*, 5 vols., Oxford, 1924

Hirsch, Samson Raphael (ed.) *Pentateuch*, trans. I. Levy, 5 vols., 1958–62

Hugo, Adèle V. *Victor Hugo raconté par un témoin de sa vie*, 2 vols., 1863

Hugo, Victor. *Œuvres complètes*, ed. J. Massin, 18 vols., 1967–9
Œuvres poétiques, ed. Pierre Albouy, 3 vols., 1964–74
Post-scriptum de ma vie, ed. H. Guillemin, Neuchâtel, 1961

Hulme, T. E. *Speculations: Essays on Humanism and the Philosophy of Art*, 1926

Husband, T. F. and M. F. A. *Punctuation: Its Principles and Practice*, 1905

In Principio: interprétation des premiers versets de la Genèse, 1973

Jakobson, Roman. *Essais de linguistique générale*, 1963

Jaspers, Karl. *Anselm and Nicholas of Cusa*, trans. Ralph Manheim, ed. Hannah Arendt, New York, 1963

Jespersen, Otto. *Language, its Nature, Development and Origin*, 1922

Bibliography

John of the Cross, Saint. *The Poems of Saint John of the Cross*, ed. and trans. Roy Campbell, 1976

Jules-Verne, Jean. *Jules Verne*, 1973

Jules Verne et les sciences humaines: colloque de Cerisy, 1978

Jung, C. G. *Collected Works*, trans. R. F. C. Hull, ed. Herbert Read, Michael Fordham, and Gerhard Adler, 20 vols., 1950–79

Kaiser, Walter. *Praisers of Folly*, 1964

Kermode, Frank. *The Sense of an Ending*, New York, 1967

Kline, Morris. *Mathematics: The Loss of Certainty*, New York, 1980

Koyré, Alexandre. *Etudes d'histoire de la pensée scientifique*, 1973

Kristeva, Julia. *Le Texte du roman*. The Hague, 1970

Kuhn, Thomas S. *The Structure of Scientific Revolutions*, Chicago, 1962

Lamartine, M. de. *Voyages en Orient*, ed. Lofty Fam, 1961

Las Cases, Le Comte de. *Le Mémorial de Sainte-Hélène*, ed. Gérard Walter, 2 vols., 1957 (English translation, 4 vols., 1823)

Leach, Edmund. *Genesis as Myth and Other Essays*, 1969

Leff, Gordon. *The Dissolution of the Medieval Outlook*, New York, 1976

Leibniz, Gottfried Wilhelm. *Philosophical Papers and Letters*, ed. L. E. Loemaker, Dordrecht, 1969

Lejeune, Philippe. *L'Ombre et la lumière dans 'Les Contemplations' de Victor Hugo*, 1968

Levi, A. H. T. (ed.) *Humanism in France at the End of the Middle Ages and in the Early Renaissance*, Manchester, 1970

Lévi-Strauss, C. *Mythologiques I: le cru et le cuit*, 1964

Mythologiques III: l'origine des manières de table, 1968

'Le Triangle culinaire', *L'Arc*, 26, Aix-en-Provence (1966), 19–28

Tristes tropiques, 1955

Lloyd, G. E. R. *Polarity and Analogy*, Cambridge, 1966

Lovejoy, Arthur O. *The Great Chain of Being*, Cambridge, Mass., 1936

'The Supposed Primitivism of Rousseau's *Discourse on Inequality*', *Essays in the History of Ideas*, Baltimore, 1948

McFarlane, Ian D. *Renaissance France 1470–1589*, 1974

Macherey, Pierre. 'Jules Verne ou le récit en défaut', *Pour une théorie de la production littéraire*, 1966

Martel (ed.), see under Bonaparte

Masson and Biagi (eds.), see under Bonaparte

Michaux, Henri. *Un Barbare en Asie*, 1933

Midrash Rabbah, trans. H. Freedman and M. Simon, 10 vols., 1961

Milton, John. *The Poetical Works of John Milton*, ed. H. C. Beeching, Oxford, 1969

Montaigne, Michel de. *Essais*, ed. Albert Thibaudet, 1939

Montesquieu, Charles de Secondat, baron de. *Œuvres complètes*, ed. Daniel Oster, 1964

Moré, Marcel. *Le Très Curieux Jules Verne: le problème du père dans les 'Voyages extraordinaires'*, 1960

Bibliography

Moreau, Pierre. *Chateaubriand, l'homme et l'œuvre*, 1956
    Le Classicisme des romantiques, 1932
Musset, Alfred de. *Œuvres complètes en prose*, ed. M. Allem and Paul
    Courant, 1960
    Premières poésies, poésies nouvelles, ed. Geneviève Bulli, 1966
Nabokov, Vladimir. *The Real Life of Sebastian Knight*, Harmondsworth,
    1964
Napoléon, see under Bonaparte
Nicholas of Cusa. *Of Learned Ignorance*, trans. Germaine Heron, 1954
    Opera, Basel, 1565
    Opera omnia, Vol. I–, Leipzig, 1932–
    The Vision of God, trans. E. G. Salter, 1928
Nietzsche, Friedrich. *Complete Works*, ed. Levy, 18 vols., 1909–13
    Twilight of the Idols, trans. R. J. Hollingdale, Harmondsworth, 1968
Nowottny, Winifred. *The Language Poets Use*, 1962
Partridge, E. H. *You Have a Point There*, 1953
Pascal, Blaise. *Pensées*, ed. Dominique Descotes, 1976
Pasteur, Louis. *Œuvres complètes*, ed. P. Valléry-Radot, 7 vols., 1922
Peirce, Charles Sanders. *Collected Papers of C. S. Peirce*, ed. C.
    Hartshorne, P. Weiss, and A. W. Burke, 8 vols., Cambridge, Mass.,
    1931–58
Pérès, J.-B. *Comme quoi Napoléon n'a jamais existé ou grand erratum
    source d'un nombre infini d'errata à noter dans l'histoire du XIXe
    siècle*, 1909 (first edition, 1827)
Périvier, A. *Napoléon journaliste*, 1918
Phillips, Derek B. *Wittgenstein and Scientific Knowledge*, 1977
Poe, Edgar Allan. *Collected Works*, ed. Thomas O. Mabbott, 3 vols.,
    Cambridge, Mass., 1969–78
Popkin, Richard H. *The History of Scepticism from Erasmus to Descartes*,
    Assen, 1960
Popper, Karl R. *The Logic of Scientific Discovery*, 1959
Porter, Charles A. *Chateaubriand, Composition, Imagination, and Poetry*,
    Stanford, 1978
Poulet, Georges. *Les Métamorphoses du cercle*, 1961
Prendergast, Christopher. *Balzac: Fiction and Melodrama*, 1978
Procès-verbaux de l'Académie des Sciences, 1808–11, Vol. IV, Hendaye,
    1913
Proust, Marcel. *A la recherche du temps perdu*, ed. Pierre Clarac and
    André Ferré, 3 vols., 1954
Quine, W. V. O. *From a Logical Point of View*, Cambridge, Mass., 1961
Rabelais, François. *Œuvres complètes*, ed. Jacques Boulenger and Lucien
    Scheller, 1955
Rad, Gerhard von. *Genesis: A Commentary*, 1961
Rashi (Solomon ben Isaac). *The Pentateuch and Rashi's Commentary*, ed.
    and trans. M. Rosenbaum and A. M. Silberman, 3 vols., New York,
    1929–31

Bibliography

Rémusat, Madame de. *Lettres, 1804–1814*, 2 vols., 1881

Mémoires, 3 vols., 1880

Rescher, Nicholas. *Scepticism: A Critical Reappraisal*, Oxford, 1980

Reverdin, Olivier. 'Napoléon, correcteur de style de Rousseau', *Annales de la Société Jean-Jacques Rousseau*, XXX, Geneva (1943–5), 143–8

Richard, Jean-Pierre. *Etudes sur le romantisme*, 1970

Littérature et sensation, 1954

Paysage de Chateaubriand, 1967

Riffaterre, Michael. *Essais de stylistique structurale*, 1971

Robertson, J. *An Essay on Punctuation*, 1785

Robin, Christian. *Un Monde connu et inconnu: Jules Verne*, Nantes, 1978

Roederer, Comte P. L. *Journal: autour de Bonaparte*, 1909

Rorty, Richard. *Philosophy and the Mirror of Nature*, Princeton, 1980

Rousseau, Jean-Jacques. *Essai sur l'origine des langues*, ed. Charles Porset, 1970

Œuvres complètes, ed. Bernard Gagnebin and Marcel Raymond, 4 vols., 1959–69

Rousseau juge de Jean-Jacques, introduction by Michel Foucault, 1962

Russell, Bertrand. *The Analysis of Mind*, 1922

An Inquiry into Meaning and Truth, 1962

The Problems of Philosophy, 1967

Said, Edward W. *Beginnings: Intention and Method*, Baltimore and London, 1975

Orientalism, New York, 1978

Sainte-Beuve, Charles Augustin. *Causeries du lundi*, 8 vols., 1868–80

Nouveaux lundis, 13 vols., 1865–9

Sartre, Jean-Paul. *L'Etre et le néant*, 1943

Situations, I, 1947

Scève, Maurice. *Microcosme*, ed. Enzo Guidici, Paris and Cassino, 1976

Schwab, Raymond. *La Renaissance orientale*, 1950

Scott, Walter. *The Life of Napoleon Buonaparte*, 9 vols., Edinburgh, 1827

Screech, M. A. *Ecstasy and the 'Praise of Folly'*, 1980

Serres, Michel. *Jouvences sur Jules Verne*, 1974

Sharratt, Peter (ed.) *French Renaissance Studies 1540–70: Humanism and the Encyclopedia*, Edinburgh, 1976

Shaw, George Bernard. *London Music in 1888–89 as Heard by Corno di Bassetto (Later Known as Bernard Shaw) with Some Further Autobiographical Particulars*, 1937

Simone, Franco. *The French Renaissance: Medieval Tradition and Italian Influence in Shaping the Renaissance in France*, trans. H. Gaston Hall, 1969

Per una storia della storiografia letteraria francese, Turin, 1966

Smith, George. *The Chaldean Account of Genesis*, 1876

Solignac, see under *In Principio*

Sonnenfeld, see under *Yale French Studies*

Soriano, Marc. *Jules Verne (le cas Verne)*, 1978

Bibliography

Sprat, Thomas. *History of the Royal Society*, 1667

Starobinski, Jean. *Jean-Jacques Rousseau: la transparence et l'obstacle*, 1971

    Montaigne en mouvement, 1982

Staub, Hans. *Le Curieux Désir: Scève et Peletier du Mans, poètes de la connaissance*, Geneva, 1967

Suvin, Darko. *Metamorphoses of Science Fiction*, New Haven and London, 1979

Suzuki, Daisetz Teitaro. *Essays in Zen Buddhism (Second Series)*, 1930

    The Zen Doctrine of No-Mind, 1965

    Zen and Japanese Culture, New York, 1959

Tanner, Tony. *Adultery in the Novel*, Baltimore, 1979

Terrasse, Jean. *Jean-Jacques Rousseau et la quête de l'âge d'or*, Brussels, 1970

Thibaudet, Albert. *Histoire de la littérature française de 1789 à nos jours*, 1936

    Montaigne, 1963

Thiry, Jean. *Bonaparte en Egypte*, 1973

Tieghem, Paul van. *Le Préromantisme: études d'histoire littéraire européenne*, 3 vols., 1947–8

Tomiche, N. *Napoléon écrivain*, 1952

Touati, Charles. *La Pensée philosophique et théologique de Gersonide*, 1973

Touttain, Pierre-André (ed.) *Jules Verne*, 1974

Verne, Jules. *Discours prononcé par M. Jules Verne à la distribution des prix du lycée de jeunes filles*, 1893

    'Edgar Poe et ses œuvres', *Musée des familles* (1864), 193–208

    Voyages extraordinaires, 80 vols., published by Michel de l'Ormeraie, 1975–81 (this is the only complete edition available at present)

Vierne, Simone. *Jules Verne et le roman initiatique*, 1973

Villiers, Charles. *L'Univers métaphysique de Victor Hugo*, 1970

Volney, Comte François de. *Voyage en Egypte et en Syrie*, ed. Jean Gaulmier, 1959

Vonnegut, Kurt. *Breakfast of Champions*, 1973

Watts, Alan W. *The Way of Zen*, 1966

Wilkins, John. *An Essay towards a Real Character, and a Philosophical Language*, 1668

Williams, Kathleen M. *Twentieth-Century Interpretations of the 'Praise of Folly'*, New York, 1969

Wittgenstein, Ludwig. *Philosophical Investigations*, trans. G. E. M. Anscombe, Oxford, 1967

Wolff, Philippe. *The Awakening of Europe*, trans. Anne Carter, Harmondsworth, 1968

Yale French Studies, 26, *The Myth of Napoleon*, Fall–Winter 1960–1

Zeldin, Theodore. *France 1848–1945*, 2 vols., Oxford, 1973–7

INDEX